MW01612641

UNITED NATIONS HANDBOOK 2007 | 2008

UNITED NATIONS HANDBOOK

AN ANNUAL GUIDE FOR THOSE WORKING WITH AND WITHIN THE UNITED NATIONS

First published in 1961 and reprinted annually as a revised edition
(with the exception of 1970 and 1976).

Forty-fifth edition

© Crown Copyright Reserved 2007

ISBN: 0-477-10200-X

Published by the Ministry of Foreign Affairs and Trade/Manatū Aorere,
Private Bag 18–901, Wellington, New Zealand.

Cover designed by Typeface, Wellington, New Zealand.

Printed by Printlink, Wellington, New Zealand.

Copies may be purchased from:

Ministry of Foreign Affairs and Trade/Manatū Aorere, Private Bag 18–901, Wellington, New Zealand.

Website: www.mfat.govt.nz

Telephone: (64 4) 439 8000, Fax: (64 4) 439 8511.

Email: ipd@mft.govt.nz

Selected bookstores and New Zealand Embassies, High Commissions and Consulates-General.

CONTENTS

LIST OF ABBREVIATIONS

Country names

The following abbreviations of the names of UN Member States are used throughout this Handbook.

Andorra	Principality of Andorra
Bahrain	Kingdom of Bahrain
Congo	Republic of the Congo
DPRK	Democratic People's Republic of Korea
DR Congo	Democratic Republic of the Congo
Iran	Islamic Republic of Iran
Kazakhstan	Republic of Kazakhstan
Lao PDR	Lao People's Democratic Republic
Libyan AJ	Libyan Arab Jamahiriya
Mauritania	Islamic Republic of Mauritania
Micronesia	Federated States of Micronesia
Monaco	Principality of Monaco
Morocco	Kingdom of Morocco
Netherlands	Kingdom of the Netherlands
Oman	Sultanate of Oman
ROK	Republic of Korea
Sri Lanka	Democratic Socialist Republic of Sri Lanka
Syrian AR	Syrian Arab Republic
UAE	United Arab Emirates
UK or United Kingdom	United Kingdom of Great Britain and Northern Ireland
UR of Tanzania	United Republic of Tanzania
USA	United States of America
Venezuela	Bolivarian Republic of Venezuela
Viet Nam	Socialist Republic of Viet Nam

RT HON WINSTON PETERS

FOREWORD

New Zealand Minister of Foreign Affairs

E nga waka, e nga mana, e nga reo,
E nga pu korero o nga hau e wha,
E rau rangatira ma,
Tena koutou, tena koutou, tena koutou katoa.

To the many peoples of the world, to those who hold authority, to those from different languages,
To the great orators from the four winds,
To the many leaders of the world,
I bring greetings to you, one and all.

Since New Zealand began publishing the United Nations Handbook 46 years ago the international environment has changed enormously, but the United Nations has remained at the heart of the multilateral system and international affairs.

As the international agenda has continued to grow and become more complex, the United Nations has needed to evolve and adapt its processes. This was recognised by world leaders at their Summit meeting in 2005. Reaffirming their commitment to the organisation and their belief in the vital importance of an effective multilateral system, they agreed to a challenging process of reform and revitalisation.

Significant progress has been achieved. This includes the establishment of the Peacebuilding Commission and the Human Rights Council, and work for greater coherence amongst the United Nations and its partner agencies. But much remains to be done to make the vision of a more effective and efficient organisation a reality.

Any organisation is only as strong as it members will allow it to be. Only through the genuine support and commitment of the entire United Nations membership will it be possible to implement fully the outcomes agreed at the Summit.

New Zealand is a strong supporter of the reform effort and of the hard work undertaken by Member States, by former Secretary-General Kofi Annan and now by Secretary-General Ban Ki-moon, and by the Secretariat, to improve and modernise the United Nations so that it can realise the hopes we have all placed in it.

We regard the annual production of this Handbook as a small contribution by New Zealand to increasing understanding of this vitally important organisation.

No reira tena koutou, tena koutou, tena koutou katoa,
Once again, I extend warm greetings to you all

Rt Hon Winston Peters
MINISTER OF FOREIGN AFFAIRS, NEW ZEALAND

WHAT THIS BOOK DOES

The United Nations Handbook is published by the New Zealand Government as a ready reference guide intended particularly for delegates, diplomats and foreign ministry officials concerned with UN matters. It is also widely used by the media, non-government organisations, government officials, business organisations, university staff and students, and interested members of the public.

The publishers are indebted to the various bodies and agencies of the UN for the considerable assistance they provide each year in making sure the Handbook is as up-to-date and comprehensive as possible.

The Handbook is not intended to be a historical record. It sets out to provide current information on all the organisations of the UN family: the basis of their existence, their aims and structures, and their membership. It also provides an overview of their activities as defined in the relevant mandates.

The book has at its heart information on the six principal organs of the UN established by the Charter: the General Assembly, Security Council, Economic and Social Council, Trusteeship Council, International Court of Justice and the Secretariat.

It also contains information on subsidiary organs established in accordance with the Charter, related UN organs and programmes, specialised agencies and autonomous bodies brought into relationship with the UN, and various ad hoc organs and programmes. Some bodies are shown as subsidiary to, or associated with, one or other of the principal organs while others are shown under the heading 'Other Bodies Subsidiary or Related to the UN'. The specialised agencies of the UN are included under this heading.

Non-government organisations with UN connections are not included; neither, generally, are other inter-government (but non-UN) organisations or political groupings.

All money values are in US dollars unless otherwise stated.

Postal addresses, telephone and fax numbers, as well as email and website addresses, are specified where possible. Agencies without specified contact details can be reached through UN Headquarters in New York.

Details of all General Assembly, Security Council, and Economic and Social Council resolutions can be found via the Main Bodies section of the UN website: www.un.org/aboutun/mainbodies.

Many websites of the UN system are indexed at: www.unsystem.org

Listed below are the contact details for UN Headquarters in New York, Geneva and Vienna:

United Nations Headquarters	United Nations Office at Geneva (UNOG)	United Nations Office at Vienna (UNOV)
United Nations Plaza		
New York, NY 10017	Palais des Nations	Vienna International Centre
United States of America	8–14 Avenue de la Paix	PO Box 500
Telephone: (+1 212) 963 1234	1211 Geneva 10	A–1400 Vienna
Fax: (+1 212) 963 4879	Switzerland	Austria
Website: www.un.org	Telephone: (+41 22) 917 1234	Telephone: (+43 1) 26 060
	Fax: (+41 22) 917 0123	Fax: (+43 1) 263 3389
	Website: www.unog.ch	Website: www.unvienna.org

Note: The information in this Handbook is intended to be accurate as at 31 May 2007 unless otherwise stated. The fluidity of the UN and its processes means entries may not be definitive after that date.

SECURITY COUNCIL

Subsidiary Bodies

PBC Peacebuilding Commission

Military Staff Committee

Standing committees and ad hoc bodies

ICTY International Criminal Tribunal for the Former Yugoslavia

ICTR International Criminal Tribunal for Rwanda

UNMOVIC UN Monitoring, Verification and Inspection Commission (Iraq)

UNCC United Nations Compensation Commission

Peacekeeping Missions, Peacebuilding Missions, Political Missions

GENERAL ASSEMBLY

Subsidiary Bodies

Main committees

Other sessional committees

Standing committees and ad hoc bodies

Other subsidiary organs

Programmes and Funds

UNCTAD United Nations Conference on Trade and Development

ITC International Trade Centre (UNCTAD/WTO)

UNDCP United Nations Drug Control Programme

UNEP United Nations Environment Programme

UNICEF United Nations Children's Fund

UNDP United Nations Development Programme

UNIFEM United Nations Development Fund for Women

UNV United Nations Volunteers

UNCDF United Nations Capital Development Fund

UNFPA United Nations Population Fund

UNHCR Office of the United Nations High Commissioner for Refugees

WFP World Food Programme

UNRWA United Nations Relief and Works Agency for Palestine Refugees in the Near East

UN-HABITAT United Nations Human Settlements Programme

Research and Training Institutes

UNICRI United Nations Interregional Crime and Justice Research Institute

UNITAR United Nations Institute for Training and Research

UNRISD United Nations Research Institute for Social Development

UNIDIR United Nations Institute for Disarmament Research

INSTRAW International Research and Training Institute for the Advancement of Women

Other UN Entities

Agencies in this group report directly to the GA but also have links to ECOSOC.

OHCHR Office of the United Nations High Commissioner for Human Rights

UNOPS United Nations Office for Project Services

UNU United Nations University

UNAIDS Joint United Nations Programme on HIV/AIDS

Related organisations

IAEA International Atomic Energy Agency

The IAEA also reports to the Security Council.

CTBTO PrepCom Preparatory Committee for the Nuclear-Test-Ban Treaty Organization

OPCW Organization for the Prohibition of Chemical Weapons

The OPCW reports directly to the GA.

INTERNATIONAL COURT OF JUSTICE

There are no subsidiary or related bodies.

TRUSTEESHIP COUNCIL

There are no subsidiary or related bodies. The Trusteeship Council has now completed its decolonisation tasks and is inactive.

SECRETARIAT

Departments and Offices include:

UNOG UN Office at Geneva
UNOV UN Office at Vienna
UNON UN Office at Nairobi
OSG Office of the Secretary-General
OIOS Office of Internal Oversight Services
OLA Office of Legal Affairs
DPA Department of Political Affairs
ODA Office for Disarmament Affairs
DPKO Department of Peacekeeping Operations

OCHA Office for the Coordination of Humanitarian Affairs
DESA Department of Economic and Social Affairs
DGACM Department for General Assembly and Conference Management
DPI Department of Public Information
DM Department of Management
UNODC United Nations Office on Drugs and Crime

ECONOMIC AND SOCIAL COUNCIL

Functional Commissions on:

Human Rights
Crime Prevention and Criminal Justice
Science and Technology for Development
Sustainable Development
Status of Women
Population and Development
Social Development
Statistics

Regional Commissions

ECA Economic Commission for Africa
ECE Economic Commission for Europe
ECLAC Economic Commission for Latin America and the Caribbean
ESCAP Economic and Social Commission for Asia and the Pacific
ESCWA Economic and Social Commission for Western Asia

Other Bodies including:

UNFF United Nations Forum on Forests
Sessional and standing committees
Expert, ad hoc and related bodies

Specialised Agencies

Specialised agencies are autonomous organisations working with the UN and each other through the coordinating machinery of ECOSOC at the inter-governmental level, and through the Chief Executives Board for Coordination (CEB) at the inter-secretariat level. These agences are linked to ECOSOC but do not have a direct reporting relationship.

ILO International Labour Organization
FAO Food and Agriculture Organization of the United Nations
UNESCO United Nations Educational, Scientific and Cultural Organization
WHO World Health Organization
IMF International Monetary Fund
ICAO International Civil Aviation Organization
IMO International Maritime Organization
ITU International Telecommunication Union
UPU Universal Postal Union
WMO World Meterological Organization
WIPO World Intellectual Property Organization

IFAD International Fund for Agricultural Development
UNIDO United Nations Industrial Development Organization
UNWTO World Tourism Organization
IMF International Monetary Fund

World Bank Group

IBRD International Bank for Reconstruction and Development
IDA International Development Association
IFC International Finance Corporation
MIGA Multilateral Investment Guarantee Agency
ICSID International Centre for Settlement of Investment Disputes

GENERAL ASSEMBLY

GENERAL ASSEMBLY

CHARTER PROVISIONS

The General Assembly consists of all members of the UN. It may discuss any questions or matters within the scope of the UN Charter, or relating to the powers and functions of any organ provided for in the Charter. It may make recommendations to UN members or the Security Council or both on any such questions or matters except disputes or situations in respect of which the Security Council is currently exercising its functions.

General Assembly decisions on important questions are made by a two-thirds majority of the members present and voting, and on other questions by a simple majority. Categories of questions requiring a two-thirds majority are listed in article 18 of the Charter. This article also provides that decisions on other questions, including the determination of additional categories of questions to be decided by a two-thirds majority, are made by a simple majority.

The General Assembly receives and considers reports from the other organs of the UN. It elects the 10 non-permanent members of the Security Council and the 54 members of the Economic and Social Council. Together with the Security Council, but voting independently, it elects the members of the International Court of Justice. On the recommendation of the Security Council it appoints the Secretary-General. The General Assembly considers and approves the regular budget of the UN and apportions expenses among members.

The Charter provisions concerning the General Assembly are contained in chapter IV (articles 9–22), which defines its composition, functions and powers, voting and procedure. Other provisions relating to the General Assembly are contained in articles 1, 2, 4–7, 23, 24, 35, 60–64, 66, 85–88, 93, 96, 97, 98, 101, 105, 108 and 109 of the Charter, and articles 4, 7–15, 32, 33 and 69 of the Statute of the International Court of Justice.

MEMBERSHIP

As at 30 June 2007, 192 states were represented in the General Assembly. These states, together with their dates of admission to the UN, are:

Afghanistan	19 Nov 1946[1]	Bahamas	18 Sep 1973
Albania	14 Dec 1955	Bahrain	21 Sep 1971[2]
Algeria	8 Oct 1962	Bangladesh	17 Sep 1974
Andorra	28 Jul 1993	Barbados	9 Dec 1966
Angola	1 Dec 1976	Belarus	24 Oct 1945*
Antigua and Barbuda	11 Nov 1981	Belgium	27 Dec 1945*
Argentina	24 Oct 1945*	Belize	25 Sep 1981
Armenia	2 Mar 1992	Benin	20 Sep 1960
Australia	1 Nov 1945*	Bhutan	21 Sep 1971
Austria	14 Dec 1955	Bolivia	14 Nov 1945*
Azerbaijan	2 Mar 1992	Bosnia and Herzegovina	22 May 1992[8]

Botswana	17 Oct 1966		Grenada	17 Sep 1974
Brazil	24 Oct 1945*		Guatemala	21 Nov 1945*
Brunei Darussalam	21 Sep 1984		Guinea	12 Dec 1958
Bulgaria	14 Dec 1955		Guinea-Bissau	17 Sep 1974
Burkina Faso	20 Sep 1960		Guyana	20 Sep 1966
Burundi	18 Sep 1962		Haiti	24 Oct 1945*
Cambodia	14 Dec 1955		Honduras	17 Dec 1945*
Cameroon	20 Sep 1960		Hungary	14 Dec 1955
Canada	9 Nov 1945*		Iceland	19 Nov 1946
Cape Verde	16 Sep 1975		India	30 Oct 1945*
Central African Republic	20 Sep 1960		Indonesia	28 Sep 1950[6]
Chad	20 Sep 1960		Iran	24 Oct 1945*
Chile	24 Oct 1945*		Iraq	21 Dec 1945*
China	24 Oct 1945*[3]		Ireland	14 Dec 1955
Colombia	5 Nov 1945*		Israel	11 May 1949
Comoros	12 Nov 1975		Italy	14 Dec 1955
Congo	20 Sep 1960		Jamaica	18 Sep 1962
Costa Rica	2 Nov 1945*		Japan	18 Dec 1956
Côte d'Ivoire	20 Sep 1960		Jordan	14 Dec 1955
Croatia	22 May 1992[8]		Kazakhstan	2 Mar 1992
Cuba	24 Oct 1945*		Kenya	16 Dec 1963
Cyprus	20 Sep 1960		Kiribati	14 Sep 1999
Czech Republic	19 Jan 1993*[4]		Kuwait	14 May 1963
DPRK	17 Sep 1991		Kyrgyzstan	2 Mar 1992
DR Congo	20 Sep 1960		Lao PDR	14 Dec 1955
Denmark	24 Oct 1945*		Latvia	17 Sep 1991
Djibouti	20 Sep 1977		Lebanon	24 Oct 1945*
Dominica	18 Dec 1978		Lesotho	17 Oct 1966
Dominican Republic	24 Oct 1945*		Liberia	2 Nov 1945*
Ecuador	21 Dec 1945*		Libyan AJ	14 Dec 1955
Egypt	24 Oct 1945*		Liechtenstein	18 Sep 1990
El Salvador	24 Oct 1945*		Lithuania	17 Sep 1991
Equatorial Guinea	12 Nov 1968		Luxembourg	24 Oct 1945*
Eritrea	28 May 1993		Madagascar	20 Sep 1960
Estonia	17 Sep 1991		Malawi	1 Dec 1964
Ethiopia	13 Nov 1945*		Malaysia	17 Sep 1957
Fiji	13 Oct 1970		Maldives	21 Sep 1965
Finland	14 Dec 1955		Mali	28 Sep 1960
France	24 Oct 1945*		Malta	1 Dec 1964
Gabon	20 Sep 1960		Marshall Islands	17 Sep 1991
Gambia	21 Sep 1965		Mauritania	27 Oct 1961
Georgia	31 Jul 1992		Mauritius	24 Apr 1968
Germany	18 Sep 1973[5]		Mexico	7 Nov 1945*
Ghana	8 Mar 1957		Micronesia	17 Sep 1991
Greece	25 Oct 1945*		Monaco	28 May 1993

Mongolia	27 Oct 1961
Montenegro	28 June 2006[8]
Morocco	12 Nov 1956
Mozambique	16 Sep 1975
Myanmar	19 Apr 1948
Namibia	23 Apr 1990
Nauru	14 Sep 1999
Nepal	14 Dec 1955
Netherlands	10 Dec 1945*
New Zealand	24 Oct 1945*
Nicaragua	24 Oct 1945*
Niger	20 Sep 1960
Nigeria	7 Oct 1960
Norway	27 Nov 1945*
Oman	7 Oct 1971
Pakistan	30 Sep 1947
Palau	15 Dec 1994
Panama	13 Nov 1945*
Papua New Guinea	10 Oct 1975
Paraguay	24 Oct 1945*
Peru	31 Oct 1945*
Philippines	24 Oct 1945*
Poland	24 Oct 1945*
Portugal	14 Dec 1955
Qatar	21 Sep 1971
ROK	17 Sep 1991
Republic of Moldova	2 Mar 1992
Romania	14 Dec 1955
Russian Federation	24 Oct 1945*[7]
Rwanda	18 Sep 1962
Saint Kitts and Nevis	23 Sep 1983
Saint Lucia	18 Sep 1979
Saint Vincent and the Grenadines	16 Sep 1980
Samoa	15 Dec 1976
San Marino	2 Mar 1992
Sao Tome and Principe	16 Sep 1975
Saudi Arabia	24 Oct 1945*
Senegal	28 Sep 1960
Serbia	1 Nov 2000[8]
Seychelles	21 Sep 1976
Sierra Leone	27 Sep 1961

Singapore	21 Sep 1965
Slovakia	19 Jan 1993*[4]
Slovenia	22 May 1992[8]
Solomon Islands	19 Sep 1978
Somalia	20 Sep 1960
South Africa	7 Nov 1945*
Spain	14 Dec 1955
Sri Lanka	14 Dec 1955
Sudan	12 Nov 1956
Suriname	4 Dec 1975
Swaziland	24 Sep 1968
Sweden	19 Nov 1946
Switzerland	10 Sep 2002
Syrian AR	24 Oct 1945*[9]
Tajikistan	2 Mar 1992
Thailand	16 Dec 1946
The Former Yugoslav Republic of Macedonia	8 Apr 1993[8]
Timor-Leste	27 Sep 2002
Togo	20 Sep 1960
Tonga	14 Sep 1999
Trinidad and Tobago	18 Sep 1962
Tunisia	12 Nov 1956
Turkey	24 Oct 1945*
Turkmenistan	2 Mar 1992
Tuvalu	5 Sep 2000
Uganda	25 Oct 1962
Ukraine	24 Oct 1945*
UAE	9 Dec 1971
UK	24 Oct 1945*
UR of Tanzania	14 Dec 1961[10]
USA	24 Oct 1945*
Uruguay	18 Dec 1945*
Uzbekistan	2 Mar 1992
Vanuatu	15 Sep 1981
Venezuela	15 Nov 1945*
Viet Nam	20 Sep 1977
Yemen	30 Sep 1947[11]
Zambia	1 Dec 1964
Zimbabwe	25 Aug 1980

Notes

* Original members, ie. those that participated in the UN Conference on International Organisation at San Francisco or had previously signed the UN Declaration of 1 January 1942, and that signed and ratified the Charter. Although Poland was not represented at San Francisco, it was agreed that it should sign the Charter subsequently as an original member.

1 On 22 December 2001 the Islamic State of Afghanistan informed the UN it had changed its name to Afghanistan.

2 On 14 February 2002 the State of Bahrain informed the UN it had changed its name to the Kingdom of Bahrain.

3 By GA res. 2758 (XXVI) (1971) the General Assembly decided to restore all its rights to the People's Republic of China and to recognise the representatives of its Government as the only legitimate representatives of China in the UN.

4 Formerly part of Czechoslovakia, an original member of the UN from 24 October 1945.

5 Through the accession of the German Democratic Republic to the Federal Republic of Germany, with effect from 3 October 1990, the two German states united to form one sovereign state. As from the date of reunification, the Federal Republic of Germany acts in the UN under the designation 'Germany'.

6 Indonesia withdrew from membership of the UN in 1965, but resumed full participation in 1966.

7 The USSR was an original member of the UN from 24 October 1945. In 1991 the Russian Federation informed the Secretary-General that the membership of the Soviet Union in the Security Council and all other UN organs was being continued by the Russian Federation with the support of the 11 member countries of the Commonwealth of Independent States.

8 The Socialist Federal Republic of Yugoslavia was an original member of the UN (the Charter having been signed on its behalf on 26 June 1945 and ratified on 19 October 1945) until its dissolution following the establishment and subsequent admission as new members of Bosnia and Herzegovina, the Republic of Croatia, the Republic of Slovenia, the Former Yugoslav Republic of Macedonia, and the Federal Republic of Yugoslavia. The Federal Republic of Yugoslavia did not automatically succeed to memberships held by the former Socialist Federal Republic of Yugoslavia. On 4 February 2003 the Federal Republic of Yugoslavia informed the UN that it had changed its name to Serbia and Montenegro. On 3 June 2006 the Republic of Serbia notified the UN that the membership of the State Union of Serbia and Montenegro in the UN, including all organs and organisations of the UN system, was continued by the Republic of Serbia on the basis of article 60 of the Constitutional Charter of Serbia and Montenegro, activated by the Declaration of Independence adopted by the National Assembly of Montenegro on 3 June 2006. The Republic of Montenegro was admitted as a member of the UN on 28 June 2006.

9 Syria withdrew in 1958 to unite with Egypt as the United Arab Republic, but resumed its independent status and separate membership of the UN in 1961.

10 Tanganyika was a member of the UN from 1961 and Zanzibar from 1963. After 1964 they continued as a single member, the United Republic of Tanganyika and Zanzibar, which later became the United Republic of Tanzania.

11 On 22 May 1990 Democratic Yemen and the Arab Republic of Yemen became a single sovereign state called the Republic of Yemen. Both had previously been members of the UN, Democratic Yemen since 14 December 1967 and the Arab Republic of Yemen since 30 September 1947.

MEMBERS OF THE GENERAL ASSEMBLY ARRANGED IN CURRENT REGIONAL GROUPS

African states

Algeria	Cameroon	Côte d'Ivoire
Angola	Cape Verde	DR Congo
Benin	Central African Republic	Djibouti
Botswana	Chad	Egypt
Burkina Faso	Comoros	Equatorial Guinea
Burundi	Congo	Eritrea

Ethiopia
Gabon
Gambia
Ghana
Guinea
Guinea-Bissau
Kenya
Lesotho
Liberia
Libyan AJ
Madagascar
Malawi

Mali
Mauritania
Mauritius
Morocco
Mozambique
Namibia
Niger
Nigeria
Rwanda
Sao Tome and Principe
Senegal
Seychelles

Sierra Leone
Somalia
South Africa
Sudan
Swaziland
Togo
Tunisia
Uganda
UR of Tanzania
Zambia
Zimbabwe

Asian states

Afghanistan
Bahrain
Bangladesh
Bhutan
Brunei Darussalam
Cambodia
China
Cyprus
DPRK
Fiji
India
Indonesia
Iran
Iraq
Japan
Jordan
Kazakhstan
Kuwait

Kyrgyzstan
Lao PDR
Lebanon
Malaysia
Maldives
Marshall Islands
Micronesia
Mongolia
Myanmar
Nauru
Nepal
Oman
Pakistan
Palau
Papua New Guinea
Philippines
Qatar
ROK

Samoa
Saudi Arabia
Singapore
Solomon Islands
Sri Lanka
Syrian AR
Tajikistan
Thailand
Timor-Leste
Tonga
Turkmenistan
Tuvalu
UAE
Uzbekistan
Vanuatu
Viet Nam
Yemen

Eastern European states

Albania
Armenia
Azerbaijan
Belarus
Bosnia and Herzegovina
Bulgaria
Croatia
Czech Republic

Estonia
Georgia
Hungary
Latvia
Lithuania
Montenegro
Poland
Republic of Moldova

Romania
Russian Federation
Serbia
Slovakia
Slovenia
The Former Yugoslav Republic
   of Macedonia
Ukraine

Latin American and Caribbean states

Antigua and Barbuda
Argentina
Bahamas
Barbados
Belize
Bolivia
Brazil
Chile
Colombia
Costa Rica
Cuba
Dominica

Dominican Republic
Ecuador
El Salvador
Grenada
Guatemala
Guyana
Haiti
Honduras
Jamaica
Mexico
Nicaragua
Panama

Paraguay
Peru
Saint Kitts and Nevis
Saint Lucia
Saint Vincent and the
   Grenadines
Suriname
Trinidad and Tobago
Uruguay
Venezuela

Western European and Other states

Andorra	Iceland	Norway
Australia	Ireland	Portugal
Austria	Israel	San Marino
Belgium	Italy	Spain
Canada	Liechtenstein	Sweden
Denmark	Luxembourg	Switzerland
Finland	Malta	Turkey
France	Monaco	UK
Germany	Netherlands	
Greece	New Zealand	

Notes

The United States of America is not a member of any regional group, but attends meetings of the Western European and Other States Group (WEOG) as an observer and is considered to be a member of that group for electoral purposes. Turkey participates fully in both the Asian group and WEOG, but for electoral purposes is considered a member of WEOG only. Israel became a full member of WEOG on a temporary basis on 28 May 2000. As at 31 May 2007 Kiribati was not a member of any regional group.
In addition to Member States, the Holy See is a non-Member State that has observer status in the UN.

By GA res. 52/250 (1998) the General Assembly conferred upon Palestine, in its capacity as observer, additional rights and privileges of participation. These included the right to participation in the general debate of the General Assembly but did not include the rights to vote or put forward candidates.

SESSIONS AND OFFICERS

RULES GOVERNING SESSIONS

GA res. 57/301 (2002) amended rule 1 of the rules of procedure of the Assembly to read: "The General Assembly shall meet every year in regular session commencing on the Tuesday of the third week in September, counting from the first week that contains at least one working day." It was further decided that, with effect from the 58th regular session, the general debate of the General Assembly should open on the Tuesday following the opening of the regular session and should be held without interruption over a period of nine working days. Sessions are held at UN Headquarters (New York), unless convened elsewhere in pursuance of a decision of the General Assembly at a previous session, or at the request of a majority of UN members.

Special sessions may be summoned by the General Assembly, at the request of the Security Council, or at the request or concurrence of a majority of UN members. Unless the date for a special session has been fixed by the General Assembly, it must be held within 15 days of receipt by the Secretary-General of the request or notification of concurrence. The Secretary-General must notify members at least 14 days in advance of the opening of a special session summoned at the request of the Security Council; otherwise 10 days' notice is required.

Emergency special sessions must be convened within 24 hours of receipt by the Secretary-General of a request from the Security Council, on the vote of any nine of its members, or of a request or notification of concurrence from a majority of UN members. Members must be given at least 12 hours' notice.

SESSIONS AND PRESIDENTS OF THE GENERAL ASSEMBLY SINCE 1946

The President of the General Assembly and the 21 Vice-Presidents are elected by the General Assembly. They hold office until the close of the session at which they are elected.

1st Regular, 1946:
Paul-Henri Spaak, Belgium

1st Special, Apr 1947
Question of Palestine:
Oswaldo Aranha, Brazil

2nd Regular, 1947:
Oswaldo Aranha, Brazil

2nd Special, Apr 1948
Question of Palestine:
Jose Arce, Argentina

3rd Regular, 1948–49:
H V Evatt, Australia

4th Regular, 1949:
Brigadier-General
Carlos P Romulo, Philippines

5th Regular, 1950–51:
Nasrollah Entezam, Iran

6th Regular, 1951–52:
Luis Padilla Nervo, Mexico

7th Regular, 1952–53:
Lester B Pearson, Canada

8th Regular, 1953:
Vijaya Lakshmi Pandit, India

9th Regular, 1954:
E N van Kleffens, Netherlands

10th Regular, 1955:
Jose Maza, Chile

1st Emergency Special,
Nov 1956
Suez Canal:
Rudecindo Ortega, Chile

2nd Emergency Special,
Nov 1956
Situation in Hungary:
Rudecindo Ortega, Chile

11th Regular, 1956–57:
Prince Wan Waithayakon,
Thailand

12th Regular, 1957:
Sir Leslie Munro,
New Zealand

3rd Emergency Special,
Aug 1958
Situation in Lebanon:
Sir Leslie Munro,
New Zealand

13th Regular, 1958:
Charles Malik, Lebanon

14th Regular, 1959:
V A Belaunde, Peru

4th Emergency Special,
Sep 1960
*Situation in the Congo
(Leopoldville):*
V A Belaunde, Peru

15th Regular, 1960–61:
Frederick Boland, Ireland

3rd Special, Aug 1961
Grave Situation in Tunisia:
Frederick Boland, Ireland

16th Regular, 1961–62:
Mongi Slim, Tunisia

17th Regular, 1962:
Sir M Zafrulla Khan, Pakistan

4th Special, May 1963
*Consideration of the Financial
Situation of the Organisation:*
Sir M Zafrulla Khan, Pakistan

18th Regular, 1963:
C Sosa Rodriguez, Venezuela

19th Regular, 1964–65:
Alex Quaison-Sackey, Ghana

20th Regular, 1965:
Amintore Fanfani, Italy

21st Regular, 1966:
Abdul Rahman Pazhwak,
Afghanistan

5th Special, Apr 1967
*South West Africa and the
Postponement to 1968 of the
UN Conference on the
Exploration and Peaceful
Uses of Outer Space:*
Abdul Rahman Pazhwak,
Afghanistan

5th Emergency Special,
Jun 1967
*Humanitarian Assistance:
Question of the Middle East:*
Abdul Rahman Pazhwak,
Afghanistan

22nd Regular, 1967–68:
Corneliu Manescu, Romania

23rd Regular, 1968:
E Arenales, Guatemala

24th Regular, 1969:
Angie Brooks, Liberia

25th Regular, 1970:
Edvard Hambro, Norway

26th Regular, 1971:
Adam Malik, Indonesia

27th Regular, 1972:
Stanislaw Trepczynski, Poland

28th Regular, 1973:
Leopoldo Benites, Ecuador

6th Special, Apr 1974
*New International Economic
Order:*
Leopoldo Benites, Ecuador

29th Regular, 1974:
Abdelaziz Boutefliika, Algeria

7th Special, Sep 1975
*Development and International
Economic Cooperation and
Establishment of a New
International Economic Order:*
Abdelaziz Boutefliika, Algeria

30th Regular, 1975:
Gaston Thorn, Luxembourg

31st Regular, 1976:
H Shirley Amerasinghe,
Sri Lanka

32nd Regular, 1977:
Lazar Mojsov, Yugoslavia

8th Special, Apr 1978
*Financing of UN Interim
Force in Lebanon:*
Lazar Mojsov, Yugoslavia

9th Special, Apr 1978
Namibia:
Lazar Mojsov, Yugoslavia

10th Special, Jun 1978
Disarmament:
Lazar Mojsov, Yugoslavia

33rd Regular, 1978–79:
I Lievano, Colombia

34th Regular, 1979–80:
Salim A Salim, UR of
Tanzania

6th Emergency Special, Jan
1980
Situation in Afghanistan:
Salim A Salim, UR of
Tanzania

7th Emergency Special,
Jul 1980
Question of Palestine:
Salim A Salim, UR of
Tanzania

11th Special, Aug 1980
*Critical Economic Situation of
Many Developing Countries:*
Salim A Salim, UR of
Tanzania

35th Regular, 1980–81:
Rüdiger von Wechmar, FR
Germany

8th Emergency Special,
Sep 1981
Question of Namibia:
Rüdiger von Wechmar,
FR Germany

36th Regular, 1981–82:
Ismat T Kittani, Iraq

9th Emergency Special,
Jan 1982
*Situation in the Occupied Arab
Territories, the Syrian Golan
Heights:*
Ismat T Kittani, Iraq

7th Emergency Special
(resumed),
Apr, Jun, Aug, Sep 1982
Question of Palestine;
Presided over by:
Ismat T Kittani, Iraq,
Apr, Jun, Aug 1982
Imre Hollai, Hungary,
Sep 1982

12th Special, Jun 1982
Disarmament:
Ismat T Kittani, Iraq

37th Regular, 1982–83:
Imre Hollai, Hungary

38th Regular, 1983–84:
Jorge E Illueca, Panama

39th Regular, 1984–85:
Paul J F Lusaka, Zambia

40th Regular, 1985–86:
Jaime de Pinies, Spain

13th Special, May 1986
*Critical Economic Situation
in Africa:*
Jaime de Pinies, Spain

41st Regular, 1986–87:
H R Choudhury, Bangladesh

14th Special, Sep 1986
Namibia:
H R Choudhury, Bangladesh

42nd Regular, 1987–88:
Peter Florin, German DR

15th Special, May–Jun 1988
Disarmament:
Peter Florin, German DR

43rd Regular, 1988–89:
Dante M Caputo, Argentina

44th Regular, 1989–90:
Joseph N Garba, Nigeria

16th Special, 1989
*Apartheid and its Destructive
Consequences in Southern Africa:*
Joseph N Garba, Nigeria

17th Special, Feb 1990
*Question of International
Cooperation Against Illicit
Production, Supply, Demand,
Trafficking and Distribution
of Narcotic Drugs:*
Joseph N Garba, Nigeria

18th Special, Apr 1990
*Devoted to International
Economic Cooperation,
in particular to the
Revitalisation of Economic
Growth and Development
of Developing Countries:*
Joseph N Garba, Nigeria

45th Regular, 1990–91:
Guido de Marco, Malta

46th Regular, 1991–92:
Samir Shihabi, Saudi Arabia

47th Regular, 1992–93:
Stoyan Ganev, Bulgaria

48th Regular, 1993–94:
Samuel R Insanally, Guyana

49th Regular, 1994–95:
Amara Essy, Côte d'Ivoire

50th Regular, 1995–96:
Diogo Freitas do Amaral,
Portugal

51st Regular, 1996–97:
Razali Ismail, Malaysia

10th Emergency Special,
Apr 1997
*Illegal Israeli Actions in Occupied
East Jerusalem and the Rest of the
Occupied Palestinian Territory:*
Razali Ismail, Malaysia

19th Special, Jun 1997
*Review and Appraisal of the
Implementation of Agenda 21:*
Razali Ismail, Malaysia

10th Emergency Special (resumed),
Jul, Nov 1997, Mar 1998, Feb 1999, Oct 2000
Illegal Israeli Actions in Occupied East Jerusalem and the Rest of the Occupied Palestinian Territory;
Presided over by:
Razali Ismail, Malaysia, Jul 1997
Hennadiy Udovenko, Ukraine, Nov 1997, Mar 1998
Didier Opertti Badan, Uruguay, Feb 1999
Harri Holkeri, Finland, Oct 2000

52nd Regular, 1997–98:
Hennadiy Udovenko, Ukraine

20th Special, Jun 1998
Devoted to Countering the World Drug Problem Together:
Hennadiy Udovenko, Ukraine

53rd Regular, 1998–99:
Didier Opertti Badan, Uruguay

21st Special, Jun–Jul 1999
Review and Appraisal of the Implementation of the Programme of Action of the International Conference on Population and Development:
Didier Opertti Badan, Uruguay

54th Regular, 1999–2000:
Theo-Ben Gurirab, Namibia

22nd Special, Sep 1999
Review and Appraisal of the Implementation of the Programme of Action for the Sustainable Development of Small Island Developing States:
Theo-Ben Gurirab, Namibia

23rd Special, 5–9 Jun 2000
Women 2000: Gender Equality, Development and Peace for the Twenty-First Century:
Theo-Ben Gurirab, Namibia

24th Special, 26–30 Jun 2000
World Summit for Social Development and Beyond: Achieving Social Development for All in a Globalising World:
Theo-Ben Gurirab, Namibia

55th Regular, 2000–01:
Harri Holkeri, Finland

25th Special, 6–8 Jun 2001
Overall Review and Appraisal of the Implementation of the Outcome of the UN Conference on Human Settlements (Habitat II):
Harri Holkeri, Finland

26th Special, 25–27 Jun 2001
HIV/AIDS:
Harri Holkeri, Finland

56th Regular, 2001–02:
Han Seung-Soo, ROK

10th Emergency Special (resumed),
Dec 2001, May 2002, Aug 2002
Illegal Israeli Actions in Occupied East Jerusalem and the Rest of the Occupied Palestinian Territory:
Han Seung-Soo, ROK

27th Special, 8–10 May 2002
Children:
Han Seung-Soo, ROK

57th Regular, 2002–03:
Jan Kavan, Czech Republic

58th Regular, 2003–04:
Julian Hunte, Saint Lucia

10th Emergency Special (resumed),
Sep, Oct, Dec 2003
Illegal Israeli Actions in Occupied East Jerusalem and the Rest of the Occupied Palestinian Territory:
Julian Hunte, Saint Lucia

59th Regular, 2004–05:
Jean Ping, Gabon

60th Regular, 2005–06:
Jan Eliasson, Sweden

61st Regular, 2006–07:
Haya Rashed Al Khalifa, Bahrain

OFFICE HOLDERS: 62ND REGULAR SESSION

Session dates
From 18 September 2007

President
Srgjan Kerim, The Former Yugoslav Republic of Macedonia

21 Vice-Presidents
Comprising the representatives of the five permanent members of the Security Council and 16 elected by the General Assembly. (Not appointed at the time of printing.)

First Committee: Disarmament and International Security

Chair	Vice-Chairs	Rapporteur
Paul Badji, Senegal	Bassam Darwish, Syrian AR	Dainius Baublys, Lithuania
	Roman Hunger, Switzerland	
	Ricardo Morote, Peru	

Second Committee: Economic and Financial

Chair	Vice-Chairs	Rapporteur
Kirsti Lintonen, Finland	Not appointed	Not appointed

Third Committee: Social, Humanitarian and Cultural

Chair	Vice-Chairs	Rapporteur
Raymond Wolfe, Jamaica	Takashi Ashiki, Japan Alan Gibbons, Ireland Kristine Malinovska, Latvia	Tebatso Future Baleseng, Botswana

Fourth Committee: Special Political and Decolonization

Chair	Vice-Chairs	Rapporteur
Abdalhaleem Mohamad, Sudan	Hossein Maleki, Iran Viktoriia Kuvshynnykova, Ukraine Third Vice-Chair not appointed	Reniery Valladares, Honduras

Fifth Committee: Administrative and Budgetary

Chair	Vice-Chairs	Rapporteur
Hamidon Ali, Malaysia	Alejandro Torres Lepori, Argentina Tomáš Micánek, Czech Republic Klaus de Rijk, Netherlands	Steven Ssenabulya, Uganda

Sixth Committee: Legal

Chair	Vice-Chairs	Rapporteur
Alexei Tulbure, Republic of Moldova	Jerzy Makarowski, Sweden Alvaro Sandoval Bernal, Colombia Karen Odaba-Mosoti, Kenya	Adam Mulawarman Tugio, Indonesia

OFFICE HOLDERS: 61ST REGULAR SESSION

Session dates
From 12 September 2006

President
Haya Rashed Al Khalifa, Bahrain

21 Vice-Presidents
Comprising the representatives of the five permanent members of the Security Council and also:

Bhutan	Haiti	Nigeria
Cameroon	Indonesia	Philippines
Chile	Kuwait	Uganda
Colombia	Libya	Zimbabwe
Croatia	Liechtenstein	
Guinea	Netherlands	

First Committee: Disarmament and International Security

Chair	Vice-Chairs	Rapporteur
Mona Juul, Norway	Bostjan Malovrh, Slovenia	Abdelhamid Gharbi, Tunisia
	Federico Perazza, Uruguay	
	Andy Rachmianto, Indonesia	

Second Committee: Economic and Financial

Chair	Vice-Chairs	Rapporteur
Tiina Intelmann, Estonia	Prayono Atiyanto, Indonesia	Vanessa Gomes, Portugal
	Aboubacar Sadikh Barry, Senegal	
	Benedito Fonseca Filho, Brazil	

Third Committee: Social, Humanitarian and Cultural

Chair	Vice-Chairs	Rapporteur
Hamid Al Bayati, Iraq	Jorge Ballesteros, Costa Rica	Elena Molaroni, San Marino
	Lamin Faati, Gambia	
	Sergei A Rachkov, Belarus	

Fourth Committee: Special Political and Decolonization

Chair	Vice-Chairs	Rapporteur
Madhu Raman Acharya, Nepal	Urban Andersson, Sweden	Rana Salayeva, Azerbaijan
	Mahieddine Djeffal, Algeria	
	Monica Bolanos Perez, Guatemala	

Fifth Committee: Administrative and Budgetary

Chair	Vice-Chairs	Rapporteur
Youcef Yousfi, Algeria	Ilgar Mammadov, Azerbaijan	Diego Simancas, Mexico
	Alexios Mitsopoulos, Greece	
	Tirtha Raj Wagle, Nepal	

Sixth Committee: Legal

Chair	Vice-Chairs	Rapporteur
Juan Manuel Gomez Robledo, Mexico	Stefan Barriga, Liechtenstein	Mamadou Moustapha Loum, Senegal
	Sivagurunathan Ganeson, Malaysia	
	Theodor Casmin Onisii, Romania	

STRUCTURE

The following are established under the General Assembly's rules of procedure:

- Main committees
- Procedural committees
- Standing committees
- Subsidiary bodies.

A number of treaty bodies established by human rights conventions also report to the General Assembly on their activities.

MAIN COMMITTEES

Internet: www.un.org/ga/61/background/committees.shtml

Purpose

The Main Committees correspond to the major fields of responsibility of the General Assembly. They consider agenda items referred to them by the General Assembly and prepare recommendations and draft resolutions for submission to the General Assembly plenary.

Evolution

GA res. 2837 (XXVI) (1971) increased the number of Vice-Chairs of the Main Committees to two per committee. By GA res. 47/233 (1993) the General Assembly decided to merge the Special Political Committee and the Fourth Committee, thereby reducing the number of Main Committees from seven to six. In GA res. 48/264 (1994) the General Assembly decided upon a pattern for election of the six Chairs of the Main Committees. It decided to review this arrangement at its 53rd session. By GA res. 52/163 (1997) the General Assembly decided that each Main Committee would elect a Chair, three Vice-Chairs and a Rapporteur. GA res. 56/509 (2002) provided for the election of President, Vice-Presidents and Chairs of the Main Committees at least three months before the opening of the session over which they were to preside. GA res. 58/126 (2003) provided for the election of the full Bureaux of the Main Committees three months in advance of the next session.

Structure

Although it is the practice to refer most items to a committee, the General Assembly may decide to deal with certain items without prior reference to a committee. All UN members have the right to be represented on each of these committees. Each committee elects its own officers. Decisions are made by a majority of the members present and voting. A majority of the committee constitutes a quorum.

PROCEDURAL COMMITTEES

General Committee

Internet: www.un.org/ga/61/general/general.shtml

Purpose

The General Committee considers the provisional agenda and the supplementary list, considers requests for the inclusion of additional items on the agenda, allocates items to committees and submits its report for the approval of the General Assembly. It assists the President in drawing up the agenda for plenary meetings, determining the priority of agenda items, coordinating the proceedings of the committees and in the general conduct of the work of the General Assembly that falls within the President's competence. The General Committee may also make recommendations to the General Assembly concerning the closing date of the session. It may not decide any political question.

Membership

The General Committee comprises the President of the General Assembly, the 21 Vice-Presidents of the General Assembly and the Chairs of the six Main Committees. No two members of the General Committee can be members of the same delegation and the Committee is constituted to ensure its representative character.

Credentials Committee

Internet: www.un.org/ga/61/credent/credent.shtml

Purpose

The Credentials Committee examines and reports on the credentials of representatives. Any representative to whose admission a member has objected is seated provisionally in the General Assembly, with the same rights as other representatives, until the Committee has reported and the Assembly has given its decision.

Membership

The Committee consists of nine members appointed at the beginning of each session by the General Assembly on the proposal of the President. Members appointed at the 61st session were:

China	Madagascar	Russian Federation
Guyana	Monaco	Tonga
Kenya	Peru	USA

STANDING COMMITTEES

Two standing committees have been established, in accordance with the General Assembly's rules of procedure, to deal with continuing problems during and between its regular sessions.

Advisory Committee on Administrative and Budgetary Questions (ACABQ)

Internet: www.un.org/docs/acabq/

Purpose

ACABQ, which was set up at the first session of the General Assembly by GA res. 14(I) A (1946), examines and reports on the regular and peacekeeping budgets and the accounts of the UN, and the administrative budgets of the specialised agencies. The Committee also advises the General Assembly on other administrative and financial matters referred to it. Its membership has been expanded a number of times, most recently by GA res. 32/103 (1977), and now stands at 16.

Membership

Members of the Committee are appointed by the General Assembly, on the recommendation of the Fifth Committee, on the basis of broad geographical representation, personal qualifications and experience. They serve for three years, retire by rotation and are eligible for reappointment. Rules 155 and 156 of the rules of procedure state that the Committee shall include at least three financial experts of recognised standing and that these financial experts may not retire simultaneously. The 16 members of the Committee are:

Term ending 31 Dec 2007	Term ending 31 Dec 2008	Term ending 31 Dec 2009
Jorge Flores Callejas, Honduras	Guillermo Kendall, Argentina	Andrzej Abraszewski, Poland (Vice-Chair)
Ronald Elkhuizen, Netherlands	Igor Khalevinski, Russian Federation	Collen V Kelapile, Botswana
Jerry Kramer, Canada	Susan McLurg, USA	Stafford Neil, Jamaica
Sun Minqin, China	Tommo Monthe, Cameroon	Mohammad Tal, Jordan
Rajat Saha, India (Chair)	Christina Vasak, France	Nonye Udo, Nigeria
Jun Yamazaki, Japan		

Committee on Contributions

Internet: follow links from www.un.org/ga/subsidiary/

Purpose

The Committee on Contributions was established by GA res. 14(I) (1946) and advises the General Assembly on the apportionment among members of the expenses of the UN, assessments for new members, appeals by members for a change of assessment and application of article 19 in cases of arrears in the payment of assessments.

Meetings

The 67th session of the Committee was held in New York from 11 to 29 June 2007.

Membership

Membership has been expanded a number of times, most recently by GA res. 31/96 (1976), and now stands at 18.

Members are selected by the General Assembly on the recommendation of the Fifth Committee on the basis of broad geographical representation, personal qualifications and experience. They serve for three years, retire by rotation and are eligible for reappointment.

The members are:

Term ending 31 Dec 2007	Term ending 31 Dec 2008	Term ending 31 Dec 2009
Gordon Eckersley, Australia	Vyacheslav Anatolievich Logutov, Russian Federation	Kenshiro Akimoto, Japan
Paul Ekorong à Dong, Cameroon	Richard Moon, UK	Petru Dumitru, Romania
Bernardo Greiver del Hoyo, Uruguay	Hae-yun Park, ROK	Ihor V Humenny, Ukraine
Hassan Mohammed Hassan, Nigeria	Henrique da Silveira Sardinha Pinto, Brazil	Meshal Al-Mansour, Kuwait
Eduardo Iglesias, Argentina	Thomas Thomma, Germany	Gobona Susan Mapitse, Botswana
Eduardo Ramos, Portugal	Wu Gang, China	Lisa P Spratt, USA

SUBSIDIARY AND AD HOC BODIES OF THE GENERAL ASSEMBLY

INTER-GOVERNMENTAL BODIES

Human Rights Council (HRC)

Secretariat of the Human Rights Council
OHCHR
Palais Wilson
52 Rue des Paquis
CH-1201 Geneva
Switzerland
Telephone: (+41 22) 917 9219
Fax: (+41 22) 917 9011
Internet: www.ohchr.org/english/bodies/hrcouncil

Purpose

The Human Rights Council was established in accordance with GA res. 60/251 (2006) to replace the Commission on Human Rights.

The Council is responsible for promoting universal respect for the protection of all human rights and fundamental freedoms for all, without distinction of any kind and in a fair and equal manner. It is mandated to consider violations of human rights, including gross and systemic violations, and make recommendations on these. The Council is also expected to promote the effective coordination and the mainstreaming of human rights within the UN system.

Structure

The Council is a subsidiary body of the General Assembly. It meets for no fewer than three sessions and for no less than 10 weeks each year. It is able to convene special sessions at the request of a Council member and with the support of one third of the Council membership.

Membership

The Council comprises 47 members, which are elected by the General Assembly. Membership is based on equitable geographical distribution on the basis: Africa 13 seats, Asia 13, Eastern Europe six, Latin America and Caribbean eight, Western European and Other states seven. The standard term of membership is three years, but the terms of the inaugural members of the Council (2006) are staggered. After two consecutive terms members are not eligible for immediate re-election.

Membership as of 19 June 2007 was:

African states

Angola	2007–10	Mali	2006–08
Cameroon	2006–09	Mauritius	2006–09
Djibouti	2006–09	Nigeria	2006–09
Egypt	2007–10	Senegal	2006–09
Gabon	2006–08	South Africa	2007–10
Ghana	2006–08	Zambia	2006–08
Madagascar	2007–10		

Asian states

Bangladesh	2006–09	Pakistan	2006–08
China	2006–09	Philippines	2007–10
India	2007–10	Qatar	2007–10
Indonesia	2007–10	ROK	2006–08
Japan	2006–08	Saudi Arabia	2006–09
Jordan	2006–09	Sri Lanka	2006–08
Malaysia	2006–09		

Eastern European states

Azerbaijan	2006–09	Russian Federation	2006–09
Bosnia and Herzegovina	2007–10	Slovenia	2007–10
Romania	2006–08	Ukraine	2008–08

Latin American and Caribbean states

Bolivia	2007–10	Mexico	2006–09
Brazil	2006–08	Nicaragua	2007–10
Cuba	2006–09	Peru	2006–08
Guatemala	2006–08	Uruguay	2006–09

Western European and Other states

Canada	2006–09	Netherlands	2007–10
France	2006–08	Switzerland	2006–09
Germany	2006–09	United Kingdom	2006–08
Italy	2007–10		

WORKING GROUPS OF THE HUMAN RIGHTS COUNCIL

Human Rights Council Advisory Committee (CAC)

Purpose

The CAC provides expertise to the Human Rights Council, focusing mainly on studies and research-based advice. It is intended to function as a think-tank to the Council and to work at its direction.

Evolution

The Human Rights Council agreed on 18 June 2007 (A/HRC/5/L.2) that it would decide at its sixth session (September 2007) on the most appropriate mechanisms to continue the work of four working groups. These were established under the Sub-Commission on the Promotion and Protection of Human Rights (a subsidiary body of the former Commission on Human Rights):

- Indigenous Populations
- Contemporary Forms of Slavery
- Minorities
- Social Forum.

Structure

The Advisory Committee is to comprise 18 experts, acting in their personal capacity and elected by Council members. The geographic distribution of experts serving on the CAC will be: Africa five, Asia five, Eastern Europe two, Latin America and Caribbean three, Western European and Others three.

The Committee may convene up to two sessions each year, for a maximum of 10 days per year, and additional sessions may be scheduled on an ad hoc basis with the prior approval of the Council. The CAC may not adopt resolutions or decisions.

Optional Protocol to the International Covenant on Economic, Social and Cultural Rights

Chair: Catarina de Albuquerque, Portugal

Purpose

Res. 2002/24 of the former Commission on Human Rights (endorsed by ECOSOC decision 2002/254) established an open-ended Working Group of the Commission to consider options for an optional protocol to the International Covenant on Economic, Social and Cultural Rights (ICESCR).

Evolution

The mandate of the Working Group was transferred to the Human Rights Council in June 2006 (A/HRC/1/102). At that meeting the Human Rights Council extended the Working Group's mandate for two years in order to develop an optional protocol to the ICESCR (A/HRC/2006/3).

Meetings

The Working Group met in Geneva from 16 to 27 July 2007.

Membership

Membership is open to all Member States and Observers of the UN.

Ad Hoc Committee on the Elaboration of Complementary Standards under the Convention on the Elimination of Racial Discrimination

Chair: vacant

Purpose

In December 2006 the Human Rights Council established an Ad Hoc Committee on the Elaboration of Complementary Standards to develop complementary standards in the form of either a convention or additional protocol(s) to the International Convention on the Elimination of Racial Discrimination (A/HRC/3/3).

Meetings

The Ad Hoc Committee is to convene annual sessions of 10 working days, beginning after the completion of the sixth session of the Working Group on the Effective Implementation of the Durban Declaration and Programme of Action. This was scheduled to take place from 3 to 7 September 2007.

The Ad Hoc Committee is to consider the base document outlining the substantive gaps in the International Convention on the Elimination of All Forms of Racial Discrimination.

Membership

Membership is open to all Member States and Observers of the UN.

The Right to Development

Chair: Ibrahim Salama, Egypt

Structure

In its decision 1998/269 ECOSOC endorsed a Commission on Human Rights recommendation (res 1998/72) to establish a mechanism to make further progress towards realisation of the right to development.

Evolution

In June 2006 the Human Rights Council extended the Working Group's mandate on the Right to Development for one year. It also extended the High Level Task Force's mandate on the implementation of the Right to Development (A/HRC/1/4).

The High-Level Task Force held its third meeting in Geneva from 22 to 26 January 2007. The Working Group held its eighth session in Geneva from 26 February to 2 March 2007. The Human Rights Council decided in March 2007 to extend the Working Group's mandate and the High-Level Task Force for two years (A/HRC/4/4).

Structure

The High-Level Task Force was established in 2004 to assist the Working Group in its analysis of progress, dissemination of best practices and consideration of possible solutions for the implementation of the right to development (CHR 2004/7). It comprises five experts and includes representatives from trade, finance and development institutions. The current members of the High-Level Task Force are:

Solita Collas Monsod, Philippines	Nicolaas Schrijver, Netherlands	Jorge Vargas Gonzalez, Colombia
Stephen Marks, USA	Margaret Sekaggya, Uganda	

Membership

The Working Group is open to all Member States and Observers of the UN.

Intergovernmental Working Group on the Effective Implementation of the Durban Declaration and Programme of Action

Chair: S E M Juan Martabit, Chile

Purpose

The Intergovernmental Working Group was created in 2002 to follow up on the World Conference against Racism, Racial Discrimination, Xenophobia and Related Intolerance (Durban, South Africa, 2001).

Evolution

During its inaugural session, held from 21 to 31 January and on 21 March 2003, the Intergovernmental Working Group decided to include a thematic approach in its future sessions, focusing on critical areas affecting the well-being of the victims of racism (W/CN.4/2003/20).

The mandate of the Working Group was transferred from the Commission on Human Rights to the Human Rights Council in June 2006 (GA Res 60/251). At its first session the Human Rights Council endorsed the conclusions and recommendations contained in the report of the Working Group's fourth session and agreed to extend the Working Group's mandate for a further three years (A/HRC/1/L.8).

Meetings

The fifth session of the Intergovernmental Working Group was held from 5 to 9 March 2007. This session was devoted to a thematic analysis of the role of national plans of action in combating racism, racial discrimination, xenophobia and related intolerance.

The Working Group was scheduled to hold its sixth session from 3 to 7 September 2007.

Membership

Membership is open to all Member States and Observers of the UN.

Preparatory Committee for the Review of the Implementation of the Durban Declaration and Programme of Action

Chair: A chair was to be elected at the organisational meeting of the Preparatory Committee in August 2007.

Purpose

Under its res. 61/149 the General Assembly has decided to review in 2009 the implementation of the Durban Declaration and Programme of Action. It has agreed that the Human Rights Council will act as the Preparatory Committee for the review.

Evolution

In December 2006 the Human Rights Council agreed that the Preparatory Committee would make preparations for the conference, including deciding on its objectives, its level, regional preparatory initiatives, date and venue (A/HRC/3/2).

Meetings

The first organisational session of the Preparatory Committee was scheduled to take place in Geneva from 27 to 31 August 2007. The Human Rights Council also agreed that the Preparatory Committee would hold two substantive sessions of 10 working days per year each in 2007 and 2008 (to be scheduled).

Membership

Membership is open to all Member States and Observers of the UN.

Group of Independent Eminent Experts

Purpose

The Durban Programme of Action (2001), adopted at the World Conference against Racism, Racial Discrimination, Xenophobia and Related Intolerance, recommended that the UN High Commissioner for Human Rights cooperate with five independent eminent experts to follow the implementation of the provisions of the Durban Declaration and Programme of Action.

Evolution

The Secretary-General appointed five independent eminent experts on 16 June 2003, with the former Commission on Human Rights defining their terms of reference in its res. 2002/68. The terms of reference were adjusted by res. 2003/30.

The Independent Eminent Experts have met twice, once in 2003 and once in 2005 (E/CN.4/2005/125). At their second meeting the Experts discussed how best to follow, in cooperation with the UN High Commissioner for Human Rights, the implementation of the provisions of the Durban Declaration and Programme of Action. Dates for the third meeting are under consideration.

Membership

Martti Oiva Kalevi Ahtisaari, Finland

Prince El Hassan bin Talal, Jordan

Salim Ahmed Salim, Tanzania

Edna Maria Santos Roland, Brazil

Hanna Suchocka, Poland

Arbitrary Detention

Purpose

Res. 1991/42 of the former Commission on Human Rights (approved by ECOSOC in decision 1991/243) established, initially for a three-year period, a working group composed of five independent experts. They had the task of investigating cases of detention imposed arbitrarily or otherwise inconsistently with the international standards set forth in the Universal Declaration of Human Rights or the relevant international legal instruments accepted by the states concerned.

Evolution

Res. 2003/31 extended the Working Group's mandate for a further three-year period. The Human Rights Council decided on 18 June 2007 (A/HRC/5/L.2) to renew the mandate of the working group until the date on which it could be considered by the Council. The Council was expected to agree its programme of work by September 2007 and is likely to consider the mandate of the Working Group later in 2007 or 2008.

Membership

Members of the working group as at 30 June 2007 were:

Tamás Ban, Hungary (Vice-Chair)

Manuela Carmena Castrillo, Spain

Seyyed Mohammad Hashemi, Iran

Soledad Villagra, Paraguay

Lella Zerrougui, Algeria (Chair and Rapporteur)

Enforced or Involuntary Disappearances

Purpose

CHR res. 20 (XXXVI) (1980) established for one year a working group consisting of five members, serving as experts in their individual capacities, to examine questions relevant to enforced or involuntary disappearances of persons.

Structure

The Working Group is made up of five independent experts.

Evolution

The Working Group held three sessions in 2006. The 81st Session took place in Geneva in March 2007. The 82nd Session took place in Geneva in June 2007.

In its second session in June 2007 the Human Rights Council decided (A/HRC/5/L.2) to renew the mandate of the Working Group until the date on which it could be considered by the Council.

The Council is expected to agree its programme of work by September 2007 and to consider the mandate of the working group later in 2007 or 2008. The 83rd Session of the Working Group is scheduled to be held in Geneva in the second half of 2007.

Membership

As at 30 June 2007 the members of the Working Group were:

Joel Adebayo Adekanye, Nigeria

Santiago Corcuera, Mexico (Chair)

Darko Gottlicher, Croatia

Saied Rajaie Khorasani, Iran

Stephen J Toope, Canada

Use of Mercenaries

Purpose

The Working Group on the Use of Mercenaries as a Means of Violating Human Rights and Impeding the Exercise of the Rights of Peoples to Self-determination was established in July 2005 (CHR/2005/3).

Structure

The Working Group is made up of five independent experts, one from each regional group. The working group reports annually to the Human Rights Council and the General Assembly. It is mandated to:
- Elaborate proposals on new standards, guidelines or principles on the right of peoples to self-determination while facing current and emergent threats posed by mercenaries
- Monitor mercenaries and mercenary activities in all their forms
- Study and identify emerging issues relating to mercenaries or mercenary-related activities
- Monitor and study the effects of the activities of private companies offering military assistance.

Membership

As at 30 June 2007 the members of the Working Group were:

Najat Al-Hajjaji, Libyan AJ

Amada Benavides, Colombia

José Luis Gomez del Prado, Spain (Chair and Rapporteur)

Alexander Nikitin, Russian Federation

Sahista Shameem, Fiji

Working Group of Experts on People of African Descent

Purpose

In 2002 the former Commission on Human Rights established the Working Group of Experts on People of African Descent to study the problems of racial discrimination faced by people of African descent and to propose measures to address those problems (res. 2002/68). The move followed the World Conference against Racism, Racial Discrimination, Xenophobia and Related Intolerance held in Durban, South Africa in 2001.

Evolution

In 2006 the mandate of the Working Group was transferred from the Commission on Human Rights to the Human Rights Council (GA Res 60/251) and extended for one year (A/HRC/1/102). The Working Group held its sixth session from 29 January to 2 February 2007.

The Human Rights Council agreed in June 2007 to renew the mandate of the Working Group until it could be considered by the Council (A/HRC/5/L.2). The Council was expected to agree to the Working Group's programme of work by September 2007.

Membership

Joseph Frans, Sweden	Peter Lesa Kasanda, Zambia, (Chair and Rapporteur)	Irina Moroianu-Zlatescu, Romania
George Nicolas Jabbour, Syrian AR		

Working Groups on Communications and Situations (Complaint Procedure)

Purpose

The Human Rights Council agreed in June 2007 (A/HRC/5/L.2) to establish a complaint procedure to address "consistent patterns of gross and reliably attested violations of all human rights and fundamental freedoms". The former Commission on Human Rights complaint procedure served as a working basis for the Council's complaint procedure and was enhanced as appropriate.

Structure

The Human Rights Council has decided to establish two working groups:
- The Working Group on Communications (WGC), which will decide on the admissibility of a communication in accordance with the guidance agreed by the Council in its decision A/HRC/5/L.2 and will assess the merits of the allegations of violations. It will comprise five members of the Council's Advisory Committee (CAC) appointed for a three-year term, renewable only once.
- The Working Group on Situations (WGS), which will bring to the Council's attention consistent patterns of gross and reliably attested violations of human rights and make recommendations on them. It will comprise five Council members, serving in their personal capacity, appointed by the respective regional groups for one-year terms. Each member's term will be renewable once, provided the state concerned is a Council member.

Both Working Groups are to work as much as possible on the basis of consensus, but will have the capacity to vote and establish their own rules of procedure. Each will meet in closed session at least twice a year, for five working days per session. The Working Groups are expected to be operational in early 2008.

The complaint procedure is confidential, in order to enhance cooperation with the State concerned. The Working Groups can recommend, however, that the Council consider a situation in public. The Council will consider these cases on a priority basis at its subsequent session.

Universal Periodic Review

Purpose

The General Assembly agreed in its res. 60/25 (2006) that the Human Rights Council would "undertake a universal periodic review, based on objective and reliable information, of the fulfilment by each State of its human rights obligations and commitments in a manner which ensures universality of coverage and equal treatment with respect to all States".

Evolution

The Council adopted the provisions of the Universal Periodic Review (UPR) in June 2007 (A/HRC/5/L.2), including the decision that the review of each State would be conducted in a Working Group chaired by the President of the Council and comprising the 47 members of the Council.

Structure

The Working Group will convene three sessions per year of two weeks each. The initial review cycle will be four years, with 48 countries to be reviewed by the Working Group per year.

The Working Group will spend three hours conducting the review of each country by way of a dialogue, and half an hour adopting a report. The review will be based on information prepared by the state under review. In addition, the Office of the High Commissioner for Human Rights will prepare a compilation of information from UN documents and a summary of information provided by other relevant stakeholders. The report of the Working Group will be submitted to the Council for its consideration in plenary. The Council plenary will adopt an outcome report in respect of each state.

The Working Group is expected to be operational at the beginning of 2008. The Human Rights Council was scheduled to agree at its September 2007 session on the guidelines for the information to be submitted by states under review.

Ad Hoc Committee on the Indian Ocean

Internet: follow links from www.un.org/ga/subsidiary/

Purpose

The Ad Hoc Committee on the Indian Ocean was established pursuant to GA res. 2992 (XXVII) (1972) to study the implications of the Declaration of the Indian Ocean as a Zone of Peace (GA res. 2832 (XXVI) (1971)).

Evolution

Following GA res. 32/86 (1977) a meeting of the coastal and hinterland states of the Indian Ocean was held in New York in 1979 as a step towards convening a conference on the Indian Ocean. However, efforts at reaching a consensus on when the conference should be held have not been successful. GA res. 46/49 (1991) decided that the conference should be structured in more than one stage and that the first stage of the conference should be convened in Colombo in 1993, or as soon as possible. The Committee has not yet been able to reach consensus on the implementation of the declaration. GA res. 60/48 (2006) requested the Chair of the Committee to continue his informal consultations with members of the Committee and report through the Committee to the General Assembly at its 62nd session.

Membership

Originally comprising 15 members, the Committee has been progressively enlarged, most recently by GA res. 34/80 (1979). Following the 6 April 1990 withdrawal from the Committee of France, UK and USA; the reunification of Germany; and the GA resolutions regarding the Socialist Federal Republic of Yugoslavia, the Committee now comprises 43 members:

Australia, Vice-Chair	Japan	Russian Federation
Bangladesh	Kenya	Seychelles
Bulgaria	Liberia	Singapore
Canada	Madagascar, Rapporteur	Somalia
China	Malaysia	Sri Lanka, Chair
Djibouti	Maldives	Sudan
Egypt	Mauritius	Thailand
Ethiopia	Mozambique, Vice-Chair	Uganda
Germany	Netherlands	UAE
Greece	Norway	UR of Tanzania
India	Oman	Yemen
Indonesia, Vice-Chair	Pakistan	Zambia
Iran	Panama	Zimbabwe
Iraq	Poland	
Italy	Romania	

Nepal, South Africa and Sweden are observers.

Ad Hoc Committee established by the General Assembly in its resolution 51/210 of 17 December 1996

Internet: www.un.org/law/terrorism/index.html

Purpose

GA res. 51/210 (1996) established an ad hoc committee to develop an international convention for the suppression of terrorist bombings and, subsequently, an international convention for the suppression of acts of nuclear terrorism, to supplement related existing international instruments and address ways of further developing a comprehensive legal framework of conventions dealing with international terrorism. This mandate continued to be renewed and revised on an annual basis by the General Assembly in its resolutions on measures to eliminate international terrorism.

Under GA res. 61/40 (2006) the Committee continues to develop the draft comprehensive convention on international terrorism and to discuss the question of convening a high-level conference under the auspices of the UN (GA res. 54/110 (1996)).

Since its establishment, the three treaties have been adopted:
- The International Convention for the Suppression of Terrorist Bombings (1997)
- The International Convention for the Suppression of the Financing of Terrorism (1999)
- The International Convention for the Suppression of Acts of Nuclear Terrorism (2005).

The Committee began the preparation of a draft comprehensive convention on international terrorism in 2000, which is still continuing.

The Committee normally holds one session each year. Its eleventh session was held from 5 to 6 and 15 February 2007. The work will be continued in the framework of a Working Group of the Sixth Committee during the 62nd session of the General Assembly.

Membership

Membership of the Committee is open to all Member States, members of the specialised agencies and of the International Atomic Energy Agency.

The officers of the Committee are:

Chair	Vice-Chairs	Rapporteur
Rohan Perera, Sri Lanka	Dieogo Malpede, Argentina	Lublin Dilja, Albania
	Maria Telalian, Greece	
	Sabelo Sivuyile, South Africa	

Ad Hoc Committee on the Criminal Accountability of United Nations Officials and Experts on Mission

Internet: www.un.org/law/criminalaccountability/index.html

Purpose

GA res. 61/29 (2006) established an ad hoc committee for the purpose of considering the report of the Group of Legal Experts established by the Secretary-General pursuant to GA res. 59/300 (document A/60/980), in particular its legal aspects.

Structure

The Committee held its first session from 9 to 13 April 2007, where it recommended that the Sixth Committee, at the 62nd session of the General Assembly, establish a working group with a view to continuing the consideration of the report of the Group of Legal Experts, taking into account the views expressed in the Ad Hoc Committee.

Membership

Membership of the Committee is open to all Member States, members of the specialised agencies and the International Atomic Energy Agency.

The officers of the Committee are:

Chair	Vice-Chairs	Rapporteur
Maria Telalian, Greece	El Hadj Lamine, Algeria	Martin Roger, Estonia
	Ruddy José Flores Monterrey, Bolivia	
	Ganeson Sivagurunathan, Malaysia	

Ad Hoc Committee on a Comprehensive and Integral International Convention on the Protection and Promotion of the Rights and Dignity of Persons with Disabilities

GA res. 56/168 (2001) established an ad hoc committee to consider proposals for a comprehensive and integral international convention to promote and protect the rights and dignity of persons with disabilities. The Committee was charged with taking a holistic approach to the work done in the fields of social development, human rights and non-discrimination.

The eighth session of the Ad Hoc Committee was held from 14 to 25 August 2006.

The Ad Hoc Committee was wound up following the signing in New York on 30 March 2007 of the Convention on the Rights of Persons with Disabilities.

Committee on Conferences

Internet: www.un.org/Depts/DGAACS/committeeonconf.html

Purpose

After consultation, the Committee on Conferences recommends to the General Assembly a draft calendar of conferences and meetings. Overlapping of meetings in the same sector of activity is avoided wherever possible. The Committee is also mandated to:
- Recommend the best use of conference-servicing resources, including the introduction of new technology in the interpretation, translation and documentation areas
- Advise on current and future requirements
- Monitor the organisation's publications policy.

Evolution

The Committee was established by GA res. 3351 (XXIX) (1974). GA res. 43/222(B) (1988) retained the Committee as a permanent subsidiary organ and set the membership of the Committee at 21 on the basis of six members from African states, five from Asian states, four from Latin American and Caribbean states, two from Eastern European states, and four from Western European and Other states. Members are appointed by the President of the General Assembly, after consultations with the chairs of the regional groups, for terms of three years. One-third of the Committee's membership retires annually and retiring members are eligible for reappointment.

At its 1999 substantive session the Committee agreed to a procedure for the participation of observers in the work of the Committee.

Meetings

The Committee is scheduled to hold its next substantive session from 10 to 14 September 2007.

Membership

Membership of the Committee is:

Term ending 31 Dec 2007	Term ending 31 Dec 2008	Term ending 31 Dec 2009
Austria	Burundi	Belarus
China	El Salvador	Germany
Egypt	France	Grenada
Jamaica	Lesotho	Honduras
Kenya	Malaysia	Nigeria
Nepal	Philippines	Senegal
USA	Russian Federation	Syria

The officers of the Committee are:

Chair	Vice-Chairs	Rapporteur
Yury G Yaroshevich, Belarus	Hilario G Davide Jr, Philippines	Anthony Andanje, Kenya
	Barbara Kaudel, Austria	
	Norma E Taylor Roberts, Jamaica	

Committee on Information

Internet: www.un.org/ga/coi/

Purpose

GA res. 33/115C (1978) established a committee to review UN public information policies and activities. The Committee comprised 41 Member States appointed by the President of the General Assembly, after consultations with regional groups, on the basis of equitable geographical distribution. It was mandated to report to the General Assembly on the policies and activities of the public information services of the UN.

Evolution

GA res. 34/182 (1979) changed the Committee's name to the UN Committee on Information and its membership was increased to 66. By this resolution the Committee was requested to:

- Continue to examine UN public information policies and activities in the light of the evolution of international relations, particularly during the past two decades, and the imperatives of the establishment of the new international economic order and a new world information and communication order
- Evaluate and follow up the efforts made and progress achieved by the UN system in the field of information and communications
- Promote the establishment of a new, more just and more effective world information and communication order, intended to strengthen peace and international understanding. This would be based on the principles of free circulation and wider and better balanced dissemination of information. Recommendations would be made to the General Assembly.

Meetings

The Committee held its 29th session in New York from 30 April to 11 May 2007.

Membership

The 110 members of the Committee are:

African states

Algeria	Ethiopia	Niger
Angola	Gabon	Nigeria
Benin	Ghana	Senegal
Burkina Faso	Guinea	Somalia
Burundi	Kenya	South Africa
Cape Verde	Liberia	Sudan
Congo	Libyan AJ	Togo
Côte d'Ivoire	Madagascar	Tunisia
DR Congo	Morocco	UR of Tanzania
Egypt	Mozambique	Zimbabwe

Asian states

Bangladesh	Kazakhstan	Singapore
China	Lebanon	Solomon Islands
Cyprus	Mongolia	Sri Lanka
DPRK	Nepal	Syrian AR
India	Pakistan	Thailand
Indonesia	Philippines	Viet Nam
Iran	Qatar	Yemen
Japan	ROK	
Jordan	Saudi Arabia	

Eastern European states

Armenia	Czech Republic	Romania
Azerbaijan	Georgia	Russian Federation
Belarus	Hungary	Slovakia
Bulgaria	Poland	Ukraine
Croatia	Republic of Moldova	

Latin American and Caribbean states

Argentina	Dominican Republic	Peru
Belize	Ecuador	Saint Vincent and the
Brazil	El Salvador	Grenadines
Chile	Guatemala	Suriname
Colombia	Guyana	Trinidad and Tobago
Costa Rica	Jamaica	Uruguay
Cuba	Mexico	Venezuela

Western European and Other states

Austria	Iceland	Netherlands
Belgium	Ireland	Portugal
Denmark	Israel	Spain
Finland	Italy	Switzerland
France	Luxembourg	Turkey
Germany	Malta	UK
Greece	Monaco	USA

Office holders for 2007–08 are:

Chair	Vice-Chairs	Rapporteur
Rudolf Christen, Switzerland	Estevão Umba Alberto, Angola	Hossein Maleki, Iran
	Marc Emillian Morar, Romania	
	Marcelo Suárez Salvia, Argentina	

Committee on Relations with the Host Country

Internet: follow links from www.un.org/ga/subsidiary/

Purpose

The Committee on Relations with the Host Country is authorised to deal with questions of security of missions accredited to the UN and the safety of their staff, the responsibilities of missions and issues relating to diplomatic parking. It may also advise the host country on issues arising in connection with the implementation of the Headquarters Agreement between the UN and the USA.

Evolution

GA res. 2819 (XXVI) (1971) established the Committee by replacing the Informal Joint Committee on Host Country Relations established under GA res. 2618 (XXIV) (1969).

Membership

Until 1998, the Committee comprised the host country and 14 Member States chosen by the President of the General Assembly. GA res. 53/104 (1998) increased the Committee's membership by four members (one each from African, Asian, Latin American and Caribbean, and Eastern European states), bringing the total membership of the Committee to 19.

The Committee has been chaired since 1971 by successive permanent representatives of Cyprus. The members are:

African states

Côte d'Ivoire, Vice-Chair	Mali
Libyan AJ	Senegal

Asian states

China	Iraq
Cyprus, Chair	Malaysia

Eastern European states

Bulgaria, Vice-Chair	Russian Federation
Hungary	

Latin American and Caribbean states

Costa Rica, Rapporteur	Honduras
Cuba	

Western European and Other states

Canada, Vice-Chair	UK
France	USA
Spain	

Committee on the Exercise of the Inalienable Rights of the Palestinian People

Internet: www.un.org/depts/dpa/qpalnew/committee.htm

Purpose

By GA res. 3376 (XXX) (1975) the General Assembly established a 20-member committee to consider and recommend to it a programme that would enable the Palestinian people to exercise the rights recognised in GA res. 3236 (XXIX) (1974).

Evolution

By GA res. 61/22 (2007) the General Assembly requested that the Committee continue to exert all efforts to promote the realisation of the inalienable rights of the Palestinian people, support the Middle East peace process and mobilise international support for and assistance to the Palestinian people. The General Assembly authorised the Committee to adjust its approved work programme as it considered appropriate and necessary, and report to the General Assembly at its 62nd session and thereafter. It also asked the Committee to continue to keep under review the question of Palestine, and to report and make suggestions to the General Assembly, the Security Council or the Secretary-General as appropriate. The General Assembly asked the Committee to continue to extend its cooperation and support to Palestinian and other civil society organisations in order to mobilise international solidarity and support for the achievement by the Palestinian people of their inalienable rights and a peaceful settlement of the question of Palestine, and to involve additional civil society organisations in its work.

Membership

Since 1976 the membership has expanded and now consists of 22 Member States and 26 Observers. The members of the Committee are:

Afghanistan	Lao PDR	Senegal
Belarus	Madagascar	Sierra Leone
Cuba	Malaysia	South Africa
Cyprus	Mali	Tunisia
Guinea	Malta	Turkey
Guyana	Namibia	Ukraine
India	Nigeria	
Indonesia	Pakistan	

The following officers comprise the Bureau of the Committee:

Chair	Vice-Chairs	Rapporteur
Paul Badji, Senegal	Rodrigo Malmierca Díaz, Cuba	Victor Camilleri, Malta
	Zahir Tanin, Afghanistan	

Committee on the Peaceful Uses of Outer Space (COPUOS)

Office for Outer Space Affairs
Vienna International Centre
PO Box 500
A–1400 Vienna, Austria
Telephone: (+43 1) 26060 4950
Fax: (+43 1) 26060 5830
Email: oosa@unvienna.org
Internet: www.unoosa.org/oosa/COPUOS/copuos.html
Director: Dr Sergio Camacho-Lara, Mexico (since December 2002) (appointed by the UN Secretary-General)

Purpose

The tasks of COPUOS are to:
- Review the scope of international cooperation in peaceful uses of outer space
- Devise programmes in this field that would be undertaken under UN auspices
- Encourage continued research and disseminate information on research
- Study legal problems arising from the exploration of outer space.

Evolution

By GA res. 1472 (XIV) (1959) the General Assembly established COPUOS as a permanent body. It succeeded the 18-nation ad hoc committee of the same name established by GA res. 1348 (XIII) (1958).

Meetings

The General Assembly has authorised the convening of three conferences on the exploration and peaceful uses of outer space. All three were held in Vienna, in 1968, 1982 and 1999.

The third, UNISPACE III, adopted 'The Space Millennium: Vienna Declaration on Space and Human Development', which was endorsed by the General Assembly in GA res. 54/68 (1999).

The 50th session of the Committee was held in Vienna from 6 to 15 June 2007.

Membership

The Committee originally comprised 24 members whose terms of office expired at the end of 1961. By GA res. 1721 (XVI) (1961) the General Assembly decided to continue the Committee and increased the membership to 28. The membership now stands at 67 following GA res. 59/116 (2004).

The Committee members are:

African states

Algeria	Egypt	Nigeria
Benin	Kenya	Senegal
Burkina Faso	Libyan AJ	Sierra Leone
Cameroon	Morocco	South Africa
Chad	Niger	Sudan

Asian states

China	Kazakhstan	ROK
India	Lebanon	Saudi Arabia
Indonesia	Malaysia	Syrian AR
Iran	Mongolia	Thailand
Iraq	Pakistan	Viet Nam
Japan	Philippines	

Eastern European states

Albania	Hungary	Russian Federation
Bulgaria	Poland	Slovakia
Czech Republic	Romania	Ukraine

Latin American and Caribbean states

Argentina	Cuba	Peru
Brazil	Ecuador	Uruguay
Chile	Mexico	Venezuela
Colombia	Nicaragua	

Western European and Other states

Australia	Germany	Spain
Austria	Greece	Sweden
Belgium	Italy	Turkey
Canada	Netherlands	UK
France	Portugal	USA

The Committee has two standing sub-committees of the whole:
- Scientific and Technical Sub-committee
- Legal Sub-committee.

The officers of the Committee are:

Chair	First Vice-Chair	Second Vice-Chair and Rapporteur
Gérard Brachet, France	Elöd Both, Hungary	Paul R Tiendrébéogo, Burkina Faso

Conference on Disarmament (CD)

Palais des Nations
1211 Geneva 10
Switzerland
Telephone: (+41 22) 917 2281
Fax: (+41 22) 917 0034
Telex: 412962
Internet: follow link from www.unog.ch/disarmament
Secretary-General of the CD and Personal Representative of the Secretary-General of the UN to the
CD: Sergei Ordzhonikidze, Russian Federation (since 2002) (appointed by the UN Secretary-General)

Purpose

Based in Geneva, the CD is the sole multilateral forum for negotiating disarmament.

Evolution

Agreement on the establishment of the Conference on Disarmament (CD) was reached at the General Assembly's First Special Session on Disarmament in 1978 (UNSSOD I res. S10/2). It succeeded the Conference of the Eighteen-Nation Committee on Disarmament (GA res. 1722 (XVI) (1961)) and the Conference of the Committee on Disarmament (GA res. 2602 (XXIV) (1969)), which had met annually in Geneva since 1962 under the co-chairing of the former USSR and the USA.

In 1979, following UNSSOD I, the Conference committed itself to promoting general and complete disarmament under effective international control. It also decided that it would deal with the arms race and disarmament in 10 areas (the 'decalogue'):
• Nuclear weapons in all aspects
• Chemical weapons
• Other weapons of mass destruction
• Conventional weapons
• Reduction of military budgets
• Reduction of armed forces
• Disarmament and development
• Disarmament and international security
• Collateral measures, confidence-building measures and effective verification methods in relation to appropriate disarmament measures, acceptable to all parties concerned
• Comprehensive programme of disarmament leading to general and complete disarmament under effective international control.

Between 1979 and 1984 the Conference on Disarmament was known as the Committee on Disarmament.

The CD draws its annual agenda from the decalogue, taking into account the recommendations made to it by the General Assembly, proposals presented by Member States of the Conference and the decisions of the Conference. Item Two of the decalogue ceased to be current after the completion of negotiations on the Chemical Weapons Convention in 1992.

The Conference has its own rules of procedure. It has a special relationship with the UN. It is funded from the UN regular budget, holds its meetings on UN premises and is serviced by the UN staff of the Geneva Branch of the Office of the High Representative for Disarmament Affairs. The Conference reports to the General Assembly annually.

Membership

The CD is a body of limited composition (currently 65 Members) that takes its decisions on the basis of consensus. Its annual session is divided into three parts of 10, seven and seven weeks respectively, under a presidency that rotates among the membership every four working weeks. The Conference pursues its mandate in plenary meetings and through subsidiary bodies or special coordinators established under individual agenda items. In 1996 it completed negotiations on a Comprehensive Nuclear-Test-Ban Treaty.

The membership is:

Algeria	Germany	Peru
Argentina	Hungary	Poland
Australia	India	ROK
Austria	Indonesia	Romania
Bangladesh	Iran	Russian Federation
Belarus	Iraq	Senegal
Belgium	Ireland	Slovakia
Brazil	Israel	South Africa
Bulgaria	Italy	Spain
Cameroon	Japan	Sri Lanka
Canada	Kazakhstan	Sweden
Chile	Kenya	Switzerland
China	Malaysia	Syrian AR
Colombia	Mexico	Tunisia
Cuba	Mongolia	Turkey
DPRK	Morocco	Ukraine
DR Congo	Myanmar	UK
Ecuador	Netherlands	USA
Egypt	New Zealand	Venezuela
Ethiopia	Nigeria	Viet Nam
Finland	Norway	Zimbabwe
France	Pakistan	

Special Committee on Peacekeeping Operations

Internet: www.un.org/Depts/dpko/dpko/ctte/CTTEE.htm

Purpose

GA res. 2006 (XIX) (1965) authorised the President of the General Assembly to establish a special committee on peacekeeping operations. The Committee was asked to undertake a comprehensive review of peacekeeping operations.

Evolution

GA res. 51/136 (1996) expanded the Committee's membership to include all past or present personnel contributors to UN peacekeeping operations and observers. It also decided that Member States that became personnel contributors in the future, or that participated as observers for three consecutive years, could become members.

Membership

At the 2007 session of the Committee, from 26 February to 16 March, membership comprised the following 133 states:

Afghanistan	Australia	Belarus
Algeria	Austria	Belgium
Argentina	Azerbaijan	Benin
Armenia	Bangladesh	Bolivia

Brazil
Bulgaria
Burkina Faso
Cambodia
Cameroon
Canada
Central African Republic
Chad
Chile
China
Colombia
Congo
Costa Rica
Côte d'Ivoire
Croatia
Cuba
Cyprus
Czech Republic
Denmark
Djibouti
Dominican Republic
Ecuador
Egypt
El Salvador
Estonia
Ethiopia
Fiji
Finland
France
Gabon
Gambia
Georgia
Germany
Ghana
Greece
Grenada
Guatemala
Guinea
Guyana
Honduras
Hungary

Iceland
India
Indonesia
Iran
Iraq
Ireland
Italy
Jamaica
Japan
Jordan
Kazakhstan
Kenya
Kuwait
Kyrgyzstan
Lao PDR
Lebanon
Libyan AJ
Lithuania
Luxembourg
Madagascar
Malawi
Malaysia
Mali
Mauritania
Mauritius
Mexico
Mongolia
Morocco
Mozambique
Namibia
Nepal
Netherlands
New Zealand
Niger
Nigeria
Norway
Pakistan
Palau
Paraguay
Peru
Philippines

Poland
Portugal
ROK
Republic of Moldova
Romania
Russian Federation
Rwanda
Saudi Arabia
Samoa
Senegal
Serbia[1]
Sierra Leone
Singapore
Slovakia
Slovenia
South Africa
Spain
Sri Lanka
Sudan
Swaziland
Sweden
Switzerland
Syrian AR
Thailand
The Former Yugoslav Republic
of Macedonia
Timor-Leste
Togo
Tunisia
Turkey
Uganda
Ukraine
UK
UR of Tanzania
USA
Uruguay
Venezuela
Yemen
Zambia
Zimbabwe

Observers

Angola
Burundi
Comoros
DPRK
Eritrea
European Community

Haiti
Holy See
International Committee of
the Red Cross
International Criminal Police
Organisation (Interpol)

Israel
Lesotho
Permanent Observer for the
Sovereign Military Order
of Malta
Viet Nam

Chair

Aminu Bashir Wali, Nigeria

Vice-Chairs

Diego Limeres, Argentina

Akio Miyajima, Japan

Beata Peksa-Krawiec, Poland

Henri-Paul Normandin,
Canada

Rapporteur

Amr El-Sherbini, Egypt

Note

[1]   On 3 June 2006 the Republic of Serbia notified the UN that the membership of the State Union of Serbia
and Montenegro in the UN, including all organs and organisations of the UN system, was continued by the
Republic of Serbia on the basis of article 60 of the Constitutional Charter of Serbia and Montenegro, activated
by the Declaration of Independence adopted by the National Assembly of Montenegro on 3 June 2006.

Special Committee on the Charter of the UN and on the Strengthening of the Role of the Organization

Internet: www.un.org/law/chartercomm/

Purpose

The Ad Hoc Committee on the Charter of the UN, which was established in 1974 under GA res. 3349 (XXIX), was reconvened under GA res. 3499 (XXX) (1975) as the Special Committee on the Charter. The resolution requested the Special Committee to examine in detail suggestions and proposals received from governments concerning:

- The Charter
- The strengthening of the role of the UN with regard to the maintenance and consolidation of international peace and security
- The development of cooperation among all nations and the promotion of the rules of international law in relations between states
- Any additional specific proposals made by governments with a view to enhancing the ability of the UN to achieve its purpose.

The Special Committee's mandate has been renewed in successive years, most recently in GA res. 61/38 (2006).

Meetings

The most recent meeting was from 7 to 15 February 2007.

Membership

Under GA res. 50/52 (1995) the Committee's membership was expanded to include all Member States. Bureau officers elected at the Committee's February 2007 meeting were:

Chair	Vice-Chair	Rapporteur
Andrzej Towpik, Poland	Yasir Abdelsalam, Sudan	Gustavo Álvarez, Uruguay

Special Committee on the Implementation of the Declaration on Decolonization (Committee of Twenty-Four)

Internet: Follow links from www.un.org/Depts/dpi/decolonization

Purpose

GA res. 1654 (XVI) (1961) established a special committee of 17 members to examine the application of the Declaration on the Granting of Independence to Colonial Countries and Peoples (GA res. 1514 (XV) (1960)), and make suggestions and recommendations on the implementation of the Declaration.

Membership

GA res. 1810 (XVII) (1962) enlarged the membership of the Special Committee to 24. With the General Assembly's decision on 10 December 2004 to extend membership to Dominica and Timor-Leste, the total now stands at 27.

Antigua and Barbuda	Côte d'Ivoire	Grenada
Bolivia	Cuba	India
Chile	Dominica	Indonesia
China	Ethiopia	Iran
Congo	Fiji	Iraq

Mali
Papua New Guinea
Russian Federation
Saint Kitts and Nevis
Saint Lucia

Saint Vincent and the
   Grenadines
Sierra Leone
Syrian AR
Timor-Leste

Tunisia
UR of Tanzania
Venezuela

Chair	Vice-Chairs	Rapporteur
Margaret Hughes Ferrari, Saint Vincent and the Grenadines	Rodrigo Malmierca Díaz, Cuba	Bashar Ja'afari, Syrian AR
	Luc Joseph Okio, Congo	

The Special Committee's Sub-committee on Small Territories, Petitions, Information and Assistance was integrated into the Special Committee in January 1997.

Special Committee to Investigate Israeli Practices Affecting the Human Rights of the Palestinian People and Other Arabs of the Occupied Territories

Internet: follow links from www.unhchr.ch/html/menu2/7/a/moatsc.htm

Purpose

GA res. 2443 (XXIII) (1968) established the Special Committee to Investigate Israeli Practices Affecting the Human Rights of the Palestinian People and Other Arabs of the Occupied Territories. It was to be composed of three Member States appointed by the President of the General Assembly.

The Occupied Territories within the scope of the Special Committee's terms of reference are the occupied Syrian Golan, the West Bank (including East Jerusalem) and the Gaza Strip.

The Special Committee's mandate has been renewed annually, most recently by GA res. 61/116 (2006).

Membership

The membership of the Committee is:

Chair
Prasad Kariyawasam, Sri Lanka

Members
Hamidon Ali, Malaysia
Moussa Bocar Ly, Senegal

UN Conciliation Commission for Palestine

Purpose

GA res. 194 (III) (1948) established the United Nations Conciliation Commission for Palestine to:
• Help with the repatriation of refugees
• Arrange for compensation for the property of those choosing not to return
• Assist Israel and the Arab states to achieve a final settlement of all questions outstanding between them.

GA res. 61/112 (2006) requested the Commission to continue its work.

Membership

The members of the Commission are France, Turkey and USA. As set out in GA res. 194 (III) (1948), they were selected by a committee of the General Assembly consisting of the five permanent members of the Security Council.

UN Disarmament Commission (UNDC)

Internet: http://disarmament2.un.org/undiscom.htm

Purpose

In the Final Document of its tenth Special Session in 1978, GA res. S-10/2 para. 118, the General Assembly decided to establish, as successor to the Commission established by GA res. 502 (VI) (1952), a Disarmament Commission composed of all UN members. It decided that the Commission should be a deliberative body, required to consider and make recommendations on disarmament problems, and follow up decisions and recommendations of the tenth Special Session.

Evolution

GA res. 37/78H (1982) requested the Commission to direct its attention to specific subjects, taking into account the relevant resolutions of the General Assembly, and to make concrete recommendations to the subsequent session of the General Assembly. In 1998, by its decision 52/492, the General Assembly decided that from 2000 the Commission's agenda would normally comprise two substantive items.

Meetings

The UNDC normally meets in one three-week session annually, and operates by way of plenary meetings and working groups. The number of working groups depends on the number of substantive items on its agenda. The five regional groups take turns assuming the chair of the Commission. The chairs of the working groups are selected in accordance with the principle of equitable geographical representation.

The Commission held its 2007 substantive session from 9 to 27 April in New York.

Membership

The Chair and other officers elected for the 2007 session were:

Chair	Vice-Chairs	Rapporteur
Elbio Rosselli, Uruguay	Jacek Januchowski, Poland	Bassam Darwish, Syrian AR
	Bernd Heinze, Germany	
	Roman Hunger, Switzerland	
	Mohsen Naziri, Iran	
	Ricardo Morote, Peru	
	Raff Bukun-olu Wole Onemola, Nigeria	
	Zeljko Vukobratovic, Bosnia and Herzegovina	
	Jean-Francis Régis Zinsou, Benin	

Chair of Working Group I	Chair of Working Group II
Jean-Francis Régis Zinsou, Benin	Carlos Duarte, Brazil

UN Scientific Committee on the Effects of Atomic Radiation (UNSCEAR)

Vienna International Centre
PO Box 500
A–1400 Vienna
Austria
Telephone: (+43 1) 26060 4330
Fax: (+43 1) 26060 5902
Internet: www.unscear.org
Secretary: Malcolm Crick, UK (August 2005–July 2009) (selected by the Executive Director of UNEP)

Purpose

UNSCEAR was established by GA res. 913 (X) (1955). The resolution requested the Committee to receive radiological information furnished by Member States of the UN or members of the specialised agencies, summarise reports received on radiation levels and radiation effects, and propose research projects.

The Committee submits annual progress reports to the General Assembly and periodically publishes comprehensive reports. These contain systematic assessments of all the major sources of exposure to ionising radiation in the human environment and reviews of selected topics in the field of radiation effects.

Meetings

The 44th session was held in Vienna from 29 May to 2 June 2006. The 55th session was held from 21 to 25 May 2007, also in Vienna.

Membership

Originally 15, the membership of UNSCEAR has been increased, most recently by GA res. 3154 (XXVIII) (1973), and now stands at 21. The members, appointed by the President of the General Assembly in consultation with the chairs of the regional groups, are:

African states

Egypt	Sudan

Asian states

China	Indonesia
India	Japan

Eastern European states

Poland	Slovakia
Russian Federation	

Latin American and Caribbean states

Argentina	Mexico
Brazil	Peru

Western European and Other states

Australia	Germany
Belgium	Sweden
Canada	UK
France	USA

Working Group on the Financing of the UN Relief and Works Agency for Palestine Refugees in the Near East

Purpose

The Working Group was established by GA res. 2656 (XXV) of 7 December 1970 to study all aspects of financing of the agency.

Each year the General Assembly has endorsed the efforts of the Working Group and requested it to continue, most recently in GA res. 61/114 (2007).

Membership

The nine members designated by the Secretary-General are:

France	Lebanon	Turkey (Chair)
Ghana	Norway, Rapporteur	UK
Japan (Vice-Chair)	Trinidad and Tobago	USA

UN Open-Ended Informal Consultative Process on Oceans and the Law of the Sea (Oceans Consultative Process)

Internet: www.un.org/Depts/los/consultative_process/consultative_process.htm

Purpose

Following a 1999 review by the Commission on Sustainable Development of the sectoral theme of 'Oceans and Seas', the General Assembly decided in GA res. 54/33 (1999) to establish an open-ended informal consultative process to facilitate its annual review of developments in ocean affairs.

The Consultative Process meets once a year to consider the Secretary-General's annual report on Oceans and the Law of the Sea, as well as any particular resolution or decision of the General Assembly, relevant special reports of the Secretary-General and relevant recommendations of the Commission on Sustainable Development, and to carry out three interrelated tasks:

- To study developments in ocean affairs consistent with the legal framework provided by the Convention on the Law of the Sea and the goals of Chapter 17 of the global environmental action plan Agenda 21
- To identify particular issues to be considered by the General Assembly against the backdrop of overall developments of all relevant oceans issues
- To place emphasis on areas where coordination and cooperation at inter-government and inter-agency levels should be enhanced.

Evolution

In GA resolutions 57/141 (2002) and 60/30 (2005), the General Assembly decided to extend the Consultative Process for further periods of three years. A further review is scheduled to take place at the 63rd session of the General Assembly.

Meetings

The eighth meeting of the Consultative Process was held in New York from 25 to 29 June 2007 in accordance with GA res. 61/222 (2006).

Membership

The Consultative Process is open to all UN Member States, States Members of the specialised agencies and all parties to the Convention. It is also open to entities that have received a standing invitation to participate as observers in the work of the General Assembly and inter-government organisations with competence in ocean affairs. Discussion panels allow input from representatives of the major groups identified in Agenda 21.

The two Co-Chairs appointed by the Acting President of the General Assembly for the eighth meeting were Lori Ridgeway, Canada, and Cristián Maquieira, Chile.

AD HOC OPEN-ENDED WORKING GROUPS

High-Level Open-Ended Working Group on the Financial Situation of the United Nations

Purpose

Following a statement by the Secretary-General on 12 October 1994 on the precarious financial situation of the Organisation, the General Assembly decided in GA res. 49/143 (1995) to establish a high-level open-ended working group under the Chair of the President of the Assembly.

Meetings

The Working Group met in 1995, 1996 and 1997 to consider additional measures aimed at ensuring a sound and viable financial basis for the UN. It has not met since 16 June 1997, when it was agreed that the Working Group would be resumed 'when appropriate', after consultations with Member States.

Membership

Membership of the Working Group is open to all members of the UN.

Open-Ended Working Group on the Question of Equitable Representation and Increase in the Membership of the Security Council

Purpose

GA res. 48/26 (1993) established an open-ended working group to consider all aspects of the question of an increase in the membership of the Security Council, and other matters related to the Security Council.

Evolution

By GA res. 53/30 (1998) the General Assembly determined not to adopt any resolution or decision on the question of equitable representation on, or increase in, the membership of the Security Council and related matters without the affirmative vote of at least two-thirds of the members of the Assembly. In the United Nations Millennium Declaration, Heads of State and Government resolved to intensify their efforts to achieve comprehensive reform. In the 2005 World Summit Outcome of 16 September 2005, Heads of State and Government expressed further support for early reform of the Security Council and recommended that it continue to adapt its working methods.

Meetings

The Working Group has met regularly since its first session on 19 January 1994. The latest report of the Working Group to the General Assembly is contained in A/60/47.

Membership

Membership of the Working Group is open to all members of the UN. Office holders are:

Haya Rashed Al Khalifa, Bahrain (Chair)

ADVISORY BODIES

Advisory Board on Disarmament Matters

Internet: Follow links from http://disarmament.un.org

Purpose

The functions of the Advisory Board are to:
- Advise the Secretary-General on matters within the area of arms limitation and disarmament, including on studies and research under the auspices of the UN or institutions within the UN
- Serve as the Board of Trustees of the UN Institute for Disarmament Research (UNIDIR)
- Advise the Secretary-General on the implementation of the UN Disarmament Information Programme.

Evolution

The Advisory Board on Disarmament Matters was established in 1978 under paragraph 124 of the Final Document of the tenth Special Session of the General Assembly in 1978 (GA res. S10/2, para. 124). The Board received its current mandate through GA res. 54/418 of 1 December 1999.

Meetings

The Advisory Board usually holds two sessions each year, alternating between New York and Geneva.

Membership

The Secretary-General chooses the members of the Board from all regions of the world for their knowledge and experience in the field of disarmament and international security. There are normally 22 members on the Advisory Board (excluding the Director of UNIDIR), but four of the positions are currently vacant. The 18 members of the Advisory Board are:

Hasmy Agam, Malaysia	Perla Carvalho Soto, Mexico	Ho-Jin Lee, ROK
Christiane Isabelle Agboton Johnson, Senegal	Michael Clarke, UK	U Joy Ogwu, Nigeria
	Gelson Fonseca Jr, Brazil	Jayant Prasad, India
Anatoly Antonov, Russian Federation	Carolina Hernandez, Philippines	Stephen G Rademaker, USA
		Adam Daniel Rotfield, Poland
Elisabet Borsiin Bonnier, Sweden	Jeremy Issacharoff, Israel	Kongit Sinegiorgis, Ethiopia
Philippe Carré, France	Mahmoud Karem, Egypt	Zhang Yan, China

The Director of the UNIDIR is an ex officio member of the Advisory Board.

Advisory Committee of the UN Programme of Assistance in the Teaching, Study, Dissemination and Wider Appreciation of International Law

Internet: www.un.org/law/programmeofassistance/

Purpose

The General Assembly established a programme of assistance and exchange in the field of international law through GA res. 2099 (XX) (1965). This resolution set up the Committee to advise the Secretary-General on substantive aspects of the programme. The following year, by GA res. 2204 (XXI) (1966), the Advisory Committee was given its current title.

The Programme of Assistance was established to contribute to a better knowledge of international law and provide direct assistance by means of:
- Fellowship programmes, regional courses and symposia in international law
- The preparation and dissemination of publications and other information relating to international law.

The Secretary-General reports every second year to the General Assembly on the implementation of the programme and is then authorised to carry out activities for the next two years.

Evolution

Through GA res. 60/19 (2005) the General Assembly authorised the provision of a number of international law fellowships for 2006 and 2007 and, subject to the Programme's overall resources, a travel grant for one participant from each developing country is invited to regional courses that might be organised in 2006 and 2007. These grants are financed primarily from voluntary contributions. The Programme also provides for a minimum of one scholarship in both 2006 and 2007 under the Hamilton Shirley Amerasinghe Memorial Fellowship on the Law of the Sea. This is to be financed by voluntary contributions.

Membership

GA res. 58/73 (2003) appointed 25 Member States to serve on the Committee for a four-year period from 1 January 2004 to 31 December 2007. New members will be elected at the General Assembly's 62nd session, with terms beginning 1 January 2008.

African states

Ethiopia	Nigeria
Ghana	Sudan
Kenya	UR of Tanzania

Asian states

Cyprus	Malaysia
Iran	Pakistan
Lebanon	

Latin American and Caribbean states

Colombia	Trinidad and Tobago
Jamaica	Uruguay
Mexico	

Eastern European states

Czech Republic	Ukraine
Russian Federation	

Western European and Other states

Canada	Italy
France	Portugal
Germany	USA

EXPERT BODIES

Board of Auditors

Internet: www.unsystem.org/auditors/

Purpose

GA res. 74 (I) (1946) established the Board of Auditors to serve as external auditor of UN accounts, funds and programmes, and the International Court of Justice. It submits reports to the General Assembly annually or every two years, depending on the financial periods of the respective organisations.

Structure

The Board is composed of the Auditors-General (or officers holding equivalent title) of three Member States of the UN. GA res. 55/248 (2001) extended the term of Board members from three years to a non-consecutive term of six years from 1 July 2002. Board members are appointed by the General Assembly on the recommendation of the Fifth Committee and retire by rotation. Each member provides an audit staff of approximately 50 professional officers for four months a year and a full-time Director.

To enable the Board to carry out its mandate, an Audit Operations Committee was established at Headquarters, comprising three full-time Directors of External Audit, each representing a member of the Board.

Meetings

The board's next annual session is scheduled to be held in New York from 25 to 27 June 2008.

Membership

The three present members of the Board of Auditors, or their equivalent, are the:

Philippines (until 30 June 2008), Chair of the Philippine Commission on Audit	France (until 30 June 2010), First President of the Court of Accounts of Finance	South Africa (until 30 June 2012), Auditor-General of the Republic of South Africa

International Civil Service Commission (ICSC)

Internet: http://icsc.un.org

Purpose

The ICSC was established by GA res. 3042 (XXVII) (1972). It is responsible for the regulation and coordination of conditions of service of staff within the UN, the specialised agencies and other international organisations that participate in the UN common system. The Commission also has some decision-making functions with respect to post-adjustment indices, daily subsistence allowances, methodologies to determine salary levels and job classification standards. For other compensation issues and on human resource matters it makes recommendations to the General Assembly or the executive heads of the participating organisations.

Membership

The Commission comprises 15 independent experts appointed in their individual capacities by, and answerable as a body to, the General Assembly. Only the Chair and the Vice-Chair serve in a full-time capacity. Members are appointed for four years by the General Assembly, on the recommendation of the Fifth Committee, from a list of candidates compiled by the Secretary-General. Members may be reappointed.

The members are:

Term ending 31 Dec 2008	Term ending 31 Dec 2009	Term ending 31 Dec 2010
Fatih Bouayad-Agha, Algeria	Minoru Endo, Japan	Emmanuel Oti Boateng, Ghana
Shamsher Chowdhury, Bangladesh	Lucretia Myers, USA	Guillermo Enrique Gonzalez, Argentina
Vladimir Morozov, Russian Federation	Wolfgang Stöckl, Germany, Vice-Chair	Kingston Papie Rhodes, Sierra Leone (Chair)
Xiaochu Wang, China	Gian Luigi Valenza, Italy	Anita Szlazak, Canada
El Hassane Zahid, Morocco	Gilberto Paranhos Velloso, Brazil	Eugeniusz Wyzner, Poland

International Law Commission (ILC)

Internet: www.un.org/law/ilc/

Purpose

GA res. 174 (II) (1947) established the ILC with a membership of 15 people of recognised competence in international law and with the function of encouraging the progressive development and codification of international law.

The seventh edition of the publication *Work of the International Law Commission*, issued in April 2007, provides a comprehensive review of the Commission's work over nearly six decades.

Meetings

The 59th session of the Commission took place in Geneva from 7 May to 5 June 2007 and was scheduled to continue from 9 July to 10 August 2007.

Membership

The membership of the Commission has been increased a number of times, most recently by GA res. 36/39 (1981), and now stands at 34. By GA res. 36/39 (1981) the General Assembly decided that the members should be elected according to the following pattern: eight from African states, seven from Asian states, three from Eastern European states, six from Latin American and Caribbean states, and eight from Western European and Other states. They would be joined by one from African or Eastern European states in rotation and one from Asian and Latin American and Caribbean states in rotation.

The members of the Commission are elected by the General Assembly for a five-year term and are eligible for re-election. They are not government representatives but are elected on a personal basis and sit in their personal capacity as experts. Casual vacancies during the term, following resignation or death, are filled by the Commission.

The Commission's membership, elected by the 61st session of the General Assembly, with terms from 1 January 2007 to 31 December 2011, is:

Ali Mohsen Fetais Al-Marri, Qatar

Ian Brownlie, UK

Lucius Caflisch, Switzerland

Enrique J A Candioti, Argentina

Pedro Comissario Afonso, Mozambique

Christopher John Robert Dugard, South Africa

Paula Escarameia, Portugal

Salifou Fomba, Mali

Giorgio Gaja, Italy

Zdzislaw Galicki, Poland

Hussein A Hassouna, Egypt

Mahmoud D Hmoud, Jordan

Marie G Jacobsson, Sweden

Maurice Kamto, Cameroon

Fathi Kemicha, Tunisia

Roman A Kolodkin, Russian Federation

Donald M McRae, Canada

Teodor V Melescanu, Romania

Bernd H Niehaus, Costa Rica

Georg Nolte, Germany

Bayo Ojo, Nigeria

Alain Pellet, France

A Rohan Perera, Sri Lanka

Ernest Petric, Slovenia

Gilberto Vergne Saboia, Brazil

Narinder Singh, India

Eduardo Valencia-Ospina, Colombia

Edmundo Vargas Carreño, Chile

Stephen C Vasciannie, Jamaica

Marcelo Vázquez-Bermudez, Ecuador

Amos S Wako, Kenya

Nugroho Wisnumurti, Indonesia

Xue Hanqin, China

Chusei Yamada, Japan

Investments Committee

Purpose

GA res. 155 (II) (1947) established the Committee to advise the Secretary-General on the investment of the UN Joint Staff Pension Fund, the UN Library Endowment Fund and the UN University Endowment Fund.

Meetings

The Committee meets four or five times a year including one meeting held in conjunction with the UN Pension Board. The meetings are normally held in New York and, on occasion, in another UN member country.

Membership

Committee members are appointed by the Secretary-General for three-year terms, following consultation with the UN Joint Staff Pension Board and the Advisory Committee on Administrative and Budgetary Questions. Appointments are subject to confirmation by the General Assembly. In addition to the nine regular members, the Secretary-General may appoint additional members to ensure geographical representation and expertise in specific sectors and markets. Such additional members are referred to as ad hoc members. The regular members are eligible for reappointment with a limit of five terms of three years each, while the ad hoc member appointments are renewed every year.

Membership has been expanded a number of times, most recently by GA res. 31/196 (1976), and now stands at nine.

The members (as of 31 May 2007) are:

Term ending 31 Dec 2007	Term ending 31 Dec 2008	Term ending 31 Dec 2009
William McDonough, USA	Masakazu Arikawa, Japan	Emilio J Cardenas, Argentina
Hélène Ploix, France	Madhav Dar, India	Fernando G Chico Pardo, Mexico
Jürgen Reimnitz, Germany	Nemir Kirdar, Iraq	Khaya Ngqula, South Africa

Joint Inspection Unit (JIU)

Internet: www.unjiu.org/

Purpose

GA res. 2150 (XXI) (1966) established the JIU, which began work in 1968. By GA res. 31/192 (1976) the General Assembly approved the Statute of the JIU.

The Unit is to satisfy itself through evaluations, inspections and investigations that activities undertaken by the UN participating organisations are carried out in the most economical manner and that optimum use is made of the resources available. Its reviews and recommendations are aimed at improving management and achieving greater coordination between organisations. Inspectors have broad powers of investigation in all matters bearing on efficiency and the proper use of funds.

The JIU's mandate covers the UN, its separately administered funds and programmes, and the specialised agencies that have accepted the Statute. The Unit reports to the General Assembly and the relevant organs of other participating organisations.

Structure

The Unit, which is located in Geneva, is assisted by an Executive Secretary, and a group of research and support staff. Its budget is included in the regular budget of the UN as a jointly financed activity, the expenditure of which is shared by the participating organisations.

Membership

The Unit consists of not more than 11 inspectors with special experience in administrative and financial matters, serving in their personal capacity for a term of five years that can be renewed once. Inspectors are appointed by the General Assembly, on the nomination of the President, with due regard to the principles of equitable geographical distribution and reasonable rotation.

The inspectors are:

Term ending 31 Dec 2007	Term ending 31 Dec 2008	Term ending 31 Dec 2010
Even Fontaine Ortiz, Cuba	Juan Luis Larrabure, Peru (Vice-Chair)	Gérard Biraud, France
Guangting Tang, China		Papa Louis Fall, Senegal
Victor Vislykh, Russian Federation	Term ending 31 Dec 2009	Istvan Posta, Hungary
Deborah Wynes, USA (Chair)	Tadanori Inomata, Japan	Cihan Terzi, Turkey
Muhammad Yussuf, UR of Tanzania		

Panel of External Auditors

Internet: www.unsystem.org/auditors/external.htm

Purpose

GA res. 1438 (XIV) (1959) established the Panel of External Auditors. The Panel exists to further coordinate and exchange information on the audits for which its members are responsible, and to direct efforts towards achieving a greater degree of uniformity of audit standards and use of common accounting principles within the UN system. The Panel may submit to the executive heads of the participating organisations observations or recommendations in relation to the accounts and financial procedures of their organisations. Conversely, the executive heads of the participating organisations may, through their auditor(s), submit requests to the Panel for its advice or opinion.

Meetings
The Panel's next annual session was scheduled to be held in Manila from 26 November to 4 December 2007.

Membership
The membership, which stands at eight, comprises the members of the UN Board of Auditors, along with the appointed external auditors of the specialised agencies and the International Atomic Energy Agency (IAEA).

UN Administrative Tribunal

Internet: www.un.org/staff/panelofcounsel/atun.htm

Purpose
The UN Administrative Tribunal was established by GA res. 351A (IV) (1949) to judge applications alleging non-observance of employment contracts or terms of appointment of staff members of the UN Secretariat.

Evolution
The General Assembly has agreed to reform the system of internal justice in the UN. Under GA res. 61/261 (2007), the Joint Appeals Boards and the Joint Disciplinary Committees are to be replaced by a new, decentralised first-instance Dispute Tribunal and the second tier of justice is to be represented by a United Nations Appeals Tribunal (replacing the UN Administrative Tribunal). The General Assembly plans to implement the new two-tiered system of internal justice no later than January 2009.

Meetings
The Tribunal normally holds two sessions per year, in June/July and October/November.

Membership
The seven members of the Tribunal are appointed by the General Assembly on the recommendation of the Fifth Committee. Only three members may sit on any particular case unless a significant question of law is involved, in which case the matter may be referred to the Tribunal as a whole. Members are appointed for four years and may be reappointed once. Present members are:

Term ending 31 Dec 2007	Term ending 31 Dec 2008	Term ending 31 Dec 2010
Julio Barboza, Argentina	Spyridon Flogaitis, Greece	Bob Hepple, UK
Dayendra Sena Wijewardane, Sri Lanka	Goh Joon Seng, Singapore	Jacqueline R Scott, USA
	Brigitte Stern, France	

UN Commission on International Trade Law (UNCITRAL)

Vienna International Centre
PO Box 500
A–1400 Vienna
Austria
Telephone: (+43 1) 26060 4060
Fax: (+43 1) 26060 5813
Email: uncitral@uncitral.org
Internet: www.uncitral.org
Secretary: Jernej Sekolec, Slovenia (since 2001) (appointed by the UN Secretary-General)

Purpose

The General Assembly established UNCITRAL under GA res. 2205 (XXI) (1966) to promote the harmonisation and unification of the law of international trade. The Commission has since come to be the core legal body in the UN system in the field of international trade law.

Membership

Under GA res. 57/20 (2003) the General Assembly increased the membership of the Commission to 60 states. Member States are elected for a term of six years, with the terms of half the members expiring every three years.

By GA res. 31/99 (1976) members take office at the beginning of the first day of the Commission's regular annual session immediately following their election. Terms of office expire on the day prior to the opening of the seventh regular annual session following their election.

Since the first day of the 37th session of the Commission (14 June 2004), when the additional members took office, the Commission has observed the following distribution of seats: 14 members from African states, 14 from Asian states, eight from Eastern European states, 10 from Latin American and Caribbean states, and 14 from Western European and Other states.

Meetings

The Commission's 40th session was held in Vienna from 25 June to 12 July 2007.

The 60 members of UNCITRAL are, as of 10 July 2007:

Member	Term of office expires	Member	Term of office expires
Algeria	2010	China	2013
Armenia	2013	Colombia	2010
Australia	2010	Czech Republic	2010
Austria	2010	Ecuador	2010
Bahrain	2013	Egypt	2013
Belarus	2010	El Salvador	2013
Benin	2013	Fiji	2010
Bolivia	2013	France	2013
Bulgaria	2013	Gabon	2010
Cameroon	2013	Germany	2013
Canada	2013	Greece	2013
Chile	2013	Guatemala	2010

Member	Term of office expires	Member	Term of office expires
Honduras	2013	Pakistan	2010
India	2010	Paraguay	2010
Iran	2010	Poland	2010
Israel	2010	ROK	2013
Italy	2010	Russian Federation	2013
Japan	2013	Senegal	2013
Kenya	2010	Serbia[1]	2010
Latvia	2013	Singapore	2013
Lebanon	2010	South Africa	2013
Madagascar	2010	Spain	2010
Malaysia	2013	Sri Lanka	2013
Malta	2013	Switzerland	2010
Mexico	2013	Thailand	2010
Mongolia	2010	Uganda	2010
Morocco	2013	UK	2013
Namibia	2013	USA	2010
Nigeria	2010	Venezuela	2010
Norway	2013	Zimbabwe	2010

Note

[1] On 3 June 2006 the Republic of Serbia notified the UN that the membership of the State Union of Serbia and Montenegro in the UN, including all organs and organisations of the UN system, was continued by the Republic of Serbia on the basis of article 60 of the Constitutional Charter of Serbia and Montenegro, activated by the Declaration of Independence adopted by the National Assembly of Montenegro on 3 June 2006.

UN Joint Staff Pension Fund

Internet: www.unjspf.org

Purpose

The Joint Staff Pension Fund was established under regulations adopted by the General Assembly in GA res. 248 (III) (1948) to provide retirement, death, disability and related benefits for staff upon cessation of their services with the UN. The regulations, which have been amended at various times, provide for the admission of other organisations to the Fund. Twenty-two organisations, including the UN, are members.

GA res. 42/222 (1987) amended the regulations of the Fund, together with the composition and size of the Board. These changes took effect on 1 January 1989.

Structure

The member organisations jointly administer the Fund through the UN Joint Staff Pension Board, which has 33 members. Twelve members are from the UN (four chosen by the General Assembly, four by the Secretary-General and four by the participants) and 21 are from the other member organisations.

The Board reports every two years to the General Assembly on the operations of the Fund and the investment of its assets and, when necessary, recommends to the Assembly amendments to the regulations governing its activities. Expenses incurred by the Board in the administration of the Fund, principally the cost of its central secretariat at UN Headquarters in New York and the management expenses of its investments, are met by the Fund.

Membership

The UN Staff Pension Committee, consisting of 12 members and their alternates, serves the UN participants in the Fund. The terms of those appointed by the General Assembly are four years, ending on 31 December 2008.

The membership is:

Appointed by the General Assembly

Members and alternates

Kenshiro Akimoto, Japan

Aizaz Ahmad Chaudhry, Pakistan

Valeria Maria González Posse, Argentina

Andrei Vitalievitch Kovalenko, Russian Federation

Gerhard Küntzle, Germany

Lovemore Mazemo, Zimbabwe

Philip Richard Okanda Owade, Kenya

Thomas Repasch, USA

Appointed by the Secretary-General

Members

Alicia Barcena, Mexico

Jan Beagle, New Zealand

Kumiko Matsuura-Mueller, Japan

Jay William Pozenel, USA

Alternates

Regina Pawlik, Germany

Sharon Van Buerle, Australia

Elected by the participants for terms expiring on 31 December 2008

Members

Adebowale Adeniyi, Nigeria

Ajay Lakhanpal, India

Shuibao Liu, China

Carlos Santos Tejada, Ecuador

Alternate members

Jean-Michel Jakobowicz, France

Noriko Nagayoshi, Japan

SECURITY COUNCIL

SECURITY COUNCIL

CHARTER PROVISIONS

Pursuant to article 24 of the UN Charter, the members of the UN have conferred on the Security Council primary responsibility for the maintenance of international peace and security. The functions of the Council fall mainly under two headings:
- Pacific settlement of disputes
- Action with respect to threats to the peace, breaches of the peace, and acts of aggression.

Decisions on procedural matters are made by an affirmative vote of any nine members. Decisions on other matters are made by an affirmative vote of nine members, including the concurring votes of the five permanent members of the Council. Parties to a dispute must abstain from voting on measures for the pacific settlement of that dispute.

The Charter provisions relating to the Security Council are contained in chapter V (articles 23–32), chapter VI (articles 33–38), chapter VII (articles 39–51), chapter VIII (articles 52–54), and articles 76 and 82–84 of chapter XII. Other provisions are found in articles 1, 2, 4–7, 10–12, 15, 18, 20, 65, 93, 94, 96–99, 106, 108 and 109 of the Charter and articles 4, 7–15, 35, 41 and 69 of the Statute of the International Court of Justice.

MEMBERSHIP

The Security Council consists of five permanent members and 10 non-permanent members. Five of the non-permanent members are elected each year by the General Assembly for a term of two years. China, France, the Russian Federation*, the UK and the USA are the permanent members.

In electing the Council's non-permanent members, the General Assembly is required by the Charter to pay due regard, in the first instance, to the contribution of UN members to the maintenance of international peace and security, the other purposes of the organisation, and also to equitable geographical distribution. A retiring member is not eligible for immediate re-election.

The Presidency is held in turn by Council members in English alphabetical order of their country names, each holding office for one month.

By GA res. 1991A (XVIII) (1963), the General Assembly adopted, and submitted for ratification by Member States of the UN, amendments to the Charter provisions relating to membership of the Council (articles 23 and 27). It was decided that the 10 non-permanent members should be elected according to the following pattern: five from African and Asian states, one from Eastern European states, two from Latin American and Caribbean states, and two from Western European and Other states.

---

* The Russian Federation informed the UN on 24 December 1991 that the membership of the Soviet Union in the Security Council and all other UN organs was being continued by it, and that the Russian Federation remains responsible for all the rights and obligations of the former Soviet Union.

These amendments took effect in 1965, having been ratified by more than two-thirds of UN Member States, including all the permanent members of the Security Council. The first expanded Council was elected in 1965.

	Previous membership	Current membership
African and Asian states		
Algeria	1968–69 88–89 2004–05	
Angola	2003–04	
Bahrain	1998–99	
Bangladesh	1979–80 2000–01	
Benin	1976–77 2004–05	
Botswana	1995–96	
Burkina Faso	1984–85	
Burundi	1970–71	
Cameroon	1974–75 2002–03	
Cape Verde	1992–93	
Congo	1986–87	2006–07
Côte d'Ivoire	1964–65 90–91	
DR Congo	1982–83 90–91	
Djibouti	1993–94	
Egypt	1946 49–50 61–62 84–85 96–97	
Ethiopia	1967–68 89–90	
Gabon	1978–79 98–99	
Gambia	1998–99	
Ghana	1962–63 86–87	2006–07
Guinea	1972–73 2002–03	
Guinea-Bissau	1996–97	
India	1950–51 67–68 72–73 77–78 84–85 91–92	
Indonesia	1973–74 95–96	2007–08
Iran	1955–56	
Iraq	1957–58 74–75	
Japan	1958–59 66–67 71–72 75–76 81–82 87–88 92–93 97–98 2005–06	
Jordan	1965–66 82–83	
Kenya	1973–74 97–98	
Kuwait	1978–79	
Lebanon	1953–54	
Liberia	1961[1]	
Libyan AJ	1976–77	
Madagascar	1985–86	
Malaysia	1965[1] 89–90 1999–2000	
Mali	1966–67 2000–01	
Mauritania	1974–75	
Mauritius	1977–78 2001–02	
Morocco	1963–64 92–93	
Namibia	1999–2000	
Nepal	1969–70 88–89	
Niger	1980–81	
Nigeria	1966–67 78–79 94–95	
Oman	1994–95	
Pakistan	1952–53 68–69 76–77 83–84 93–94 2003–04	
Philippines	1957[1] 63[1] 80–81 2004–05	
Qatar		2006–07
ROK	1996–97	

	Previous membership	Current membership
Rwanda	1994–95	
Senegal	1968–69 88–89	
Sierra Leone	1970–71	
Singapore	2001–02	
Somalia	1971–72	
South Africa		2007–08
Sri Lanka	1960–61	
Sudan	1972–73	
Syrian AR[6]	1947–48 70–71 2002–03	
Thailand	1985–86	
Togo	1982–83	
Tunisia	1959–60 80–81 2000–01	
Uganda	1966 81–82	
UAE	1986–87	
UR of Tanzania	1975–76 2005–06	
Yemen	1990–91	
Zambia	1969–70 79–80 87–88	
Zimbabwe	1983–84 91–92	

Eastern European states[2, 3]

	Previous membership	Current membership
Belarus	1974–75	
Bulgaria	1966–67 86–87 2002–03	
Czech Republic	1994–95	
Hungary	1968–69 92–93	
Poland	1946–47[1] 60 70–71 82–83 96–97	
Romania	1962[1] 76–77 90–91 2004–05	
Serbia[4]		
Slovakia		2006–07
Slovenia	1998–99	
Ukraine	1948–49 84–85 2000–01	

Latin American and Caribbean states

	Previous membership	Current membership
Argentina	1948–49 59–60 66–67 71–72 87–88 94–95 1999–2000 05–06	
Bolivia	1964–65 78–79	
Brazil	1946–47 51–52 54–55 63–64 67–68 88–89 93–94 98–99 2004–05	
Chile	1952–53 61–62 96–97 2003–04	
Colombia	1947–48 53–54 57–58 69–70 89–90 2001–02	
Costa Rica	1974–75 97–98	
Cuba	1949–50 56–57 90–91	
Ecuador	1950–51 60–61 91–92	
Guyana	1975–76 82–83	
Honduras	1995–96	
Jamaica	1979–80 2000–01	
Mexico	1946 80–81 2002–03	
Nicaragua	1970–71 83–84	
Panama	1958–59 72–73 76–77 81–82	2007–08
Paraguay	1968–69	
Peru	1955–56 73–74 84–85	2006–07
Trinidad and Tobago	1985–86	
Uruguay	1965–66	
Venezuela	1962–63 77–78 86–87 92–93	

	Previous membership	Current membership

Western European and Other states

	Previous membership	Current membership
Australia	1946–47 56–57 73–74 85–86	
Austria	1973–74 91–92	
Belgium	1947–48 55–56 71–72 91–92	2007–08
Canada	1948–49 58–59 67–68 77–78 89–90 1999–2000	
Denmark	1953–54 67–68 85–86 2005–06	
Finland	1969–70 89–90	
Germany[5]	1977–78 87–88 95–96 2003–04	
Greece	1952–53 2005–06	
Ireland	1962[1] 81–82 2001–02	
Italy	1959–60 71–72 75–76 87–88 95–96	2007–08
Malta	1983–84	
Netherlands	1946 51–52 65–66 83–84 1999–2000	
New Zealand	1954–55 66[7] 93–94	
Norway	1949–50 63–64 79–80 2001–02	
Portugal	1979–80 97–98	
Spain	1969–70 81–82 93–94 2003–04	
Sweden	1957–58 75–76 97–98	
Turkey	1951–52 54–55 61[1]	

Notes

[1]   Split term.

[2]   Czechoslovakia served on the Council in 1964 and 1978–79.

[3]   The Socialist Federal Republic of Yugoslavia served on the Council in 1950–51, 1956 (split term), 1972–73 and 1988–89. It was not automatically succeeded by any of the new states succeeded following its dissolution.

[4]   On 3 June 2006 the Republic of Serbia notified the UN that the membership of the State Union of Serbia and Montenegro in the UN, including all organs and organisations of the UN system, was continued by the Republic of Serbia on the basis of article 60 of the Constitutional Charter of Serbia and Montenegro, activated by the Declaration of Independence adopted by the National Assembly of Montenegro on 3 June 2006.

[5]   The German Democratic Republic served a term on the Council in 1980–81.

[6]   The United Arab Republic served on the Council in 1961.

[7]   One-year term pursuant to elections held in accordance with article 23(2) of the Charter.

STRUCTURE

- Standing committees
- Ad hoc working groups
- Military Staff Committee
- Counter-Terrorism Committee
- Sanctions committees
- Peacekeeping operations
- Political and peacebuilding missions
- Commissions
- International tribunals
- Other organisations

STANDING COMMITTEES

The Committee of Experts on Rules of Procedure, the Committee on Council Meetings away from Headquarters and the Committee on the Admission of New Members each comprises representatives of all the members of the Security Council. The Presidency of the Council provides the chair in each case.

AD HOC WORKING GROUPS

Internet: follow links from www.un.org/Docs/sc/unsc_structure.html

Informal Working Group on Documentation and Procedural Questions

Established in June 1993, the Informal Working Group is concerned with the Council's documentation and other procedural questions. It comprises representatives of all Council members.

The Informal Working Group Chair is Peter Burian, Slovakia, who was elected to serve until 31 December 2007 (S/2007/20).

Working Group on Peacekeeping Operations

Established on 31 January 2001 (S/PRST/2001/3), the Working Group addresses both generic peacekeeping issues relevant to the responsibility of the Council and technical aspects of individual peacekeeping operations. This is done without prejudice to the competence of the General Assembly's Special Committee on Peacekeeping Operations.

The Chair is Rezlan Ishar Jenie, Indonesia, who has been elected to serve until 31 December 2007 (S/2007/20).

Ad Hoc Working Group on Conflict Prevention and Resolution in Africa

The Working Group was established on 1 March 2002 (S/2002/207) to monitor and implement the recommendations contained in Presidential Statement S/PRST/2002/2 (of 31 January 2002), and previous presidential statements and resolutions regarding conflict prevention and resolution in Africa. The Group is also mandated to propose recommendations on the enhancement of cooperation between the Security Council and the Economic and Social Council, as well as with other UN agencies dealing with Africa. In particular, it is asked to examine regional and cross-conflict issues that affect the Council's work on African conflict prevention and resolution, and to propose recommendations to the Security Council to enhance cooperation on conflict prevention and resolution among the UN, regional (Organization of African Unity) and sub-regional organisations.

The Chair is Basile Ikouebe, Congo, who was elected to serve until 31 December 2007 (S/2007/20).

Working Group Established Pursuant to Resolution 1566 (2004)

By res. 1566 (2004) the Security Council established the Working Group to examine:
- Practical measures to be imposed on individuals, groups or entities involved in or associated with terrorist activities, other than those designated by the Al-Qaida/Taliban Sanctions Committee
- The possibility of establishing an international fund to compensate victims of terrorist acts and their families.

The Chair is Jorge Voto-Bernales, Peru, who was elected to serve until 31 December 2007 (S/2007/20).

Working Group on Children and Armed Conflict

The Working Group on Children and Armed Conflict (CAAC) was established in July 2005 pursuant to Security Council res. 1612 (2005) to:
- Review the reports of the monitoring and reporting mechanism referred to in paragraph 3 of res. 1612 (2005)
- Review progress in the development and implementation of the action plans mentioned in paragraph 5(a) of res. 1539 (2004) and paragraph 7 of res. 1612 (2005)
- Consider other relevant information presented to it
- Make recommendations to the Council on possible measures to promote the protection of children affected by armed conflict, including through recommendations on appropriate mandates for peacekeeping missions and recommendations with respect to parties to the conflict
- Address requests, as appropriate, to other bodies within the UN system for action to support implementation of res. 1612 (2005) in accordance with their respective mandates.

The Chair of the Working Group is Jean-Marc de La Sablière, France, who was elected to serve until 31 December 2007 (S/2007/20).

Ad Hoc Committee on Mandate Review

Established in a note from the President of the Security Council to the Secretary-General on 31 May 2006 (S/2006/354), the Ad Hoc Committee was formed to conduct the review of Security Council mandates called for in the World Summit Outcome Document (GA res. 60/1) and to follow up on the recommendations contained in the Secretary-General's report *Mandating and Delivering* (A/60/733 and Corr.1).

The Chairs of the Ad Hoc Committee are Dumisani Shadrack Kumalo, South Africa, and Peter Burian, Slovakia, who were elected to serve until 31 December 2007 (S/2007/20).

MILITARY STAFF COMMITTEE

The Military Staff Committee, established under article 47 of the Charter, comprises the senior military advisers or attachés of the Security Council permanent members, or their representatives. Its function is to advise and assist the Council on all questions relating to:
- The military requirements for maintaining peace and security
- The employment and command of forces placed at its disposal
- The regulation of armaments and possible disarmament.

The Committee's advice and assistance is expected to be sought for:
- Actions requiring the use of military forces under article 42
- Agreements to provide military forces to the Council under articles 43 and 44
- The readiness of immediately available air force contingents for combined international enforcement action under article 45
- Planning for the application of armed force under article 46. The Committee's task in assisting the Council in formulating plans for the regulation of armaments is addressed under article 26.

GA res. 1235 (XII) (1957) authorised the integration of the civilian staff of the Military Staff Committee with the UN Secretariat.

The World Summit 2005 (A/RES/60/1) requested the Security Council to consider the composition, mandate and working methods of the Military Staff Committee.

COUNTER-TERRORISM COMMITTEE (CTC)

Internet: www.un.org/sc/ctc

By SC res. 1373 (2001) the Security Council adopted measures to counter the threats to international peace and security posed by terrorist acts. By SC res. 1373 (2001) the Security Council also established the Counter-Terrorism Committee (CTC) to monitor, with appropriate expert help, implementation of the resolution. The resolution requires Member States to:
- Deny all forms of financial support for terrorist groups
- Suppress the provision of safe haven, sustenance or support for terrorists and eliminate the supply of weapons to terrorists
- Cooperate with other governments in the investigation, detection, arrest and prosecution of those involved in such acts
- Criminalise active and passive assistance for terrorism in domestic laws and bring violators of these laws to justice
- Take the necessary steps to prevent the commission of terrorist acts and prevent the movement of terrorists by effective controls of borders and travel documents
- Share information with other governments on any groups practising or planning terrorist acts.

The resolution also calls upon all states to become party as soon as possible to the relevant international conventions and protocols relating to terrorism.

The CTC asks every state to take specific action, based on the circumstances in each country, to meet the requirements of the resolution. The CTC is not a sanctions committee and does not have a list of terrorist organisations or individuals.

By SC res. 1373 (2001) Member States are also required to report to the Committee, initially within 90 days and thereafter according to a timetable established by the Committee, on the steps they have taken to implement the resolution. The Committee has established three sub-committees, each chaired by one of the Committee's Vice-Chairs, to consider Member States' reports.

Following a review in early 2004 the Security Council adopted SC res. 1535 (2004), which was aimed at revitalising the Committee. The resolution established a Counter-Terrorism Committee Executive Directorate (CTED) to enhance the Committee's ability to monitor the implementation of SC res. 1373 and to improve the capacity-building work of the Committee. In December 2005 the Security Council issued Presidential Statement 2005/64 welcoming the CTED's expanded mandate and further expanding it to include monitoring implementation of SC res. 1624 (2005) relating to incitement to commit a terrorist act.

In 2006 the Committee instituted the new analytical tool of Preliminary Implementation Assessments (PIAs), which have the aim of facilitating a more targeted, tailor-made dialogue with Member States on their implementation of the resolution.

2007 Chair
Panama

Sub-Committee A Chair
Peru

Sub-Committee B Chair
South Africa

Sub-Committee C Chair
Qatar

CTED Executive Director
Javier Rupérez, Spain

SANCTIONS COMMITTEES

Internet: www.un.org/sc/committees/

There are 12 Security Council sanctions committees, each comprising all 15 Council members, which meet in closed session. Office holders are elected by the Council in early January for terms that run to 31 December. The work of each committee and related expert groups, as well as the specifics of the sanctions measures currently in effect, are detailed on committee websites. Because of the frequent changes to the various sanctions regimes, up-to-date information on all Security Council sanctions should be sought from the website.

As part of its commitment to ensure that fair and clear procedures exist for placing individuals and entities on sanctions lists and for removing them, as well as for granting humanitarian exemptions, the Security Council, on 19 December 2006, adopted SC res. 1730 (2006). This requested the Secretary-General to establish a focal point to receive de-listing requests and to perform the tasks described in the annex to that resolution. Contact details for the focal point can be found at: www.un.org/sc/committees/dfp.shtml

SC Res. 751 Committee – Somalia

Internet: www.un.org/sc/committees/751/index.shtml

The Committee was established by SC res. 751 (1992) on 24 April 1992 to oversee the sanctions on Somalia imposed under SC res. 733 (1992). As at 30 June 2007 an arms embargo, first imposed on 23 January 1992, remained in effect.

By SC res. 1425 (2002) a Panel of Experts was established to generate information on violations of the arms embargo with a view toward strengthening it. In 2003 the Panel was succeeded by a Monitoring Group to focus on the ongoing arms embargo violations. The Monitoring Group continues to be in operation. Its mandate was most recently extended by SC res. 1766 (2006) to 26 January 2008.

Chair	Vice-Chairs
South Africa	Ghana and Slovakia

SC Res. 918 Committee – Rwanda

Internet: www.un.org/sc/committees/918/index.shtml

The Committee was established by SC res. 918 (1994) on 17 May 1994 to oversee the arms embargo imposed under the same resolution. SC res. 1011 (1996) lifted the embargo in terms of the Government of Rwanda, but retained it with regard to non-government forces.

As at 30 June 2007 an embargo on the sale or supply of arms to Rwanda, with the exception of sale or supply to the Government of Rwanda, remained in effect. An embargo on the sale or supply of arms to persons in states neighbouring Rwanda for use in Rwanda was also in effect.

Chair	Vice-Chair
Indonesia	Italy

SC Res. 1132 Committee – Sierra Leone

Internet: www.un.org/sc/committees/1132/index.shtml

The Committee was established by SC res. 1132 (1997) on 8 October 1997 to oversee an oil and arms embargo, as well as restrictions on the travel of members of the military junta that ruled Sierra Leone at the time. By SC res. 1156 (1998) the oil embargo was terminated. By SC res. 1171 (1998) the Council removed the remaining prohibitions but imposed a new travel ban on leading members of the former military junta, as well as an arms embargo on parties other than the Government of Sierra Leone. By SC res. 1299 (2000) the arms embargo was lifted for Member States cooperating with UNAMSIL (now UNIOSIL) and the Sierra Leone Government.

By SC res. 1306 (2000) the Council imposed a ban on imports of all rough diamonds that were not controlled by the Sierra Leone Government. The Council announced in June 2003 it would not renew these sanctions.

As at 30 June 2007 an arms embargo on non-state actors and a travel ban on individuals as designated by the Committee remained in effect.

Chair	Vice-Chairs
Qatar	Congo and Panama

SC Res. 1267 Committee – Al-Qaida and the Taliban

Internet: www.un.org/sc/committees/1267/index.shtml

The Committee was established by SC res. 1267 (1999) on 15 October 1999 to oversee aviation and financial sanctions imposed on the Taliban in Afghanistan under that same resolution. The aim was to secure the surrender of Osama bin Laden to the appropriate authorities for prosecution and to close down terrorist camps in Afghan territory.

The sanctions regime has been expanded considerably since 1999. As at 30 June 2007 an assets freeze, travel ban and arms embargo on individuals and entities associated with Al-Qaida, Osama bin Laden and/or the Taliban were in effect. A list of such individuals and entities is maintained by the Committee on the basis of information provided by Member States and regional organisations.

The Committee is one of three subsidiary bodies established by the Security Council that deal with terrorism related issues. The other two are the Counter-Terrorism Committee (CTC) and the 1540 Committee. The three committees and their experts coordinate their work, cooperate closely and, when possible, brief the Security Council on their activities in joint meetings.

Chair	Vice-Chairs
Belgium	Ghana and the Russian Federation

SC Res. 1518 Committee – Iraq

Internet: www.un.org/sc/committees/1518/index.shtml

The Committee was established by SC res. 1518 (2003) on 24 November 2003 as the successor body to the Security Council Committee established by SC res. 661 (1990) concerning Iraq and Kuwait. The 1518 Committee's role is to continue to identify senior officials of the former Iraqi regime and their immediate family members, including entities owned or controlled by them or by persons acting on their behalf, who are subject to the arms embargo and assets freeze measures imposed in SC res. 1483 (2003).

By SC res. 1546 (2004) the Security Council exempted the Government of Iraq and multinational force from the embargo on arms and related material, but noted that the exemption did not include chemical, biological or nuclear weapons, or missiles or materials related to these.

As at 30 June 2007 an assets freeze, and transfer measures concerning senior officials of the former Iraqi regime and their immediate family, as designated by the Committee, were in effect. A partial arms embargo was also in effect.

Chair	Vice-Chair
Ghana	Belgium

SC Res. 1521 Committee – Liberia

Internet: www.un.org/sc/committees/1521/index.shtml

The Committee was established by SC res. 1521 (2003) on 22 December 2003 as the successor to the Committee established by SC res. 1343 (2001). This had imposed an arms embargo, a ban on the import of rough diamonds from Liberia and travel restrictions on senior members of the Government of Liberia, its armed forces and their spouses, and any other individuals providing financial and military support to armed rebel groups in neighbouring countries. SC res. 1478 (2003) also imposed a prohibition against the importation of Liberian timber and timber products.

SC res. 1521 (2003) acknowledged changed circumstances in Liberia. The Security Council recognised the new transitional government but also imposed for 12 months revised prohibitions in connection with arms, diamonds, timber and travel of designated individuals. By SC res. 1532 (2004) the Security Council decided all states should freeze the funds of, and other financial assets controlled by, the former President of Liberia, Charles Taylor, as well as Jewell Howard Taylor, Charles Taylor Jr and/or other individuals designated by the Committee.

The arms embargo and travel sanctions have been consistently renewed, most recently by SC res. 1731 (2006), which expires on 20 December 2007. However, the Security Council decided to allow the timber sanctions to expire on 20 June 2006 in light of the Government of Liberia's commitment to transparent management of the country's forestry resources. With the adoption of SC res. 1753 (2007) on 27 April 2007, the Council also decided to terminate the diamond sanctions.

Chair	Vice-Chairs
Qatar	Indonesia and South Africa

SC Res. 1533 Committee – Democratic Republic of the Congo

Internet: www.un.org/sc/committees/1533/index.shtml

The Committee was established by SC res. 1533 (2004) on 12 March 2004 to oversee the sanctions originally imposed by SC res. 1493 (2003) and subsequently expanded by further resolutions.

The Security Council first imposed an arms embargo on all foreign and Congolese armed groups and militias operating in the territory of North and South Kivu and Ituri, and on groups not party to the Global and All-inclusive Agreement in the Democratic Republic of the Congo as at 28 July 2003. The sanctions regime has since been modified and strengthened, including by broadening the scope of the arms embargo and imposing a travel ban and assets freeze on individuals and entities as designated by the Committee.

SC res. 1698 (2006) most recently renewed the sanctions until 31 July 2007. As well as renewing the arms embargo, which at 30 June 2007 covered the entire DRC territory, the resolution extended the travel and financial measures to include political and military leaders recruiting or using children in armed conflict and individuals violating international law involving the targeting of children in arms conflict.

Chair	Vice-Chairs
Peru	Indonesia and Qatar

SECURITY COUNCIL

SC Res. 1540 Committee (Non-Proliferation of WMD to Non-State Actors)

Internet: http://disarmament2.un.org/Committee1540/index.html

SC res. 1540 (2004) adopted measures to counter the threat of proliferation of weapons of mass destruction (WMDs) to non-state actors. Para. 9 of that resolution established a committee comprising all Council members that would report on the implementation of the resolution. Member States are required to report to the Committee, initially within six months of the adoption of the resolution, on steps they have taken or intend to take in its implementation.

On 22 October 2004 the Committee decided to establish three sub-committees, each chaired by Vice-Chairs of the Committee, to consider Member States' reports. The Committee also appointed experts to assist it. By SC res. 1673 (2006) the Security Council extended the mandate of the Committee until 27 April 2008. It further decided the Committee should intensify its efforts to promote the full implementation of SC res. 1540, and submit a report on compliance with the resolution to the Council by 27 April 2008.

Chair	Sub-Committee A Chair
Slovakia	UK
Sub-Committee B Chair	Sub-Committee C Chair
Ghana	Indonesia

SC Res. 1572 Committee – Côte d'Ivoire

Internet: www.un.org/sc/committees/1572/index.shtml

By SC res. 1572 (2004) the Security Council imposed an arms embargo for a period of 12 months on Côte d'Ivoire, and established on 15 November 2004 a committee to oversee sanctions imposed under the same resolution.

The sanctions have subsequently been modified and extended, most recently by SC res. 1727 (2006). They include an arms embargo, travel ban and assets freeze on individuals designated by the Committee, and a ban on the importation of rough diamonds from Côte d'Ivoire. The Security Council underlined that it was fully prepared to impose targeted measures against people responsible for attacking or obstructing the UN Operations in Côte d'Ivoire (UNOCI), the French forces, the High Representative for the Elections, the International Working Group, or the Mediator, as well as for serious violations of human rights and international humanitarian law, and for inciting public hatred and violating the arms embargo.

In light of progress achieved in the peace and national reconciliation process in Côte d'Ivoire, the Council is scheduled to review the sanctions regime by 31 October 2007.

Chair	Vice-Chairs
Belgium	Italy and South Africa

SC Res. 1591 Committee – Sudan

Internet: www.un.org/sc/committees/1591/index.shtml

The Security Council first imposed an arms embargo on all non-government entities and individuals, including the Janjaweed, operating in the states of North Darfur, South Darfur and West Darfur on 30 July 2004 with the adoption of SC res. 1556 (2004).

By SC res. 1591 (2005) the Committee was established on 29 March 2005 to oversee the sanctions. The same resolution also expanded the scope of the arms embargo and imposed additional measures, including a travel ban and an assets freeze on individuals and entities designated by the Committee.

As at 30 June 2007 an embargo on the supply of arms and related material and also of technical training and assistance to the following actors was in effect: all non-government entities and individuals, including all Janjaweed; all parties to the N'djamena Ceasefire Agreement; and any other belligerents. A travel ban on designated individuals and an assets freeze on designated individuals and entities were also in effect.

Chair

Italy

Vice-Chairs

Panama and Slovakia

SC Res. 1636 Committee

Internet: www.un.org/sc/committees/1636/index.shtml

The Committee was established by SC res. 1636 (2005) on 31 October 2005 to register a travel ban and assets freeze on any individuals, as designated by the International Independent Investigation Commission or Government of Lebanon, suspected of involvement in the 14 February 2005 terrorist bombing in Beirut, Lebanon, that killed former Lebanese Prime Minister Rafiq Hariri and 22 others.

As at 30 June 2007 no individuals had been registered.

Chair

Ghana

Vice-Chairs

Belgium and Slovakia

SC Res. 1718 Committee – Democratic People's Republic of Korea (DPRK)

Internet: www.un.org/sc/committees/1718/index.shtml

The Security Council decided by SC res. 1718 (2006) that the DPRK should suspend all activities related to its ballistic missile programme, abandon all nuclear weapons and existing nuclear programmes, and abandon all other existing weapons of mass destruction and ballistic missile programmes in a complete, verifiable and irreversible manner. The Committee was established by the same resolution on 14 October 2006 to oversee arms embargo, assets freeze and travel ban sanctions.

To ensure compliance with the sanctions regime, the Security Council called on all states to take cooperative action, including through inspection of cargo to and from the DPRK as necessary. Member States were also obliged to report to the Council by 14 November 2006 on steps taken to effectively implement the sanctions. As of 22 June 2007, 70 countries and the European Union had reported.

As at 30 June 2007 an embargo prohibiting the sale and supply to and from the DPRK of heavy weapons, and of items and technology contained in Security Council documents (S/2006/814, S/2006/815 and S/2006/853), was in effect. An embargo on the sale of luxury goods to the DPRK was also in effect. No individuals or entities had been designated by the Committee in relation to the assets freeze and travel ban sanctions.

Chair   Vice-Chairs

Italy   Ghana and Peru

SC Res. 1737 Committee (2006) – Non-proliferation (Iran)

Internet: www.un.org/sc/committees/1737/index.shtml

The Committee was established by SC res. 1737 (2006) on 23 December 2006 to oversee the sanctions imposed under that same resolution. These included a nuclear and ballistic missile programmes-related embargo, and an assets freeze and travel notification requirements on persons and entities, as designated by the Security Council or Committee. In addition, the Council called on all states to prevent specialised teaching or training of Iranian nationals in disciplines that would contribute to Iran's proliferation of sensitive nuclear activities and development of nuclear weapon delivery systems.

SC res. 1747 (2007) imposed a ban on exports of arms from Iran. It also designated additional persons and entities as subject to the assets freeze and travel notification requirements. In addition, the Council called on all states to exercise vigilance and restraint in the provision of heavy weapons and related services to Iran, and called on all states and international financial institutions not to enter into new commitments for grants, financial assistance and concessional loans to the Government of Iran, except for humanitarian and developmental purposes. The resolution also obliged states to report to the Committee, within 60 days of the adoption of the resolution (on 24 March 2007), on steps taken to implement specific paragraphs of the resolution. As of 12 April 2007, 62 states and the European Union had reported to the Committee.

The Security Council affirmed that it would review Iran's actions following an International Atomic Energy Agency (IAEA) report, due to be submitted within 60 days of the adoption of the resolution.

As at 30 June 2007 the nuclear and ballistic missile programmes-related embargo remained in effect, as did the ban on the export of all arms from Iran, the assets freeze and travel notification requirements.

Chair   Vice-Chairs

Belgium   Ghana and Peru

Terminated Sanctions Regimes

No sanctions regimes were terminated between 1 June 2006 and 31 May 2007.

Internet: www.un.org/depts/dpko/dpko/index.asp

More than 60 UN peacekeeping operations have been deployed since 1948. They have involved more than 1.2 million military and civilian police personnel, and cost around $41 billion. There were approximately 82,755 uniformed (military and police) and 18,927 civilian personnel serving as at 31 March 2007. The estimated annual cost of the 18 operations in place in 2006/2007 was approximately $5.28 billion.

Two operations, the UN Truce Supervision Organization (UNTSO) and the UN Military Observer Group in India and Pakistan (UNMOGIP), are funded from the UN regular budget, while the other 16 are financed from their own separate accounts on the basis of legally binding assessments on all states. The mandates of most operations are renewed periodically or are subjected to reviews. Figures for operational strength, which may include both military and civilian police personnel, vary from month to month owing to the rotation of contingents and personnel.

One mission, the UN Operation in Burundi (ONUB), was successfully concluded in December 2006. It was replaced by a special political mission, the UN Integrated Office in Burundi (BINUB).

Three of the missions – the UN Assistance Mission in Afghanistan (UNAMA), the UN Integrated Office in Sierra Leone (UNIOSIL) and the UN Integrated Office in Burundi (BINUB) – are political or peacebuilding missions. These are, however, directed and supported by the Department of Peacekeeping Operations (DPKO), so are included here.

Operations are listed below in chronological order of establishment.

UN Truce Supervision Organization (UNTSO)

PO Box 490
Jerusalem 91004
Israel
Telephone: (+1 212) 963 2802 (New York: general enquiries for peacekeeping missions)
Internet: www.un.org/Depts/dpko/missions/untso
Chief of Staff: Major-General Ian Gordon, Australia

SC res. 50 (1948) formed the basis of what would become UNTSO. It provided for military observers to help the UN Mediator in Palestine, in concert with the Truce Commission, to supervise the observance of the truce in Palestine. Since then, UNTSO has performed various tasks entrusted to it by the Security Council, including the supervision of the General Armistice Agreements of 1949 and the observation of the ceasefire in the Suez Canal area and the Golan Heights following the Arab-Israeli war of June 1967.

At present, UNTSO assists and cooperates with the UN Disengagement Observer Force (UNDOF) on the Golan Heights in the Israel-Syria sector and the UN Interim Force in Lebanon (UNIFIL) in the Israel-Lebanon sector. UNTSO is also present in the Egypt-Israel sector in the Sinai. It has offices in Beirut and Damascus.

The authorised strength of UNTSO is 152. Its strength as at 31 March 2007 was 152 military observers, supported by 108 international civilian personnel and 120 local civilian staff. The following states contribute personnel to UNTSO:

Argentina	Australia	Austria

Belgium	France	Russian Federation
Canada	Ireland	Slovakia
Chile	Italy	Slovenia
China	Nepal	Sweden
Denmark	Netherlands	Switzerland
Estonia	New Zealand	USA
Finland	Norway	

UN Military Observer Group in India and Pakistan (UNMOGIP)

(Nov–Apr)	(May–Oct)
UNMOGIP	UNMOGIP
PO Box 68	PO Box 58
Rawalpindi	Srinagar
Pakistan	India

Telephone: (+1 212) 963 2802 (New York: general enquiries for peacekeeping missions)
Internet: www.un.org/Depts/dpko/missions/unmogip/
Chief Military Observer: Major-General Dragutin Repinc, Croatia

SC res. 39 (1948) established a three-member UN Commission for India and Pakistan (UNCIP) to investigate and mediate the dispute over the status of Kashmir. By the terms of resolutions adopted by UNCIP on 13 August 1948 and 5 January 1949, UNMOGIP was established to assist in the implementation of the ceasefire agreement of 1 January 1949. Following the termination of UNCIP, the Security Council, by SC res. 91 (1951), decided UNMOGIP should continue to supervise the ceasefire in Kashmir.

Following the outbreak of hostilities in Kashmir in 1965, the Security Council in SC res. 210 (1965) asked the Secretary-General to strengthen UNMOGIP. A number of governments agreed to provide additional observers. As a result, the UN India-Pakistan Observation Mission (UNIPOM) was created as a temporary measure to supervise a ceasefire called for in SC res. 211 and to supervise withdrawals. After fulfilling its function, UNIPOM was disbanded and UNMOGIP reverted to its original strength.

The authorised strength of UNMOGIP is 45. At the end of March 2007, its strength was 44 military observers from:

Chile	Finland	Sweden
Croatia	Italy	Uruguay
Denmark	ROK	

UN Force in Cyprus (UNFICYP)

PO Box 21642	PO Box 5838
1590 Nicosia	Grand Central Station
Cyprus	New York, NY 10163–5838
	United States of America

Telephone: (+357 22) 614 479 (Cyprus) or (+1 212) 963 2802 (New York: general enquiries for peacekeeping missions)
Fax: (+357 22) 614 493
Internet: www.unficyp.org/
Force Commander: Major-General Rafael José Barni, Argentina

SC res. 186 (1964) established, in consultation with the Governments of Cyprus, Greece, Turkey and the UK, a peacekeeping force in Cyprus. The Force was declared operational on 27 March 1964 with a mandate of three months. There have been successive extensions, the latest being by SC res. 1758 (2007), which extended the mission to 15 December 2007.

UNFICYP's principal functions are to supervise the ceasefire and to control the buffer zone in which civilian activities continue under escort.

Until recently the cost of UNFICYP was met by the governments that provided the military contingents and by voluntary contributions. However, by SC res. 831 (1993), the Security Council agreed that costs of UNFICYP not otherwise met by voluntary contributions should be met, from the time of the June 1993 mandate renewal, from assessed contributions. This was confirmed by the General Assembly in its GA res. 47/236 (1993).

As of March 2007 the strength of UNFICYP was 850 military, including 40 military observers/liaison officers (MOLO) and 65 civilian police. At the end of March 2007 the military and civilian police involved in UNFICYP were made up of personnel from:

Argentina	Chile	Italy
Australia	Croatia	Netherlands
Austria	El Salvador	Paraguay
Bolivia	Hungary	Peru
Bosnia and Herzegovina	India	Slovakia
Canada	Ireland	UK

UN Disengagement Observer Force (UNDOF)

PO Box 5368
Damascus
Syrian AR
Telephone: (+1 212) 963 2802 (New York: general enquiries for peacekeeping missions)
Internet: www.un.org/Depts/dpko/missions/undof
Force Commander: Major-General Wolfgang Jilke, Austria

By SC res. 350 (1974), and following a ceasefire agreement between Syria and Israel, the Security Council established UNDOF for an initial period of six months. The Force was deployed in the Golan Heights in June 1974, membership being drawn from UN Truce Supervision Organization (UNTSO) observers in the area.

The UNDOF mandate has been renewed periodically by successive Council resolutions, the latest being SC res. 1759 (2007), which extended the period until 31 December 2007. The authorised strength of UNDOF is 1047. As of the end of May 2007 its strength was 1046 troops and 57 UNTSO military observers. Troops were provided by:

Austria	Japan	Slovakia
Canada	Nepal	
India	Poland	

UN Interim Force in Lebanon (UNIFIL)

PO Box 75
Nahariya 22100
Israel
Telephone: (+1 212) 963 2802 (New York: general enquiries for peacekeeping missions)
Internet: www.un.org/Depts/dpko/missions/unifil
Force Commander: Major-General Claudio Graziano, Italy

Following a request from the Government of Lebanon, the Security Council decided by SC res. 425 (1978) to set up under its authority a UN Interim Force for Southern Lebanon. SC res. 426 (1978) established the Force for an initial period of six months and approved the Secretary-General's report containing terms of reference for it. The Force's mandate has since been extended for varying periods by successive Council resolutions.

In July 2006 conflict broke out between Israel and Lebanon. On 11 August 2006 SC res. 1701 was adopted, providing a new and enhanced mandate for UNIFIL, including an authorised force of 15,000 troops and a Maritime Task Force capability, and extending its mandate to 31 August 2007. SC res. 1757 (2007) established a Special Tribunal for Lebanon.

As at 31 May 2007 UNIFIL's strength stood at 13,225 military personnel, comprising units and staff officers from:

Belgium	Hungary	Poland
China	India	Portugal
Cyprus	Indonesia	Qatar
Denmark	Ireland	ROK
Finland	Italy	Slovakia
France	Luxembourg	Slovenia
Germany	Malaysia	Spain
Ghana	Nepal	Sweden
Greece	Netherlands	Turkey
Guatemala	Norway	UR of Tanzania

There are also approximately 50 UNTSO observers.

UN Mission for the Referendum in Western Sahara (MINURSO)

PO Box 5846
Grand Central Station
New York, NY 10163–5846
United States of America
Telephone: (+1 212) 963 2802 (New York: general enquiries for peacekeeping missions)
Email: minurso-informationofficer@un.org
Internet: www.minurso.unlb.org
Force Commander: Major-General Kurt Mosgaard, Denmark

MINURSO (a Spanish acronym) was established by SC res. 690 (1991), in accordance with settlement proposals, which provided for a transitional period for the preparation of a referendum in which the people of Western Sahara would choose between independence and integration with Morocco. The resolution also agreed a plan for a referendum involving civilian, security and military units of MINURSO supervising the repatriation of Western Saharans identified as eligible to vote. Only part of MINURSO has so far been deployed. By SC res. 973 (1995) the MINURSO Identification Commission was expanded in order to accelerate the voter identification and registration process. By SC res. 995 (1995), and in the context of concern at practices hampering progress towards the implementation of the Settlement Plan, the Security Council decided to send a mission to the region.

The Mission's mandate has since been extended, most recently by SC res. 1754 (2007), until 31 October 2007. This was done with the expectation that the parties, under the auspices of the Secretary-General's Personal Envoy, would continue to try to resolve the multiple problems relating to the implementation of the Settlement Plan and try to agree on a mutually acceptable political solution to their dispute over Western Sahara.

The mandated strength of MINURSO is 231 military and six civilian police personnel. As at 31 March 2007 its strength stood at 229, comprising military observers, civilian police and support units from the following states:

Argentina	Bangladesh	Croatia
Austria	China	Denmark

Egypt	Hungary	Pakistan
El Salvador	Ireland	Poland
France	Italy	Russian Federation
Ghana	Kenya	Sri Lanka
Greece	Malaysia	Uruguay
Guinea	Mongolia	Yemen
Honduras	Nigeria	

UN Observer Mission in Georgia (UNOMIG)

PO Box 4712
Grand Central Station
New York, NY 10163–4712
United States of America
Telephone: (+1 212) 963 9563
Fax: (+1 212) 963 9561
Internet: www.unomig.org
Chief Military Observer: Major-General Niaz Mohammed Khan Khattak, Pakistan
Senior Police Adviser: Colonel Oleksiy Telychkin, Ukraine

SC res. 858 (1993) established UNOMIG for a period of six months to verify compliance with the ceasefire agreement reached on 27 July 1993 and investigate reports of violations of the ceasefire agreement. SC res. 937 (1994) approved the expansion of UNOMIG to include monitoring and verifying (in cooperation with the Commonwealth of Independent States Peacekeeping Force) the implementation of the ceasefire agreement signed in Moscow on 14 May 1994. SC res. 1494 (2003) approved the addition of 20 civilian police. The mandate was renewed by SC res. 1752 (2007) until 15 October 2007.

The authorised strength of UNOMIG is 136. As at 16 April 2007, 136 uniformed personnel (121 military observers and 13 police) were deployed from the following countries:

Albania	Greece	Russian Federation
Austria	Hungary	Sweden
Bangladesh	Indonesia	Switzerland
Croatia	Jordan	Turkey
Czech Republic	Lithuania	Ukraine
Denmark	Pakistan	UK
Egypt	Poland	USA
France	ROK	Uruguay
Germany	Republic of Moldova	Yemen
Ghana	Romania	

UN Interim Administration Mission in Kosovo (UNMIK)

Bulevar Ilinden BB
9100 Skopje
Former Yugoslav Republic of Macedonia
Telephone: (+1 212) 963 2802 (New York: general enquiries for peacekeeping missions)
Internet: www.unmikonline.org
Police Commissioner: Mr Richard Monk, UK
Chief Military Liaison Officer: Major-General Raul Cunha, Portugal

UNMIK was established by SC res. 1244 (1999). Its mandate includes:
* Promoting the establishment, pending a final settlement, of substantial autonomy and self-government in Kosovo
* Performing basic civilian administrative functions

- Holding elections
- Facilitating a political process to determine Kosovo's future status
- Supporting reconstruction
- Maintaining civil law and order
- Protecting and promoting human rights
- Assuring the safe and unimpeded return of all refugees and displaced persons to their homes.

The strength of UNMIK at the end of April 2007 was 38 military personnel and 2050 civilian police contributed by:

Argentina	Hungary	Poland
Austria	India	Portugal
Bangladesh	Ireland	Romania
Bolivia	Italy	Russian Federation
Brazil	Jordan	Slovenia
Bulgaria	Kenya	Spain
Chile	Kyrgyzstan	Sweden
China	Lithuania	Switzerland
Croatia	Malawi	Timor-Leste
Czech Republic	Malaysia	Turkey
Denmark	Nepal	Uganda
Egypt	Netherlands	Ukraine
Finland	New Zealand	UK
France	Nigeria	USA
Germany	Norway	Zambia
Ghana	Pakistan	Zimbabwe
Greece	Philippines	

UN Organization Mission in the Democratic Republic of the Congo (MONUC)

PO Box 4653
Grand Central Station
New York, NY 10163–4653
United States of America
Telephone: (+1 212) 963 0103
Fax: (+1 212) 963 0205
Internet: www.monuc.org
Special Representative of the Secretary-General: William Lacy Swing, USA
Force Commander: Lieutenant General Babacar Gaye, Senegal
Acting Deputy Force Commander: Brigadier-General Duma Mdutyana, South Africa
Police Commissioner: Daniel Cure, France

The Democratic Republic of the Congo and five regional states signed the Lusaka Ceasefire Agreement in July 1999. SC res. 1258 (1999) authorised the deployment of UN military liaison personnel and other staff following the signing of the agreement. To maintain liaison with the parties and carry out other tasks, the Security Council set up MONUC on 30 November 1999 (SC res. 1279), incorporating UN personnel authorised in earlier resolutions.

The Security Council has extended and expanded MONUC's mandate a number of times, including SC resolutions 1669 and 1671 (2006), which authorised the temporary deployment of forces from the UN Operation in Burundi (ONUB) and the European Union reserve force to support MONUC. The organisation's mandate was increased most recently by SC res. 1756 (2007) to 31 December 2007.

MONUC's strength as of 31 May 2007 was 936 international civilian personnel, 2028 local civilian staff, 607 UN Volunteers and 18,357 uniformed personnel. The latter included 728 military observers and 1036 civilian police contributed by:

Algeria	Guinea	Peru
Argentina	India	Poland
Bangladesh	Indonesia	Romania
Belgium	Ireland	Russian Federation
Benin	Jordan	Senegal
Bolivia	Kenya	Serbia
Bosnia and Herzegovina	Malawi	South Africa
Burkina Faso	Malaysia	Spain
Cameroon	Mali	Sri Lanka
Canada	Mongolia	Sweden
China	Morocco	Switzerland
Czech Republic	Mozambique	Togo
Denmark	Nepal	Tunisia
Egypt	Niger	Ukraine
France	Nigeria	UK
Ghana	Pakistan	Uruguay
Guatemala	Paraguay	Zambia

UN Mission in Ethiopia and Eritrea (UNMEE)

PO Box 4611
Grand Central Station
New York, NY 10163–4611
United States of America
Telephone: (+1 212) 963 2802 (New York: general enquiries for peacekeeping missions)
Internet: www.unmeeonline.org and/or www.un.org/Depts/dpko/missions/unmee/
Force Commander: Major-General Mohammad Taisir Masadeh, Jordan

In June 2000, after two years of fighting in a border dispute, Ethiopia and Eritrea signed a cessation of hostilities agreement. SC res. 1312 (2000) established UNMEE for six months. The Mission was to consist of up to 100 military observers and operate in anticipation of a peacekeeping operation, with a mandate to establish and maintain liaison with the parties. SC res. 1320 (2000) expanded UNMEE to a maximum strength of 4200 military personnel including 220 military observers. The mandate included monitoring the temporary security zone (TSZ) to assist in ensuring compliance with the Agreement on Cessation of Hostilities. It has since been extended, most recently by SC res. 1767 (2007) to 31 January 2008.

The current strength of UNMEE is 1463 troops, 218 military observers (as of 31 May 2007), 146 international civilian staff and 203 local staff (as of 30 April 2007) contributed by:

Algeria	Greece	Romania
Austria	Guatemala	Russian Federation
Bangladesh	India	South Africa
Bosnia and Herzegovina	Iran	Spain
Bulgaria	Jordan	Sweden
China	Kenya	Switzerland
Croatia	Malaysia	Tunisia
Czech Republic	Namibia	Ukraine
Denmark	Nepal	UR of Tanzania
Finland	Nigeria	USA
France	Norway	Uruguay
Gambia	Paraguay	Zambia
Germany	Peru	
Ghana	Poland	

UN Assistance Mission in Afghanistan (UNAMA)

Charrabi-Yi Sherpur
Near Wazir Akbar
Khan Street
Kabul
Afghanistan
Telephone: (+1 212) 963 2668/2670 (New York)
Fax: (+1 212) 963 2669/2674 (New York)
Internet: www.unama-afg.org
Head of Assistance Mission and Special Representative of the Secretary-General: Tom Koenigs, Germany

UNAMA succeeds the Special Mission to Afghanistan (UNSMA), which was established by GA res. 48/208 (1993). UNAMA was established by SC res. 1401 (2002). Its original mandate was aimed at supporting the process of rebuilding and national reconciliation outlined in the Bonn Agreement of 5 December 2001 (S/2001/1154).

Afghanistan has moved on from the Bonn Process and the Mission's work has adapted accordingly. Since March 2006 UNAMA's mandate, which is renewed annually, contains six main elements. These are:
- Providing political and strategic advice for the peace process
- Providing good offices
- Assisting Afghanistan's government towards implementation of the Afghanistan Compact
- Promoting human rights
- Providing technical assistance
- Continuing to manage all UN humanitarian relief, recovery, reconstruction and development activities in coordination with the government.

UNAMA's mandate was most recently extended to 23 March 2008 (SC res. 1746 (2007)).

The Secretary-General is required to report to the Council every six months on the progress of the Mission.

UNAMA comprises a political section and a humanitarian, recovery and reconstruction section, each led by a Deputy Special Representative. The Mission, as well as parts of the Office for Coordination of Humanitarian Affairs (OCHA), has its headquarters in Kabul, with eight regional offices around the country and several sub-offices. In addition, it has two liaison offices, in Islamabad and Tehran.

The strength of UNAMA at the end of March 2007 was 184 international civilian staff, 744 local civilian staff, 13 military liaison officers and eight civilian police. The uniformed personnel are from:

Australia	New Zealand	Sweden
Bangladesh	Poland	UK
Denmark	ROK	Uruguay
Germany	Romania	

UN Mission in Liberia (UNMIL)

PO Box 4677
Grand Central Station
New York, NY 10163–4677
United States of America
Telephone: (+1 212) 963 9925
Fax: (+1 212) 963 9924
Internet: www.unmil.org
Special Representative of the Secretary-General: Alan Doss, UK
Force Commander: Lieutenant-General Chikadibia Obiakor, Nigeria
Police Commissioner: Mohammad Alhassan, Ghana

The UN Peace-building Support Office in Liberia (UNOL) was established on 1 November 1997 following consultations with the Government of Liberia and the Security Council. Its role was to support the Government of Liberia to consolidate peace, promote national reconciliation and strengthen its democratic institutions, as well as to strengthen the engagement of the UN system in post-conflict peacebuilding. In September 2003 UNOL ceased when the Security Council, under SC res. 1509 (2003), established UNMIL, initially for 12 months.

UNMIL's mission is to:
- Support the implementation of the ceasefire agreement and the peace process
- Protect UN staff, facilities and civilians
- Support humanitarian and human rights activities
- Assist in national security reform, including national police training and the formation of a new, restructured military.

SC res. 1750 (2007) extended UNMIL to 30 September 2007 and gave it an authorised strength of up to 15,256 military personnel, including 214 military observers and up to 1201 UN police officers. At the end of May 2007 UNMIL had 15,296 uniformed personnel from:

Argentina	Indonesia	Romania
Bangladesh	Ireland	Russian Federation
Benin	Jamaica	Rwanda
Bolivia	Jordan	Samoa
Bosnia and Herzegovina	Kenya	Senegal
Brazil	Kyrgyzstan	Serbia
Bulgaria	Malawi	Sri Lanka
China	Malaysia	Sweden
Croatia	Mali	The Former Yugoslav Republic
Czech Republic	Mongolia	of Macedonia
Denmark	Namibia	Togo
Ecuador	Nepal	Turkey
Egypt	Niger	Uganda
El Salvador	Nigeria	Ukraine
Ethiopia	Norway	UK
Fiji	Pakistan	USA
Finland	Paraguay	Uruguay
France	Peru	Yemen
Gambia	Philippines	Zambia
Germany	Poland	Zimbabwe
Ghana	ROK	
India	Republic of Moldova	

SECURITY COUNCIL

UN Operations in Côte d'Ivoire (UNOCI)

08 BP 588
08 Abidjan
Côte d'Ivoire
Telephone: (+1 212) 963 2802 (New York: general enquiries for peacekeeping missions)
Internet: www.un.org/Depts/dpko/missions/unoci
Special Representative of the Secretary-General: vacant
Acting Officer in Charge: Abon Moussa, Chad
Acting Force Commander: Brigadier General Fernand Marcel Amoussou, Benin
Police Commissioner: Major-General Gerardo Cristian Chaumont, Argentina

UNOCI replaced the UN Mission in Côte d'Ivoire (MINUCI), a political mission set up by the Security Council in May 2003 with a mandate to facilitate the implementation of the peace agreement signed in January 2003. UNOCI was established on 27 February 2004 by SC res. 1528 for an initial period of 12 months. (MINUCI's mandate ended with the Secretary-General transferring authority from MINUCI and Economic Community of West African States (ECOWAS) forces to UNOCI in April 2004.) SC res. 1765 (2007) extended UNOCI's mandate to 15 January 2008.

The strength of UNOCI as of 31 May 2007 was 7848 troops, 195 military observers and 1162 UN police. Personnel are contributed by:

Argentina	Guatemala	Romania
Bangladesh	Guinea	Russian Federation
Benin	India	Rwanda
Bolivia	Ireland	Senegal
Brazil	Jordan	Serbia
Cameroon	Kenya	Switzerland
Canada	Madagascar	Togo
Central African Republic	Morocco	Tunisia
Chad	Namibia	Turkey
China	Nepal	Uganda
Croatia	Niger	UR of Tanzania
Djibouti	Nigeria	Uruguay
Dominican Republic	Pakistan	Vanuatu
Ecuador	Paraguay	Yemen
El Salvador	Peru	Zambia
Ethiopia	Philippines	Zimbabwe
France	Poland	
Ghana	Republic of Moldova	

UN Stabilization Mission in Haiti (MINUSTAH)

PO Box 5008
Grand Central Station
New York, NY 10163–5008
United States of America
Telephone: (+1 212) 963 2802 (New York: general enquiries for peacekeeping missions)
Internet: www.un.org/Depts/dpko/missions/minustah
Special Representative of the Secretary-General: Hédi Annabi, Tunisia
Force Commander: Major-General Carlos Alberto dos Santos Cruz, Brazil
Police Commissioner: Mamadou Mountaga Diallo, Guinea

SC res. 1529 (2004) authorised the Multinational Interim Force (MIF). It also declared the Security Council ready to establish a follow-on UN stabilisation force to support the continuation of a peaceful and constitutional political process, and the maintenance of a secure and stable environment. SC res. 1542 (2004) established MINUSTAH, transferring authority from the MIF on 1 June 2004.

SC res. 1743 (2007) extended MINUSTAH to 15 October 2007.

The strength of MINUSTAH at the end of March 2007 was 8836 military personnel and 1813 UN police contributed by:

Argentina	France	Philippines
Benin	Ghana	Romania
Bolivia	Grenada	Russian Federation
Brazil	Guatemala	Rwanda
Burkina Faso	Guinea	Senegal
Cameroon	Jordan	Sierra Leone
Canada	Madagascar	Spain
Chad	Mali	Sri Lanka
Chile	Mauritius	Togo
China	Nepal	Turkey
Colombia	Niger	USA
Croatia	Nigeria	Uruguay
Ecuador	Pakistan	Vanuatu
Egypt	Paraguay	Yemen
El Salvador	Peru	

UN Mission in the Sudan (UNMIS)

Plot 110 Garden City
PO Box 69
Khartoum, 11111
Sudan
Telephone: (+249 187) 086 000
Fax: (+249 187) 086 200
Internet: www.unmis.org
Special Representative of the Secretary-General: Vacant
Acting Special Representative of the Secretary-General: Taye Brook Zerihoun, Ethiopia
Force Commander: Lieutenant-General Jasbir Singh Lidder, India
Police Commissioner: Kay Vittrup, Denmark

UNMIS was established by SC res. 1590 (2005). It subsumed the UN Advance Mission in Sudan (UNAMIS), which had been established by SC res. 1547 (2004). The UNMIS mandate includes:
- Supporting implementation of the Comprehensive Peace Agreement (CPA)
- Supporting the voluntary return of refugees and internally displaced persons
- Providing humanitarian assistance.

Because of continuing unrest in Darfur, Security Council resolutions have encouraged UNMIS to provide maximum possible assistance to the African Union-led Mission in the Sudan (AMIS). They have also asked UNMIS, jointly with the African Union, to carry out early planning for a 'hybrid' AMIS/UN operation. This is to include options for UNMIS to reinforce the effort for peace in Darfur.

SC res. 1755 (2007) enhances previous resolutions and extends the UNMIS mandate to 31 October 2007. The mandated strength of UNMIS is 17,300 military personnel, including 750 military observers and 715 UN police. At the end of March 2007 UNMIS' strength was 10,027 uniformed personnel (8766 troops, 599 military observers and 662 UN police) from:

Argentina	Ghana	Philippines
Australia	Greece	Poland
Austria	Guatemala	ROK
Bangladesh	Guinea	Republic of Moldova
Belgium	India	Romania
Benin	Indonesia	Russian Federation
Bolivia	Jamaica	Rwanda
Bosnia and Herzegovina	Jordan	Samoa
Botswana	Kenya	South Africa
Brazil	Kyrgyzstan	Sri Lanka
Cambodia	Malawi	Sweden
Canada	Malaysia	Thailand
China	Mali	Turkey
Croatia	Mongolia	Uganda
Denmark	Mozambique	Ukraine
Ecuador	Namibia	UK
Egypt	Nepal	UR of Tanzania
El Salvador	Netherlands	USA
Fiji	New Zealand	Uruguay
Finland	Nigeria	Vanuatu
France	Norway	Yemen
Gabon	Pakistan	Zambia
Gambia	Paraguay	Zimbabwe
Germany	Peru	

UN Integrated Office in Sierra Leone (UNIOSIL)

PO Box 4670
Grand Central Station
New York, NY 10163–4670
United States of America
Telephone: (+1 212) 963 2802 (New York: general enquiries for peacekeeping missions)
Internet: follow links from www.ohchr.org/english/countries/sl/index.htm
Executive Representative: Victor da Silva Angelo, Portugal

UNIOSIL succeeded the peacekeeping operation UN Assistance Mission in Sierra Leone (UNAMSIL), which was deployed in Sierra Leone from October 1999 to December 2005.

By SC res. 1620 (2005) UNIOSIL was established on 1 January 2006 for 12 months. By SC res. 1734 (2006) the mandate was extended until 31 December 2007.

UNIOSIL's mandate is to:
• Assist the Government of Sierra Leone to strengthen the capacity of state institutions and advance the rule of law, human rights, security sector reform, transparency and the capacity to hold free and fair elections in 2007
• Report on the security situation
• Coordinate with regional actors in dealing with cross-border challenges such as illicit movement of small arms and human trafficking
• Coordinate with the Special Court for Sierra Leone.

The strength of UNIOSIL at the end of April 2007 was 82 international civilian staff, 192 local staff, 40 uniformed personnel (13 military observers and 27 police). The uniformed personnel are contributed by:

Bangladesh	Gambia	Kenya
China	Ghana	Malaysia
Egypt	India	Nepal

Nigeria	Russian Federation	Turkey
Pakistan	Spain	UK
Portugal	Sweden	Zambia

UN Mission in Timor-Leste (UNMIT)

Reserve Bank Building
6 Bennet Street
Darwin
Australia 8000
Telephone: (+670) 331 2210
Fax: (+670) 332 2007/8
Internet: www.unmiset.org
Special Representative of the Secretary-General: Atul Kare, India
Police Commissioner: Commander Rodolfo Asel Tor, Philippines

PO Box 4758
Grand Central Station
New York, NY 10163–4758
United States of America

SC res. 1704 (2006) established UNMIT as an integrated mission. It replaced the UN Office in Timor-Leste (UNOTIL) on 20 May 2005 and was to remain in Timor-Leste for one year. On 28 February 2007 SC res. 1745 (2007) extended the mandate of UNMIT for one year to 28 February 2008.

The authorised strength is 34 military liaison officers and 1748 UN police officers. In April 2007 the total number of military officers and UN police was 1588, from:

Australia	Malaysia	Singapore
Bangladesh	Namibia	Spain
Brazil	Nepal	Sri Lanka
Canada	New Zealand	Sweden
China	Nigeria	Thailand
Croatia	Pakistan	Turkey
Egypt	Philippines	Uganda
El Salvador	Portugal	Ukraine
Fiji	ROK	USA
Gambia	Romania	Uruguay
India	Russian Federation	Vanuatu
Japan	Samoa	Yemen
Jordan	Senegal	Zambia
Kyrgyzstan	Sierra Leone	Zimbabwe

UN Integrated Office in Burundi (BINUB)

BINUB – Burundi
PO Box 4884
Grand Central Station
New York, NY 10163–4884
United States of America
Telephone: (+1 212) 963 2802 (New York: general enquiries for peacekeeping missions)
Internet: www.binub.org
Executive Representative of the Secretary-General: Yousef Mahmoud

SC res. 1719 (2006) established BINUB for an initial period of 12 months, beginning 1 January 2007. It replaces the UN Operation in Burundi (ONUB), which successfully completed its mandate on 31 December 2006.

The BINUB mandate includes supporting the Burundi Government in peace consolidation and democratic governance, including the promotion and protection of human rights.

SECURITY COUNCIL

The current strength of BINUB is 14 military advisers and police contributed from:

Benin	Côte d'Ivoire	Niger
Burkina Faso	Madagascar	Pakistan
Cameroon	Netherlands	Turkey

POLITICAL AND PEACEBUILDING MISSIONS

Internet: www.un.org/depts/dpa/

UN peacemaking and peacebuilding efforts include a number of special representatives and envoys of the Secretary-General, as well as field-based missions and offices established for the prevention, control and resolution of conflicts and to facilitate peacebuilding activities and assistance.

These missions and offices are established by the Secretary-General, where necessary in consultation with the Security Council, in the exercise of his global responsibilities under the UN Charter relating to the maintenance of international peace and security. Most are supported by the Department of Political Affairs of the UN Secretariat. However, three political or peacebuilding missions – the UN Assistance Mission in Afghanistan (UNAMA), the UN Integrated Office in Burundi (BINUB) and the UN Integrated Office in Sierra Leone (UNIOSIL) – are directed and supported by the Department of Peacekeeping Operations and these missions are covered in the preceding section.

As of 31 March 2007 the special political and peacebuilding missions and offices of the UN comprised 840 international civilian personnel, 401 military personnel and civilian police, and 1673 local civilian personnel.

UN Political Office for Somalia (UNPOS)

PO Box 20
Grand Central Station
New York, NY 10163
United States of America
Telephone: (+1 212) 963 3096
Fax: (+1 212) 963 3095
Internet: www.un-somalia.org/index.asp
Representative of the Secretary-General and Head of Office: François Lonseny Fall, Guinea

UNPOS was established on 15 April 1995 to monitor the situation in Somalia and restore national reconciliation and peace. In consultation with the Security Council, the Secretary-General has extended its mandate several times, most recently until 8 May 2008. However, in doing so, the Security Council expressed its hope that the Secretary-General would revisit the mandate in October 2007 given the possibility that the UN might decide to change the nature of its presence in Somalia during the period.

As of the end of March 2007, UNPOS consisted of 18 international civilian and 10 local civilian staff.

UN Peace-building Support Office in Guinea-Bissau (UNOGBIS)

Rua Rui Djassi
Box 1011
Bissau
Guinea-Bissau
Telephone: (+1 212) 963 1976; (+1 212) 963 3756 (New York)
Fax: (+1 212) 963 1758 (New York)
Internet: www.un.org/depts/dpa/guinea-bissau.html
Representative of the Secretary-General and Head of Office: Shola Omoregie, Nigeria

Following SC res. 1216 (1998) and consultations between the Secretary-General and the Security Council, UNOGBIS was established with a mandate to:

- Help create an enabling environment for restoring and consolidating peace, democracy and the rule of law and for the organisation of free and democratic elections in Guinea-Bissau
- Work with the Government of National Unity, the Monitoring Group (ECOMOG) of the Economic Community of West African States (ECOWAS) and other national and international partners to facilitate the implementation of the Abuja Agreement
- Seek the commitment of the Government and other parties to adopt a programme of voluntary arms collection, disposal and destruction
- Provide the political framework and leadership for harmonising and integrating the activities of the UN system in the country, particularly during the transitional period leading up to general and presidential elections.

The Secretary-General, in consultation with the Security Council, has extended the mandate of UNOGBIS, most recently until 31 December 2007. The strength of UNOGBIS at the end of March 2007 was nine international civilian staff, two military advisers, one civilian police adviser and 10 local civilian staff.

UN Peace-building Office in the Central African Republic (BONUCA)

PO Box 4661
Grand Central Station
New York, NY 10163–4661
Internet: www.un.org/depts/dpa/car.html
Representative of the Secretary-General and Head of Office: General Lamine Cissé, Senegal

BONUCA was established in accordance with SC res. 1271 (1999) and became operational on 15 February 2000. Its primary mission is to:

- Support the efforts of the Government of the Central African Republic to consolidate peace and national reconciliation
- Strengthen democratic institutions
- Facilitate the mobilisation of international political support and resources for both national reconstruction and economic recovery.

The Secretary-General, in consultation with the Security Council, has extended the mandate of BONUCA, most recently until 31 December 2007.

The strength of BONUCA at the end of March 2007 was 28 international civilian staff, five military advisers, six civilian police and 51 local civilian staff.

Office of the Special Representative of the Secretary-General for the Great Lakes Region

The Secretary-General decided in 1999 to appoint a Special Representative for the Great Lakes Region to sound out views on the organisation of an international conference and address the regional dimensions of the conflict in the Democratic Republic of the Congo.

The Office was decommissioned following the December 2006 signing by 11 African countries of the Pact on Security, Stability and Development in the Great Lakes Region (the Nairobi Security Pact).

UN Tajikistan Office of Peace-building (UNTOP)

UNTOP was established on 1 June 2000 following the withdrawal of the UN Mission of Observers in Tajikistan (UNMOT) in May 2000. It was set up to consolidate peace, and provide support and assistance for recovery and reconstruction.

In response to a request by the Republic of Tajikistan Government, the Security Council decided on 18 May 2007 that UNTOP's mandate would be completed by 31 July 2007.

Office of the Special Representative of the Secretary-General for West Africa

Lot 14
Ouest Almadies
Dakar
Senegal
Telephone: (+221) 869 8585
Fax: (+221) 820 4638
Special Representative of the Secretary-General: Ahmedou Ould-Abdallah, Mauritania

The Secretary-General announced his decision to establish the Office of the Special Representative of the Secretary-General for West Africa in a letter to the Security Council President dated 29 November 2001.

At the end of March 2007 the Office of the Special Representative consisted of eight international civilian and nine local civilian staff.

UN Assistance Mission for Iraq (UNAMI)

PO Box 5859
Grand Central Station
New York, NY 10163–5859
United States of America
Telephone: (+962 6) 550 4700
Fax: (+962 6) 550 4705
Internet: follow links from www.uniraq.org
Special Representative of the Secretary-General: Ashraf Jehangir Qazi, Pakistan

Following SC res. 1483 (2003) the position of the Special Representative of the Secretary-General for Iraq was established with a mandate to coordinate with the administering Authority (USA and UK) to:
• Coordinate humanitarian and reconstruction assistance by UN agencies and between UN agencies and non-government organisations

- Promote the safe, orderly and voluntary return of refugees and displaced persons
- Work intensively with the Authority, the people of Iraq, and others concerned to advance efforts to restore and establish national and local institutions for representative governance, including by working together to facilitate a process leading to an internationally recognised, representative government of Iraq
- Facilitate the reconstruction of key infrastructure, in cooperation with other international organisations
- Promote economic reconstruction and the conditions for sustainable development, including through coordination with national and regional organisations, civil society, donors and the international financial institutions
- Encourage international efforts to contribute to basic civilian administration functions
- Promote the protection of human rights
- Encourage international efforts to rebuild the capacity of the Iraqi civilian police force
- Encourage international efforts to promote legal and judicial reform.

UNAMI was established by SC res. 1500 (2003). It had the role, initially for 12 months, of supporting the Secretary-General in the fulfilment of his mandate under SC res. 1483. Subsequent SC resolutions 1546 (2003), 1557 (2004), 1619 (2005) and 1700 (2006) have consolidated tasks, increased UNAMI's maximum strength to 1014 personnel, and extended its mandate to 10 August 2007.

At the end of March 2007 UNAMI consisted of 281 international civilian staff, 347 local civilian staff, 223 military personnel and seven military observers.

Office of the UN Special Coordinator for the Middle East (UNSCO)

Government House
PO Box 490
Jerusalem 91004
Israel
Telephone: (+1 212) 963 9568 (New York)
Fax: (+1 212) 963 9567 (New York)
Internet: www.unsco.org
Special Coordinator for the Middle East Peace Process and Personal Representative of the Secretary-General to the Palestine Liberation Organisation and the Palestinian Authority: Michael Williams, UK

On 6 May 2005 the Secretary-General appointed Alvaro de Soto, Peru, as the UN Special Coordinator for the Middle East Peace Process and as his Personal Representative to the Palestine Liberation Organisation and the Palestinian Authority. Alvaro de Soto resigned in May 2007 and has been replaced by Michael Williams, UK. The Special Coordinator represents the Secretary-General in discussions with the parties and the international community on all matters related to continuing UN support for the peace process.

At the end of March 2007, UNSCO consisted of 29 international civilian and 21 local civilian staff.

United Nations Mission in Nepal (UNMIN)

UN House
Pulchowk
GPO Box 107
Kathmandu
Nepal
Telephone: (+ 977) 1 554 8553
Fax: (+ 997) 1 554 8597
Internet: www.un.org.np/unmin.php
Special Representative of the Secretary-General in Nepal and Head of Mission: Ian Martin, UK

UNMIN was established by the Security Council on 23 January 2007 for one year, with a mandate to monitor the ceasefire and assist in the election of a Constituent Assembly. The Mission's mandate will be extended or terminated at the request of the Nepalese Government.

At the end of March 2007, UNMIN consisted of 34 international civilian staff and 86 military observers.

COMMISSIONS

Peacebuilding Commission (PBC)

Internet: www.un.org/peace/peacebuilding/

Purpose

At the UN World Summit in September 2005 Leaders agreed to establish the PBC as an inter-government advisory body to assist countries emerging from conflict. The key objectives of the PBC are to:
- Provide advice on, and propose integrated strategies for, peacebuilding and post-conflict recovery
- Ensure predictable financing for early recovery activities and sustained financial investment over the medium to long term
- Extend the period of attention of the international community to post-conflict recovery
- Focus attention on reconstruction and institution building efforts
- Develop best practices on issues that require collaboration and cooperation among key political, military, humanitarian and development participants.

On the request of the Security Council (PBC/OC/1/2) the PBC has engaged with Sierra Leone and Burundi as its first two country-specific situations.

Structure

The PBC's institutional structures, including its membership and procedures, were established by GA res. 60/180 (2005) and SC resolutions 1645 (2005) and 1646 (2005).

GA res. 60/180 provides for a review of the PBC's founding arrangements in five years to ensure that they are appropriate to fulfil the agreed functions of the Commission. Both the General Assembly and the Security Council would need to concur with any amendments to the PBC's structure and operations.

The PBC Organisational Committee is composed of seven members selected by the Security Council; seven members elected by the Economic and Social Council (ECOSOC); seven members elected by the General Assembly; the five top providers of assessed contributions to UN budgets and voluntary contributions to UN funds, programmes and agencies; and the five top providers of military personnel and civilian police to UN missions.*

Membership

At the end of March 2007, membership of the PBC Organisational Committee was:

Members selected by the Security Council

China	South Africa	USA
France	Russian Federation	
Panama	UK	

Members elected by the General Assembly

Burundi	Egypt	Jamaica
Chile	El Salvador	
Croatia	Fiji	

Members elected by the ECOSOC

Angola	Guinea-Bissau	Sri Lanka
Brazil	Indonesia	
Czech Republic	Luxembourg	

Top providers of assessed and voluntary contributions

Germany	Japan	Norway
Italy	Netherlands	

Top providers of military personnel and civilian police

Bangladesh	India	Pakistan
Ghana	Nigeria	

At the end of March 2007, the Chair and Vice-Chairs were:

Chair	Vice-Chairs
Ismael Gaspar Martins, Angola	Carmen Maria Gallardo Hernandez, El Salvador
	Johan L Løvald, Norway

Note

* Arrangements for the election of members from the General Assembly were agreed in GA res. 60/261 (2006). Given the over-representation of Western European and Other states (WEOG) in other categories of the Organisational Committee, it was agreed that during the first elections for the General Assembly category that WEOG would not have a regional seat.

SECURITY COUNCIL

UN Monitoring, Verification and Inspection Commission (UNMOVIC)

United Nations Headquarters
Alcoa Building
866 UN Plaza
New York, NY 10017
United States of America
Telephone: (+1 212) 963 3018 or (+1 212) 963 3022
Fax: (+1 212) 963 3922
Email: info@unmovic.org
Internet: www.unmovic.org
Acting Executive Chairman: Demetrius Perricos, Greece (appointed by the UN Secretary-General)

UNMOVIC was established by SC res. 1284 (1999) to replace the former UN Special Commission (UNSCOM) established under SC res. 687 (1991). The mandate of UNMOVIC included the former UNSCOM's responsibilities regarding verification of Iraq's compliance with its obligations under SC res. 687 and other related resolutions, and the establishment and operation of a reinforced system of monitoring and verification to ensure that Iraq did not reacquire the same capabilities or weapons prohibited to it by the Security Council.

Following the beginning of military action in Iraq in March 2003, UNMOVIC's activities on the ground in Iraq under SC res. 1284 (1999) were suspended, though work at Headquarters continued. SC res. 1483 (2003), adopted at the end of military action in Iraq, reaffirmed Iraq's disarmament obligations and highlighted the Council's intention to revisit UNMOVIC's mandate. This was reiterated in SC res 1546 (2004).

On 29 June 2007 SC res. 1762 (2007) terminated UNMOVIC's mandate as of that date.

UN Compensation Commission (UNCC)

Villa la Pelouse
Palais des Nations
1211 Geneva 10
Switzerland
Telephone: (+41 22) 917 3600
Fax: (+41 22) 917 0069
Email: unccwebmaster@uncc.ch
Internet: www2.unog.ch/uncc
Officer-in-charge: Mojtaba Kazazi, Iran (since 2007) (appointed by the UN Secretary-General)

Purpose

By SC res. 687 (1991) the Security Council reaffirmed Iraq's liability under international law for any direct loss, damage, including environmental damage and the depletion of natural resources, or injury to foreign governments, nationals and corporations resulting from Iraq's unlawful invasion and occupation of Kuwait. By SC res. 692 (1991) the Security Council established both the UN Compensation Fund to pay compensation for claims that fell within these categories, and a commission to administer the Fund.

Nineteen panels of Commissioners, which have now concluded their work, reviewed and evaluated the claims submitted by governments, companies and individuals. The panels reported their recommendations to the Governing Council for approval.

Approximately 2.7 million claims, with an asserted value of approximately $352.5 billion, were filed with the Commission. With the approval of the final reports and recommendations of the panels of Commissioners by the Governing Council in June 2005, the Compensation

Commission completed its processing of all submitted claims. The total compensation awarded amounts to approximately $52.5 billion.

Currently the Commission's principal areas of activity relate to the payment of outstanding awards and the Follow-Up Programme for Environmental Awards established by the Council at its 58th session in December 2005 for the purpose of monitoring the expenditures by claimant governments of environmental awards. As of June 2007 the Commission had paid out approximately $22 billion to claimants.

Structure

The 15-member Governing Council is the principal organ of the Commission and is composed of representatives of the current members of the Security Council. The Governing Council elects its own President and two Vice-Presidents, each for two-year terms.

The secretariat of the Commission, headed by the Executive Secretary, provides support and assistance to the Governing Council. At its height the secretariat had a staff of approximately 300. This decreased to fewer than 30 employees, with that number continuing to diminish in mid-2007. The secretariat will be further downsized into a residual format in accordance with the decision on successor arrangements taken by the Governing Council at its 58th session in December 2005.

Funds to pay compensation are drawn from the Compensation Fund, which currently receives 5 percent of the revenue derived from Iraqi oil exports as provided by SC res. 1483 (2003).

Membership

The current membership of the Governing Council is:

Permanent members

China	Russian Federation	USA
France	UK	

Non-permanent members with mandate until end of 2007

DR Congo (Vice-President)	Peru	Slovakia
Ghana	Qatar	

Non-permanent members with mandate until end of 2008

Belgium (President)	Italy	South Africa
Indonesia (Vice-President)	Panama	

SECURITY COUNCIL

INTERNATIONAL TRIBUNALS

International Criminal Tribunal for the Former Yugoslavia (ICTY)

Churchillplein 1
PO Box 13888
2517 JW The Hague
The Netherlands
Telephone: (+31 70) 512 5000
Fax: (+31 70) 512 3355
Internet: www.un.org/icty
Registrar: Henry Adam Holthuis, Netherlands

SC res. 808 (1993) established an international tribunal for the prosecution of people responsible for serious violations of international humanitarian law committed in the former Yugoslavia since 1991.

By SC res. 827 (1993) the Security Council, acting under chapter VII of the UN Charter, adopted the Statute of the International Tribunal for the Former Yugoslavia.

There are 16 permanent ICTY judges, elected by the General Assembly or, in the event of a vacancy arising, appointed directly by the Secretary-General after consultation with the Presidents of the Security Council and of the General Assembly. On 19 November 2004 the General Assembly elected the following 14 permanent judges, for a term of four years, beginning on 17 November 2005 and expiring on 16 November 2009:

Fausto Pocar, Italy (President)

Kevin Parker, Australia (Vice-President)

Patrick Lipton Robinson, Jamaica (Presiding Judge)

Carmel A Agius, Malta (Presiding Judge)

Alphonsus Martinus Maria Orie, Netherlands (Presiding Judge)

Mohamed Shahabuddeen, Guyana

Mehmet Güney, Turkey

Liu Daqun, China

Andresia Vaz, Senegal

Theodor Meron, USA

Wolfgang Schomburg, Germany

O-gon Kwon, South Korea

Jean-Claude Antonetti, France

Iain Bonomy, UK

Christine Van Den Wyngaert, Belgium

Bakone Justice Moloto, South Africa

In addition to the permanent judges, the Security Council decided by SC res. 1329 (2000) to establish a pool of ad litem judges, elected by the General Assembly. On 24 August 2005 the General Assembly elected the following ad litem judges for a term of four years, commencing on 24 August 2005:

Krister Thelin, Sweden

Janet Nosworthy, Jamaica

Frank Höpfel, Austria

Árpád Prandler, Hungary

Stefan Trechsel, Switzerland

Antoine Mindua, DR Congo

Ali Nawaz Chowhan, Pakistan

Tsvetana Kamenova, Bulgaria

Kimberly Prost, Canada

Ole Bjørn Støle, Norway

Frederik Harhoff, Denmark

Flavia Lattanzi, Italy

The Tribunal discharges its judicial functions through three Trial Chambers and an Appeals Chamber. Each Trial Chamber consists of three permanent judges. There may also be up to six ad litem judges in a given Trial Chamber. If ad litem judges are assigned to serve in a Trial Chamber, that Trial Chamber may be divided into a maximum of three sections of three judges each. Three judges sit on a given trial. At least one of the three must be a permanent judge. SC res. 1660 (2006) permits the Secretary-General to appoint, at the request of the ICTY, reserve judges from the ICTY pool of ad litem judges to specific trials. Reserve judges are present at each stage of a trial and replace a judge on the bench if she or he is unable to continue sitting.

Seven of the judges are members of the Appeals Chamber. Only permanent judges may be members of this Chamber. Each appeal is heard by five members of the Appeals Chamber. The members of the ICTY Appeal Court also serve as the members of the Appeals Chamber of the International Criminal Tribunal for Rwanda (ICTR). Five ICTY Appeals Chamber judges are drawn from the permanent ICTY judges, and two are drawn from the ICTR permanent judges.

The Prosecutor is appointed by the Security Council, upon nomination by the Secretary-General, for a term of four years and is eligible for re-appointment. On 4 September 2003, the Security Council reappointed Carla Del Ponte, Switzerland, as the ICTY Chief Prosecutor for a second four-year term commencing on 15 September 2003. The Prosecutor acts independently as a separate organ of the Tribunal.

International Criminal Tribunal for Rwanda (ICTR)

Arusha International Conference Centre
PO Box 6016
Arusha
United Republic of Tanzania
Telephone: (+255) 27 250 4372
Fax: (+255) 27 250 4373
Internet: www.ictr.org
Registrar: Adama Dieng, Senegal

SC res. 955 (1994), adopted under chapter VII of the UN Charter, established an international tribunal for the prosecution of persons committing genocide and other serious violations of international humanitarian law during 1994 in the territory of Rwanda, and of Rwandan citizens committing such crimes in neighbouring territories. SC res. 955 (1994) also adopted the Statute of the ICTR under chapter VII of the UN Charter.

The Tribunal consists of three organs:
- The Chambers and the Appeals Chamber
- The Office of the Prosecutor – in charge of investigations and prosecutions
- The Registry – responsible for providing overall judicial and administrative support to the Chambers and the Prosecutor.

The three Trial Chambers and the Appeals Chamber are composed of 16 independent judges elected by the General Assembly from a list submitted by the Security Council. No two judges may be nationals of the same state. They are initially selected from a list of nominees submitted by UN Member States. Nominations must take account of adequate representation of the principal legal systems of the world. The judges are elected for a term of four years, and are eligible for re-election.

Three judges sit in each of the Trial Chambers and five judges sit in the Appeals Chamber, which is shared with the International Criminal Tribunal for the former Yugoslavia.

Judges in order of precedence:

Charles Michael Dennis Byron, Saint Kitts and Nevis (President ICTR; Member, Trial Chamber III)

Khalida Rachid Khan, Pakistan (Vice-President ICTR; Presiding Judge, Trial Chamber III)

Fausto Pocar, Italy (Presiding Judge, Appeals Chamber)

William Sekule, UR of Tanzania (Presiding Judge, Trial Chamber II)

Erik Møse, Norway (Presiding Judge, Trial Chamber I)

Mohamed Shahabuddeen, Guyana (Member, Appeals Chamber)

Mehmet Güney, Turkey (Member, Appeals Chamber)

Liu Daqun China (Member, Appeals Chamber)

Andrésia Vaz, Senegal (Member, Appeals Chamber)

Theodor Meron, US (Member, Appeals Chamber)

Wolfgang Schomburg, Germany (Member, Appeals Chamber)

Arlette Ramaroson, Madagascar (Member, Trial Chamber II)

Jai Ram Reddy, Fiji (Member, Trial Chamber I)

Sergei Alekseevich Egorov, Russian Federation (Member, Trial Chamber I)

Inés Mónica Weinberg de Roca, Argentina (Member, Trial Chamber III)

Joseph Asoka Nihal De Silva, Sri Lanka (Member, Trial Chamber II)

By SC res. 1431 (2002) the Security Council decided to establish a pool of 18 ad litem judges. At any one time, a maximum of four ad litem judges may be attached to the Trial Chambers. SC res 1512 (2003) increased the number of ad litem judges who may serve on the Tribunal at any one time from four to nine.

The ad litem judges are:

Solomy Balungi Bossa, Uganda (Member, Trial Chamber II)

Lee Gacugia Muthoga, Kenya (Member, Trial Chamber II)

Florence Rita Arrey, Cameroun (Member, Trial Chamber III)

Emile Francis Short, Ghana (Member, Trial Chamber II)

Taghrid Hikmet, Jordan (Member, Trial Chamber II)

Seon Ki Park, Republic of Korea (Member, Trial Chamber II)

Gberdao Gustave Kam, Burkina Faso (Member, Trial Chamber III)

Robert Fremr, Czech Republic (Member, Trial Chamber III)

Vagn Joensen, Denmark (Member, Trial Chamber III)

OTHER ORGANISATIONS

UN Command in Korea

UNIT #15259, APO AP 96205–0032
Telephone: (+82 2) 7913 0032
Fax: (+82 2) 7913 3537
Commander: General BB Bell, USA

By SC res. 84 (1950) the Security Council requested all Member States providing military forces in Korea to make them available to a unified command under the leadership of the USA. Combatant units were provided by 16 Member States:

Australia
Belgium
Canada
Colombia
Ethiopia
France

Greece
Luxembourg
Netherlands
New Zealand
Philippines
South Africa

Thailand
Turkey
UK
USA

In addition, five Member States provided medical units:

Denmark
India

Italy
Norway

Sweden

The Republic of Korea also placed its military forces under the unified command.

As a signatory to the Armistice Agreement of 27 July 1953, the Commander-in-Chief of the UN Command (UNC) accepted responsibility (with the other signatories, the Supreme

Commander of the Korean People's Army and the Commander of the Chinese People's Volunteers) for implementing and maintaining the Armistice until the Armistice Agreement was expressly superseded either by mutually acceptable amendments and additions or by provision in an appropriate agreement for a peaceful settlement at a political level between both sides.

The composition of the command is not restricted or limited, except that the USA designates the commander. The 16 Member States that provided combat forces during the war are not obligated to provide support to the Commander-in-Chief of the UNC.

Fifteen Liaison Groups are accredited to the UNC. Their responsibilities include formulating policies and procedures for integration of the contingents into the UNC, and acting as their states' senior representatives to coordinate administrative, logistical and fiscal matters with the UNC. They also carry out Military Armistice Commission (MAC) duties. The Liaison Groups come from:

Australia	France	Philippines
Belgium	Greece	Thailand
Canada	Netherlands	Turkey
Colombia	New Zealand	UK
Denmark	Norway	USA

Coalition members actively participate in Armistice maintenance activities. Some Sending States provide officers to augment the MAC in Armistice maintenance duties. These countries include Australia, France, New Zealand and the UK.

ECONOMIC AND SOCIAL COUNCIL

ECONOMIC AND SOCIAL COUNCIL

CHARTER PROVISIONS

The UN is charged by its Charter with promoting in the economic and social fields:
- Higher standards of living, full employment and conditions of economic and social progress and development
- Solutions to international economic, social, health and related problems, and international cultural and educational cooperation
- Universal respect for, and observance of, rights and fundamental freedoms for all, without distinction as to race, sex, language or religion.

Responsibility for discharging these functions is vested in the General Assembly and, under its authority, the Economic and Social Council (ECOSOC).

ECOSOC makes or initiates studies and reports with respect to international economic, social, cultural, educational, health and related matters. It makes recommendations on these to the General Assembly, members of the UN and the specialised agencies concerned. It also makes recommendations for the purpose of promoting respect for, and observance of, human rights. ECOSOC prepares draft conventions for submission to the General Assembly and convenes international conferences when necessary. It enters into agreements with specialised agencies and makes arrangements for consultation with non-government organisations.

The Charter provisions relating to ECOSOC are contain in chapter IX (articles 55–60), which sets forth the objectives and functions of the UN in the sphere of international economic and social cooperation, and chapter X (articles 61–72), which defines the composition, functions and powers, and voting and procedure of the Council. Other provisions are to be found in articles 1, 2, 7, 15, 17, 18, 91, 96, 98 and 101.

MEMBERSHIP

Membership of ECOSOC, originally 18, was increased to 27 by amendment to article 61 of the UN Charter in accordance with GA res. 1991B (XVIII) (1963), which came into operation on 31 August 1965. GA res. 2847 (XXVI) (1971) enlarged the Council to 54 and amended article 61 accordingly. This enlargement took effect on 12 October 1973.

The pattern for the geographical distribution of seats was established in GA res. 2847 (XXVI) (1971): 14 members from African states, 11 from Asian states, six from Eastern European states, 10 from Latin American and Caribbean states, and 13 from Western European and Other states.

Eighteen members of ECOSOC are elected each year. Members serve three-year terms of office, with their terms expiring on 31 December.

	Previous membership	Current membership

African states

	Previous membership	Current membership
Algeria	1964–66 73–81 83–85 90–92 1998–2000	2007–09
Angola	1992–94 2000–02	2006–08
Benin	1966–67 82–84 92–94 2000–05	2006–08
Botswana	1983–85 91–93	
Burkina Faso	1968–70 77–79 90–92 2000–02	
Burundi	1972–74 81–83 2002–04	
Cameroon	1966–67 78–83 89–91 2000–02	
Cape Verde	1997–99	2007–09
Central African Republic	1978–80 96–98	
Chad	1968–70	2005–07
Comoros	1998–2000	
Congo	1968–70 74–76 83–85 95–97 1999–2001 03–05	
Côte d'Ivoire	1974–76 95–97	
DR Congo	1971–77 80–82 84–95 1999–2001	2005–07
Djibouti	1983–88 97–99	
Egypt	1952–57 74–76 86–88 94–96 2001–03	
Ethiopia	1961–63 74–77 80–82 92–94 2001–03	
Gabon	1965–67 75–77 86–88 93–98	
Gambia	1997–99	
Ghana	1970–72 79–81 88–90 94–96 2002–04	
Guinea	1974–75 85–93	2005–07
Guinea-Bissau	1999–2001	2006–08
Kenya	1970–72 74–77 81–83 89–91 2003–05	
Lesotho	1978–80 88–90 1998–2000	
Liberia	1974–76 82–84 88–90	
Libyan AJ	1967–69 80–82 88–90 93–95 2002–04	
Madagascar	1971–73 92–94	2006–08
Malawi	1980–82	2007–09
Mali	1973–75 82–84	
Mauritania	1977–79	2006–08
Mauritius	1998–2000 04–06	
Morocco	1966–68 79–81 85–87 91–93 1999–2001	
Mozambique	1986–88 97–99 2003–05	
Namibia	2004–06	
Niger	1971–73 89–91	
Nigeria	1976–78 80–82 85–87 93–95 2001–06	
Rwanda	1977–79 84–92 1999–2001	
Senegal	1962–64 74–75 79–81 85–87 94–96 2003–05	
Sierra Leone	1966–69 83–88 1998–2000	
Somalia	1977–79 84–89 91–93	2007–09
South Africa	1995–97 2001–03	2005–07
Sudan	1958–60 69–71 77–79 81–83 87–89 95–97 2000–02	2007–09
Swaziland	1982–84 92–94	
Togo	1976–78 91–98	
Tunisia	1970–72 76–78 82–84 89–91 96–98 2004–06	
Uganda	1973–78 84–86 95–97 2001–03	
UR of Tanzania	1966–69 78–80 94–96 2004–06	
Zambia	1974–76 79–81 89–91 97–99	
Zimbabwe	1985–87 94–96 2002–04	

Asian states

	Previous membership	Current membership
Afghanistan	1959–61 76–78	
Bahrain	1990–92 2000–02	
Bangladesh	1976–78 81–83 85–87 92–94 96–98 2004–06	
Bhutan	1993–95 2002–04	
China	1946–60 1972–2004	2005–07
Cyprus	1979–81	
Fiji	1974–75 81–83 2000–02	
India	1946–47 53–55 62–64 66–70 74 78–83 85–90 1992–2000 02–04	2005–07
Indonesia	1956–58 69–71 74–75 79–81 84–86 89–91 94–96 1999–2000 04–06	2007–09
Iran	1950–52 66–68 74–79 87–92 2001–03	
Iraq	1964–66 77–82 86–91	2007–09
Japan	1960–65 68–70 72–80 1982–2005	2006–08
Jordan	1961–63 74–76 80–82 89–91 96–98	
Kazakhstan		2007–09
Kuwait	1967–69 92–94	
Lebanon	1946–49 71–73 83–85 96–98	
Malaysia	1971–73 76–78 83–85 91–93 95–97 2003–05	
Mongolia	1973–75	
Nepal	1980–82 2001–03	
Oman	1987–89 1998–2000	
Pakistan	1954–59 65–67 69–71 74–77 79–84 86–88 90–92 94–96 1998–2003	2005–07
Papua New Guinea	1984–86	
Philippines	1951–53 66–68 77–79 86–88 92–97	2007–09
Qatar	1982–84 2002–04	
ROK	1993–95 97–99 2003–06	
Saudi Arabia	1983–85 88–90 1999–2001 03–05	2006–08
Sri Lanka	1970–72 84–89 93–95 97–99	2006–08
Syrian AR	1977–79 86–88 91–93 1999–2001	
Thailand	1974–76 80–85 89–91 95–97	2005–07
UAE	1978–80 2004–06	
Viet Nam	1998–2000	

Eastern European states[1, 2]

	Previous membership	Current membership
Albania		2005–07
Armenia	2004–06	
Azerbaijan	2003–05	
Belarus	1947–49 81–83 86–88 1992–2000	2007–09
Bulgaria	1959–61 68–70 75–77 80–85 87–92 94–96 1999–2001	
Croatia	2000–02	
Czech Republic	1996–2001	2006–08
Georgia	2001–03	
Hungary	1971–73 78–80 2002–04	
Latvia	1997–99	
Lithuania		2005–07
Poland	1948–53 57–62 72–74 77–79 81–89 1992–2000 04–06	
Romania	1965–67 74–76 78–80 82–87 90–98 2001–03	2007–09

	Previous membership	Current membership
Russian Federation	1947–2004	2005–07
Ukraine	1946 77–79 89–91 93–95 2002–04	

Latin American and Caribbean states

	Previous membership	Current membership
Argentina	1952–57 63–65 68–70 74–86 91–93 96–98 2001–03	
Bahamas	1980–82 89–91 93–95	
Barbados	1979–81	2007–09
Belize	1987–89 2004–06	
Bolivia	1972–74 76–78 87–89 1999–2001	2007–09
Brazil	1948–50 56–58 60–62 70–87 1989–2003	2005–07
Chile	1946–47 58–60 64–66 72–74 80–82 91–99 2002–04	
Colombia	1946 62–64 74–79 82–90 1992–2000 04–06	
Costa Rica	1958–60 84–86 94–96 2000–02	2005–07
Cuba	1946–47 52–54 76–78 88–90 93–95 1997–2005	2006–08
Dominican Republic	1955–57 78–80	
Ecuador	1954–56 64–66 79–81 83–85 90–92 2003–05	
El Salvador	1961–63 97–99 2002–04	2007–09
Guatemala	1967–69 74–75 2002–04	
Guyana	1984–86 96–98	2006–08
Haiti	1971–73 85–87	2006–08
Honduras	1999–2001	
Jamaica	1969–71 74–79 86–88 90–92 95–97 2003–05	
Mexico	1950–52 57–59 67–69 74–85 90–95 1997–2002	2005–07
Nicaragua	1981–83 89–91 96–98 2003–05	
Panama	1966–68 86–88 2004–06	
Paraguay	1994–96	2006–08
Peru	1946–51 65–67 70–72 75–77 81–83 86–88 91–93 2001–03	
Saint Lucia	1982–84 1998–2000	
Suriname	1983–85 92–94 2000–02	
Trinidad and Tobago	1973–75 78–80 88–93	
Uruguay	1951–53 61–63 69–71 87–89	
Venezuela	1947–49 53–55 59–61 66–68 74–90 94–96 1999–2001	

Western European and Other states

	Previous membership	Current membership
Andorra	2001–03	
Australia	1948–50 53–55 62–64 74–76 80–82 86–88 92–97 2002–06	
Austria	1963–65 76–78 82–84 91–93 2000–02	2006–08
Belgium	1946 49–54 67–69 74–76 80–82 86–88 92–94 1998–2000 04–06	
Canada	1946–48 50–52 56–58 65–67 74–77 1981–2001 04–06	2007–09
Denmark	1948–50 60–62 75–77 81–83 87–89 93–95 1999–2001	2005–07
Finland	1957–59 72–74 78–80 84–86 90–92 96–98 2002–04	
France	1946–2005	2006–08
Germany	1974–2005	2006–08
Greece	1946 56–58 66 70–72 76–78 82–84 88–90 94–96 2000 2003–05	2007–08
Iceland	1985–87 97–99	2005–07

	Previous membership	Current membership
Ireland	1968–70 79–81 88–90 94–96 2003–05	
Italy	1961–63 70–72 74–82 86–94 1998–2003 04–06	
Luxembourg	1964–66 83–85 95–97	2007–09
Malta	1978–80 2001–02	
Netherlands	1947–48 55–60 73–75 77–79 83–85 89–91 95–97 2001–03	2007–09
New Zealand	1947–49 59–61 71–73 77–79 83–85 89–91 1998–2000	2007
Norway	1946–47 54–56 69–71 75–77 81–83 87–89 93–95 1999–2001	
Portugal	1976–78 82–84 88–90 94–96 2000–01	2007
Spain	1959–61 73–75 79–81 85–87 91–93 97–99 2002–06	
Sweden	1951–53 66–68 74 78–80 84–86 90–92 96–98 2002–04	
Turkey	1947–49 53–55 67–69 74–75 79–81 85–87 91–93 97–99 2003–06	
UK	1947–2004	2005–07
USA	1946–2006	2007–09

Countries that have never served on the Council are not listed.

Notes

[1] The former Socialist Federal Republic of Yugoslavia served on ECOSOC for the following periods: 1946, 1962–64, 1969–71, 1974–78, 1980–82, 1984–86 and 1988–92. It was not automatically succeeded by any of the new states created following its dissolution.

[2] Czechoslovakia served on ECOSOC from 1946–47, 1950–52, 1954–56, 1963–68, 1974–77 and 1989–91.

SESSIONS AND OFFICERS

Until 1991 ECOSOC usually held two sessions a year, as well as a brief organisational meeting. It established, as required, the following sessional committees: Economic Committee, Social Committee, and Policy and Programme Committee.

By GA res. 45/264 (1991) the General Assembly decided, with effect from February 1992, that ECOSOC would hold one substantive session annually between May and July, to take place in alternate years in New York and Geneva. The substantive session would have a four-day high-level segment open to all Member States, with ministerial participation. This would be devoted to consideration of one or more major economic and/or social themes.

There would also be a one-day policy dialogue on important developments in the world economy and on international economic cooperation, with invited participation from the heads of the international financial and trade institutions of the UN system. The high-level segment would be followed by coordination, operational activities and committee segments when economic, social and related issues would be considered in two separate committees meeting simultaneously.

These arrangements remain current, except that GA res. 48/162 (1993) replaced the committee segment with a general segment and GA res. 50/227 (1996) limited the substantive session to four weeks in July.

In paragraphs 155 and 156 of the World Summit Outcome Document, ECOSOC was mandated to hold Annual Ministerial Reviews to assess progress with implementing outcomes of the major UN conferences and summits of the past 15 years, including the internationally agreed development goals. It also asked ECOSOC to convene emergency meetings, serve as a quality platform of engagement on global policies and trends in the economic, social, environmental and humanitarian fields, and hold biennial Development Cooperation Forums to review trends in international development cooperation.

In the July 2007 substantive session, the high-level segment comprised a thematic discussion on strengthening efforts at all levels to promote pro-poor sustained economic growth, including through equitable macroeconomic policies, and an Annual Ministerial Review on strengthening efforts to eradicate poverty and hunger, including through the global partnership for development. The biennial Development Cooperation Forum was launched.

ECOSOC decisions are taken by a simple majority of members present and voting. An organisational session of not more than four days is held in late January/early February. Elections, appointments and nominations take place at a resumed organisational session, normally in late April/early May. GA res. 48/162 (1993) also specifies issues to be addressed in the future regarding restructuring and revitalisation of the UN in the economic, social and related fields.

In 2007 ECOSOC held organisational sessions on 17 January, 6 to 9 February, 25 to 26 April and 24 May. A special high-level meeting with Bretton Woods Institutions, WTO and UNCTAD was held on 16 April. The substantive session of the Council was held from 2 to 27 July in Geneva.

The following Bureau was elected at the organisational session in January 2007:

President
Dalius Cekuolis, Lithuania

Vice-Presidents
Hilario G Davide, Philippines
Hjálmar W Hannesson, Iceland
Leo Merores, Haiti
Youcef Yousfi, Algeria

SUBSIDIARY BODIES OF ECOSOC

Article 68 of the Charter provides for ECOSOC to set up commissions:
- In economic and social fields
- For the promotion of human rights
- In other fields required for the performance of its functions.

FUNCTIONAL COMMISSIONS

Commission on Narcotic Drugs (CND)

United Nations Office on Drugs and Crime
Vienna International Centre
PO Box 500
A–1400 Vienna
Austria
Telephone: (+43 1) 260 600
Fax: (+43 1) 26060 5866
Email: unodc@unodc.org
Internet: www.unodc.org/unodc/en/cnd.html
Secretary: Andrés Finguerut, UK (since 2005)

Purpose

The CND was established in 1946 by the Economic and Social Council in ECOSOC res. 9 (I) as the central policy-making body within the UN system for dealing with drug-related matters. The Commission analyses the world drug situation and develops proposals to strengthen international drug control, as well as carrying out functions assigned to it by international drug control treaties. Its mandate was enlarged by the Council in ECOSOC res. 1991/38 and by the General Assembly in GA res. 46/185 C section XVI to include serving as the governing body of the Fund of the United Nations International Drug Control Programme (UNDCP).

The CND provides legislative overview and policy guidance on international drug control matters to the United Nations Office on Drugs and Crime (UNODC). It approves the budgets of the UNDCP Fund and the administrative and programme support costs. It holds its regular sessions annually. UNODC provides substantive secretariat support to the Commission.

Under the operational segment of its agenda, the Commission functions as the governing body of UNODC's drug programme. The Commission also carries out treaty-related functions, such as the scheduling of substances for international control. It provides policy guidance and strategic direction to UNODC, as well as considering budgetary and administrative matters.

Evolution

In the Political Declaration adopted by the twentieth special session of the General Assembly devoted to countering the world drug problem, held in New York from 8 to 10 June 1998, the Assembly mandated the Commission to carry out the follow-up on countries' implementation of the goals and targets for 2003 to 2008. It also strengthened the Commission's role as the global forum for international cooperation in combating the world drug problem and its functions as the governing body of the drug programme of UNODC.

Meetings

The Commission held its 49th session in Vienna from 13 to 17 March 2006. The thematic debate was on alternative development as an important drug control strategy and establishing alternative development as a cross-cutting issue. Resolutions on the subject called for strengthening international cooperation for alternative development, with due regard for environmental protection; and using alternative development programmes to reduce cannabis cultivation.

The 50th session of the Commission was held in Vienna from 12 to 16 March 2007.

Membership

By ECOSOC res. 1991/49, the Commission's membership was enlarged from 40 to 53 members, with a term of four years. The Council elects, at two-year intervals, 20 and 33 members respectively for four-year terms. Members are elected:
- From among UN Member States and States Parties to the international drug control treaties
- With due regard to adequate representation of countries that are important producers of opium or coca leaves, of countries that are important in the manufacture of narcotic drugs, and of countries where drug addiction or the illicit traffic in narcotic drugs is an important problem
- Taking into account the principle of equitable geographical distribution.

The Commission has 11 members from African states, 12 from Asian states, six from Eastern European states, 10 from Latin American and Caribbean states, and 14 from Western European and Other states. One seat rotates between Asian states and Latin American and Caribbean states every four years.

	Previous membership	Current membership
African states		
Algeria	1978–81 84–87 96–99	2004–07
Angola	2000–03	
Benin	2000–03	
Burkina Faso	2002–05	
Cameroon		2004–07
Côte d'Ivoire	1984–85 88–91 1994–2001	
DR Congo	1982–85	2004–07
Egypt	1946–77 1988–2003	
Gabon	1992–95	
Gambia	1990–93 2002–05	
Ghana	1964–71 1990–2001	
Guinea	1994–97	
Kenya	1973–79	
Lesotho	1992–95	
Liberia	1994–97	
Libyan AJ	1990–93 2000–03	
Madagascar	1962 76–95	2004–07
Malawi	1980–83	
Mali	1986–89	
Mauritius	1997–2001	
Morocco	1962–65 67–77 84–87 92–99	
Mozambique	2000–03	

	Previous membership	Current membership
Namibia		2006–09
Niger		2006–09
Nigeria	1966–68 72–75 82–89 92–99 2002–05	2006–09
Senegal	1982–93	2006–09
Sierra Leone	1997–2001	
South Africa	1996–99 2002–05	
Sudan	1996–2003	2004–07
Swaziland	2000–03	
Togo	1970–81	
Tunisia	1978–81 92–99	
Uganda		2004–07
Zambia	1986–89	2004–07

Asian states

	Previous membership	Current membership
China	1946–69 1986–2005	
India	1946–85 1988–2003	2004–07
Indonesia	1973–81 86–93 96–99 2002–05	
Iran	1946–72 74–81 84–87 1992–2003	2004–07
Japan	1962–2005	2006–09
Kazakhstan	2000–03	
Kyrgyzstan	2000–03	
Lao PDR	1997–2001	2004–07
Lebanon	1970–73 88–91 1994–2001	2004–07
Malaysia	1982–93 96–99	2004–07
Myanmar		2004–07
Pakistan	1969–99 2002–05	
Philippines	1992–95 2000–03	
ROK	1963–68 82–85 1992–2003	2006–09
Saudi Arabia	2006–09	
Sri Lanka	1984–87 94–97	
Syrian AR	1992–99	
Tajikistan		2006–09
Thailand	1973–2003	2004–07
UAE		2004–07

Eastern European states[1,2]

	Previous membership	Current membership
Belarus	2002–05	
Bosnia and Herzegovina		2004–07
Bulgaria	1982–93 96–99	
Croatia		2004–07
Czech Republic	1993–2003	
Hungary	1957–93	2004–07
Poland	1946–56 62–63 88–99	2006–09
Romania	1973–77 1994–2001	
Russian Federation	1946–2005	2006–09
Slovakia	2000–03	
The Former Yugoslav Republic of Macedonia	2000–03	
Ukraine	1994–2005	2006–09

Latin American and Caribbean states

	Previous membership	Current membership
Argentina	1965–67 72–89 2000–03	2004–07

	Previous membership	Current membership
Bahamas	1982–85 90–97	
Bolivia	1988–2003	2006–09
Brazil	1962–64 67–81 84–91 1996–2003	2004–07
Chile	1973–77 92–95 1997–2001	2004–07
Colombia	1976–87 1990–2005	2006–09
Cuba	1996–2003	2004–07
Dominican Republic	1968–71	
Ecuador	1986–93 1996–2003	
Guatemala		2004–07
Jamaica	1967–77 92–99 2002–05	2006–09
Mexico	1946–2005	2006–09
Nicaragua	1992–95 2002–05	
Panama	1978–85	
Paraguay	1994–97	
Peru	1946–75 84–95 2000–03	2004–07
Uruguay	1992–95 1997–2001	
Venezuela	1986–89 1992–2003	

Western European and Other states

	Previous membership	Current membership
Australia	1973–2005	2006–09
Austria	1957–59 84–85 2000–03	2004–07
Belgium	1978–97	2006–09
Canada	1946–79 1984–2003	2006–09
Denmark	1988–91 2000–03	
Finland	1984–87 94–97	
France	1946–2003	2004–07
Germany	1963–2003	2004–07
Greece	1954–56 84–87 1996–2003	
Israel		2004–07
Italy	1976–2003	2004–07
Netherlands	1946–53 60–62 84–99 2002–05	
Norway	1980–83 92–95	2004–07
Portugal	1996–2003	
Spain	1980–83 1986–2005	
Sweden	1969–79 90–93 96–99	2004–07
Switzerland	1961–75 88–95 1997–2001	2004–07
Turkey	1946–89 92–95 1997–2005	2006–09
UK	1946–2005	2006–09
USA	1946–2003	2004–07

Notes

[1] The former Socialist Federal Republic of Yugoslavia served on the Commission from 1946 to 1992. It was not automatically succeeded by any of the states created following its dissolution.

[2] Czechoslovakia served on the Commission in 1992.

Subcommission on Illicit Drug Traffic and Related Matters in the Near and Middle East

Internet: Follow links from www.unodc.org/unodc/index.html

The Subcommission on Illicit Drug Traffic and Related Matters in the Near and Middle East was established as a subsidiary body of the Commission on Narcotic Drugs by ECOSOC res. 1776 (LIV) (1973) and res. 6 (XXV) (1973) of the Commission on Narcotic Drugs.

The Subcommission consists of representatives of:

Afghanistan	Kazakhstan	Syrian AR
Azerbaijan	Kuwait	Tajikistan
Bahrain	Kyrgyzstan	Turkey
Egypt	Lebanon	Turkmenistan
India	Oman	UAE
Iran	Pakistan	Uzbekistan
Iraq	Qatar	Yemen
Jordan	Saudi Arabia	

States from outside the region may attend as observers.

Regional meetings of Heads of National Drug Law Enforcement Agencies (HONLEA)

The Commission has four additional regional subsidiary HONLEA. Meetings of these agencies are held annually, except for HONLEA (Europe), which meets every two years. The four agencies are:

- HONLEA, Asia and the Pacific, established by ECOSOC res. 1845/LVI (1973)
- HONLEA, Africa, established by ECOSOC res. 1985/11
- HONLEA, Latin America and the Caribbean, established by ECOSOC res. 1987/34
- HONLEA, Europe, established by ECOSOC res. 1990/30.

HONLEA meetings are held to promote regional cooperation in drug law enforcement and coordinate activities directed against illicit drug traffic in each region. Their recommendations are conveyed to the Commission. Membership is open to any state or territory that is a member of the relevant regional United Nations Economic Commission. Other states may attend as observers.

Commission on Population and Development (CPD)

2 United Nations Plaza, DC2–1950
New York, NY 10017
United States of America
Telephone: (+1 212) 963 3179
Fax: (+1 212) 963 2147
Internet: www.un.org/esa/population/
Hania Zlotnik, Director, UN Population Division

Purpose

Established by ECOSOC res. 3 (III) (1946) the Population Commission was tasked with studying and advising ECOSOC on population changes, including migration, and their effect on economic and social conditions.

Following the International Conference on Population and Development (ICPD) in 1994, the name of the Commission was changed to the Commission on Population and Development

ECONOMIC AND SOCIAL COUNCIL

(GA res. 49/128 (1994)). GA res. 49/128 also decided that the Commission should meet annually from 1996 and be charged with monitoring and assessing the implementation of the ICPD Programme of Action at the national, regional and international levels. In line with its new mandate, new terms of reference for the Commission were later endorsed by ECOSOC res. 1995/55.

Under its terms of reference the Commission assists ECOSOC by:
- Arranging for studies and advising the Council on:
  - Population issues and trends
  - Integrating population and development strategies
  - Population and related development policies and programmes
  - Population assistance, upon request, to developing countries and, on a temporary basis, to countries with economies in transition, and
  - Any other population and development questions referred to it by either the principal or subsidiary UN organs or its specialised agencies.
- Monitoring, reviewing and assessing implementation of the Programme of Action of the International Conference on Population and Development
- Providing appropriate recommendations to the Council on the basis of an integrated consideration of the reports and issues related to the implementation of the Programme of Action.

Meetings

The Commission held its 40th session in New York from 9 to 13 April 2007. Its theme was The Changing Age Structures of Population and their Implications for Development.

Membership

Originally 12, the membership has been increased several times and now stands at 47 (GA res. 50/124 (1995)). Members are elected by ECOSOC for a four-year term on the following basis: 12 from African states, 11 from Asian states, five from Eastern European states, nine from Latin American and Caribbean states, and 10 from Western European and Other states. Representatives of governments on the Commission are expected to have a relevant background in population and development.

ECOSOC decided (2005/13) that the term of office for members of the Commission should run for four regular sessions of the Commission, beginning after the conclusion of the Commission's regular session.

Four new members were elected to the Commission at ECOSOC's 2006 resumed Organisational Session. Their terms were to begin at the 41st session in 2007 and expire at the close of the 44th session in 2011. The Council postponed elections to fill the four remaining vacancies. At the 2007 Organisational Session, ECOSOC elected Spain for a term beginning on 25 April 2007 and expiring at the close of the 44th session.

	Previous membership	Current membership
African states (12 members)		
Algeria	1996–98 2000–03	
Benin		2007–11
Botswana	1990–93 2002–06	
Burkina Faso	1969–72	
Burundi	1986–89 1999–2002	

	Previous membership	Current membership
Cameroon	1966–69 85–88 1993–2004	2005–09
Central African Republic	1968–71	
Comoros		2005–09
Congo	1996–98	
Côte d'Ivoire	1997–2000	
DR Congo	1977–84 2003–07	
Egypt	1968–75 78–81 84–87 89–92 96–99 2001–04	
Equatorial Guinea		2007–11
Ethiopia	1997–2000	
Gabon	1970–73	
Gambia	2002–06	2007–10
Ghana	1962–79 2001–04	
Guinea	1999–2002	
Kenya	1969–72 1996–2003	2004–08
Lesotho	1996–97	
Libyan AJ		2004–08
Madagascar	1992–95	2004–08
Malawi	1967–68 78–81 86–89 1998–2001	
Mauritania	1974–77 2003–07	
Mauritius	1985–88	
Morocco	1972–75 80–83	2005–09
Niger	1967 73–76 1998–2001	
Nigeria	1967–68 80–91 1996–2006	
Rwanda	1967–69 73–84 88–95	
Sierra Leone	1976–83	2007–10
South Africa	1998–2001	2007–10
Sudan	1982–85 92–99	
Togo	1984–91	
Tunisia	1964–67 70–77 94–97	
Uganda	1976–79 89–92 96 2000–03	
UR of Tanzania	1993–96	
Zambia	1982–85 90–93 96–97 2002–06	2007–10

Asian states (11 members)

	Previous membership	Current membership
Bangladesh	1989–2004	2005–09
China	1947–67 1982–2006	2007–10
India	1965–72 74–81 84–87 1994–2006	2007–10
Indonesia	1952–54 68–69 76–83 96–99 2001–04	2005–09
Iran	1953–55 70–73 86–93 1996–2007	2007–11
Iraq	1988–91	
Israel	1956–59	
Japan	1958–85 1988–2003	2004–08
Lebanon	2002–2006	2007–10
Malaysia	1984–87 1997–2004	2005–09
Nepal	1996	
Oman		2007–10
Pakistan	1967–71 92–96 2000–03	2004–08
Philippines	1967–69 72–79 1996–2001 03–07	
ROK	1996–2001	
Sri Lanka	1961–64 80–83	2007–11
Syria	1950–52 54–56 62–65 96–98	
Thailand	1973–88 1997–2000 02–06	
Yemen	1999–2002	

	Previous membership	Current membership

Eastern European states (5 members)[1]

	Previous membership	Current membership
Armenia		2004–08
Belarus	2000–03	
Bulgaria	1984–87 96–99	2005–09
Croatia	1999–2002	
Hungary	1977–84 1993–2000 03–07	
Lithuania	2001–04	
Poland	1988–95 2002–06	2007–11
Romania	1973–76	
Russian Federation	1947–2006	2007–10
The Former Yugoslav Republic of Macedonia	1996–98	
Ukraine	1947–83 85–92 1996–2001	2007–10

Latin American and Caribbean states (9 members)

	Previous membership	Current membership
Argentina	1954–60	
Barbados	1970–73 78–81	
Bolivia	1982–85 88–91 2003–2007	
Brazil	1947–60 69–80 85–92 1996–2003	2005–09
Chile	1967–68 1999–2002	
Colombia	1985–96	
Costa Rica	1954–57 73–76 84–87 1999–2000	
Cuba	1986–89 96	
Dominican Republic	1977–80	
Ecuador	1967–69 74–77 80–83	
El Salvador	1958–65 1996–2001 03–07	
Guyana	2002–04	2005–09
Haiti	1970–73 1999–2002	2005–08
Honduras	1981–84 92–95	
Jamaica	1967–71 1994–2006	2007–10
Mexico	1961–64 76–79 1982–2006	2007–10
Nicaragua	1993–96 2002–06	
Panama	1965–68 74–81 90–93 1997–2000	
Paraguay	1999–2000	
Peru	1966–69 72–75 81–84 96–98 2001–04	2005–09
Uruguay	1961–64	2007–10
Venezuela	1969–72 96–97	

Note: there are two vacancies in this regional group.

Western European and Other states (10 members)

	Previous membership	Current membership
Australia	1947–49 52–53 65–68	
Austria	1965–68 2001–04	
Belgium	1951–64 1989–2004	2005–09
Canada	1947–49 54–60 1993–2000	2005–09
Denmark	1969–76	
Finland	1976–83 96	
France	1947–2003	2004–08
Germany	1985–2004	2005–09
Greece	1962–64 81–84	
Ireland	2002–06	
Italy	1960–63 96–97 1999–2002	
Luxembourg	2003–07	

	Previous membership	Current membership
Malta	1996–98	
Netherlands	1947–50 65–68 73–88 1992–2003	2004–08
New Zealand	1969–72	
Norway	1950–61 77–84 2002–06	
Spain	1969–72 77–80	2008–11
Sweden	1950–55 64–75 84–91 1998–2006	2007–10
Switzerland		2005–09
Turkey	1973–76 85–92 1997–2004	
UK	1947–2001	2007–10
USA	1947–2006	2007–10

Note

[1] The former Socialist Federal Republic of Yugoslavia served on the Commission from 1947–53 and 65–68. It was not automatically succeeded by any of the new states created following its dissolution.

Commission on Science and Technology for Development (CSTD)

Palais de Nations
8–14, Av. de la Paix
1211 Geneva 10
Switzerland
Internet: http://stdev.unctad.org/
Email: stdev@unctad.org

Purpose

ECOSOC res. 1992/218 established CSTD in accordance with GA res. 46/235 (1992) on the restructuring and revitalisation of the UN in the economic, social and related fields. It provides the General Assembly and the Economic and Social Council with high-level advice on relevant issues through analysis and appropriate policy recommendations or options in order to enable those organs to guide the future work of the UN, develop common policies and agree on appropriate actions. The Commission replaced the Intergovernmental Committee on Science and Technology for Development and its subsidiary body, the Advisory Committee on Science and Technology for Development.

The Commission acts as a forum for:
- Examining science and technology questions and their implications for development
- Advancing understanding on science and technology policies, particularly in respect of developing countries
- Formulating recommendations and guidelines on science and technology matters within the UN system.

The United Nations Conference on Trade and Development (UNCTAD) serves as the Secretariat for the Commission.

Evolution

ECOSOC res. 1992/62 reaffirmed the mandate of the Commission as set forth in ECOSOC and General Assembly resolutions including GA res. 34/218 (1979), 41/183 (1986), 42/192 (1987), 44/14 (1989) and 46/235 (1991). ECOSOC res. 2002/37 requested the Commission to meet annually, starting from the sixth session held in May 2003.

The tenth regular session took place in Geneva from 21 to 25 May 2007. Its theme was promoting the building of a people-centred, development-oriented and inclusive information society, and the role of the CSTD in the UN System-wide Follow-up to the World Summit on the Information Society (WSIS). ECOSOC res. 1998/46 decided that the Commission should work more closely with the Commission on Sustainable Development and UNCTAD.

Membership

ECOSOC res. 2006/46 increased the Commission's membership from 33 to 43. Members are elected for four-year terms by ECOSOC on the basis of the following regional allocation of seats: 11 from African states, nine from Asian states, five from Eastern European states, eight for Latin American and Caribbean states, and 10 from Western European and Other states.

Current members of the Commission and expiry dates for their terms are:

Commission member	Expiry of term	Commission member	Expiry of term
African states		**Latin American and Caribbean states**	
Angola	2008	Argentina	2010
Burkina Faso	2010	Brazil	2008
DR Congo	2008	Chile	2008
Eritrea	2010	Cuba	2010
Equatorial Guinea	2008	Dominican Republic	2010
Gambia	2008	El Salvador	2010
Lesotho	2010	Jamaica	2008
Sierra Leone	2008	Peru	2008
Sudan	2010		
Tunisia	2010		
Uganda	2010	**Western European and Other states (plus Japan)**	
		Austria	2008
Asian states		Belgium	2010
China	2010	Finland	2008
India	2010	France	2010
Iran	2010	Germany	2010
Jordan	2008	Italy	2008
Malaysia	2010	Switzerland	2008
Oman	2008	Turkey	2010
Pakistan	2008	UK	2008
Philippines	2010	USA	2010
Sri Lanka	2008		
Eastern European states			
Belarus	2010		
Latvia	2010		
Russian Federation	2008		
Slovakia	2008		

Commission on Sustainable Development (CSD)

Division for Sustainable Development
Department of Economic and Social Affairs
2 United Nations Plaza, DC2–2220
New York, NY 10017
United States of America
Telephone: (+1 212) 963 8102
Fax: (+1 212) 963 4260
Internet: www.un.org/esa/sustdev/csd

Purpose

ECOSOC res. 1993/207 established CSD in accordance with GA res. 47/191 (1991). Its task is to monitor progress in the implementation of Agenda 21, which was agreed at the 1992 UN Conference on Environment and Development in Rio de Janeiro. The Commission, part of the ECOSOC Division for Sustainable Development, promotes sustainable development through technical cooperation and capacity building at international, regional and national levels.

Evolution

A Programme for Further Implementation of Agenda 21 was agreed at the UN General Assembly Special Session held from 23 to 27 June 1997.

GA res. 55/199 (2000) decided the tenth session of the Commission would be an open-ended preparatory committee for the World Summit on Sustainable Development (WSSD), with full participation by all states. WSSD, held in Johannesburg, South Africa from 26 August to 4 September 2002, decided that the Commission should continue its role as the high-level forum within the UN for discussion of sustainable development issues, but that it needed to be strengthened to place more emphasis on implementation issues.

The eleventh session of the Commission, held in New York from 28 April to 9 May 2003, made specific recommendations on the work of the Commission. These were adopted by ECOSOC res. 2003/61 and included organising the work of the Commission on the basis of two-year implementation cycles, including review and policy sessions. The Commission also recommended that its multi-year work programme after 2003 be organised on the basis of seven two-year thematic clusters of issues. The current and next of these are:
*   2006–07: Energy for sustainable development, industrial development, air pollution/ atmosphere and climate change
*   2008–09: Agriculture, rural development, land, drought, desertification and Africa.

The fifteenth session of the Commission was held in New York from 30 April to 11 May 2007.

Membership

ECOSOC res. 1993/207 decided that the Commission should include 53 members elected from the Member States of the UN and members of the specialised agencies for a term of three years. Members were to be elected according to the following allocation of seats: 13 from African states, 11 from Asian states, six from Eastern European states, 10 from Latin American and Caribbean states, and 13 for Western European and Other states. ECOSOC res. 1997/63 decided that at the end of each regular session the first meeting of the subsequent regular session would be convened for the sole purpose of electing the new bureau.

Current members of the Commission and their terms of office are as follows:

	Previous membership	Current membership
African states		
Algeria	1993–94 1998–2001 04–07	
Angola	1999–2002	
Benin	1993–94 96–99	
Burkina Faso	1993–95 2004–07	
Burundi	1995–98	
Cameroon	1999–2002	2005–08
Cape Verde		2007–10
Central African Republic	1996–99	
Côte d'Ivoire	1998–2001	
DR Congo	1999–2005	2005–08
Djibouti	1997–2000	2006–09
Egypt	1993–94 1997–2000 02–05	
Ethiopia	1995–98 2003–06	
Gabon	1993–99 2002–05	
Gambia		2007–10
Ghana	1995–98 2001–04 04–07	
Guinea	1993–96	2007–10
Guinea-Bissau	2003–06	
Lesotho	2002–05	
Madagascar	2000–03	
Malawi	1993–95	
Mali	2000–03	
Mauritania	1998–2001	
Mauritius	1998–2001	
Morocco	1993–96 2001–04	
Mozambique	1996–2002	
Namibia	1993–95	
Niger	1997–2000	
Nigeria	1993–94 2001–04	
Senegal	1995–98 2001–04	2006–09
Sierra Leone	2004–07	
South Africa	2002–05	2007–10
Sudan	1997–2006	2006–09
Tunisia	1993–95 1999–2002	2005–08
Uganda	1993–96 2003–06	
UR of Tanzania	1994–96	2006–09
Zambia		2005–08
Zimbabwe	1996–99	2005–08
Asian states		
Bahrain		2007–10
Bangladesh	1995–98	
China	1993–2005	2005–08
DPRK	1998–2001	2005–08
Fiji	2003–06	
India	1993–2004	2007–10
Indonesia	1993–95 1997–2004	2006–09
Iran	1995–2007	2007–10
Japan	1993–2006	2007–10
Kazakhstan	1999–2002 04–07	

	Previous membership	Current membership
Kuwait		2006–09
Lebanon	1999–2002	
Malaysia	1993–96	
Mongolia	2001–04	
Nepal	2002–05	
Pakistan	1993–2003 04–07	
Papua New Guinea	1995–98	
Philippines	1993–2001	
Qatar	2004–07	
ROK	1993–95 1999–2006	2007–10
Saudi Arabia	1996–99 2002–05	2005–08
Singapore	1993–94	
Sri Lanka	1993–94 1998–2001	
Thailand	1996–2003	2005–08
Vanuatu	1993–94	
Uzbekistan	2002–05	

Eastern European states

	Previous membership	Current membership
Azerbaijan	2002–05	
Belarus	1993–96 2000–03	2005–08
Bulgaria	1993–2000	
Croatia	2002–05	2007–10
Czech Republic	1993–94 1998–2001	2006–09
Georgia	2004–07	
Hungary	1993–2001 03–06	
Poland	1993–2003	2007–10
Republic of Moldova	2001–04	
Russian Federation	1993–2006	2006–09
Serbia[1]		2005–08
Slovakia	1997–2004	
The Former Yugoslav Republic of Macedonia	1999–2002 04–07	
Ukraine	1995–98	

Latin American and Caribbean states

	Previous membership	Current membership
Antigua and Barbuda	1993–99 2002–05	2006–09
Argentina	2002–05	
Bahamas	1995–98	
Barbados	1993–96	
Belize		2005–08
Bolivia	1993–2003	2005–08
Brazil	1993–2007	
Chile	1993–95	2006–09
Colombia	1993–94 1996–2002 04–07	
Costa Rica	2002–05	2007–10
Cuba	1993–94 1999–2002	2005–08
Ecuador	2001–04	
Guatemala	2000–03	2007–10
Guyana	1996–2002	
Haiti		2007–10
Honduras	2003–06	
Jamaica	2003–06	
Mexico	1993–2003	2005–08

	Previous membership	Current membership
Nicaragua	1998–2001	
Panama	1997–2000	
Paraguay	1999–2002 04–07	
Peru	1995–2005	2006–09
Saint Lucia	2003–06	
Uruguay	1993–95	
Venezuela	1993–2004	

Western European and Other states

	Previous membership	Current membership
Australia	1993–98 2000–06	2006–09
Austria	1993–94 2001–07	
Belgium	1993–2005	2005–08
Canada	1993–2000 02–05	2005–08
Denmark	2000–02	
Finland	1995–99 2004–07	
France	1993–2007	2007–10
Germany	1993–2005	2005–08
Greece	2000–03	
Iceland	1993–95 2001–04	
Israel		2005–08
Ireland	1997–2000	
Italy	1993–96 1999–2002	2005–08
Luxembourg	2004–07	
Monaco		2007–10
Netherlands	1993–2006	2007–10
New Zealand	1998–2001	
Norway	1993–94 2002–05	
Portugal	1998–2001	
Spain	1995–2001	2006–09
Sweden	1996–98	2007–10
Switzerland	1996–99 2001–04	
Turkey	1993–95 2002–05	
UK	1993–2006	2006–09
USA	1993–2006	2006–09

Note

[1] On 3 June 2006, the Republic of Serbia notified the UN that the membership of the State Union of Serbia and Montenegro in the UN, including all organs and organisations of the UN system, was continued by the Republic of Serbia on the basis of article 60 of the Constitutional Charter of Serbia and Montenegro, activated by the Declaration of Independence adopted by the National Assembly of Montenegro on 3 June 2006.

Commission on the Status of Women (CSW)

Division for the Advancement of Women
Department of Economic and Social Affairs
United Nations Headquarters
New York, NY 10017
United States of America
Telephone: (+1 212) 963 3153
Fax: (+1 212) 963 3463
Email: daw@un.org
Internet: www.unorg/womenwatch/daw/csw/

Purpose

The CSW was established by ECOSOC res. 11 (II) (1946) to prepare reports for ECOSOC on matters concerning the promotion of women's rights in the political, economic, social and educational fields, and to make recommendations to the Council on problems requiring immediate attention in the field of women's rights. Its mandate was expanded in 1987 to include promoting the objectives of equality, development and peace.

Evolution

The Commission was transferred to New York from Vienna in 1993.

It was decided by GA res. 50/203 (1995) that the Commission would have a central role in monitoring implementation of the Platform for Action of the Fourth World Conference on Women (Beijing, 1995). This role was reaffirmed by GA res. 55/71 (2000) with the inclusion of monitoring implementation of the outcome of the 23rd Special Session of the General Assembly.

The Working Group on Communications on the Status of Women, established by ECOSOC res. 1983/27, consists of five Commission members selected with regard to geographical representation. The Working Group has closed meetings during each session of the Commission to consider communications received, including the replies of governments. This is done with a view to bringing to the Commission's attention to communications that appear to reveal a consistent pattern of reliably attested injustice and discriminatory practices against women.

Meetings

The Commission meets annually and held its 51st session from 26 February to 9 March 2007.

Membership

Originally 15, membership of the CSW has been enlarged a number of times, most recently by ECOSOC res. 1989/45 (1989). It now stands at 45. Members are elected for four-year terms on the basis of 13 from African states, 11 from Asian states, four from Eastern European states, nine from Latin American and Caribbean states, and eight from Western European and Other states.

	Previous membership	Current membership
African states		
Algeria	1993–96 2003–07	
Angola	1995–98	
Benin	2000–04[2]	
Botswana	1968–70 2002–06	
Burkina Faso	1988–91 2002–06	
Burundi	1999–2003[1]	
Cameroon (Vice-Chair)		2007–10
Central African Republic	1971–74	
Congo	1995–98 2003–07	
Côte d'Ivoire	1987–94 1998–2001	
Djibouti		2007–10
DR Congo	1971–78 81–84 87–94	
Egypt	1962–76 81–84 90–93 1999–2003[1]	
Ethiopia	1976–79 1997–2000	
Gabon	2002–06	2007–11

ECONOMIC AND SOCIAL COUNCIL

	Previous membership	Current membership
Ghana	1962–70 79–82 90–93 1997–2000	2004–08
Guinea	1964–69 73–76 94–97 2001–05[3]	
Guinea-Bissau	1993–96	
Kenya	1967 72–75 83–86 94–97	
Lesotho	1980–83 88–91 1998–2001	2007–10
Liberia	1966–75 83–86	
Libyan AJ	1977–80 94–97	
Madagascar	1968–69 73–80 92–95	
Malawi	2000–04[2]	
Mali	1996–99	2005–09
Mauritania	1967–68 70–72	
Mauritius	1985–88	2004–08
Morocco	1969–71 89–92 1997–2000	2005–09
Namibia	1994–97	2007–11
Niger	1977–80	2007–11
Nigeria	1971–74 80–83 90–93 2003–07	
Rwanda	1991–94 1998–2001	
Senegal	1975–78 79–82 1999–2003[1]	
Sierra Leone	1963–65 83–86	
South Africa	2002–06	
Sudan	1981–96 1998–2006	
Swaziland	1996–99	
Togo	1976–79 84–87 95–98	2007–10
Tunisia	1967–72 85–88 94–97 2001–05[3]	
Uganda	1967 79–82 90–93 1998–2001	
UR of Tanzania	1989–92 2001–05[3]	2005–09
Zambia	1984–90 92–95	2007–10
Zimbabwe	1990–93	

Asian states

	Previous membership	Current membership
Bangladesh	1987–94	
Cambodia		2007–11
China	1947–63 65–67 73–76 1980–2004	2004–08
Cyprus	1968–70 90–97	
DPRK	1999–2003[1]	
India	1947–51 73–88 1990–2001 03–07	
Indonesia	1955–57 62–65 71–78 83–86 90–93 95–98 2002–06	2007–10
Iran	1952–54 62 64–72 76–79 1990–2001 02–06	2007–10
Iraq	1967–72 79–82	
Israel	1956–61	
Japan	1958–63 65–70 72–75 1977–2005[3]	2005–09
Kazakhstan		2004–08
Kyrgyzstan	2000–04[2]	
Lebanon	1950–55 96–99	
Malaysia	1967–71 79–82 1990–2001 02–06	2007–10
Mongolia	1999–2003[1]	
Myanmar	1952–54	
Nepal	1964–66	
Pakistan	1952–60 76–95 2001–05[3]	2007–11
Philippines	1961–75 83–98	
Qatar		2005–09
ROK (Vice-Chair)	1994–2001 02–06	2006–10
Sri Lanka	1998–2001	
Syrian AR	1947–49	

	Previous membership	Current membership
Thailand	1971–78 1989–2000 03–07	
UAE	2002–06	2007–10

Eastern European states[4]

	Previous membership	Current membership
Armenia (Vice-Chair)	2003–07	2007–11
Azerbaijan	2001–05[3]	2007–11
Belarus	1952–57 67–78 85–88 93–96	
Bulgaria	1977–80 91–98	
Croatia	2000–04[2]	2005–09
Hungary	1964–76	2004–08
Lithuania	1999–2003[1]	
Poland	1951–68 89–92 1997–2000	
Romania	1969–75	
Russian Federation	1947–2007	
Slovakia	1993–99	
Ukraine	1981–84 91	

Latin American and Caribbean states

	Previous membership	Current membership
Argentina	1955–61 72–75 2001–05[3]	
Bahamas	1990–97	
Belize		2005–09
Bolivia	1998–2001 03–07	
Brazil	1952–54 85–92 1996–2004[2]	2007–10
Chile	1952–54 66–75 1992–2004[2]	
Colombia	1960–65 70–76 89–96	
Costa Rica	1947–50 69–75 88–91 94–97	
Cuba	1952–62 76–79 80–91 93–96 1998–2001 02–06	
Dominican Republic	1951–59 64–66 68–78 1996–2004	2004–08
Ecuador	1984–87 90–97	2007–10
El Salvador		2004–08
Guatemala	1967–69 80–83 88–91 2002–06	
Haiti	1949–51 53–55	
Honduras	1966–68 80–83	
Jamaica	1990–93	
Mexico	1947–52 57–68 76–79 1983–2003[1]	2007–10
Nicaragua	1969–71 73–76 84–87 2002–06	
Panama	1979–82	
Paraguay (Vice-Chair)	1997–2000	2007–11
Peru	1963–65 67–69 77–80 92–95 1997–2005[3]	2005–09
Saint Lucia	1998–2001	
Suriname		2004–08
Uruguay	1970–72	
Venezuela	1953–58 67 76–79 81–88 92–95	

Western European and Other states

	Previous membership	Current membership
Australia	1955–57 61–63 67–69 83–90 93–96	
Austria	1965–67 70–72 89–96	
Belgium (Chair)	1956–58 70–80 1995–2003 03–07	2007–11
Canada	1958–60 70–76 81–92 2003–07	
Denmark	1947–50 76–79 84–87 2000–04[2]	
Finland	1960–68 71–74 79–82 92–95	
France	1947–83 1985–2000	
Germany	1976–90 1997–2005[3]	2005

	Previous membership	Current membership
Greece	1949–51 59–61 73–76 85–88 95–98	
Iceland		2004–08
Italy	1981–84 87–94 1999–2003[1]	
Netherlands	1951–53 59–64 66–69 91–94 2001–05[3]	2005–09
New Zealand	1952–53 77–80	
Norway	1969–75 80–83 96–99	
Portugal	1995–98	
Spain	1962–64 68–70 81–84 92–95	2007–11
Sweden	1954–59 75–78 88–91	
Turkey	1947–50 67–69 88–91 1999–2003[1] 03–07	2007–11
UK	1947–86 1997–2005[3]	2005–09
USA	1947–94 1996–2004	2004–08

Notes

[1] ECOSOC decision 2002/234 decided to extend the terms of office for members of the Commission whose terms were to expire on 31 December 2002 until the conclusion of the 47th session.

[2] ECOSOC decision 2002/234 decided to extend the terms of office for members of the Commission whose terms were to expire on 31 December 2003 until the conclusion of the 48th session.

[3] ECOSOC decision 2002/234 decided to extend the terms of office for members of the Commission whose terms were to expire on 31 December 2004 until the conclusion of the 49th session.

[4] The former Socialist Federal Republic of Yugoslavia served on the Commission from 1954 to 56. It was not automatically succeeded by any of the new states created following its dissolution.

Statistical Commission

2 United Nations Plaza
New York, NY 10017
United States of America
Fax: (+1 212) 963 9851
Internet: follow links from http://unstats.un.org/
Email: statistics@un.org

Purpose

The Statistical Commission was established by ECOSOC res. 8 (I) (1946). Its terms of reference are set out in ECOSOC res. 8 (I), 8 (II) (1946) and 1566 (L) (1971). The Commission helps the Council to:
- Promote the development of national statistics and improve their comparability
- Coordinate the statistical work of specialised agencies and the development of the central statistical services of the Secretariat
- Advise the organs of the UN on general questions relating to the collection, analysis and dissemination of statistical information
- Promote the improvement of statistics and statistical methods generally.

The Statistical Commission considers special issues of concern in international statistical development, methodological issues, coordination and integration of international statistical programmes, support of technical cooperation activities in statistics and organisational matters. The Commission submits a report on each session to ECOSOC.

Meetings

ECOSOC decision 1999/223 decided that the Commission should meet annually in New York, beginning in 2000, for a period of four working days. The Commission held its 38th session from 27 February to 2 March 2007.

Membership

Originally 12, membership of the Commission has been increased a number of times, most recently by ECOSOC res. 1147 (XLI) (1966), and now stands at 24. Members are elected by ECOSOC for four-year terms on the basis of five members from African states, four from Asian states, four from Eastern European states, four from Latin American and Caribbean states, and seven from Western European and Other states.

Elections for the new bureau were held at the beginning of the 38th session on 27 February 2007. The following officers were elected:

Chair	Vice-Chairs	Rapporteur
Gilberto Calvillo Vives, Mexico	Heli Jeskanen-Sundstrom, Finland	Peter Pukli, Hungary
	Pali Lehohla, South Africa	
	Xie Fuzhan, China	

	Previous membership	Current membership
African states		
Algeria	2002–05	
Botswana	1994–2001	
Cape Verde		2004–07
Côte d'Ivoire	1998–2001	
DR Congo		2006–09
Egypt	1964–71 78–81 86–89	
Ethiopia	1978–81	
Gabon	1974–77	
Ghana	1967–95 2002–05	
Kenya	1972–87 90–97	2004–07
Libyan AJ	1970–73 82–85	
Mali	1967–68	
Mauritania		2006–09
Morocco	1966–73 88–95 2000–03	
Nigeria	1982–85	
Sierra Leone	1974–77	
South Africa	2002–05	2006–09
Sudan	1962–63 96–99	
Togo	1982–93 96–99	
Tunisia	1967–69 74–81 1998–2001	
Uganda	1970–73 2000–03	
Zambia	1986–97	
Asian states		
China	1947–67 1984–2003	2005–08
India	1947–83 85–88 1993–2004	
Indonesia	1968–71	
Iran	1953–55 89–92	2004–07
Iraq	1976–83	
Japan	1962–69 1973–2004	2005–08
Malaysia	1972–75 77–84	
Pakistan	1967–68 1984–2003	
Philippines	1951 69–72	
ROK		2004–07
Sri Lanka	1973–76	

	Previous membership	Current membership
Thailand	1969–72	

Eastern European states[1]

	Previous membership	Current membership
Bulgaria	1984–91 96–99	
Croatia		2004–07
Czech Republic	1993–95 1997–2004	
Hungary	1965–68 73–76 80–83 89–92 2000–03	2005–08
Poland	1969–72 92–95	
Romania	1957–64 77–80 1996–2003	
Russian Federation	1947–2005	2006–09
Ukraine	1947–79 81–88 93–96	2004–07

Latin American and Caribbean states

	Previous membership	Current membership
Argentina	1950–52 72–79 1982–2001	
Brazil	1960–67 69–96	
Colombia	1996–99	2005–08
Costa Rica	2002–05	
Cuba	1957–64 67–71 84–87	2004–07
Dominican Republic	1956–69	
Ecuador	1967–69 80–83	
Jamaica	1978–81 92–95 1997–2004	2006–09
Mexico	1947–49 1981–2004	2005–08
Panama	1965–72 77–80 88–91	
Peru	2000–03	
Uruguay	1962–68 73–76	
Venezuela	1970–77	

Western European and Other states

	Previous membership	Current membership
Australia	1952–57 60–71 81–84 93–96 1998–2001	
Austria	1980–83	
Belgium	1966–73	
Canada	1951–59 62–69 74–81 89–92	2006–09
Denmark	1951–60 69–72 2002–05	
Finland	1981–88	2006–09
France	1947–80 82–97 2001–04	2006–09
Germany	1986–2001	2005–08
Greece	2001–04	
Iceland	1974–76 1995–2001	
Ireland	1970–73 76–79 82–85	
Netherlands	1947–61 90–93 1997–2000	2005–08
New Zealand	1956–63 74–77 85–88 2002–05	
Norway	1947–50 61–68 89–92	
Portugal	1997–2000	
Spain	1972–75 78–89 94–97 2002–05	
Sweden	1973–80 93–96	
Turkey	1947–50	
UK	1947–2004	2005–08
USA	1947–81 1984–2003	2004–07

Note

[1] The former Socialist Federal Republic of Yugoslavia served on the Commission from 1954 to 1956. It was not automatically succeeded by any of the new states created following its dissolution.

Commission for Social Development (CSocD)

Division for Social Policy and Development
Department of Economic and Social Affairs
United Nations, DC2–1320
New York, NY 10017
United States of America
Fax: (+1 212) 963 3062
Internet: www.un.org/esa/socdev/csd/index.html

Purpose

Originally known as the Social Commission, but renamed in 1966, the Commission for Social Development (CSocD) was established by ECOSOC res. 10 (II) (1946). Its purpose was to advise ECOSOC on social policies of a general character and, in particular, on all matters in the social field not covered by the specialised inter-government agencies. The Commission's mandate was further developed by ECOSOC resolutions 830J (XXXII) (1961), 1139 (XLI) (1966) and 1996/7.

Since the convening of the World Summit for Social Development in Copenhagen in 1995, the Commission has been the key UN body in charge of the follow-up and implementation of the Copenhagen Declaration and Programme of Action. Each year since then, the Commission has taken up key social development themes as part of its follow-up to the outcome of the Copenhagen Summit.

The Commission meets annually in New York. The 45th session of the Commission met from 7 to 16 February 2007.

Membership

Originally 18, the membership of the Commission has been increased a number of times and now stands at 46. Members are elected by ECOSOC for four years on the following basis: 12 from African states, 10 from Asian states, five from Eastern European states, nine from Latin American and Caribbean states, and 10 from Western European and Other states.

Until 2002, terms began on 1 January and ended on 31 December. ECOSOC decision 2002/210 decided that terms of office would begin immediately after the Commission's regular session and end at the conclusion of a regular session. Decision 2002/210 also decided that at the end of each regular session, the first meeting of the subsequent regular session would be convened for the sole purpose of electing the new bureau.

Following the adjournment of the 45th session in 2007, the first meeting of the 46th session was held immediately after the session for the sole purpose of electing the new Chair and other members of the bureau of the 46th session. Members are:

	Previous membership	Current membership
African states		
Algeria	1999–2003[1]	
Angola		2005–09
Benin	1995–98 2000–04[2]	2007–11
Botswana	1968–70	
Burkina Faso	1966–68	
Burundi	1989–92	
Cameroon	1968–74 1989–2000	2007–11
Central African Republic	1983–86 2003–07	

	Previous membership	Current membership
Chad	1979–82	
Comoros	2001–05[3]	
Congo	1969–71	
Côte d'Ivoire	1972–75 92–95	2004–08
DR Congo	1975–78	2005–09
Egypt	1956–78 95–98	2007–11
Ethiopia	1995–98	2004–08
Gabon	1963–65 69–71 75–78 96–99 2001–05[3]	
Gambia	1997–99	
Ghana	1983–94 2000–04	
Guinea	1977–80 91–94 1999–2003	
Kenya	1980–87	
Lesotho	1976–82	
Liberia	1983–90	
Libyan AJ	1987–90 2003–07	
Madagascar	1977–84 91–94	
Malawi	1997–2000	
Mali	1964–67 75–78 85–88	2004–08
Mauritania	1964–76 97–99	
Morocco	1967–69 80–87 1999–2003[1]	
Namibia		2007–11
Nigeria	1972–75 91–94 2000–04[2]	
Senegal	1979–82 2003–07	
Sierra Leone	1970–72 76–79	
Somalia	1971–74	
South Africa	1947–51 1997–2005[3]	2005–09
Sudan	1973–76 81–84 1988–2004	
Swaziland	1999–2003[1]	
Togo	1979–90 95–98	
Tunisia	1962–74	2004–08
Uganda	1964–67 88–91 1997–2000	
UR of Tanzania	1967–68 2001–05[3]	2005–09
Zambia	2003–07	
Zimbabwe	1985–88 93–96	

Asian states

	Previous membership	Current membership
Bangladesh	1987–90 2001–05[3]	2005–09
China	1947–64 66–68 1989–2005[3]	2005–09
Cyprus	1967–94	
DPRK	1999–2003	2005–09
India	1949–57 69–75 79–86 1997–2000 03–07	2007–11
Indonesia	1972–83 86–88 92–95 2000–04[2]	2004–08
Iran	1967–70 1991–2007	
Iraq	1962–65 73–80 88–91	
Israel	1951–56 61–64 66–68	
Japan	1971–78 1996–2004	2004–08
Jordan	1947–50 53–55	
Kazakhstan	2001–05[3]	
Lebanon	1969–71	
Malaysia	1962–65 84–87 97–98	
Mongolia	1976–87 95–98	
Myanmar		2005–09
Nepal	1997–99	2007–11

	Previous membership	Current membership
Pakistan	1967–69 88–95 1997–2000 03–07	
Philippines	1952–57 67–72 77–84 1989–2000	
ROK	1996–2004	2004–08
Sri Lanka	1962	
Thailand	1970–76 81–88 1999–2003[1]	
UAE		2007–11
Viet Nam	2001–05[3]	

Eastern European states[4, 5, 6]

	Previous membership	Current membership
Albania	1961–64	
Belarus	1951–60 62–71 83–86 1992–2004	
Bulgaria	1964–67 2001–05[3]	
Croatia	1999–2003	
Czech Republic	2001–05[3]	2005–09
Hungary	1976–79	
Poland	1947–50 77–92 1997–2000	
Republic of Moldova		2004–08
Romania	1968–70 75–82 84–91 1997–2000 03–07	
Russian Federation	1947–2004	2004–08
Ukraine	1972–75 80–83 91–98	2005–09

Latin American and Caribbean states

	Previous membership	Current membership
Argentina	1964–66 68–70 1983–2007	
Bolivia	1950–52 79–82 93–96	2005–09
Brazil	1950–55 60–63	
Chile	1967–2000	2004–08
Colombia	1947–49 53–59 73–76	
Costa Rica	1971–78 80–83	
Cuba	1964–67 69–71 1997–2000	2007–11
Dominican Republic	1956–59 72–79 1987–2007	
Ecuador	1957–64 77–80 83–86 89–92 1997–2004	
El Salvador	1980–87 2001–05[3]	
Grenada	1976–79	
Guatemala	1970–72 88–91 97–98 2000–04[2]	
Haiti	1984–95 1999–2003[1]	2004–08
Honduras	1964–67	
Jamaica	1971–74 1997–2005[3]	2007–11
Mexico	1968–70 75–78 92–95 2001–05[3]	2007–11
Nicaragua	1979–82	
Panama	1981–88	
Paraguay		2005–09
Peru	1947–49 67–68 1996–2004	2004–08
Suriname	2003–07	
Uruguay	1954–56 60–69 72–75	
Venezuela	1967–71 96–99	2005–09

Western European and Other states

	Previous membership	Current membership
Andorra		2007–11
Australia	1950–52 54–56 58–61	
Austria	1962–65 73–76 83–98 2001–05[3]	
Belgium	1951–56 72–75	
Canada	1961–64 67–72 84–87 1997–2000	

	Previous membership	Current membership
Denmark	1964–66 77–80 85–88 93–96 2001–05[3]	
Finland	1960–63 75–78 83–86 89–92 1997–2000	2005–09
France	1947–2004	2004–08
Germany	1987–2004	2004–08
Greece	1947–48 52–57 67–69	
Italy	1958–61 70–88 2001–05[3]	2005–09
Malta	1989–2000 03–07	
Monaco		2005–09
Netherlands	1957–60 66–71 76–83 85–88 1993–2000	2005–09
New Zealand	1947–52 57–60 73–76	
Norway	1953–55 67–69 79–82 87–90 95–98	
Spain	1957–60 68–74 89–92 1997–2003 03–07	2007–11
Sweden	1956–59 70–72 81–84 91–94 1999–2003[1]	
Switzerland	2001–05[3]	
Turkey	1949–51 77–84 1999–2007	2007–11
UK	1947–82	
USA	1947–2004	2004–08

Notes

[1] ECOSOC decision 2002/210 decided to extend the terms of office for members of the Commission whose terms were to expire on 31 December 2002 until the conclusion of the 41st session.

[2] ECOSOC decision 2002/210 decided to extend the terms of office for members of the Commission whose terms were to expire on 31 December 2003 until the conclusion of the 42nd session.

[3] ECOSOC decision 2002/210 decided to extend the terms of office for members of the Commission whose terms were to expire on 31 December 2004 until the conclusion of the 43rd session.

[4] Czechoslovakia served on the Commission from 1947–48, 1953–59 and 1964–76.

[5] The former Socialist Federal Republic of Yugoslavia served on the Commission from 1947–52, 1960–63 and 1971–74. It was not automatically succeeded by any of the new states created following its dissolution.

[6] Vacancy – Eastern European Group.

Commission on Crime Prevention and Criminal Justice (CCPCJ)

Vienna International Centre
PO Box 500
A-1400 Vienna
Austria
Telephone: +(43 1) 26060 0
Fax: +(43 1) 26060 5866
Email: unodc@unodc.org
Internet: www.unodc.org
Secretary: Andrés Finguerut, UK (since 2005)

Purpose

The CCPCJ was established by ECOSOC res. 1992/1. This resolution dissolved the Committee on Crime Prevention and Control, the expert body of the Council, pursuant to GA res. 46/152 (1991). Its main functions are to:

- Provide policy guidance to UN Member States on crime prevention and criminal justice
- Develop, monitor and review the implementation of the UN crime prevention programme
- Facilitate and help to coordinate the activities of the inter-regional and regional institutes on the prevention of crime and the treatment of offenders

- Mobilise the support of Member States
- Prepare and follow-up to the UN congresses on crime prevention and criminal justice.

The mandates of the Commission are carried out by the UN Office on Drugs and Crime (UNODC) crime programme.

Evolution

At its sixteenth session in Vienna from 23 to 27 April 2007, the Commission considered the outcome of the Eleventh United Nations Congress on Crime Prevention and Criminal Justice, held in Bangkok from 18 to 25 April 2005, including follow-up action through ECOSOC by the General Assembly at its 60th session. The Commission held a debate on maximising the effectiveness of technical assistance provided to Member States in crime prevention and criminal justice. It also discussed combating transnational crime and terrorism through international cooperation, the use and application of UN standards and norms in crime prevention and criminal justice, and strategic management and programme questions.

Membership

The Commission has 40 States Members, which are elected by ECOSOC for a term of three years on the basis of 12 from African states, nine from Asian states, four from Eastern European states, eight from Latin American and Caribbean states, and seven from Western European and Other States.

Terms begin on 1 January and end on 31 December of the years shown. The names of members elected or re-elected by ECOSOC at its resumed organisational session in May 2006 are included.

	Previous membership	Current membership
African states		
Algeria	2003–05	
Botswana	2004–06	
Burundi	2004–06	
Cameroon		2007–09
Central African Republic	2003–05	
Comoros[1]	2004–05	2006–08
DR Congo	2002–03	2006–08
Egypt	2004–06	
Ethiopia	2003–05	
Gambia	2003–05	
Libyan AJ		2006–08
Mauritania	2003–05	
Namibia		2006–08
Niger		2006–08
Nigeria	2004–06	2007–09
Sierra Leone		2007–09
Senegal		2006–08
South Africa		2007–09
Uganda	2003–06	2004–08
UR of Tanzania		2006–08
Zambia	2003–05	

	Previous membership	Current membership

Asian states

	Previous membership	Current membership
China	2003–05	2006–08
India	2004–06	2007–09
Indonesia	2004–06	2007–09
Iran	2004–06	2007–09
Japan	2003–05	2006–08
Pakistan	2003–05	2006–08
ROK	2003–05	2006–08
Saudi Arabia	2004–06	2007–09
Thailand	2004–06	2007–09

Eastern European states

	Previous membership	Current membership
Armenia		2006–08
Croatia	2003–05	
Czech Republic	2004–06	
Republic of Moldova		2007–09
Russian Federation	2003–05	2006–08
Ukraine	2004–06	2007–09

Latin American and Caribbean states

	Previous membership	Current membership
Argentina		2007–09
Bolivia		2006–08
Brazil	2004–06	2007–09
Chile		2006–08
Colombia		2007–09
Costa Rica		2006–08
Cuba	2004–06	
El Salvador	2004–06	
Guatemala		2007–09
Jamaica	2004–06	2007–09
Mexico	2004–06	
Nicaragua	2003–05	
Paraguay	2004–06	
Peru	2003–05	

Western European and Other states

	Previous membership	Current membership
Austria	2003–05	2006–08
Canada	2004–06	2007–09
Finland	2004–06	
Germany		2006–08
Italy	2003–05	2006–08
Turkey[2]	2003–05	2007–09
UK	2004–06	2007–09
USA	2004–06	2007–09

Notes

[1] Comoros replaced Sudan for the term of office ending 31 December 2005.

[2] Turkey replaced Germany for the term of office ending 31 December 2005.

Commission on Human Rights (CHR)

The Commission on Human Rights is now closed.

Following agreement in the General Assembly to establish the Human Rights Council (GA res. 60/251 of 15 March 2006), the Economic and Social Council decided to abolish the Commission on Human Rights. The decision took effect on 16 June 2006 (ECOSOC res. 2006/2).

The Commission, which had been established in 1946, held its last session on 27 March 2006. At that session the Commission decided to conclude its work and referred all reports to the Human Rights Council for further consideration (E/CN.4/2006/122, CHR res. 2006/1).

Historical information on the work of the Commission can be found on the OHCHR website: www.ohchr.org.

Please note that the following Working Groups of the Commission on Human Rights, the mandates of which were transferred to the Human Rights Council in June 2006, are included in this Handbook in the section on the Human Rights Council:
- Open-ended Working Group to Consider Options Regarding the Elaboration of an Optional Protocol to the International Covenant on Economic, Social and Cultural Rights
- Open-ended Working Group Established to Monitor and Review Progress Made in the Promotion and Implementation of the Right to Development
- Intergovernmental Working Group Established to Make Recommendations with a View to the Effective Implementation of the Durban Declaration and Programme of Action
- Working Group on Arbitrary Detention
- Working Group on the Question of the Use of Mercenaries as a Means of Violating Human Rights and Impeding the Exercise of the Right of Peoples to Self-determination
- Working Group of Experts on People of African descent
- Group of Independent Eminent Experts on the Implementation of the Durban Declaration and Programme of Action
- Working Group on Enforced or Involuntary Disappearances
- Working Group on Situations (Confidential 1503 Procedure).

The following Working Group of the Sub-Commission on the Promotion and Protection of Human Rights is now covered in this Handbook in the section on the Human Rights Council:
- Working Group on Communications (Confidential 1503 Procedure).

The following Working Groups of the Sub-Commission on the Promotion and Protection of Human Rights are no longer covered in this Handbook:
- Social Forum
- Working Group on Contemporary Forms of Slavery
- Working Group on Indigenous Populations
- Working Group on Administration of Justice
- Working Group on Minorities
- Working Group on Transnational Corporations
- Working Group on Detailed Principles and Guidelines Concerning the Promotion and Protection of Human Rights when Combating Terrorism.

The Human Rights Council decided on 18 June 2007 (A/HRC/5/L.2) that it would decide at its sixth session (September 2007) on the most appropriate mechanisms to continue the work of the Working Groups on Indigenous Populations, Contemporary Forms of Slavery, Minorities, and the Social Forum.

REGIONAL COMMISSIONS

Economic Commission for Africa (ECA)

Menelik II Avenue
PO Box 3001
Addis Ababa
Ethiopia
Telephone: (+251 11) 551 7200 (Addis Ababa) or (+1 212) 963 6905 (New York)
Fax: (+251 11) 551 0365
Email: ecainfo@uneca.org
Internet: www.uneca.org
Executive Secretary: Abdoulie Janneh, Gambia (since 2005) (appointed by the UN Secretary-General)

Purpose

Established in 1958 by ECOSOC res. 671A (XXV) (1958), ECA is one of five regional commissions under the administrative direction of UN Headquarters. As the regional arm of the UN in Africa, it is mandated to support the economic and social development of its 53 Member States, foster regional integration and promote international cooperation for Africa's development. Its work programme focuses on two areas:
• Promoting regional integration in support of the African Union vision and priorities
• Meeting Africa's special needs and emerging global challenges.

Structure

The Commission is organised around six substantive programme divisions:
• Development Policy and Management
• Economic and Social Policy
• Gender and Development
• Information for Development
• Sustainable Development
• Trade and Regional Integration.

Five sub-regional offices contribute to the work programme and support outreach.

ECA has established the following subsidiary bodies:
• Committee on Women and Development
• Committee on Development Information
• Committee on Sustainable Development
• Committee on Human Development and Civil Society
• Committee on Industry and Private Sector Development
• Committee on Natural Resources and Science and Technology
• Committee on Regional Cooperation and Integration.

Membership

The geographical scope of the Commission's work is the whole continent of Africa, Madagascar and other African islands. Membership is open to members of the UN in this region and to any state in the area that may become a member of the UN in the future. Under its terms of reference, the Commission may invite Member States of the UN to participate in its work in a consultative capacity. Switzerland participates in a consultative capacity in the work of the Commission by virtue of ECOSOC res. 925 (XXXIV) (1962).

The 53 members of ECA are:

Algeria	Ethiopia	Niger
Angola	Gabon	Nigeria
Benin	Gambia	Rwanda
Botswana	Ghana	Sao Tome and Principe
Burkina Faso	Guinea	Senegal
Burundi	Guinea-Bissau	Seychelles
Cameroon	Kenya	Sierra Leone
Cape Verde	Lesotho	Somalia
Central African Republic	Liberia	South Africa
Chad	Libyan AJ	Sudan
Comoros	Madagascar	Swaziland
Congo	Malawi	Togo
Côte d'Ivoire	Mali	Tunisia
DR Congo	Mauritania	Uganda
Djibouti	Mauritius	UR of Tanzania
Egypt	Morocco	Zambia
Equatorial Guinea	Mozambique	Zimbabwe
Eritrea	Namibia	

UN Economic and Social Commission for Asia and the Pacific (ESCAP)

United Nations Building
Rajadamnern Nok Ave
Bangkok 10200
Thailand
Telephone: (+66 2) 288 1234
Fax: (+66 2) 288 1000
Email: escap-registry@un.org
Internet: www.unescap.org
Executive Secretary: Noeleen Heyzer, Singapore (from July 2007) (appointed by the UN Secretary-General)

Purpose

ESCAP is a regional arm of the UN Secretariat. By GA res. 32/197 (1977) it is mandated to serve as the main general economic and social development centre within the UN system for the Asia-Pacific region, and as an executing agency for inter-sectoral, sub-regional, regional and inter-regional projects.

The ESCAP programme promotes economic and social development in Asia and the Pacific, with particular focus on reducing social and economic disparities within and among countries in the region. Under the new programme structure endorsed by the Commission at its 58th session (2002), ESCAP's work is focused on three key thematic areas:
- Poverty reduction
- Managing globalisation
- Addressing emerging social issues.

Its work is implemented through eight interdependent and complementary sub-programmes.

Evolution

The Economic Commission for Asia and the Far East (ECAFE) was established by ECOSOC res. 37 (IV) (1947). By its res. 1895 (LVII) (1974), ECOSOC approved the change of name to the United Nations Economic and Social Commission for Asia and the Pacific (ESCAP).

Structure

The main legislative organ of ESCAP is the Commission, which meets annually at the ministerial level and reports to ECOSOC. The Commission provides a forum for all governments of the region to review and discuss economic and social issues, and to strengthen regional cooperation.

The Advisory Committee of Permanent Representatives and Other Representatives Designated by Members of the Commission (ACPR) was established in 1974. It is composed of ESCAP members and associate members, and meets once a month to advise and exchange views with the Executive Secretary on the Commission's work, and to maintain close cooperation and consultation between Member States and the Secretariat of the Commission.

As a result of a revision of the conference structure of the Commission through resolution 61/1 (2005), the work of eight sectoral sub-committees was subsumed under three thematic committees.

The Commission is also responsible for the following regional institutions:
- Asian and Pacific Centre for Transfer of Technology (APCTT)
- Asian and Pacific Training Centre for Information and Communications Technology for Development (APCICT)
- Centre for Alleviation of Poverty through Secondary Crops' Development in Asia and the Pacific (CAPSA)
- Statistical Institute for Asia and the Pacific (SIAP)
- United Nations Asian and Pacific Centre for Agricultural Engineering and Machinery (UNAPCAEM).

The ESCAP Pacific Operations Centre (EPOC) in Suva, Fiji, provides technical assistance and advisory services to countries in the Pacific region.

The 63rd session of ESCAP was held in Almaty, Kazahkstan, from 17 to 23 May 2007. Ministers and senior officials from more than 50 countries adopted the previous session's Jakarta Declaration, which enhances regional cooperation in infrastructure development.

Membership

Members of ESCAP are states within the geographical scope of the Commission. This extends from the Russian Federation to the Cook Islands. There are also four non-regional members: France, Netherlands, UK and USA. Non-self-governing territories in the region may become associate members.

There are 53 Member States:

Afghanistan	India	Myanmar
Armenia	Indonesia	Nauru
Australia	Iran	Nepal
Azerbaijan	Japan	Netherlands
Bangladesh	Kazakhstan	New Zealand
Bhutan	Kiribati	Pakistan
Brunei Darussalam	Kyrgyzstan	Palau
Cambodia	Lao PDR	Papua New Guinea
China	Malaysia	Philippines
DPRK	Maldives	ROK
Fiji	Marshall Islands	Russian Federation
France	Micronesia	Samoa
Georgia	Mongolia	Singapore

Solomon Islands	Tonga	USA
Sri Lanka	Turkey	Uzbekistan
Tajikistan	Turkmenistan	Vanuatu
Thailand	Tuvalu	Viet Nam
Timor-Leste	UK	

Associate members

American Samoa	Guam	New Caledonia
Cook Islands	Hong Kong, China	Niue
French Polynesia	Macau, China	Northern Marianas

Economic Commission for Europe (UNECE)

Palais des Nations
1211 Geneva 10
Switzerland
Telephone: (+41 22) 917 1234
Fax: (+ 41 22) 917 0505
Email: info.ece@unece.org
Internet: www.unece.org
Executive Secretary: Marek Belka, Poland (from 3 February 2006) (appointed by the UN Secretary-General)

Purpose

UNECE was created in 1947 by ECOSOC res. 36 (IV) (1947). Its major aim is to promote pan-European economic integration. To do so, UNECE brings together 56 countries located in Europe, Central Asia and North America to work together on economic and sectoral issues.

The Commission provides analysis, policy advice and assistance to governments. In cooperation with other stakeholders, notably the business community, it gives focus to UN global economic mandates. It also sets out norms, standards and conventions to facilitate international cooperation within and outside the region.

UNECE expertise covers sectors including: economic cooperation and integration, sustainable energy, environment, housing and land management, population, statistics, timber, trade and transport.

The Commission holds a biennial public session. Meetings, mostly private, of its sectoral committees are held throughout the year.

Evolution

The Commission celebrated its 60th anniversary at its 62nd session, held from 25 to 27 April 2007. This session, which was attended by over 400 participants, considered the technical and sectoral work of UNECE in a wider context and gave members the opportunity to set strategic directions for the Commission's work over the next two years. Part of the high-level segment was devoted to two panels illustrating the UNECE's contribution to pan-European integration: the first on cooperation for stability and prosperity in the UNECE region, the other on pan-European economic integration in a globalised world.

Three further panels were devoted to promoting sustainable development in the UNECE region: (a) sustainable energy policies, (b) secure transport development, and (c) the economics of gender in the European economy.

ECONOMIC AND SOCIAL COUNCIL

Structure

UNECE's principal subsidiary bodies are:
- Committee on Economic Cooperation and Integration
- Committee on Environmental Policy
- Conference of European Statisticians
- Committee on Housing and Land Management
- Committee on Inland Transport
- Committee on Sustainable Energy
- Committee on Timber
- Committee on Trade.

Membership

The Commission is composed of the European members of the UN, plus USA, Canada, Israel and the Central Asian and Caucasian former USSR Republics. The 56 members are:

Albania	Greece	Republic of Moldova
Andorra	Hungary	Romania
Armenia	Iceland	Russian Federation
Austria	Ireland	San Marino
Azerbaijan	Israel	Serbia[1]
Belarus	Italy	Slovakia
Belgium	Kazakhstan	Slovenia
Bosnia and Herzegovina	Kyrgyzstan	Spain
Bulgaria	Latvia	Sweden
Canada	Liechtenstein	Switzerland
Croatia	Lithuania	Tajikistan
Cyprus	Luxembourg	The Former Yugoslav Republic
Czech Republic	Malta	of Macedonia
Denmark	Monaco	Turkey
Estonia	Montenegro	Turkmenistan
Finland	Netherlands	Ukraine
France	Norway	UK
Georgia	Poland	USA
Germany	Portugal	Uzbekistan

Notes

The Holy See, which is not a member of the UN, also participates in UNECE activities in a consultative capacity. Provision is also made for participation by representatives of other Member States of the UN inter-government and non-government organisations in activities of concern to them.

[1] On 3 June 2006 the Republic of Serbia notified the UN that the membership of the State Union of Serbia and Montenegro in the UN, including all organs and organisations of the UN system, was continued by the Republic of Serbia on the basis of article 60 of the Constitutional Charter of Serbia and Montenegro, activated by the Declaration of Independence adopted by the National Assembly of Montenegro on 3 June 2006.

Economic Commission for Latin America and the Caribbean (ECLAC)

Edificio Naciones Unidas
Avenida Dag Hammarskjold, 3477
Casilla 179–D
Santiago
Chile
Telephone: (+56 2) 210 2000
Fax: (+56 2) 208 0252/1946
Email: dpisantiago@eclac.cl
Internet: www.eclac.cl or www.eclac.org
Executive Secretary: José Luis Machinea, Argentina (since December 2003) (appointed by the UN
Secretary-General)

Purpose

ECLAC was founded in 1948, by ECOSOC res. 106 (VI), to coordinate policies for the promotion of Latin American economic development and to foster regional and international trade. Later, its work was extended to the Caribbean countries and its programme of action was expanded to promote social development.

In 1996 member governments updated ECLAC's mandate through res. 553 (XXVI). Under this provision, the Commission helps Member States to analyse the development process by formulating, evaluating and following up on public policies, as well as by providing assistance in areas of specialised information. ECLAC experts also offer advice, training and support for regional and international cooperation and coordination.

Structure

The work programme is carried out through the:
* Division of Economic Development
* Division of International Trade and Integration
* Division of Natural Resources and Infrastructure
* Division of Population
* Division of Production, Productivity and Management
* Division of Social Development
* Division of Statistics and Economic Projections
* Division of Sustainable Development and Human Settlements
* Latin American and Caribbean Institute for Economic and Social Planning (ILPES)
* Women and Development Unit.

In addition to its headquarters in Santiago, Chile, the Commission has sub-regional headquarters in Mexico City for Mexico and Central America, and in Port of Spain, Trinidad and Tobago, for the Caribbean.

ECLAC has a number of subsidiary organs:
* Caribbean Development and Cooperation Committee (CDCC)
* Committee of High-Level Government Experts (CEGAN)
* Committee on Central American Economic Cooperation (CCE)
* Regional Conference on Women in Latin America and the Caribbean
* Regional Council for Planning.
* Statistical Conference of the Americas of the ECLAC.

ECONOMIC AND
SOCIAL COUNCIL

Meetings

Meetings of the Commission are held every two years. The most recent was from 20 to 24 March 2006 in Montevideo, Uruguay. The next, scheduled to be held in the first semester of 2008, is to be hosted by the Government of the Dominican Republic.

The Committee of the Whole meets between sessions, most recently in New York on 5 June 2007.

Membership

The geographical scope of the Commission's work is Latin America and the Caribbean. Membership is open to UN members in North, Central and South America and in the Caribbean, and to France, Italy, Netherlands, Portugal, Germany, Japan, Spain and UK. Non-self-governing territories in the region may become associate members. The 43 members of the Commission are:

Antigua and Barbuda	El Salvador	Paraguay
Argentina	France	Peru
Bahamas	Germany	Portugal
Barbados	Grenada	Saint Kitts and Nevis
Belize	Guatemala	Saint Lucia
Bolivia	Guyana	Saint Vincent and the
Brazil	Haiti	Grenadines
Canada	Honduras	Spain
Chile	Italy	Suriname
Colombia	Jamaica	Trinidad and Tobago
Costa Rica	Japan	UK
Cuba	Mexico	USA
Dominica	Netherlands	Uruguay
Dominican Republic	Nicaragua	Venezuela
Ecuador	Panama	

Associate members

Anguilla	Montserrat	US Virgin Islands
Aruba	Netherlands Antilles	Turks and Caicos Islands
British Virgin Islands	Puerto Rico	

Economic and Social Commission for Western Asia (ESCWA)

PO Box 11–8575
Beirut
Lebanon
Telephone: (+961 1) 981 301
Fax: (+961 1) 981 510
Email: webmaster-escwa@un.org
Internet: www.escwa.org.lb
Executive Secretary: Bader al-Dafer, Qatar (from July 2007) (appointed by the UN Secretary-General)

Purpose

The Economic Commission for Western Asia (ECWA) was established under ECOSOC res. 1818 (LV) (1973). In 1985 the Commission was renamed the Economic and Social Commission for Western Asia (ESCWA) to reflect its expanded mandate to cover the social development field.

ESCWA is mandated to initiate measures that promote economic and social development in Western Asia and strengthen the economic and social relations of the countries in the region, both among themselves and with other countries.

The Commission's programme focuses on managing four region-specific priority areas central to the Millennium Declaration:

- Social policies
- Energy and water
- Globalisation
- Technology, with particular attention to information and communication technology.

Priority is given to the cross-cutting themes of gender mainstreaming, the special needs of Least Developed Countries, and countries emerging from conflict.

Structure

The biennial Commission session is the highest inter-government source of recommendations on development issues to the member Governments. It advises ECOSOC of the consolidated views of member governments on issues significant to economic and social development at the global level. The Commission sessions facilitate policy discussion among high-level government officials on the regional development agenda and emerging issues. The Commission sets mandates within the global development framework, based on the expressed needs of the member countries.

The Commission has seven inter-government committees dealing with:

- Statistics
- Water resources
- Energy
- Transport
- Social development
- International trade
- Women.

The Commission also has consultative committees on non-government organisations, and science and technology.

Membership

ESCWA has 13 members. They are:

Bahrain	Lebanon	Syrian AR
Egypt	Oman	UAE
Iraq	Palestine	Yemen
Jordan	Qatar	
Kuwait	Saudi Arabia	

STANDING COMMITTEES

Committee for Programme and Coordination (CPC)

Internet: www.un.org/ga/cpc

Structure

The CPC was established by ECOSOC res. 920 (XXXIV) (1962) and was given its present name by ECOSOC res. 1171 (XLI) (1966). Earlier legislation defining its terms of reference is consolidated in ECOSOC res. 2008 (LX) (1976), which provides that the Committee shall function as the main subsidiary organ of ECOSOC and the General Assembly for planning, programming and coordination.

The Committee is charged with:

- Reviewing UN programmes as defined in the medium-term plan
- Recommending priority programmes
- Guiding the Secretariat on translating legislation into programmes and making recommendations where duplication should be avoided
- Developing evaluation procedures
- Assisting the Council in its coordination functions.

The CPC is required to consider the activities of UN agencies on a sectoral basis and recommend guidelines for them, taking into account the need for coherence and coordination. It must also carry out periodic reviews of the implementation of important legislative decisions. It is directed to cooperate with the Advisory Committee on Administrative and Budgetary Questions (ACABQ) and consult with the Joint Inspection Unit (JIU), whose members are free to participate in its meetings.

Meetings

The CPC meets for six weeks in plan years and for four weeks in budget years. The 47th session of the Committee was held from 11 June to 6 July 2007.

Membership

Originally 11, membership of the Committee has been increased a number of times, most recently by GA res. 42/450 (1987). It now stands at 34. In accordance with GA res. 42/318 (1987) and ECOSOC res. 1987/94, members are elected by the General Assembly on the nomination of the Council and on the basis of equitable geographical distribution. Allocation of seats is according to the formula: nine members from African states, seven from Asian states, four from Eastern European states, seven from Latin American and Caribbean states, and seven from Western European and Other states. Members serve for a term of three years.

	Previous membership	Current membership
African states		
Algeria	1990–92	2005–07
Benin	1986–91 95–97 1999–2001 03–05	2006–08
Botswana	2001–03	
Burkina Faso	1987–89	
Burundi	1978–80 91–93	
Cameroon	1981–92 1994–2002	
Central African Republic	2003–05	2006–08
Comoros	1994–96 1999–2001 04–06	2007–09
Congo	1991–99	
Côte d'Ivoire	1988–90	
DR Congo	1975–77 96–98	
Egypt	1984–86 1993–2001	
Ethiopia	1983–85 2002–04	
Gabon	2000–05	
Ghana	1978–80 92–97	2005–07
Kenya	1972–80 88–90 93–95	2005–07
Liberia	1984–86	
Mauritania	2000–02	
Morocco	1981–83 90–92	
Nigeria	1983–85 91–93 97–99 2002–04	

	Previous membership	Current membership
Rwanda	1988–90	
Senegal	1981–83 94–96	2006–08
South Africa	2003–05	2006–08
Sudan	1977–82	
Togo	1974–76 93–98	
Tunisia	1987–89 2002–04	
Uganda	1972–79 88–93 1998–2000	
UR of Tanzania	1972–77 80–82 2001–03	
Zambia	1986–94 1998–2000	
Zimbabwe	1997–2002 04–06	2007–09

Asian states

Bahrain	1988–90	
Bangladesh	1985–90 2000–02	
China	1987–2004	2005–07
India	1975–86 88–96 2003–05	2006–08
Indonesia	1972–80 84–89 1991–2005	2006–08
Iran	1994–2005	2006–08
Iraq	1985–87 91–93	
Japan	1975–2004	2005–07
Pakistan	1973–84 1988–2005	2006–08
Philippines	1981–83	
ROK	1993–2004	2005–07
Sri Lanka	1990–92	
Thailand	1997–99	

Eastern European states[1]

Armenia	2003–05	2006–08
Belarus	1973–78 85–87 94–96	2006–08
Bulgaria	1976–78 91–93	2006–08
Hungary	1973–75	
Poland	1988–93 1997–2002	
Republic of Moldova	2000–05	
Romania	1979–84 88–90 94–99	
Russian Federation	1974–2003 04–06	2007–09
Ukraine	1991–2005	

Latin American and Caribbean states

Argentina	1974–88 90–92 1994–2005	2006–08
Bahamas	1988–2003 04–06	
Brazil	1975–89 1991–2005	2006–08
Chile	1976–78 83–85 91–93	
Colombia	1977–79 88–93	
Costa Rica	1980–82	
Cuba	1988–90 94–96 2005	2006–08
Guyana	1973–75	
Haiti	1974–76	2007–09
Jamaica		2005–07
Mexico	1988–90 1995–2003 04–06	
Nicaragua	1993–95 97–99 2003–05	
Peru	1986–88 2000–02	
Trinidad and Tobago	1979–99	

	Previous membership	Current membership
Uruguay	1992–94 1996–2004	2006–08
Venezuela	1989–91	2007–09

Western European and Other states[2]

Austria	1988–90 97–99	
Belgium	1973–81	
Canada	1988–90 94–96 2003–05	
Denmark	1973–78	
France	1974–2003 04–06	2007–09
Germany	1982–2005	
Israel		2006–08
Italy	1991–93 1997–2002	2006–08
Monaco	2003–05	
Netherlands	1982–87 91–96	
Norway	1979–81 91–96	
Portugal	1999–2002	2006–08
San Marino	2000–02	
Sweden	1988–90	
Switzerland	2003–05	2006–08
UK	1973–2005	
USA	1974–2003 04–06	

Notes

[1] The former Socialist Federal Republic of Yugoslavia served on the Committee from 1979 to 1990. It was not automatically succeeded by any of the new states created following its dissolution.

[2] Two seats from the Group of Western European and Other states remain to be filled.

Committee on Non-Governmental Organisations (CNGO)

Internet: www.un.org/esa/coordination/ngo/

Purpose

Established by ECOSOC res. 3 (II) (1946), the CNGO examines and reports on the consultative relationship that ECOSOC should accord to international non-government organisations (NGOs). It must also recommend what action should be taken on submissions that NGOs make to it. ECOSOC res. 1996/31 approved new criteria by which consultative arrangements between ECOSOC and NGOs may be established.

Meetings

The Committee meets annually for three weeks. If necessary, with the approval of the Council, the Committee holds a resumed session of up to two weeks annually. The 2007 regular session of the Committee was held from 22 January to 2 February 2007.

Membership

Originally five, membership was increased to seven in 1950, 13 in 1966 and 19 by ECOSOC res. 1981/50.

Membership is open to all states, with regard to equitable geographical representation: five members from African states, four from Asian states, two from Eastern European states, four from Latin American and Caribbean states, and four from Western European and Other states.

Under ECOSOC res. 70 (ORG-75) (1975) members are elected for a term of four years. Membership starts on 1 January and expires on 31 December of the year stated.

Current membership	
African states	
Angola	2007–11
Burundi	2007–11
Egypt	2007–11
Guinea	2007–11
Sudan	2007–11
Asian states	
China	2007–11
India	2007–11
Pakistan	2007–11
Qatar	2007–11
Eastern European states	
Romania	2007–11
Russian Federation	2007–11

Current membership	
Latin American and Caribbean states	
Colombia	2007–11
Cuba	2007–11
Dominica	2007–11
Peru	2007–11
Western European and Other states	
Israel	2007–11
Turkey	2007–11
UK	2007–11
USA	2007–11

EXPERT BODIES

Committee of Experts on International Cooperation in Tax Matters

Financing for Development Office
2 United Nations Plaza (DC2–2386)
New York, NY 10017
United States of America
Telephone: (+1 212) 963 2587
Fax: (+1 212) 963 0443
Internet: www.un.org/esa/ffd/ffdtaxation.htm

Purpose

The Committee of Experts on International Cooperation in Tax Matters is mandated to:
- Keep under review and update as necessary the United Nations Model Double Taxation Convention between Developed and Developing Countries and the Manual for the Negotiation of Bilateral Tax Treaties between Developed and Developing Countries
- Provide a framework for dialogue with a view to enhancing and promoting international tax cooperation among national tax authorities
- Consider how new and emerging issues could affect international cooperation in tax matters and develop assessments commentaries and appropriate recommendations
- Make recommendations on capacity-building and the provision of technical assistance to developing countries and countries with economies in transition
- Give special attention to developing countries and countries with economies in transition in dealing with all the above issues.

The Group's mandate has been broadened to include:
- Tax treaties between developed and developing countries
- International cooperation in tax matters, including transfer pricing
- Mutual assistance in collection of debts
- Treaty shopping and treaty abuses
- Interaction of tax, trade and investment
- Financial transaction and equity market development
- Tax treatment of cross-border interest income and capital flight
- Taxation of electronic commerce.

Evolution

The Ad Hoc Group of Experts on Tax Treaties between Developed and Developing Countries was established in 1968 pursuant to ECOSOC res. 1273 (XLIII) (1967). Its purpose was to promote the conclusion of treaties between developed and developing countries that were acceptable to all parties and that would fully safeguard their respective revenue interests. In 1980, the Group finalised the United Nations Model Double Taxation Convention between Developed and Developing Countries.

In ECOSOC res. 1980/13 (1980), the Group was given the title Ad Hoc Group of Experts on International Cooperation in Tax Matters. Its membership was increased from 20 to 25 tax administrators drawn from 10 developed countries and 15 developing countries and economies in transition.

ECOSOC res. 2004/69 renamed the Group the Committee of Experts on International Cooperation in Tax Matters. The second session of the Committee was held from 30 October to 3 November 2006 and the third is scheduled to take place from 29 October to 2 November 2007.

Membership

ECOSOC res. 2004/69 determined that the Committee should comprise 25 members nominated by governments and acting in their expert capacities. Nominees are required to be drawn from the fields of tax policy and tax administration, and are selected by the Secretary-General for a term of four years. The Secretary-General is required to take into account equitable geographic distribution and representation from different tax systems in making his or her selections. The current 25 members of the Committee of Experts are:

Noureddine Bensouda, Morocco (Chair)

Bernell Arrindell, Barbados (Rapporteur)

Pascal Saint-Amans, France (Vice-Rapporteur)

Moftah Jassim Al-Moftah, Qatar

Rowena G Bethel, Bahamas

Patricia A Brown, USA

José Antonio Bustos Buiza, Spain

Nahil L Hirsh Carrillo, Peru

Danies Kawama Chisenda, Zambia

Paolo Ciocca, Italy

Andrew Dawson, UK

Talmon de Paula Freitas, Brazil

Harry Msamire Kitillya, UR of Tanzania

Kyung Geun Lee, ROK

Tizhong Liao, China

Habiba Louati, Tunisia

Ronald Peter van der Merwe, South Africa

Frank Mullen, Ireland

Dmitry Vladimirovich Nikolaev, Russian Federation

Serafin U Salvador Jr, Philippines

Erwin Silitonga, Indonesia

Stig B Sollund, Norway

Yoshiki Takeuchi, Japan

Robert Waldburger, Switzerland

Armando Lara Yaffar, Mexico

Committee for Development Policy (CDP)

Secretariat of the United Nations Committee for Development Policy
2 United Nations Plaza, DC2-2102
New York, NY 10017
United States of America
Fax: (+1 212) 963 1061
Internet: www.un.org/esa/policy/devplan
Email: cdp@un.org

Purpose

ECOSOC res. 1035 (XXXVII) (1964) requested the Secretary-General to consider the establishment of a group of experts in development planning theory and practice to work as a consultative body within the UN. ECOSOC res. 1079 (XXXIX) (1965) set out the functions of this proposed group, which was appointed at the Council's 40th session and designated the Committee for Development Planning. Its functions include evaluation of the programmes of the UN organs and specialised agencies relating to economic planning, projection and proposed improvements, and the study of development policy issues.

The Committee provides inputs and independent advice to ECOSOC on emerging cross-sectoral development issues and on international cooperation for development, focusing on medium- and long-term aspects.

The Committee for Development Policy is responsible for setting the criteria for the designation of Least Developed Countries (LDCs), and reviewing the list of LDCs every three years.

ECOSOC res. 2004/66 and GA res. 59/209 re-emphasised the importance of a smooth transition for countries graduating from LDC status. It established a process whereby once a country had met the criteria for graduation at a second three-yearly review, ECOSOC would confirm the Committee's recommendation for graduation. There would then be a three-year period before graduation would take effect. This has been noted by the General Assembly.

The list of LDCs as at 31 May 2007 consisted of the following 50 states:

Afghanistan	Gambia	Rwanda
Angola	Guinea	Samoa[1]
Bangladesh	Guinea-Bissau	Sao Tome and Principe
Benin	Haiti	Senegal
Bhutan	Kiribati	Sierra Leone
Burkina Faso	Lao PDR	Solomon Islands
Burundi	Lesotho	Somalia
Cambodia	Liberia	Sudan
Cape Verde	Madagascar	Timor-Leste
Central African Republic	Malawi	Togo
Chad	Maldives	Tuvalu
Comoros	Mali	Uganda
DR Congo	Mauritania	UR of Tanzania
Djibouti	Mozambique	Vanuatu
Equatorial Guinea	Myanmar	Yemen
Eritrea	Nepal	Zambia
Ethiopia	Niger	

Note

[1] The Committee for Development Policy recommended in 2006 that Samoa graduate from LDC status.

Evolution

ECOSOC res. 1625 (LI) (1975) enlarged the membership of the Committee from 18 to 24, with effect from 1 January 1972. The Committee was suspended between 1992 and 1995, following the Secretary-General's recommendation that it be disestablished.

Following an ECOSOC review of its subsidiary bodies initiated by GA res. 50/227 (1996), the Committee was renamed (under ECOSOC res. 1998/46) the Committee for Development Policy. The resolution also determined that ECOSOC should decide the work programme for the Committee. Furthermore, the resolution decided that the Committee should continue three-yearly reviews of the status of LDCs and meet to discuss this issue once every three years. The Committee's ninth session was held from 19 to 23 March 2007 in New York.

Membership

Members serve in their individual capacities as experts and not as representatives of states. They are nominated by the Secretary-General in consultation with interested governments and appointed by ECOSOC for three-year terms. In decision E/2007/12, ECOSOC appointed 24 members for a term beginning on 1 January 2007 and ending on 31 December 2009.

Current membership of the Committee is:

Bina Agarwal, India	Stanislawa Golinowska, Poland	Fatima Sadiqi, Morocco
Jose Antonio Alonso, Spain	Patrick Guillaumont, France	Frances Stewart, UK
Lourdes Arizpe, Mexico	Philippe Hein, Mauritius	Diana Tussie, Argentina
Tariq Banuri, Pakistan	Hiroya Ichikawa, Japan	Milica Uvalic, Serbia
Albert Binger, Jamaica	Willene Johnson, USA	Anatoly Vishnevsky, Russian Federation
Olav Bjerkholt, Norway	Martin Khor, Malaysia	
Kwesi Botchwey, Ghana	Amina Mama, South Africa	Samuel Wangwe, UR of Tanzania
Gui Ying Cao, China	Hans Opschoor, Netherlands	
Ricardo Ffrench-Davis, Chile	Suchitra Punyaratabandhu, Thailand	

Committee of Experts on the Transport of Dangerous Goods and on the Globally Harmonized System of Classification and Labelling of Chemicals

Geneva Office
c/– UNECE
Transport Division
Palais des Nations
1211 Geneva 10
Switzerland
Telephone: (+41 22) 917 2456
Fax: (+41 22) 917 0039
Internet: www.unece.org/trans/danger/danger.htm
Director: J Capel Ferrer, Spain (since 1991) (appointed by the UN Secretary-General)

Purpose

The Committee is a subsidiary body of ECOSOC and was previously known as the Committee of Experts on the Transport of Dangerous Goods. It was reconfigured by the Economic and Social Council's resolution 1999/65 of 26 October 1999 as the Committee of

Experts on the Transport of Dangerous Goods and on the Globally Harmonized System of Classification and Labelling of Chemicals, with two specialised sub-committees:

- The Sub-Committee of Experts on the Transport of Dangerous Goods (TDG Sub-Committee)
- The Sub-Committee of Experts on the Globally Harmonized System of Classification and Labelling of Chemicals (GHS Sub-Committee).

The main functions of the Committee are to:

- Approve the work programmes for the sub-committees in the light of available resources
- Coordinate strategic and policy directions in areas of shared and overlapping interests
- Give formal endorsement to the recommendations of the sub-committees and provide the mechanism for channelling these to ECOSOC
- Facilitate and coordinate the smooth running of the sub-committees.

Meetings

The Committee meets every two years. Its next meeting is scheduled to take place in Geneva on 12 December 2008. Secretariat services are provided by UNECE.

Membership

The Committee comprises experts from the following 36 states:

Argentina	Greece	Portugal
Australia	India	Qatar
Austria	Iran	Russian Federation
Belgium	Ireland	Senegal
Brazil	Italy	Serbia[1]
Canada	Japan	South Africa
China	Mexico	Spain
Czech Republic	Morocco	Sweden
Denmark	Netherlands	Ukraine
Finland	New Zealand	UK
France	Norway	USA
Germany	Poland	Zambia

Observers from the following countries also participate, in accordance with Rule 72 of the Rules of Procedure of ECOSOC:

Algeria	Indonesia	Slovakia
Bulgaria	Nigeria	Slovenia
Cambodia	Philippines	Switzerland
Gambia	Romania	Thailand

ECONOMIC AND SOCIAL COUNCIL

Note

[1] On 3 June 2006 the Republic of Serbia notified the UN that the membership of the State Union of Serbia and Montenegro in the UN, including all organs and organisations of the UN system, was continued by the Republic of Serbia on the basis of article 60 of the Constitutional Charter of Serbia and Montenegro, activated by the Declaration of Independence adopted by the National Assembly of Montenegro on 3 June 2006.

Sub-Committee of Experts on the Transport of Dangerous Goods

Purpose

The Sub-Committee replaces the previous Committee of Experts on the Transport of Dangerous Goods. This was established under ECOSOC res. 468G (XV) (1953) to make a study and prepare a report which, taking account of existing practices, procedures and usage, would recommend and define groupings or classification of dangerous goods on the basis of the character of risk involved. It would also list and classify the principal dangerous goods, recommend marks or labels to identify the risk graphically and without text, and recommend the simplest possible requirements to convey the fundamental information relative to the hazard of the goods offered for transport by any mode.

The Sub-Committee develops the recommendations on the Transport of Dangerous Goods, which are updated every two years in the light of technical progress, the advent of new substances and materials, the requirements of modern transport systems and, above all, the requirement to ensure the safety of people, property and the environment.

The recommendations are addressed to governments and international organisations concerned with the regulation of the transport of dangerous goods, including hazardous wastes and environmentally hazardous substances. The aim is to achieve uniformity with respect to different modes of transport (road, rail, inland waterways, sea and air) and ensure the safety of transport without impeding the movement of goods.

The recommendations form the basis of much national legislation and of international instruments such as:
- The IMO International Maritime Dangerous Goods Code
- The ICAO Technical Instructions for the Safe Transport of Dangerous Goods by Air
- The European Agreement concerning the International Carriage of Dangerous Goods by Road (ADR)
- The European Agreement Concerning the International Carriage of Dangerous Goods by Inland Waterways (ADN)
- The Regulations concerning the International Carriage of Dangerous Goods by Rail (RID).

Meetings

The Sub-Committee meets twice a year, in July and December. Its last meeting took place in Geneva from 2 to 6 July 2007.

Membership

The Sub-Committee comprises experts from 27 states:

Argentina	France	Norway
Australia	Germany	Poland
Austria	India	Portugal
Belgium	Iran	Russian Federation
Brazil	Italy	South Africa
Canada	Japan	Spain
China	Mexico	Sweden
Czech Republic	Morocco	UK
Finland	Netherlands	USA

Observers from the following countries participate in accordance with Rule 72 of the Rules of Procedure of ECOSOC:

Algeria	Kenya	Switzerland
Bulgaria	Namibia	Thailand
Denmark	New Zealand	Tunisia
Fiji	Nigeria	Ukraine
Greece	Romania	
Ireland	Slovakia	

Sub-Committee of Experts on the Globally Harmonized System of Classification and Labelling of Chemicals

Purpose

The GHS Sub-Committee was established under ECOSOC res. 1999/65 to give effect to a Globally Harmonized System of Classification and Labelling of Chemicals developed by several organisations in the context of the follow-up to the UN Conference on Environment and Development (Rio de Janeiro, June 1992) and Agenda 21, Chapter 19, Programme Area B.

The terms of reference of the GHS Sub-Committee are to:
- Act as custodian of the Globally Harmonized System of Classification and Labelling of Chemicals (GHS), managing and giving direction to the harmonisation process
- Keep the GHS up to date as necessary, considering the need for changes to ensure its continued relevance and practical utility
- Determine the need for, and timing of, the updating of technical criteria while working with existing bodies as appropriate
- Promote understanding and use of the GHS and encourage feedback
- Make the GHS available for worldwide use and application
- Make guidance available on the application of the GHS, and on the interpretation and use of technical criteria to support consistency of application
- Prepare work programmes and submit recommendations to the Committee.

Meetings

The Sub-Committee meets twice a year, in July and December. Its last meeting took place from 9 to 11 July 2007.

Membership

The Sub-Committee comprises experts from the following 32 states:

Argentina	Germany	Qatar
Australia	Greece	Senegal
Austria	Iran	Serbia
Belgium	Ireland	South Africa
Brazil	Italy	Spain
Canada	Japan	Sweden
China	Netherlands	Ukraine
Czech Republic	New Zealand	UK
Denmark	Norway	USA
Finland	Poland	Zambia
France	Portugal	

ECONOMIC AND SOCIAL COUNCIL

Observers from the following countries also participate in accordance with Rule 27 of the Rules of Procedure of ECOSOC:

Bulgaria	Nigeria	Slovenia
Gambia	Philippines	Switzerland
Indonesia	Romania	Thailand
Mexico	Russian Federation	

Committee on Economic, Social and Cultural Rights (CESCR)

The International Covenant on Economic, Social and Cultural Rights obliges States Parties to report to ECOSOC on their implementation of the Covenant (in contrast with the other core international human rights instruments, which establish treaty bodies to examine States Parties' reports).

ECOSOC has delegated consideration of such reports to the Committee on Economic, Social and Cultural Rights (CESCR), which was established as an expert subsidiary body of ECOSOC by its res. 1985/17. Its functions had previously been carried out by an inter-government working group established under decision 1978/10.

Full information about CESCR is provided on page 230 of this Handbook, in the section on human rights treaty bodies.

Committee of Experts on Public Administration (CEPA)

Division for Public Administration and Development Management
Department of Economic and Social Affairs
United Nations
2 United Nations Plaza, DC2–1712
New York, NY 10017
United States of America
Telephone: (+1 212) 963 2926
Fax: (+1 212) 963 9681
Email: armstrong@un.org
Internet: www.unpan.org/cepa.asp

Purpose

CEPA was established by ECOSOC through its resolution 2001/45. It succeeded the Group of Experts on Public Administration, established in 1967 by ECOSOC res. 1199 (XLII).

Meetings

The Committee meets once a year, and comprises 24 experts representing different systems of public administration. Members serve in their personal capacities. They are nominated by the Secretary-General in consultation with Member States and are approved by ECOSOC.

They examine the implementation of GA res. 50/225 (1996) on the need for public administrations to be redesigned in order to meet the challenges of socio-economic development and change, and review actions to establish accountable, efficient and capable governance in all countries.

The Committee held its sixth session from 10 to 13 April 2007 in New York. At the meeting, the Committee dealt with:
- The review of the activities of the UN Programme in Public Administration
- Participatory governance and citizens' engagement in policy development, service delivery and budgeting

- A compendium of basic UN terminology in governance and public administration
- A public administration perspective on the high-level segment of ECOSOC – strengthening efforts to eradicate poverty and hunger, including through the global partnership for development
- The proposed programme of work and agenda for the next session of the Committee of Experts and preliminary review of the Draft Report of the Committee.

Based on the discussion of these topics, the Committee recommended to ECOSOC a draft resolution for its consideration and adoption. The Committee also produced a set of conclusions for consideration by ECOSOC, Member States and the UN Secretariat.

Membership

The current members of CEPA, who are serving a four-year term beginning 1 January 2006 and expiring on 31 December 2009, are:

Luis Aguilar Villanueva, Mexico	Mario Chiti, Italy	Barbara Kudrycka, Poland
Peter Anyang' Nyong'o, Kenya	Mikhail Dmitriev, Russian Federation	Florin Lupescu, Romania
Ousmane Batoko, Benin		Anthony Makrydemetres, Greece
Marie-Françoise Bechtel, France	Geraldine Fraser-Moleketi, South Africa	Jose Oscar Monteiro, Mozambique
Rachid Benmokhtar Benabdellah, Morocco	Edgar Alfonso Gonzalez Salas, Colombia	Siripurapu Rao, India
Emilia Boncodin, Philippines	Werner Jann, Germany	Prijono Tjiptoherijanto, Indonesia
Jocelyne Bourgon, Canada	Taher Kannan, Jordan	
Luiz Carlos Bresser-Pereira, Brazil	Pan Suk Kim, ROK	Wang Xiaochu, China

Permanent Forum on Indigenous Issues (UNPFII)

Secretariat of the Permanent Forum on Indigenous Issues
United Nations
2 United Nations Plaza, DC2–1772
New York, NY 10017
United States of America
Telephone: (+ 1 917) 367 5100
Fax: (+1 917) 367 5102
Email: indigenouspermanentforum@un.org
Internet: www.un.org/esa/socdev/unpfii

Purpose

The Permanent Forum on Indigenous Issues was established by ECOSOC res. 2000/22. It serves as an advisory body to ECOSOC and is mandated to discuss indigenous issues relating to economic and social development, culture, the environment, education, health and human rights and to promote the integration and coordination of activities related to indigenous issues within the UN system.

Meetings

The Forum holds an annual session for 10 working days. The sixth session was held in New York from 14 to 25 May 2007. States, UN bodies and organs, inter-government and non-government organisations, and organisations of indigenous peoples may participate in the Forum as observers.

Membership

The Forum consists of 16 members: eight nominated by governments and elected by the Council, and eight nominated by indigenous organisations and appointed by the President of the Council.

Elected members are based on traditional UN regional groupings, with each group having one seat and the other three rotating. Appointed members are based on, among other criteria, the diversity and geographical distribution of the indigenous peoples of the world. All members serve in their personal capacity as independent experts for a period of three years, with the possibility of re-election for one additional term.

Elections were held on 27 April 2007 for all 16 seats, with members serving from 1 January 2008 until 21 December 2010.

Members elected by states:

Simeon Adewale Adekanye, Nigeria

Bartolomé Clavero Salvador, Spain

Carlos Mamani Condori, Bolivia

Paimaneh Hasteh, Iran

Liliane Muzangi Mbella, DR Congo

A A Nikiforov, Russian Federation

Carsten Smith, Norway

Xiaomei Qin, China

Members elected by indigenous non-government organisations:

Lars-Andrew Baer, Sweden

Hassan Id Balkassm, Morocco

Michael Dodson, Australia

Tonya Gonella Frichner, USA

Margaret Lokawua, Uganda

Elisa Canqui Mollo, Bolivia

Pavel Suyandziga, Russian Federation

Victoria Tauli-Corpuz, Philippines

UN Group of Experts on Geographical Names (UNGEGN)

Internet: unstats.un.org/unsd/geoinfo/

Purpose

The UN Group of Experts on Geographical Names was established by ECOSOC resolutions 715A (XXVII) (1959) and 1314 (XLIV) (1968), and a decision taken by the Council on 4 May 1973 to further the standardisation of geographical names at both national and international levels.

The Group plays an active role in collecting and analysing the work of national and international bodies dealing with the standardisation of geographical names, and providing this information to interested bodies such as mapping organisations.

UNGEGN working groups play a significant role in furthering worldwide communication by developing procedures on materials on geographical names, data files and gazetteers, training courses, terminology, romanisation systems, country names, and publicity and funding.

Meetings

The 23rd session of UNGEGN was held in Vienna from 28 March to 4 April 2006. The 24th session was scheduled to take place in New York from 20 to 31 August 2007.

Structure

To implement the resolutions of the UN Conferences on the Standardisation of Geographical Names, the Group's experts from UN Member States are organised into 22 linguistic/geographical divisions. Governments may decide for themselves which division they belong to. Each division elects an expert to represent the division as a whole at the sessions of the Group.

UN System's Chief Executives Board for Coordination (CEB)

United Nations DC1–1228
New York, NY 10017
United States of America
Telephone: (+1 212) 963 5719
Fax: (+1 212) 963 4190
Internet: http://unsystemceb.org

Palais des Nations
Rooms A–503, C–553
1211 Geneva 10
Switzerland
Tel: (+41 22) 917 1760/917/3276
Fax: (+41 22) 917 0063/917 0308

Purpose

The CEB was the new name given by ECOSOC decision 2001/321 to the former Administrative Committee on Coordination (ACC), which had been set up by ECOSOC res. 13 (III) (1946). The broad task of the Board is to ensure the effective implementation of the relationship agreements between the UN and specialised agencies.

Structure

Chaired by the Secretary-General of the UN, the CEB meets twice annually. It is composed of the Executive Heads of the member organisations and is assisted by two high-level committees, the High Level Committee on Programmes (HLCP) and the High Level Committee on Management (HLCM). A number of the issues previously coordinated through ACC subsidiary machinery are now the subject of inter-agency networks that are not formally subsidiary bodies of CEB but retain a relationship with it and its high-level committees.

ECONOMIC AND SOCIAL COUNCIL

High Level Committee on Management (HLCM)

Telephone: (+41 22) 917 2743
Internet: http://hlcm.unsystemceb.org

Purpose

The HLCM is the principal UN inter-agency body for coordination in the administration and management areas, particularly regarding financial and budgetary, human resources, information and communications technology (ICT), and staff security issues within the UN system. It was established in October 2000 by the UN system's Chief Executives Board for Coordination (CEB).

Its main function is to advise CEB on administration and management issues that are of system-wide importance and to promote inter-agency cooperation and coordination on these matters on behalf of CEB. The HLCM is composed of senior representatives from member organisations with responsibilities in administration and management.

Coordination work previously carried out by ACC subsidiary bodies in the administration and management area is now being undertaken through ICT, human resource management, and finance and budget networks.

Priority items currently on the HLCM agenda include:
- Security and safety of UN staff
- Accountability and transparency
- Emergency preparedness and business continuity planning
- Improving the budgetary process
- The impact on management and programmes of the changing relationship between regular and voluntary funding
- Capitalising on technology
- Accounting standards
- The simplification of entitlements procedures and processes
- Gender mainstreaming.

The HLCM is also responsible for maintaining dialogue with staff representatives on concerns of a system-wide nature and it interacts, as appropriate, with Member States in the UN's Fifth Committee and with the Chairs of the Advisory Committee on Administrative and Budgetary Questions (ACABQ) and the International Civil Service Commission (ICSC). Following a recommendation by the HLCM's Task Force on Accounting Standards, the tenth session (October 2005) made a decision that the organisations of the UN system would adopt external accounting standards.

Meetings

The HLCM meets twice a year and undertakes consultation and coordination on a continuing basis between sessions through electronic and other means of information and communications exchange.

Membership

The current Chair is the Executive Director of the UN Population Fund (UNFPA), Thoraya Obaid. The Vice-Chair is Denis Aitken, Assistant Director-General and Director of the Office of the Director-General of the World Health Organization (WHO).

High Level Committee on Programmes (HLCP)

United Nations, DC1–1236
New York, NY 10017
United States of America
Telephone: (+1 212) 963 4832
Internet: http://hlcp.unsystemceb.org

Purpose

The HLCP is the principal mechanism for system-wide coordination in the programme area. Its main function is to advise the CEB on strategic planning, policy, programme and operational matters of system-wide importance and to foster inter-agency cooperation and coordination on these matters on behalf of the CEB.

It is composed of senior representatives of member organisations who are responsible for programme matters and are authorised to take decisions on behalf of their executive heads. The terms of reference for the HLCP are broadly to:
- Address issues of strategic planning, policy and programme development and implementation
- Foster and support the integrated and coordinated implementation and follow-up of major UN conferences and summits

- Act as a forum for inter-agency dialogue on the development and launching of new programme initiatives
- Advise the CEB on matters that require its priority attention, in the timely elaboration of strategies and policies in responding to emerging issues and challenges facing the UN system
- Contribute to the translation of strategies and policies into broad guidance for elaboration of joint and related programmes and activities, and provide broad guidance and oversight of coordination and effective programme implementation at country level
- Share experiences on policy development, programming and monitoring, and foster dialogue and propose ways in which the collaboration and interaction with the private sector, NGOs and other parts of civil society can be enhanced.

Meetings

The HLCP meets twice a year and carries out consultation and coordination between sessions through electronic and other means.

Membership

The current Chair of the HLCP is the President of the International Fund for Agricultural Development (IFAD), Lennart Båge. The Vice-Chair is World Bank Vice-President Mats Karlsson.

UN Forum on Forests (UNFF)

Secretariat of the United Nations Forum on Forests
Department of Economic and Social Affairs
DC1–1245
1 United Nations Plaza
New York, NY 10017
United States of America
Telephone: (+1 212) 963 3160/3401
Fax: (+1 917) 367 3186
Email: unff@un.org
Internet: www.un.org/esa/forests
Coordinator and Head: Pekka Patosaari, Finland (since 2002) (appointed by the UN Secretary-General)

Purpose

UNFF was established by ECOSOC res. 2000/35. Operating as a functional commission under ECOSOC, its main objective is to promote the management, conservation and sustainable development of all types of forests, and to strengthen long-term political commitment to this end.

Evolution

ECOSOC res. 2000/35 tasked the fifth session of UNFF with reviewing the effectiveness of the international arrangement on forests and the progress made with special consideration of future actions. This included consideration of a possible legal framework for all types of forests. The sixth session continued discussion on the future shape of the international arrangements on forests, and established four Global Objectives on Forests, as well as a set of new guiding principles for global forest policy.

The Global Objectives and these guiding principles will form the basis of the work programme of the UNFF, until 2015. The outcome of the sixth session called for action by ECOSOC in developing a non-legally binding instrument for all types of forests, to be concluded and adopted at the seventh session.

The UNFF gives guidance to, and is supported by, the Collaborative Partnership on Forests (CPF), which was established in April 2001 under ECOSOC res. 2000/35. The CPF is an inter-agency partnership among 14 international organisations, institutions and instruments with the capacity, programmes and substantive resources to support the UNFF and its member countries.

Meetings

UNFF held its seventh session from 16 to 27 April 2007 in New York.

Following the 2007 session, UNFF will meet every two years for up to two weeks on the basis of a focused multi-year programme of work adopted at its seventh session.

Membership

Membership of the Forum is open to all Member States of the UN and States Members of the specialised agencies.

TRUSTEESHIP COUNCIL

TRUSTEESHIP COUNCIL

Purpose

The Trusteeship Council was set up under chapters XII and XIII of the UN Charter to ensure that non-self-governing territories were administered in the best interests of their people and of international peace and security.

The Council's role was originally to consider reports submitted by the administering authority of the trust territory, accept petitions and examine them in consultation with the administering authority, provide for periodic visits to the territory, and take other actions in conformity with the trusteeship agreements.

With the termination of the Trusteeship Agreement for the Trust Territory of the Pacific Islands by SC res. 956 (1994), and Palau's admission as the 185th member of the UN, the Trusteeship Council completed the task entrusted to it under the Charter with respect to the last of the 11 territories that had been placed under the Trusteeship System. The amendment to the rules of procedure of the Trusteeship Council contained in Council res. 2200 (LXI) (1994) became operational with the end of the Trusteeship Agreement on Palau, and the Council now meets as and where required.

The Secretary-General recommended in both his 1994 report on the work of the Organisation and his 2005 report *In Larger Freedom* that the General Assembly proceed with steps to eliminate the Trusteeship Council in accordance with article 108 of the Charter. World Leaders endorsed this recommendation at the 2005 World Summit and recorded in the Outcome Document their agreement to delete chapter XIII of the Charter and references to the Council in chapter XII.

Structure

Article 86 of the Charter provides that the Trusteeship Council is to consist of members administering trust territories, the permanent members of the Security Council and enough other members elected by the General Assembly for a three-year period to make an equal division between administering and non-administering countries.

The rapid period of decolonisation in the 1960s resulted in several changes in the composition of the Council. Membership dwindled as trusteeship territories achieved independence. A legal opinion submitted by the Secretary-General concluded that the Council could be composed of the administering powers and non-administering permanent members of the Security Council until all trusteeship agreements had been terminated or, if the Charter were amended, such an amendment came into force.

The Council elected Karen Pierce (UK) as President and Jean-Pierre Lacroix (France) as Vice-President at its most recent meeting on 21 August 2006.

INTERNATIONAL
COURT OF JUSTICE

INTERNATIONAL COURT OF JUSTICE (ICJ)

Peace Palace
Carnegieplein 2
2517 KJ The Hague
The Netherlands
Telephone: (+31 70) 302 2323
Fax: (+31 70) 364 9928
Email: information@icj-cij.org
Internet: www.icj-cij.org
Registrar: Philippe Couvreur, Belgium (2000–14)

Purpose

The ICJ is the principal judicial organ of the UN. Its Statute is an integral part of the UN Charter and its Rules.

The principal function of the Court is to decide, in accordance with international law, cases that are submitted to it by states. It is directed to apply:

- International conventions establishing rules expressly recognised by the contesting states
- International custom, as evidence of a general practice accepted as law
- The general principles of law recognised by civilised nations
- Judicial decisions and the teachings of the most highly qualified international law experts, as subsidiary means for the determination of rules of law.

The Court also gives advisory opinions to the General Assembly and the Security Council on legal questions, and advisory opinions to other organs of the UN and specialised agencies that are authorised by the General Assembly to request them.

The Charter provisions concerning the Court are contained in chapter XIV (articles 92–96) article 34 para. 1 of the Statute of the Court provides that only states may be parties in cases before the Court. States entitled to appear before the Court fall into three categories:

- States Members of the UN (article 93 para. 1 of the Charter provides that all UN members are parties to the Statute)
- States not members of the UN that are parties to the Statute (article 93, para. 2 of the Charter). Conditions are to be determined in each case by the General Assembly on the recommendation of the Security Council
- States not parties to the Statute to which the Court is open (article 35 para. 2 of the Statute). The conditions upon which the Court is open to such states are to be laid down by the Security Council, but they must not place the parties in a position of inequality before the Court. These conditions were laid down in SC res. 9 (1946).

Structure

Under article 21 para. 2 of its Statute, the Court appoints its own officers. The Court elects its registrar by secret ballot from amongst candidates proposed by Members of the Court. The Registrar is elected for a term of seven years and is eligible for reappointment. The Registrar and all his or her staff are answerable to the Court itself and not to the UN Secretary-General.

The current Registrar is Philippe Couvreur, Belgium, who was re-elected for a second seven-year term in February 2007. The Deputy Registrar, elected in the same way and also for seven years, is Jean-Jacques Arnaldez, France.

Membership

The Court comprises 15 members, no two of whom may be nationals of the same state.

Candidates for membership are nominated by the national groups in the Permanent Court of Arbitration or by national groups similarly appointed. The Permanent Court of Arbitration, established under conventions of 1899 and 1907, consists of a panel of members from which arbitrators may be chosen to hear any one case. Each State Party to the conventions may name no more than four people to be members of the panel. Those chosen constitute national groups.

UN members that are not members of the Permanent Court appoint national groups for nominating the members of the ICJ, in the same way that the national groups of the Permanent Court of Arbitration are appointed. The Secretary-General of the UN draws up a list of candidates nominated. From this list the General Assembly and the Security Council, voting independently, elect the members of the Court. An absolute majority in both the General Assembly and the Council is required for election.

The members of the Court are elected for nine years and may be re-elected. The terms of five (ie. one-third) of the judges expire every three years.

The conditions under which a state that is a party to the Statute of the Court, but not a member of the UN, may participate in the election of judges were laid down on the recommendation of the Security Council by GA res. 264 (III) (1948).

The present members of the Court, whose terms end on 5 February of the year shown, are, in official order of precedence:

President
Rosalyn Higgins, UK 2009

Vice-President
Awn Shawkat Al-Khasawneh, Jordan 2009

Judges
Raymond Ranjeva, Madagascar 2009
Shi Jiuyong, China 2012
Abdul G Koroma, Sierra Leone 2012
Gonzalo Parra-Aranguren, Venezuela 2009

Thomas Buergenthal, USA 2015
Hisashi Owada, Japan 2012
Bruno Simma, Germany 2012
Peter Tomka, Slovakia 2012
Ronny Abraham, France 2009
Kenneth Keith, New Zealand 2015
Bernardo Sepúlveda Amor, Mexico 2015
Mohamed Bennouna, Morocco 2015
Leonid Skotnikov, Russian Federation 2015

SECRETARIAT

SECRETARIAT

United Nations Headquarters
United Nations Plaza
New York, NY 10017
United States of America

Charter provisions

The Secretariat, which is headed by the Secretary-General, is one of the six principal organs of the Organisation. The main Charter provisions concerning the Secretariat are contained in chapter XV (articles 97–101). Other provisions are to be found in articles 7, 12, 20, 73, 102, 105 and 110.

Secretaries-General of the United Nations

Trygve Lie, Norway .... Installed 2 February 1946

Dag Hammarskjöld, Sweden .... Installed 10 April 1953 (died in office 18 September 1961)

U Thant, Burma (now Myanmar) .... Installed 3 November 1961

Kurt Waldheim, Austria .... Installed 22 December 1971

Javier Pérez de Cuéllar, Peru .... Installed 15 December 1981

Boutros Boutros-Ghali, Egypt .... Installed 1 January 1992

Kofi Annan, Ghana .... Installed 1 January 1997

Ban Ki-moon, ROK .... Installed 1 January 2007

Deputy Secretary-General, Under-Secretaries-General, Assistant Secretaries-General and Other Senior Officers

Deputy Secretary-General
Asha-Rose Migiro, UR of Tanzania

The Secretariat consists of the major organisational units listed below, each headed by an official accountable to the Secretary-General.

For further information on the work of major individual units, please refer to p174 onwards.

Executive Office of the Secretary-General (EOSG)
Internet: www.un.org/news/ossg/sg

Chef de Cabinet	Vijay Nambiar, India
Deputy Chef de Cabinet	Kim Won-soo, ROK
Assistant Secretary-General for Policy Planning	Robert Orr, USA
Assistant Secretary-General for Political, Peacekeeping and Humanitarian Affairs	Nicholas Haysom, South Africa
Chief of Protocol	Alice Hecht, Belgium

Office of Internal Oversight Services (OIOS)
Internet: www.un.org/depts/oios

Under-Secretary-General........................Inga-Britt Ahlenius, Sweden

Office of Legal Affairs (OLA)
Internet: http://untreaty.un.org/ola

Under-Secretary-General and Legal Counsel.....Nicolas Michel, Switzerland
Assistant Secretary-General........................Larry D Johnson, USA

Department of Political Affairs (DPA)
Internet: www.un.org/depts/dpa

Under-Secretary-General........................B Lynn Pascoe, USA
Assistant Secretaries-General........................Angela Kane, Germany
Tulimeni Kalomoh, Namibia

Office for Disarmament Affairs (ODA)
Internet: http://disarmament.un.org

High Representative........................Sergio de Queiroz Duarte, Brazil

Department of Peacekeeping Operations (DPKO)
Internet: http://www.un.org/depts/dpko/dpko/index.asp

Under-Secretary-General........................Jean-Marie Guéhenno, France
Assistant Secretary-General for
Operations........................Edmond Mulet, Guatemala
Assistant Secretary-General for Logistics,
Management and Mine Action........................Jane Holl Lute, USA

Office for the Coordination of Humanitarian Affairs (OCHA)
Internet: http://ochaonline.un.org

Under-Secretary-General:
Humanitarian Affairs
Emergency Relief Coordinator........................John Holmes, UK
Assistant Secretary-General:
Deputy Emergency Relief Coordinator.............Margareta Wahlström, Sweden

The Under-Secretary-General for Humanitarian Affairs also serves as the Emergency Relief Coordinator, responsible for the UN's system-wide response to humanitarian emergencies.

Department of Economic and Social Affairs (DESA)
Internet: www.un.org/esa

Under-Secretary-General........................Zukang Sha, China
Assistant Secretary-General:
Special Adviser on Gender Issues and
Advancement of Women........................Rachel Mayanja, Uganda
Assistant Secretary-General for Policy
Coordination and Inter-Agency Affairs.............Vacant as at 30 June 2007

Assistant Secretary-General for
Economic Development................................Jomo Kwame Sundaram, Malaysia

Department for General Assembly Affairs and Conference Management (DGACM)
Internet: www.un.org/depts/DGACM

Under-Secretary-General................................Chen Jian, China

Assistant Secretary-General................................Yohannes Mengesha, Ethiopia

Department of Public Information (DPI)
Internet: www.undpi.org

Under-Secretary-General................................Kiyotaka Akasaka, Japan

Department of Management (DM)
Under-Secretary-General................................Alicia Barcena Ibarra, Mexico

Assistant Secretary-General: Programme
Planning, Budget and Accounts (Controller)....Warren Sach, UK

Assistant Secretary-General:
Human Resources Management................................Jan Beagle, New Zealand

Assistant Secretary-General:
Central Support Services................................Andrew Toh, Singapore

Assistant Secretary-General:
Executive Director, Capital Master Plan............Michael Adlerstein, USA

Other high-level posts

Office of the High Representative for the Least Developed Countries, Landlocked Developing Countries and Small Island Developing States
High Representative................................Cheikh Sidi Diarra, Mali

Office of the United Nations Security Coordinator
Assistant Secretary-General................................David Veness, UK

Away from Headquarters

UN Office at Geneva (UNOG)
Internet: www.unog.ch

Under-Secretary-General:
Director-General................................Sergei Ordzhonikidze, Russian Federation

UN Office at Nairobi (UNON)
Internet: www.unon.org

Under-Secretary-General:
Director-General................................Anna Tibaijuka, UR of Tanzania

UN Office at Vienna (UNOV)
Internet: www.unvienna.org

Under-Secretary-General:
Director-General................................Antonio Maria Costa, Italy

Special/Personal Representatives or Envoys of the Secretary-General

Internet: www.un.org/News/ossg/srsg

Afghanistan	Tom Koenigs, Germany, Special Representative
African Region	Mohamed Sahnoun, Algeria, Special Adviser on Africa (based in Geneva); Vacant as at 30 June 2007, Special Adviser on Africa (based in New York)
Alliance of Civilisations	Iqbal Riza, Pakistan, Special Adviser Jorge Sampaio, Portugal, High Representative
Avian and Human Influenza	David Nabarro, UK, Senior UN System Coordinator
Burundi	Youssef Mahmoud, Tunisia, Special Representative
Cambodia	Yash Ghai, Kenya, Special Representative on the Situation of Human Rights in Cambodia
Central African Republic	General Lamine Cissé, Special Representative and Head of the UN Peace-building Office in the Central African Republic
Children and Armed Conflict	Radhika Coomaraswamy, Sri Lanka, Special Representative
Climate Change	Gro Harlem Brundtland, Norway, Special Envoy Han Seung-soo, ROK, Special Envoy Ricardo Lagos Escobar, Chile, Special Envoy
Commonwealth of Independent States	Yuli Voronstov, Russian Federation, Special Envoy for CIS
Conference on Disarmament	Sergei Ordzhonikidze, Russian Federation, Personal Representative
Côte d'Ivoire	Abou Moussa, Chad, Acting Special Representative Gerard Stoudmann, Switzerland, Special Representative for Elections
Cyprus	Michael Moller, Denmark, Special Representative and Head of Mission
Darfur	Jan Elliason, Sweden, Special Envoy
DR Congo	William Swing, USA, Special Representative
Eritrea/Ethiopia	Azouz Ennifar, Tunisia, Acting Special Representative
Former Yugoslav Republic of Macedonia–Greece	Matthew Nimetz, USA, Personal Envoy for the Greece–FYROM Talks
Gabon and Equitorial Guinea Territorial Dispute	Yves Fortier, Canada, Adviser to the Secretary-General
Gender Issues and the Advancement of Women	Rachel N Mayanja, Uganda, Special Adviser
Georgia	Jean Arnault, France, Special Representative
Global Compact	Klaus Leisinger, Germany, Special Adviser
Great Lakes Region	Ibrahima Fall, Senegal, Special Representative
Guinea-Bissau	Shola Omoregie, Nigeria, Representative and Head of UNOGBIS
Haiti	Hédi Annabi, Tunisia, Special Representative
HIV/AIDS in Africa	Elizabeth Mataka, Botswana
HIV/AIDS in Asia	Nafis Sadik, Pakistan, Special Envoy
HIV/AIDS in the Caribbean Region	George Alleyne, Barbados, Special Envoy

HIV/AIDS in Russia, Central Asia and Eastern Europe	Lars O Kallings, Sweden, Special Envoy
Horn of Africa	Kjell Magne Bondevik, Norway, Special Humanitarian Envoy
Human Rights	Hina Jilani, Pakistan, Special Representative
Human Rights and the Business Community	John Ruggie, USA, Special Representative
Internally Displaced Persons	Walter Kälin, Switzerland, Representative
Iraq	Ashraf Jehangir Qazi, Pakistan, Special Representative
Iraq/Kuwait	Yuli Vorontsov, Russian Federation, Secretary-General's High-Level Coordinator for compliance by Iraq with its obligations regarding the repatriation or return of all Kuwaiti and third country nationals or their remains, as well as the return of all Kuwaiti property, including archives seized by Iraq
Kosovo	Joachim Rücker, Germany, Special Representative Martti Ahtisaari, Finland, Special Envoy
Latin American Region	Vacant as at 30 June 2007: Special Adviser on Latin American Issues
Least Developed Countries, Landlocked Developing Countries and Small Island Developing States	Cheikh Sidi Diarra, Mali
Lebanon	Geir O Pedersen, Norway, Personal Representative; Serge Brammertz, Belgium, Commissioner of the UN Independent Investigation Commission on the Assassination of Former Lebanese Prime Minister Rafik Hariri
Liberia	Alan Doss, UK, Special Representative
Middle East	Terje Roed-Larsen, Norway, Special Envoy for the Implementation of SC res. 1559
Migration	Peter Sutherland, Ireland, Special Representative
Millennium Development Goals	Jeffrey D Sachs, USA, Special Adviser
Myanmar	Imbrahim Gambari, Nigeria, Special Adviser
Nepal	Ian Martin, UK, Special Representative
Peacebuilding Support	Carolyn McAskie, Canada
Prevention of Genocide	Francis Deng, Sudan
Prevention and Resolution of Conflict	Jan Egeland, Norway, Special Adviser
Sierra Leone	Victor da Silva Angelo, Portugal, Executive Representative for UNIOSIL
Somalia	François Lonseny Fall, Guinea, Special Representative and Head of UNPOS
South Asia Earthquake Disaster	George Herbert Walker Bush, USA, Special Envoy
Southern Africa	James Morris, USA, Special Envoy for Humanitarian Needs in Southern Africa
Special Adviser to the Secretary-General on the International Impact for Iraq and Other Issues	Ibrahim Gambari, Nigeria
Sport for Development and Peace	Adolf Ogi, Switzerland, Special Adviser
Sudan	Taye-Brook Zerihoun, Ethiopia, Special Representative
Tajikistan	Vladimir Sotirov, Bulgaria, Representative

Territories Occupied by Israel	Michael Williams, UK, Special Coordinator for the Middle East Peace Process and Personal Representative of the Secretary-General to the Palestine Liberation Organisation and the Palestinian Authority
Timor-Leste	Atul Khare, India, Special Representative and Head of Mission
Tsunami Recovery	William Jefferson Clinton, USA, UN Special Envoy
Tuberculosis	Jorge Sampaio, Portugal, Special Envoy
Uganda (LRA)	Joaquim Chissano, Mozambique, Special Envoy for the Lord's Resistance Army-affected areas
UN International School	Silvia Fuhrman, USA, Special Representative
West Africa	Ahmedou Ould Abdallah, Mauritania, Special Representative and Head of the Office of the Special Representative
Western Sahara	Julian Harston, UK, Special Representative
	Peter van Walsum, Netherlands, Special Envoy
World Summit on Information Society	Nitin Desai, India, Special Adviser

Executive Office of the Secretary-General (EOSG)

Internet: www.un.org/News/ossg/sg
Secretary-General: Ban Ki-moon, ROK
Deputy Secretary-General: Asha-Rose Migiro, UR of Tanzania

Purpose

The Executive Office of the Secretary-General (OESG) provides the senior administrative leadership to the Secretariat and to the wider UN organisation.

The Secretary-General is the organisation's chief administrative officer. The Charter also requires the Secretary-General to perform other functions as are entrusted by the main UN organs, as well as to "bring to the attention of the Security Council any matter which in his opinion may threaten the maintenance of international peace and security".

The Secretary-General may also use the 'good offices' of the position – the value of its independence, impartiality and integrity – to try to prevent or resolve international disputes.

The Secretary-General chairs the UN System's Chief Executives Board for Coordination (CEB), which twice a year brings together the executive heads of all UN funds, programmes and specialised agencies.

Structure

OESG comprises:
• Secretary-General
• Deputy Secretary-General
• Senior Management Group
• Special Representatives and Envoys
• Messengers of Peace
• Spokesperson for the Secretary-General.

Special representatives and envoys are listed under the main Secretariat heading, see p172.

The Senior Management Group comprises senior UN managers. It serves as the Secretary-General's cabinet and the central policy planning body of the United Nations. Its objective is to ensure strategic coherence and direction in the work of the organisation. The cabinet was approved by the General Assembly in 1997 as part of the reform proposal submitted by Secretary-General.

Messengers of Peace are people who possess widely recognised talents in the fields of arts, literature, music and sports, and who have agreed to help focus worldwide attention on the work of the UN.

The Spokesperson for the Secretary-General is Michele Montas.

Office of Internal Oversight Services (OIOS)

Internet: www.un.org/depts/oios
Under-Secretary-General: Inga-Britt Ahlenius, Sweden

Purpose

OIOS provides worldwide internal auditing, investigation, monitoring, evaluation and consulting services for all UN activities.

The Office was established in 1994 under GA res. 48/218 B (1994) to strengthen oversight functions within the UN. The General Assembly stressed that the new Office would have a proactive and advisory role, that it would be operationally independent and that it should assist and provide methodological support to programme managers in the effective discharge of their responsibilities. The General Assembly gave the new organisation wider powers than former audit bodies and greater scope to investigate possible fraud and abuse within the UN system.

Evolution

The Fifth Committee of the General Assembly reviews the functions and reporting procedures of OIOS, as required in the original mandate. Reviews have resulted in a number of new provisions on OIOS as contained in GA resolutions 54/244 (1999) and 59/272 (2004).

A more detailed review of OIOS is underway as part of the independent evaluation of governance and oversight within the UN. It is being carried out by a steering committee of eminent people established by the Secretary-General. The evaluation was requested in the World Summit Outcome Document and is also a key element in the UN Secretary-General's recent reform proposals, Investing in the UN for a Stronger Organisation Worldwide (A/60/692). The review of OIOS will include the development of options for the level of independence, organisational structure and resource requirements that meet identified best practices.

Work carried out by OIOS has included:
- Around 2000 recommendations annually aimed at improving organisational efficiency
- Quantitative and qualitative measurement of programme performance
- Preparation of risk management reports
- Internal audits, including on the December 2004 tsunami response, field security procedures and compensation procedures
- Investigations into reports of abuse in peacekeeping missions, procurement and financial impropriety.

The work of the OIOS is supported by the Integrated Management Information System (IMIS), a computer system that allows for stronger monitoring and audit capabilities through electronic audit trails.

Office of Legal Affairs (OLA)

Internet: http://untreaty.un.org/ola
Under-Secretary-General and Legal Counsel: Nicolas Michel, Switzerland
Assistant Secretary-General: Larry D Johnson, USA

Purpose

OLA was established by GA res. 13(l) (1946) to provide a unified central legal service for the Secretariat and the organs of the UN. It provides secretariat functions to UN bodies, including the Sixth Committee of the General Assembly, the International Law Commission and the UN Commission on International Trade Law. It also provides legal services for UN organs and offices, and field and peacekeeping missions, on issues including respect for privileges and immunities and the legal status of the organisation.

OLA discharges the Secretariat's responsibilities under article 102 of the UN Charter regarding the registration and publication of treaties, and the Secretary-General's responsibilities as the depository for multilateral conventions. It also contributes to the development and codification of international law and assists in its teaching, study and dissemination. It prepares the Repertory of Practice of United Nations Organs (a record of the procedural practice of the General Assembly) and other legal publications.

A key purpose of OLA is to promote the strengthening, development and effective implementation of the international legal order for the seas and oceans. The Office provides information and assistance to states on law of the sea and ocean affairs, monitors and reviews reporting on related developments, services institutions and inter-governmental bodies as mandated by the UN Convention on the Law of the Sea and the General Assembly, and fulfils the Secretary-General's dispute settlement responsibilities.

OLA houses the Secretariat of the UN Administrative Tribunal (UNAT). Established by the General Assembly in 1949 (GA res. 351A (IV)(1949), UNAT hears and decides applications concerning the contracts of UN Secretariat staff members, and the UN Joint Staff Pension Fund.

Structure

OLA consists of six units:
- Office of the Legal Counsel
- General Legal Division
- Codification Division
- Division for Ocean Affairs and the Law of the Sea
- International Trade Law Division
- Treaty Section.

Department of Political Affairs (DPA)

Internet: www.un.org/depts/dpa
Under-Secretary-General: B Lynn Pascoe, USA
Assistant Secretaries-General: Tuliameni Kalomoh, Namibia, and Angela Kane, Germany

Purpose

DPA works to prevent and resolve conflict and promote lasting peace by:
*   Monitoring and assessing global political developments
*   Advising the Secretary-General on actions that could enhance the cause of peace
*   Providing support and guidance to UN peace envoys and political missions in the field
*   Serving Member States directly through electoral assistance and through the support by DPA staff for the work of the Security Council and other UN bodies.

DPA provides the Secretary-General with regular reports and briefings to inform his decisions and work regarding Member States, non-government organisations and others. It is the lead UN department for peacemaking and preventive diplomacy. It works behind the scenes using the Secretary-General's 'good offices' to attempt to prevent, limit or resolve armed conflict. In this role, DPA helps define and plan missions, and provides UN special envoys and mediators with guidance and backing from headquarters.

DPA evaluates and coordinates requests from Member States for electoral assistance.

The political and peacebuilding support offices overseen by DPA are (with their start years):
*   UN Political Office for Somalia (UNPOS), 1995
*   UN Peace-building Support Office in Guinea-Bissau (UNOGBIS), 1998
*   UN Peace-building Office in the Central African Republic (BONUCA), 2000
*   UN Tajikistan Office of Peace-building (UNTOP), 2000
*   Office of the Special Representative of the Secretary-General for West Africa, 2001
*   UN Assistance Mission for Iraq (UNAMI), 2003
*   Office of the UN Special Coordinator for the Middle East (UNSCO), 2005
*   UN Mission in Nepal (UNMIN), 2007
*   The Office of the Personal Representative of the Secretary-General for Lebanon.

The Department provides substantive and secretarial support for the Security Council and two standing committees established by the General Assembly: the Committee on the Exercise of the Inalienable Rights of the Palestinian People and the Special Committee on Decolonization.

Structure

The Department is headed by the Under-Secretary-General for Political Affairs. Two Assistant Secretaries-General have oversight of the following divisions:
*   Africa (two divisions)
*   Americas and Europe
*   Asia and Pacific
*   Electoral Assistance
*   Palestinian Rights
*   Security Council Affairs.

A Policy Planning Unit forms part of the Office of the Under-Secretary-General and a Decolonisation Unit sits alongside the divisions listed above.

Office for Disarmament Affairs (ODA)

Internet: http://disarmament.un.org
High Representative: Sergio de Queiroz Duarte, Brazil

Purpose

The Office promotes the goals of nuclear disarmament and non-proliferation, and the strengthening of the disarmament regimes for weapons of mass destruction, chemical and biological weapons. It also promotes disarmament efforts in the area of conventional weapons, especially land mines and small arms.

ODA supports disarmament through the work of the General Assembly and its First Committee, the Disarmament Commission, the Conference on Disarmament and other bodies. It fosters preventive disarmament measures including dialogue, transparency and confidence building on military matters, and encourages regional disarmament efforts. It also provides information on the United Nations disarmament efforts.

The Office supports practical post-conflict disarmament measures such as disarming and demobilising former combatants and helping them to reintegrate into society.

Evolution

In 2007 ODA replaced the former Department of Disarmament Affairs, which had been set up in January 1998 under the Secretary-General's reform programme in accordance with his report A/51/950.

The Department had been originally established in 1982 on the recommendation of the General Assembly's Second Special Session on Disarmament. From 1992 to 1997 the Department operated as a centre under the Department of Political Affairs (DPA).

Structure

ODA has five branches:
* Conference on Disarmament Secretariat and Conference Support (Geneva)
* Weapons of Mass Destruction
* Conventional Arms (including Practical Disarmament Measures)
* Regional Disarmament
* Monitoring, Database and Information.

Department of Peacekeeping Operations (DPKO)

Internet: www.un.org/Depts/dpko/dpko/index.asp
Under-Secretary-General: Jean-Marie Guéhenno, France
Assistant Secretary-General for Operations: Hédi Annabi, Tunisia
Assistant Secretary-General for Logistics, Management and Mine Action: Jane Holl Lute, USA

Purpose

DPKO is charged with planning, preparing, managing and directing UN peacekeeping operations so they can effectively fulfil their mandates under the overall authority of the Security Council and General Assembly, and under the command vested in the Secretary-General.

The Department is based at UN Headquarters in New York and provides political and executive direction to UN peacekeeping operations. It liaises with the Security Council, parties to conflicts, and contributors of both personnel and peacekeeping funds to implement Security Council mandates.

DPKO provides administrative and logistical support to missions in the field through the deployment of equipment and services, financial resources and trained personnel. It works to integrate the peacekeeping efforts of UN, government and non-government bodies. It also provides guidance and support on military police, mine action, and logistical and administrative issues to other UN political and peacebuilding missions.

Its current work priorities include:
- Ensuring there is a sufficient commitment of human and financial resources by Member States to meet the demand for peacekeeping operations
- Strengthening regional – particularly African – peacekeeping capacities
- Developing an integrated mission planning process
- Improving security for peacekeeping personnel
- Strengthening coordination and partnerships with all peacekeeping partners
- Improving the management of human resources
- Raising the profile and winning support for peacekeeping through effective public information.

The Department currently administers 18 peace operations around the world. They account for nearly 73,000 uniformed personnel, more than 5700 international civilian personnel and 12,400 local civilian personnel.

The peacekeeping operations overseen by DPKO are (with their start years):
- UN Truce Supervision Organization (UNTSO), 1948
- UN Military Observer Group in India and Pakistan (UNMOGIP), 1949
- UN Force in Cyprus (UNFICYP), 1964
- UN Disengagement Observer Force (UNDOF), 1974
- UN Interim Force in Lebanon (UNIFIL), 1978
- UN Mission for the Referendum in Western Sahara (MINURSO), 1991
- UN Observer Mission in Georgia (UNOMIG), 1993
- UN Interim Administration Mission in Kosovo (UNMIK), 1999
- UN Organization Mission in the Democratic Republic of the Congo (MONUC), 1999
- UN Mission in Ethiopia and Eritrea (UNMEE), 2000
- UN Mission in Liberia (UNMIL), 2003
- UN Operations in Côte d'Ivoire (UNOCI), 2004
- UN Stabilization Mission in Haiti (MINUSTAH), 2004
- UN Assistance Mission in Sudan (UNMIS), 2005
- UN Mission in Timor-Leste (UNMIT), 2006 – formerly known as UN Office in Timor-Leste (UNOTIL)
- UN Integrated Office in Burundi (BINUB), 2007 – formerly known as UN Operation in Burundi (ONUB).

The political or peacebuilding missions overseen by DPKO are (with their start years):
- UN Assistance Mission in Afghanistan (UNAMA), 2002
- UN Integrated Office in Sierra Leone (UNIOSIL), 2006.

Structure

The Office of the Under-Secretary-General oversees the work of the:

- Military Division
- Police Division
- Office of Operations (geographical divisions and the Situation Centre)
- Office of Mission Support (logistics and administration)
- Mine Action Service
- Change Management (including Peacekeeping Best Practices Unit and Integrated Training Services).

Office for the Coordination of Humanitarian Affairs (OCHA)

Internet: http://ochaonline.un.org
Under-Secretary-General and Emergency Relief Coordinator: John Holmes, UK
Assistant Secretary-General and Deputy Emergency Relief Coordinator: Margareta Wahlström, Sweden

Purpose

OCHA was created by the Secretary-General in 1998 during a reorganisation of the Department of Humanitarian Affairs (DHA). Its primary function is to coordinate the delivery of humanitarian assistance to the victims of disasters and other emergencies. Humanitarian advocacy is another key function.

Structure

The coordination work of OCHA is carried out mainly through the Inter-Agency Standing Committee (IASC), which ensures inter-agency consultation and joint decision-making in the response to, and management of, complex emergencies. Its work includes:

- Needs assessment
- Consolidated appeals
- Field coordination
- Humanitarian policy development.

The Standing Committee is chaired by the Emergency Relief Coordinator (ERC), a position created in 1991 by GA res. 46/182 (1991). The ERC has been assigned the status of Under-Secretary-General for Humanitarian Affairs.

The ERC has responsibilities in three main areas:

- Policy development and coordination to ensure that all humanitarian issues, including protection and assistance for internally displaced persons, are addressed
- Advocacy within the UN (notably to the Security Council) of humanitarian issues
- Coordination of responses.

OCHA has headquarters in both New York and Geneva. The New York office focuses on policy and advocacy, and works directly with the Security Council, ECOSOC, the General Assembly and other organs of the UN. Geneva concentrates on support to the field and resource mobilisation.

The Office operates through some two dozen field offices that support UN Humanitarian Coordinators and country teams. It maintains regional support offices in Abidjan, Johannesburg and Nairobi, as well as Regional Disaster Response Advisers in South Asia, the Pacific, the Caribbean and Latin America.

Department of Economic and Social Affairs (DESA)

Internet: www.un.org/esa
Under-Secretary-General: Zukang Sha, China

Purpose

DESA is a consolidation of the former Departments for Policy Coordination and Sustainable Development, the Department for Economic and Social Information and Policy Analysis, and the Department for Development Support and Management Services.

The Department aims to promote broad-based, sustainable development based on the integration of economic, social, environmental, population and gender-related factors. Its key mandate is to promote higher living standards, full employment, and economic and social development.

DESA is responsible for administering and overseeing work relating to sustainable development, conflict prevention, peacebuilding, social policy, public administration, population matters, gender issues and statistics.

The Department acts as a support mechanism for ECOSOC and for the UN Forum on Forests (UNFF).

Structure

DESA's work areas are managed by the following divisions and offices:
*   Office of the Under-Secretary-General
*   Population Division
*   Development Policy and Analysis Division
*   Division for the Advancement of Women
*   Office of the Special Adviser on Gender Issues
*   Division for Social Policy and Development
*   Division for Public Administration and Development Management
*   Division for Sustainable Development
*   Financing for Development Office
*   Statistics Division
*   Office for ECOSOC Support and Coordination
*   Secretariat of the UNFF.

Department for General Assembly and Conference Management (DGACM)

Internet: www.un.org/depts/DGACM
Under-Secretary-General: Chen Jian, China
Assistant Secretary-General: Yohannes Mengesha, Ethiopia

Purpose

DGACM provides secretariat services and other assistance to the General Assembly, ECOSOC and the Trusteeship Council. It also provides interpretation services in the six official languages of the UN and prepares verbatim records of the meetings of the General Assembly, Security Council and other bodies. The Department produces documents and publications, and translates them as required.

Structure

The Department has three divisions and one service:
- General Assembly and ECOSOC Affairs Division
- Interpretation, Meetings and Publishing Division
- Documentation Division
- Central Planning and Coordination Service.

There is also an Executive Office, a Documents Programming and Monitoring Unit, and an Information and Technology Unit.

Department of Public Information (DPI)

Internet: refer http://un.by/en/dpi/
Under-Secretary-General: Kiyotaka Akasaka, Japan

Purpose

DPI was established in 1946 to inform a worldwide audience about the purposes and activities of the UN. It conveys the work of the UN through:

The UN website
- Publications
- Press releases
- Radio and television programmes
- Documentary videos
- Special events
- Public tours
- Library facilities.

Structure

The Department, which is based in New York, comprises three divisions:
- Public Affairs Division
- News and Media Division
- Library and Information Resources Division.

The Public Affairs Division carries out public awareness campaigns to promote UN themes, conferences and programmes. The News and Media Division provides live television and radio broadcasts to correspondents and news organisations worldwide on all major UN activities. The Library and Information Resources Division oversees the work of the Dag Hammarskjöld Library, which maintains a complete collection of UN documentation and provides research and reference services.

The Department of Public Information coordinates a worldwide total of 78 UN Information Centres and Services, and UN Offices with information components.

Department of Management (DM)

Under-Secretary-General: Alicia Barcena Ibarra, Mexico
Assistant Secretary-General Programme Planning, Budget and Accounts (Controller): Warren Sach, UK
Assistant Secretary-General Human Resources Management: Jan Beagle, New Zealand
Assistant Secretary-General Central Support Services: Andrew Toh, Singapore
Assistant Secretary-General: Executive Director, Capital Master Plan: Michael Adlerstein, USA

Purpose

DM is responsible for the UN's treasury, budget and accounts, human resources management, information technology and systems, security, travel and transportation, procurement and archives.

Structure

DM offices and divisions include:

- Treasury
- Office of Human Resources Management
- Integrated Management Information System Project
- Procurement Service
- UN Postal Administration
- Archives and Records Management Section
- Capital Master Plan.

OTHER BODIES SUBSIDIARY OR RELATED TO THE UN

OTHER BODIES SUBSIDIARY OR RELATED TO THE UN

FUNDS, PROGRAMMES AND BODIES OF THE UNITED NATIONS

RECOGNISED FUNDS AND PROGRAMMES OF THE UN

UN Children's Fund (UNICEF)

UNICEF House
3 United Nations Plaza
New York, NY 10017
United States of America
Telephone: (+1 212) 326 7000
Fax: (+1 212) 888 7465/7454
Email: netmaster@unicef.org
Internet: www.unicef.org
Executive Director: Ann M Veneman, USA (since 2005) (appointed by the UN Secretary-General in consultation with the Executive Board)

Purpose

UNICEF was established by GA res. 57 (I) (1946) to provide emergency assistance to children in war-ravaged countries following World War II. GA res. 802 (VIII) (1953) placed the Fund on a permanent footing and charged it with addressing the long-term needs of children and mothers in developing countries. That resolution changed the organisation's name to the UN Children's Fund, but retained the UNICEF acronym.

The priority areas for UNICEF's work are set out in UNICEF's medium-term strategic plan for 2006 to 2009. They are:
* Young child survival and development
* Basic education and gender equality
* HIV/AIDS and children
* Child protection from violence, exploitation and abuse
* Policy advocacy and partnerships for children's rights.

Structure

UNICEF reports through its Executive Board to ECOSOC, which in turn reports to the General Assembly.

GA res. 48/162 (1993) decided that the UNICEF Executive Board should be reconstituted to comprise 36 members (previously 41). The Board is responsible for providing inter-government support to, and supervision of, the Fund's activities, and for ensuring that UNICEF is responsive to the needs and priorities of recipient countries. It also approves UNICEF's policies, country programmes and budgets. The specific functions of the Board are set out in Annex I of that resolution. The Board's work is coordinated by a bureau comprising one representative from each of the five regional groups of Member States.

The Board meets in one annual and two regular sessions per year, holding inter-sessional meetings as it deems necessary. In 2007 the first regular session of the Executive Board was held in New York from 16 to 18 January, the annual session from 4 to 7 June 2007, and the second regular session was scheduled to be held from 4 to 7 September. In addition to the scheduled Board meetings, a joint meeting of the UN Development Programme (UNDP)/UN Population Fund (UNFPA), UN Children's Fund (UNICEF) and World Food Programme (WFP) Executive Boards was held in New York on 19 and 22 January 2007.

Resources

UNICEF's resources derive from voluntary contributions from governments and the private sector. Contributions for 2006 totalled $2781 million, of which $1614 million came from governments, $799 million from non-government and private sector sources, $178 million from inter-organisation arrangements (UN System) and $190 million from other sources.

Membership

GA res. 48/162 (1993) specified that membership of the Executive Board should be based on equitable geographical representation and other relevant factors. It specified that eight members should come from African states, seven from Asian states, four from Eastern European states, five from Latin American and Caribbean states, and 12 from Western European and Other states. Board membership is normally for three years.

Bureau members of the UNICEF Executive Board in 2007 are:

President

Latin America and the Caribbean states............Javier Loayza Barea, Bolivia

Vice-Presidents

Western European and Others Group............Robert Hill, Australia

Eastern European Group............Pavle Jevremovic, Serbia

African Group............Michael Kafando, Burkina Faso

Asian Group............Kyaw Tint Swe, Myanmar

Current members of the Board and their terms are:

	Previous membership	Current membership
African states		
Algeria	1971–74 82–85 2004–06	
Angola	1991–97	
Benin	1975–78 84–90	
Botswana	1980–83	
Burkina Faso	1982–85 93–96	2006–08
Burundi	1979–82 95–97 2004–06	
Cameroon	1976–79 88–91	2007–09
Cape Verde	1997–99	
Central African Republic	1973–76 82–85 91–94	2007–09
Chad	1982–85	
Comoros	1998–2000	
Congo	1972–75 85–88 91–94 1998–2000	
Côte d'Ivoire	1981–84 2000–02	
DR Congo	2001–03	
Djibouti	1985–88 2004–06	
Egypt	1970–76 88–91	
Eritrea	2003–05	
Ethiopia	1985–88 91–94	2007–09

	Previous membership	Current membership
Gabon	1970–73 85–88 2001–03	
Gambia	2001–03	
Ghana	1978–81 93–96 2003–05	
Guinea	1968–70 75–78 2000–02	
Kenya	1995–97	
Lesotho	1983–89 2002–04	
Liberia	1987–93	
Libyan AJ	1979–82 1998–2000	
Madagascar	1982–85 2001–03	
Malawi	1970–73 2004–06	
Mali	1985–88	2007–09
Mauritania		2007–09
Morocco	1976–79 95–97 2001–03	
Mozambique	1992–95	2005–07
Namibia	1996–98	
Niger	1984–87	
Nigeria	1970–75 88–91 97–99	
Rwanda	1973–76	2006–08
Sao Tome and Principe	1988–91	
Senegal	1978–81 91–94 2004–06	
Sierra Leone	1969–71 90–93	
Somalia	1979–85	
South Africa	1946–51 1998–2000	
Sudan	1988–93 1998–2000	
Swaziland	1982–85	
Togo	1981–84	
Tunisia	1957–71 85–88	
Uganda	1974–77 88–91 95–97	
UR of Tanzania	1976–79 91–94	
Zambia	1977–80	
Zimbabwe	1989–92 1999–2001	

Asian states

	Previous membership	Current membership
Afghanistan	1977–80	
Bahrain	1982–85	
Bangladesh	1982–91 1998–2000 2004–06	
Bhutan	1984–87	
China	1958–73 1980–2004	2005–07
DPRK		2005–07
India	1950–60 62–97 2000–05	2007–09
Indonesia	1951–78 84–99 2001–03	
Iran	1957–62 2000–05	
Iraq	1968–70	
Israel	1961–68	
Jordan	1977–80	
Kazakhstan	1998–2000	
Lao PDR	2001–03	
Lebanon	1993–96 2004–06	
Malaysia		2007–09
Myanmar	2004–06	2007–09
Nepal	1982–85 92–94 2002–04	
Oman	1985–91 97–99	
Pakistan	1952–80 81–84 85–97 1999–2001	2006–08

	Previous membership	Current membership
Philippines	1963–81 87–90 92–95	
ROK	1988–97	2006–08
Sri Lanka	1951–52 90–93	
Thailand	1951–53 65–67 69–77 80–92	
UAE		
Viet Nam	1959–62 96–98	
Yemen	1991–94 1998–2003	

Eastern European states[1,2]

Armenia	2001–03	
Azerbaijan	1994–97 1998–2000	
Belarus	1978–81 88–91 94–95 2004–06	
Bulgaria	1960–65 66–78 85–88 92–94	
Croatia		2007–09
Czech Republic	1993 98–99	
Hungary	1979–85	
Poland	1986–92	
Republic of Moldova	2003–05	
Romania	1971–74 84–87 93–96 2000–02	
Russian Federation	1946–2004	2005–07
Serbia		2006–08
Slovenia	2002–04	
Ukraine	1946–50 1996–2001	2005–07

Latin American and Caribbean states

Antigua and Barbuda	1998–2000	
Argentina	1985–88	2005–07
Bahamas		2007–09
Barbados	1977–83 89–92	
Bolivia	1951 75–78 88–91 2000–02	2005–07
Brazil	1976–83 85–88 91–96	
Chile	1958–75 77–80 82–88	
Colombia	1946–50 55–59 74–77 83–89 92–94 2001–03	2006–08
Costa Rica	1970–73 92–95	
Cuba	1974–77 83–86 96–98 2001–02	
Dominican Republic	1951 54–65 67–70	
Ecuador	1965–68 2002–04	
El Salvador	1957–63 2004–06	
Guatemala		2006–08
Guyana	1986–89 1999–2001	
Jamaica	1991–99 2002–04	
Mexico	1979–91	
Nicaragua	1988–94 97–99 2003–05	
Panama	1982–85	
Paraguay	1999–2001	
Peru	1973–76 89–92 2003–05	
Suriname	1993–98	
Trinidad and Tobago	2000	
Uruguay	1971–74 87–93	
Venezuela	1968–74 78–87 95–97	

	Previous membership	Current membership
Western European and Other states (plus Japan)		
Australia	1979–82 83–95 2001–02	2005–07
Austria	1981–84 2004–06	
Belgium[3]	1980–83 84–90 97–99	2005–07
Canada	1946-58 62–96 1999–2001 03–06	
Denmark	1946–50 84–87 90–93 96–97 1999–2001 03–04	2006–07
Finland	1974–77 83–86 89–94 95 1998–2000 05–06	
France	1946–96 98–99 2001–02 04–05	
Germany	1957–95 97–99 2001–03	2006–07
Greece	1960–62 1998–2000	
Ireland	2002–03	2007
Italy	1970–79 82–97 2000–02 04–06	
Japan	1973–2004	2005–07
Luxembourg	2003	
Netherlands	1975–1997 2000–02	2005–07
New Zealand	1946–52 58–61 97–98	
Norway	1946–55 71–74 77–83 86–89 91–94 95–97 98–99 2001–03 04–05	
Portugal	2001–03	2007
Spain	1963–65 90–93 2000 03–04 06	
Sweden	1955–84 88–91 92–98 2000–03 04–06	2007–09
Switzerland	1946–94 96–99 2002–04	2006–07
Turkey	1951 59–74 86–89 93–94 96–97 2000	2006–07
UK	1946–96 1998–2000 03–05	2007–09
USA	1946–2005	2006–08

Notes

[1]   Czechoslovakia served on the Board from 1968–71 and 1990–92.

[2]   The former Socialist Federal Republic of Yugoslavia served on the Board from 1946–61, 1965–68, 1974–86 and 1987–92.

[3]   Belgium will relinquish its seat to Finland at the end of 2007.

UN Conference on Trade and Development (UNCTAD)

Palais des Nations
1211 Geneva 10
Switzerland
Telephone: (+41 22) 917 5809
Fax: (+41 22) 917 0051
Email: info@unctad.org
Internet: www.unctad.org
Secretary-General: Supachai Panitchpakdi, Thailand (since 2005) (appointed by the UN Secretary-General)

Purpose

UNCTAD's principal function is to integrate developing countries into the world economy, with a view to maximising the trade and development opportunities offered by globalisation. UNCTAD XI reaffirmed its role as the UN focal point for the integrated treatment of trade and related development issues in the areas of trade, finance, technology, investment and sustainable development.

The first session of UNCTAD took place in Geneva in 1964 in accordance with ECOSOC res. 917 (XXXIV) (1962). GA res. 1995 (XIX) (1964) established UNCTAD as a UN organ and set its mandate.

Structure

- Conference
- Trade and Development Board
- Subsidiary commissions.

Meetings

The Conference meets every four years. It adopted the São Paulo Consensus (TD/410) at its most recent session (UNCTAD XI) in São Paulo, Brazil, in June 2004. The Consensus reaffirmed that the Plan of Action (TD/386) adopted in Bangkok, Thailand, in February 2000 should continue to be a blueprint for UNCTAD's work in future years. The twelfth session of the Conference (UNCTAD XII) is scheduled to be held in Accra, Ghana, from 20 to 25 April 2008.

Membership

Membership of UNCTAD is open to any UN Member State, its specialised agencies and the International Atomic Energy Agency (IAEA). As at April 2007 there were 193 members, as listed below. Members of the Trade and Development Board are indicated with an asterisk.

Afghanistan*	Central African Republic*	Germany*
Albania*	Chad*	Ghana*
Algeria*	Chile*	Greece*
Andorra	China*	Grenada*
Angola*	Colombia*	Guatemala*
Antigua and Barbuda	Comoros	Guinea*
Argentina*	Congo*	Guinea-Bissau
Armenia*	Costa Rica*	Guyana*
Australia*	Côte d'Ivoire*	Haiti*
Austria*	Croatia*	Holy See
Azerbaijan*	Cuba*	Honduras*
Bahamas	Cyprus*	Hungary*
Bahrain*	Czech Republic*	Iceland*
Bangladesh*	DPRK*	India*
Barbados*	DR Congo	Indonesia*
Belarus*	Denmark*	Iran*
Belgium*	Djibouti	Iraq*
Belize	Dominica*	Ireland*
Benin*	Dominican Republic*	Israel*
Bhutan*	Ecuador*	Italy*
Bolivia*	Egypt*	Jamaica*
Bosnia and Herzegovina	El Salvador*	Japan*
Botswana*	Equatorial Guinea*	Jordan*
Brazil*	Eritrea	Kazakhstan
Brunei Darussalam	Estonia	Kenya*
Bulgaria*	Ethiopia*	Kiribati
Burkina Faso*	Fiji	Kuwait*
Burundi*	Finland*	Kyrgyzstan
Cambodia	France*	Lao PDR
Cameroon*	Gabon*	Latvia*
Canada*	Gambia	Lebanon*
Cape Verde	Georgia*	Lesotho*

Liberia*	Panama*	Suriname*
Libyan AJ*	Papua New Guinea*	Swaziland
Liechtenstein*	Paraguay*	Sweden*
Lithuania*	Peru*	Switzerland*
Luxembourg*	Philippines*	Syrian AR*
Madagascar*	Poland*	Tajikistan
Malawi	Portugal*	Thailand*
Malaysia*	Qatar*	The Former Yugoslav Republic
Maldives	ROK*	of Macedonia*
Mali*	Republic of Moldova*	Timor-Leste
Malta*	Romania*	Togo*
Marshall Islands	Russian Federation*	Tonga
Mauritania*	Rwanda	Trinidad and Tobago*
Mauritius*	Saint Kitts and Nevis	Tunisia*
Mexico*	Saint Lucia	Turkey*
Micronesia	Saint Vincent and the	Turkmenistan
Monaco	Grenadines	Tuvalu
Mongolia*	Samoa	Uganda*
Montenegro	San Marino	Ukraine*
Morocco*	Sao Tome and Principe*	UAE*
Mozambique*	Saudi Arabia*	UK*
Myanmar*	Senegal*	UR of Tanzania*
Namibia*	Serbia*1	USA*
Nauru	Seychelles	Uruguay*
Nepal*	Sierra Leone*	Uzbekistan
Netherlands*	Singapore*	Vanuatu
New Zealand*	Slovakia*	Venezuela*
Nicaragua*	Slovenia*	Viet Nam*
Niger	Solomon Islands	Yemen*
Nigeria*	Somalia*	Zambia*
Norway*	South Africa*	Zimbabwe*
Oman*	Spain*	
Pakistan*	Sri Lanka*	
Palau	Sudan*	

Note

1   On 3 June 2006 the Republic of Serbia notified the UN that the membership of the State Union of Serbia and Montenegro in the UN, including all organs and organisations of the UN system, was continued by the Republic of Serbia on the basis of article 60 of the Constitutional Charter of Serbia and Montenegro, activated by the Declaration of Independence adopted by the National Assembly of Montenegro on 3 June 2006.

Trade and Development Board (TDB)

Purpose

Between sessions of UNCTAD, the TDB functions under GA res. 1995 (XIX) (1964) as UNCTAD's executive body. The TDB reports to the Conference and, through ECOSOC, to the General Assembly.

The TDB's regular session is for 10 days each autumn (it is scheduled to meet from 1 to 11 October 2007). It examines interdependence and global economic issues from a trade and development perspective.

The TDB can meet in one-day executive sessions three times a year to deal with policy and management matters arising between its regular annual sessions. In 2006, as mandated by the São Paulo Consensus, a special session reviewed the results achieved since the São Paulo Conference (UNCTAD XI). The 23rd special session was held over three meetings, the first in May, the second in June and the last in September 2006.

Structure

The TDB has three subsidiary commissions that perform integrated policy work within specified terms of reference:

- Commission on Investment, Technology and Related Financial Issues
- Commission on Trade in Goods and Services, and Commodities
- Commission on Enterprise, Business Facilitation and Development.

Each Commission may convene a maximum of 10 short expert meetings a year to provide technical input into its work.

Membership

TDB membership is open to all UNCTAD Member States. In October 2006 there were 150 members of the Board. The President of the TDB for the 53rd session was Mohamed Saleck Ould Mohamed Lemine, Mauritania.

UN Development Group (UNDG)

UN Development Group Office
UN Development Programme
1 United Nations Plaza
New York, NY 10017
United States of America
Internet: www.undg.org

Purpose

The Secretary-General established UNDG in 1997 to improve the effectiveness of UN development activities at country level, including fostering greater coordination among different organisations within the UN system.

UNDG is an instrument for UN reform. It develops policies and procedures that allow member agencies to work together to analyse country issues, plan support strategies, implement support programmes, monitor results and advocate for change. These initiatives are intended to increase UN impact in helping countries achieve the Millennium Development Goals (MDGs), including poverty reduction.

Structure

UNDG's work is guided by four Executive Committee agencies: UNDP, UNFPA, UNICEF and WFP. The High Commissioner for Human Rights is an ex officio member of the Executive Committee. UNDG's work is supported by the UN Development Group Office, which is hosted by the UN Development Programme (UNDP). The Group is chaired by UNDP on behalf of the Secretary-General.

The following are the UNDG governance mechanisms:

- The UNDG Executive Committee is the four funds and programmes or 'founding members' that report directly to the Secretary-General: UNICEF, UNFPA, WFP and UNDP. (The High Commissioner for Human Rights is an ex officio member of the Committee.) The Executive Committee focuses on reforming the work methods of the funds and programmes and manages the mechanisms of the UNDG. It meets every other month and is chaired by the UNDP Administrator.
- The Support Group is the forum through which all member organisations and observers contribute to preparing the UNDG's work programme and issues for decision. It

communicates decisions for agency implementation, prepares for UNDG meetings and agrees on follow-up action as required.
- The Management Group focuses on improving the efficiency of the Resident Coordinator System. It joins with the Programme Group to simplify and harmonise programme procedures, including preparation, approval, execution, and financing. It also addresses issues of common services and common premises, including UN houses.
- The Programme Group develops policies, guidelines and procedures to improve the quality and effectiveness of UN Country Team programme collaboration. It particularly supports national efforts to implement the Millennium Declaration and achieve the MDGs.

Membership

The full UNDG membership has grown to 28, plus five observers. The group meets at least three times a year to decide on issues related to country level coordination to achieve MDGs.

UN Development Programme (UNDP)

1 United Nations Plaza
New York, NY 10017
United States of America
Telephone: (+1 212) 906 5000
Fax: (+1 212) 906 5364
Email: hq@undp.org
Internet: www.undp.org
Administrator: Kemal Derviş, Turkey (since 2005) (appointed by the UN Secretary-General)

Purpose

UNDP began operations in 1966 under GA res. 2029 (XX) (1965), which combined the UN Expanded Programme of Technical Assistance (EPTA) with the Special Fund. GA res. 2688 (XXV) (1970), which took effect in 1971, defined the organisational structure and activities.

UNDP is the main body responsible for coordinating UN development work, especially global and national efforts to reach the MDGs, with particular emphasis on halving extreme poverty by 2015. The organisation has a presence in more than 166 countries and is the largest provider of development grant assistance in the UN system. Its work focuses on:
- Achieving the MDGs and reducing human poverty
- Fostering democratic governance
- Managing sustainable development in energy and the environment
- Information and communications technology
- Supporting crisis prevention and recovery
- Responding to HIV/AIDS.

Special attention is paid to the needs of the Least Developed Countries (LDCs). UNDP administers special funds and programmes, including:
- UN Development Fund for Women (UNIFEM), see p200
- UN Volunteers (UNV), see p201
- UN Capital Development Fund (UNCDF), see p199.

The Programme publishes the annual *Human Development Report*.

UNDP/UNFPA Executive Board decision 1999/23 (1999) recognised the establishment of the multi-year funding framework (MYFF) 2004–07 as the primary tool for integrating

UNDP's programme objectives, resources and budget. This is soon to be replaced by the UNDP Strategic Plan 2008–11.

Structure

GA res. 48/162 (1993) transformed the UNDP Governing Council into an Executive Board, responsible for providing inter-government support to, and supervision of, UNDP and the UN Population Fund (UNFPA). The functions of the Executive Board are set out in that resolution.

The Board meets in one annual and two regular sessions each year. The annual session alternates between New York and Geneva. The regular sessions are held in New York. The 2007 Board meeting schedule is: first regular session from 23 to 26 January, annual session from 11 to 22 June (New York), and second regular session 10 to 14 September. In addition to the schedule of Board sessions, a joint meeting of the UNDP/UNFPA, UNICEF and WFP Executive Boards was held in New York on 19 and 22 January 2007.

Resources

UNDP's financial resources are derived primarily from voluntary contributions by participating state governments. Gross voluntary contributions to regular resources in 2006 amounted to $905 million,* up from $900 million in 2005. This was in line with the intermediate MYFF target of $900 million.

UNDP has co-financing arrangements with donor and recipient governments, as well as with multilateral financing institutions. Co-financing contributions (including cost-sharing by recipient governments and trust fund contributions) make up an increasingly significant component of UNDP's revenue and for 2006 were approximately $3.55 billion,* about the same as in 2005.

*Provisional figures as at 21 May 2007.

Membership

GA res. 48/162 (1993) specified that membership of the Executive Board should be based on equitable geographic representation and other relevant factors. It specifies that there should be 36 members: eight from African states, seven from Asian and Pacific states, four from Eastern European states, five from Latin American and Caribbean states, and 12 from Western European and Other states. Board terms are three years, unless otherwise agreed.

Bureau members of the UNDP/UNFPA Executive Board in 2007 are:

President
Western European and Others Group – Carsten Staur, Denmark
Vice-Presidents
Latin America and the Caribbean states – José Briz-Gutiérrez, Guatemala
Eastern European Group – Andriy Nikitov, Ukraine
African Group – Fernande Aviavi Houngbedji, Benin
Asian Group – Iftekhar Ahmed Chowdhury, Bangladesh

Members of the UNDP/UNFPA Board and their terms are:

	Previous membership	Current membership
African states		
Algeria		2006–08
Angola		2007–09
Benin		2006–08
Botswana	1998–2000 04–06	
Burundi	1995–97	
Cameroon	1994 2004–06	
Cape Verde	2003–05	
Central African Republic		2007–09
Comoros	2002–04	
Congo	1994 2004–06	
DR Congo	1995–2003	
Djibouti	2001–03	
Egypt	2000–02	
Eritrea	2004–06	
Ethiopia	1995–97 1999–2001	
Gabon	2001–03	
Gambia	1994–97 2004–06	
Ghana	1998–2000	
Guinea	1997–99	
Lesotho	1994	
Libyan AJ	1997–99	
Madagascar	1996–98	
Malawi		2007–09
Mauritania	2001–03	
Morocco	1994–96	
Mozambique	2001–03	
Senegal		2007–09
Sierra Leone	1994–96	
Somalia	1994	2007–09
South Africa	1998–2000	
Sudan	1994–95	
Togo	2000–02	
Tunisia	2003–05	
Uganda		2005–07
UR of Tanzania	1998–2000	
Zambia	1995–97	
Asian and Pacific states		
Bangladesh	1994–96	2006–08
Bhutan		2007–09
China	1994–2003 04–06	2007–09
DPRK		2005–07
India	1994–2001 03–05	2007–09
Indonesia	1995–97 2000–02 04–06	
Iran	2001–03 04–06	
Kazakhstan		2005–07
Kyrgyzstan	1999–2001	
Lebanon	1998–2000	
Malaysia	1996–98	
Nepal	2003–05	

	Previous membership	Current membership
Pakistan	1994–99 2002–04	2006–08
Papua New Guinea	1994	
Philippines	1994–97 2001–03	
ROK	1994–95 1998–2000	
Thailand	1997–99	
Viet Nam	2000–02	
Yemen	2002–04	

Eastern European states

Belarus	1999–2001	2005–07
Bulgaria	1994–95 2001–03	
Czech Republic	1998–2000 02–04	
Poland	1994–96 2004–06	
Romania	1996–98 2002–04	
Russian Federation	1994–95 1997–2005	2006–08
Serbia[1]		2007–09
Slovakia	1994–97	
Ukraine	1996–2001	2005–07

Latin American and Caribbean states

Antigua and Barbuda	1997–99 2002–04	2007–09
Argentina	1994–98	
Belize	1996–98	
Brazil	1997–2002	
Cuba	1994–97 1999–2001 04–06	
Ecuador	2001–03	2006–08
El Salvador	2003–05	
Guatemala	1999–2001	2005–07
Guyana		2005–07
Honduras	2000–02	
Jamaica	1998–2000	2006–08
Peru	1994–96 2002–04	
Trinidad and Tobago	1994–96	
Uruguay	1994–95 2003–05	

Western European and Other states (plus Japan)

Australia	1997–98 2003–05	
Austria	1997–99	
Belgium	1994–96 2000–02	2007–09
Canada[1]	1994–96 98–99 2001–04	2007
Denmark	1994–96 98–99 2001–02	2004–09
Finland	1996–97 2001–03	
France	1994–95 97–98 2000–04	
Germany	1994–97 1999–2003 04–06	2007
Greece[2]		2007
Ireland	1998–2000	
Italy	1994–95 1999–2001 03–05	2007–08
Japan	1994–2005	2006–08
Luxembourg	2002	
Netherlands	1996–98 2000–02 04–06	
New Zealand	1994–95 2000–01 06	
Norway	1994–95 97–98 2000–01 03–05	2006–10

	Previous membership	Current membership
Portugal	1994–96	2005–07
Spain	1996 98–99 2002	2007
Sweden	1995–97 1999–2003 04–06	
Switzerland	1996–97 1999–2000 02–04	
Turkey	2002 05–06	
UK	1994–95 97–99 2002–04	2006–07
USA	1994–2004	2005–07

Notes

On 3 June 2006 the Republic of Serbia notified the UN that the membership of the State Union of Serbia and Montenegro in the UN, including all organs and organisations of the UN system, was continued by the Republic of Serbia on the basis of article 60 of the Constitutional Charter of Serbia and Montenegro, activated by the Declaration of Independence adopted by the National Assembly of Montenegro on 3 June 2006.

[1] Canada will relinquish its seat to Australia at the end of 2007.

[2] Greece will relinquish its seat to The Netherlands at the end of 2007.

UN Population Fund (UNFPA)

220 East 42nd Street
New York, NY 10017
United States of America
Telephone: (+1 212) 297 5000
Fax: (+1 212) 370 0201
Email: hq@unfpa.org
Internet: www.unfpa.org
Executive Director: Thoraya Ahmed Obaid, Saudi Arabia (since 2001) (appointed by the UN Secretary-General)

Purpose

UNFPA's work is guided by its multi-year funding framework (MYFF). Decision 2004/7 (2004) of the UNDP/UNFPA Executive Board endorsed the Fund's second MYFF, covering the period 2004 to 2007, which sets out three goals:

- All couples and individuals enjoy good reproductive health, including family planning and sexual health, throughout life
- Countries address the interaction between population dynamics, sustainable development and poverty, including the impact of HIV/AIDS
- Gender equality and empowerment of women are achieved.

The MYFF is due to be replaced by the UNFPA Strategic Plan 2008–11.

Evolution

UNFPA was set up by the Secretary-General in 1967, after GA res. 2211 (XXI) (1966) called on UN system organisations to provide assistance in the field of population.

In 1969 the Secretary-General entrusted the Fund's management to the Administrator of UNDP and renamed it the UN Fund for Population Activities (UNFPA). GA res. 3019 (XXVII) (1972) placed the Fund under the General Assembly's authority and designated the UNDP Governing Council to be its governing body, subject to conditions to be established by ECOSOC. ECOSOC res. 1763 (LIV) (1973) set down UNFPA's aims and purposes and tasked the Fund with playing a leading UN role in promoting population programmes.

ECOSOC res. 2025 (LXI) (1976) endorsed a set of general principles for the allocation of UNFPA resources.

GA res. 34/104 (1979) reaffirmed the 1972 resolution, including the Fund's status as a subsidiary organ of the General Assembly in terms of article 22 of the Charter. GA res. 42/430 (1987) renamed the Fund the UN Population Fund (UNFPA). GA res. 48/162 (1993) transformed the governing body of UNDP/UNFPA into the UNDP/UNFPA Executive Board, to provide inter-government support to and supervision of the Fund in accordance with the overall policy guidance of the General Assembly and ECOSOC.

UNDP/UNFPA Executive Board decision 95/15 (1995) determined that UNFPA's future programme of assistance should follow the principles in Chapter II of the Programme of Action of the International Conference on Population and Development (ICPD), held in Cairo in 1994. Executive Board decision 2000/11 (2000) encouraged UNFPA to fulfil its leadership role as an advocate for reproductive health, population and development issues, and for actions agreed at ICPD and at the 21st session of the General Assembly on the ICPD+5.

Structure

UNFPA reports through its Executive Board to ECOSOC, which in turn reports to the General Assembly. See UNDP Structure and Membership sections for further information.

Resources

The Fund's integrated resources framework for 2004 to 2007 sets a target of $1.52 billion for total resources mobilised during that period.

UNFPA's resources come from voluntary contributions from governments and the private sector. Regular income for 2006 was $389.3 million. The breakdown was $360.1 million of voluntary contributions from donor governments, $15.4 million from a private endowment fund, $0.5 million from private sector sources, $10.8 million in interest income and other income of $2.5 million.

Total non-core income for 2006 was $208 million. Of that, $167.2 million was from co-financing ($98.2 million from governments and $69 million from non-government sources and the private sector), $37.7 million from procurement, $2.5 million from Junior Professional Officer (JPO) programmes and $0.6 million from other trust funds.

Committee for the UN Population Award

Purpose

The Committee was established and charged with selecting recipients of the Award by GA res. 36/201 (1981). The Award is presented annually to individuals and/or institutions in recognition of outstanding contributions to increasing awareness of population problems and developing solutions to them. It was first presented in 1983 and consists of a gold medal, a diploma and a monetary prize.

The winners for 2007 were Columbia University's Allan Rosenfield, Iran's Hosseing Malek Afzali and two institutions, Algeria's National Population Committee and Malaysia's National Population and Family Development Board.

Structure

The Committee comprises 10 UN Member States' representatives elected by ECOSOC for three years, the Secretary-General and Executive Director of UNFPA (ex officio), and five eminent individuals. The UN Secretary-General selects the latter on the basis of their significant contributions to population-related activities. They serve in an advisory capacity for renewable terms of three years. The Executive Director of UNFPA is the designated Secretary.

Membership

Current members of the Committee, whose terms expire on 31 December 2007, are:

Algeria	Guyana	Netherlands
Bangladesh	Haiti	Peru
Belarus	Iran	
Cameroon	Kenya	

ECOSOC elected the following Committee members at an organisational session in May 2007. This is for a three-year term beginning on 1 January 2008.

Algeria	Haiti	Sweden
Bangladesh	Iran	UR Tanzania
Czech Republic	Malaysia	
DR Congo	Peru	

UN Capital Development Fund (UNCDF)

2 United Nations Plaza
New York, NY 10017
United States of America
Telephone: (+1 212) 906 6119
Fax: (+1 212) 906 6479
Email: info@uncdf.org
Internet: www.uncdf.org
Deputy Executive Secretary and Officer in Charge: Henriette Keijzers (since 2003) (appointed by the Administrator of UNDP)

Purpose

GA res. 2186 (XXI) (1966) established the UNCDF as one of its autonomous organs. In 1973 the Fund's mandate was modified to give priority to Least Developed Countries (LDCs). In January 2005 the Executive Board reaffirmed that UNCDF's overarching goal was to help reduce poverty through investing with the poor, and building the productive capacity and self-reliance of poor communities by strengthening their influence over investments that directly affect their lives and livelihoods. This is achieved through helping developing countries strengthen their economies by supplementing existing sources of capital assistance with grants and loans that are flexible, high-risk and innovative. It is channelled primarily to poor rural areas in LDCs, where capacity and governance challenges are typically the greatest, to reduce poverty and support efforts towards achieving the objectives of the Brussels Programme of Action for LDCs and Millennium Development Goals (MDGs).

UNCDF currently invests $125 million in 28 LDCs, focused on local development and microfinance. Its local development programmes provide communities with access to social services and economic infrastructure. Its microfinance investments provide better access to financial services and direct support for start-up and emerging microfinance institutions.

Structure

The Fund is a member of the UNDP group and is represented at country level by UNDP resident representatives. In accordance with GA res. 2321 (XXII) (1967), the UNDP/UNFPA Executive Board operates as the Executive Board of the Fund. UNDP provides $5 million annually to cover UNCDF administrative expenses.

Resources

The Fund's resources come from voluntary contributions by Member States and from co-financing by governments, international organisations and the private sector.

UN Development Fund for Women (UNIFEM)

304 East 45th Street, 15th Floor
New York, NY 10017
United States of America
Telephone: (+1 212) 906 6400
Fax: (+1 212) 906 6705
Email: unifem@undp.org
Internet: www.unifem.org
Director: Noeleen Heyzer, Singapore (since 1994) (appointed by the Administrator of UNDP, in consultation with the Consultative Committee)

Purpose

UNIFEM was established by GA res. 39/125 (1984) as an autonomous organisation working in close association with UNDP. The Fund works with countries to formulate and implement laws and policies that eliminate gender discrimination and promote gender equality. It also aims to transform institutions to be more accountable to gender equality and women's rights, strengthen the capacity and voice of women's rights advocates, and help change harmful and discriminatory practices.

UNIFEM provides financial and technical assistance to innovative programmes and strategies that promote women's rights, political participation and economic security. Its mandate is to:

- Support innovative and experimental activities benefiting women, in line with national and regional priorities
- Serve as a catalyst, with the goal of ensuring the involvement of women in mainstream development activities
- Play an innovative role in relation to the overall UN system of development cooperation.

UNIFEM focuses on four key areas:

- Reducing women's poverty and exclusion
- Ending violence against women
- Reversing the spread of HIV/AIDS among women and girls
- Supporting women's leadership in governance and post-conflict reconstruction.

Two international agreements frame UNIFEM's work: the Beijing Platform for Action resulting from the Fourth World Conference on Women in 1995, and the Convention on the Elimination of All Forms of Discrimination against Women (CEDAW).

Structure

UNIFEM is governed by the UNDP Executive Board. UNIFEM also has a five-member Consultative Committee that meets once a year to provide guidance on programme and policy matters. The Committee was established by GA res. 31/133 (1976), and its mandate was renewed and modified by GA res. 39/125 (1984) upon the establishment of UNIFEM. The Committee's 47th session was held from 14 to 15 February 2007.

The Fund's multi-year funding framework for 2004 to 2007 provides strategic policy and management direction for UNIFEM to increase development effectiveness, strengthen strategic partnerships and mobilise resources. This is due to be replaced by the UNIFEM Strategic Plan 2008–11.

Resources

UNIFEM is financed from voluntary contributions from both government and private donors (approximately $20 million in 2006).

Membership

The General Assembly President designates five Member States to serve on the Consultative Committee for a term of three years, taking account of voluntary contributions to the Fund and equitable geographical distribution. The members, whose terms are from 1 January 2006 to 31 December 2008, are:

Estonia	Mexico	Sudan
Jordan	Norway	

UN Volunteers (UNV)

Hermann-Ehlers-Str 10
53153 Bonn
Germany
Telephone: (+49 228) 815 2000
Fax: (+49 228) 815 2001
Email: information@unvolunteers.org
Internet: www.unv.org
Executive Coordinator: Ad de Raad, Netherlands (since 2004)

Purpose

The UNV programme was created under GA res. 2659 (XXV) (1970) as an operational partner in international development. Administered by UNDP, UNV is the focal point for volunteerism in the UN system. It advocates the role and benefits of volunteerism, integrates civic engagement into development programmes and helps to mobilise volunteers worldwide.

UNV volunteers support sustainable human development globally in key areas such as poverty reduction, democratic governance, energy, the environment, crisis prevention and recovery, and health. UNV helps set up national volunteer schemes, starts creative and pioneering volunteer activities, and develops research capacity on volunteerism in developing countries.

Since 1971 UNV has mobilised some 40,000 mid-career professionals to serve the causes of peace and development. In 2006, 7600 UNV volunteers, representing 163 nationalities, served in 144 countries worldwide. Reaffirming the programme's commitment to promoting

South-South cooperation, the majority of volunteers (76 percent) are nationals of developing countries.

Since 2000, UNV has run an online volunteering service that has attracted 30,000 people, of whom more than half have engaged in an online assignment with some of the 960 registered development organisations.

UN Environment Programme (UNEP)

PO Box 30552
United Nations Avenue
Gigiri, Nairobi 00100
Kenya
Cable Address: Uniterra, Nairobi
Telephone: (+254 20) 762 1234
Fax: (+254 20) 762 4489/90
Email: unepinfo@unep.org
Internet: www.unep.org
Telex: 22068, 22173
Executive Director: Achim Steiner, Germany (2006–10) (elected by the UN General Assembly)

Purpose

UNEP was established by GA res. 2997 (XXVII) (1972), following the Stockholm Conference on the Human Environment. It aims to provide leadership and encourage partnerships in caring for the environment by inspiring, informing and enabling nations and people to improve their quality of life, without compromising future generations.

In 1997, the Governing Council adopted the Nairobi Declaration on the Role and Mandate of the United Nations Environment Programme, which established the following core mandate for UNEP. It is to:

- Analyse the state of the global environment and assess global and regional environmental trends, provide policy advice and early warning information on environmental threats, and catalyse and promote international cooperation and action, based on the best scientific and technical capabilities available
- Further the development of international environmental law aiming at sustainable development, including the development of coherent linkages among existing international environmental conventions
- Advance the implementation of agreed international norms and policies, monitor and foster compliance with environmental principles and international agreements, and stimulate cooperative action to emerging environmental challenges
- Strengthen its role in coordinating environmental activities in the UN system, and as its role as an implementing agency of the Global Environment Facility
- Promote greater awareness and facilitate effective cooperation in implementing the international environmental agenda, and serve as an effective link between the scientific community and policy-makers at national and international levels
- Provide policy and advisory services in key areas of institution-building to governments and other relevant institutions.

Evolution

In 2002 the Governing Council/Global Ministerial Environment Forum adopted the report of the Open-ended Inter-governmental Group of Ministers or their Representatives on International Environmental Governance. This was endorsed in the Johannesburg Plan of

Implementation of the World Summit on Sustainable Development. It recommended an increased role for UNEP in country-level capacity-building and training, and national-level coordination of the environmental component of sustainable development.

In 2005 the Governing Council/Global Ministerial Environment Forum adopted the Bali Strategic Plan for Technology Support and Capacity-building. This was developed to meet the urgent need for technology support and capacity-building of developing countries and countries with economies in transition.

Structure

- Governing Council
- Secretariat
- Environment Fund (voluntary)
- Committee of Permanent Representatives.

The Governing Council reports to the General Assembly through ECOSOC, and its regular sessions are held every two years. GA res. 53/242 (1999) instituted an annual, ministerial-level, global environmental forum, constituted by the Governing Council in the years that it meets in regular session and, in alternate years, by a special session of the Governing Council.

The 24th session/Global Ministerial Environment Forum was held in Nairobi from 5 to 9 February 2007. The tenth special session of the Governing Council/Global Ministerial Environment Forum will be held in the Principality of Monaco from 20 to 22 February 2008. The 25th session of the Governing Council/Global Ministerial Environment Forum will be held in Nairobi from 16 to 20 February 2009.

Membership

The Governing Council comprises 58 members elected by the General Assembly for four-year terms on the basis of 16 seats for African states, 13 for Asian states, six for Eastern European states, 10 for Latin American and Caribbean states, and 13 for Western European and Other states.

	Previous membership	Current membership
African states		
Algeria	1978–80 84–86 96–99	2006–09
Angola		2006–09
Benin	1996–2003	2006–09
Botswana	1979–95 1998–2001	2006–09
Burkina Faso	1996–2003	2004–07
Burundi	1973–75 79–84 1987–2001	2006–09
Cameroon	1973–74 83–85 92–95 1998–2001	2004–07
Cape Verde		2004–07
Central African Republic	1973–78 96–99	
Chad	1977–79 2002–05	
Comoros	1998–2001	
Congo	1986–88 92–95 2002–05	
Côte d'Ivoire	1974–79 83–85 89–95	
DR Congo	1975–97	2006–09
Egypt	1975–77 81–83 2000–03	
Equatorial Guinea	2000–03	

	Previous membership	Current membership
Ethiopia	1980–82	
Gabon	1973–76 80–82 87–97	
Gambia	1990–97 2000–03	
Ghana	1973–79 81–83 85–88	2004–07
Guinea	1979–84	
Guinea-Bissau	1994–97	
Kenya	1973–83 85–99	2002–09
Lesotho	1983–85 89–93	
Liberia	1976–81	
Libyan AJ	1975–83 85–91 2000–03	
Madagascar	1973–75	
Malawi	1973–74 79–81 1998–2001	
Mauritania	1980–82 87–89 96–99	
Mauritius	1989–93	
Morocco	1973–76 82–84 96–99	2004–07
Namibia	2002–05	
Niger	1985–88	
Nigeria	1973–75 83–88 92–95 1998–2005	
Rwanda	1976–78 84–86 89–95	
Senegal	1973–75 77–79 82–84 87–89 92–95 2000–03	2004–07
Sierra Leone	1973–76 80–82	
Somalia	1973–74 76–78	2004–07
South Africa		2006–09
Sudan	1973 75–77 80–82 84–86 89–91 1994–2005	
Swaziland	1986–88	
Togo	1976–78 84–86 89–91	
Tunisia	1973–74 78–80 85–88 90–93 96–99	
UR of Tanzania	1973–75 77–79 82–84	2004–07
Uganda	1976–81 83–91 2000–03	2006–09
Zambia	1986–88 94–97 2002–05	
Zimbabwe	1989–2005	

Asian states

	Previous membership	Current membership
Afghanistan	1982–84	
Bangladesh	1977–82 89–95	2004–07
Bhutan	1992–95	
China	1973–2001	2002–09
Cyprus	1976–78	
DPRK	1994–97	
India	1973–77 1979–2003	2004–07
Indonesia	1973–2005	2006–09
Iran	1973–80 87–89 1992–2003	2004–07
Iraq	1973–81 87–89	
Japan	1973–2005	2006–09
Jordan	1973–75 85–91	
Kazakhstan	1998–2001	2004–07
Kuwait	1973–74 76–81 84–86 90–93	
Kyrgyzstan		2004–07
Lebanon	1973–76	
Malaysia	1975–86 92–95	
Marshall Islands	1996–2003	
Myanmar	2002–05	

	Previous membership	Current membership
Nepal	1984–86	
Oman	1982–91	
Pakistan	1973–75 78–83 1989–2003	2006–09
Papua New Guinea	1983–88	
Philippines	1973–79 83–85 90–93 96–99	
ROK	1987–89 1994–2005	2006–09
Samoa	1996–2003	
Saudi Arabia	1980–85 89–91 2000–03	2004–07
Sri Lanka	1973–75 81–83 85–95	
Syrian AR	1973–79 86–88 1994–2005	
Thailand	1976–84 86–88 90–93 1996–2003	2006–09
Tuvalu		2004–07
UAE	1980–82	

Eastern European states

	Previous membership	Current membership
Belarus	1979–84 1998–2001	
Bulgaria	1977–82 85–91 94–97	2004–07
Czech Republic*	1996–99 2002–05	2006–09
Hungary	1976–78 83–85 1994–2001	2004–07
Poland	1973–78 1982–2003	2004–07
Republic of Moldova	2000–03	
Romania	1973–80 92–95 2002–05	2006–09
Russian Federation	1973–2005	2006–09
Serbia and Montenegro	1973–93	
Slovakia*	1993–2003	
Ukraine	1981–93	

Latin American and Caribbean states

	Previous membership	Current membership
Antigua and Barbuda	1998–2005	2006–09
Argentina	1973–2005	2006–09
Bahamas	2000–03	2004–07
Barbados	1986–93	
Brazil	1973–97 2000–03	2004–07
Chile	1973–75 80–99	2006–09
Colombia	1975–80 1982–2003	2004–07
Costa Rica	1989–91 94–97	2004–07
Cuba	1998–2005	
Dominican Republic	1987–89	
Grenada	1976–78	
Guatemala	1973–79	
Guyana	1989–95	
Haiti	1981–86	2006–09
Jamaica	1973–79 82–88 1998–2001	
Mexico	1973–2003	2004–07
Nicaragua	1973–75 94–97 2002–05	
Panama	1973–75 79–81 85–88 96–99	
Peru	1973–74 76–78 80–85 90–93 96–99	
Suriname	2000–03	
Trinidad and Tobago	1979–81	
Uruguay	1976–84 92–95	2002–09
Venezuela	1973–2001	

	Previous membership	Current membership

Western European and Other states

	Previous membership	Current membership
Australia	1973–75 79–81 83–89 92–99	2006–09
Austria	1973–74 78–80 84–86 90–93 1998–2001	2006–09
Belgium	1976–78 80–82 84–86 1998–2001	2002–09
Canada	1973–79 82–91 1994–2001	2002–09
Denmark	1978–80 86–88 92–95 2000–03	
Finland	1975–77 83–85 89–91 96–99	
France	1973–2001	2002–09
Germany	1973–2001	2002–09
Greece	1976–78 82–84 87–89 2002–05	
Iceland	1973–74 81–83	
Israel		2004–07
Italy	1973–77 79–81 83–85 1996–2003	
Malta	1985–91	
Monaco		2004–07
Netherlands	1973–75 78–83 1986–2003	2004–07
New Zealand	1976–78 80–82 90–93 2000–03	
Norway	1977–79 84–86 90–93 1998–2001	
Portugal	1992–95	
Spain	1973–79 82–84 90–97	
Sweden	1973–76 80–82 87–89 94–97	2004–07
Switzerland	1975–77 81–83 87–89 94–97 2002–05	
Turkey	1973–75 79–81 85–91 1996–2003	2004–07
UK	1973–2003	2004–07
USA	1973–2001	2002–09

Note

*   Insofar as they formed part of Czechoslovakia until 31 December 1992, the Czech Republic and Slovakia were members of the Governing Council 1973–76 and 1986–92.

Office of the UN High Commissioner for Refugees (UNHCR)

94 Rue Montbrillant
Case Postale 2500
1211 Geneva 2
Switzerland
Telephone: (+41 22) 739 8111
Fax: (+41 22) 731 9546
Email: hqpi00@unhcr.org
Internet: www.unhcr.org
Telex: 415740 UNHCR Ch
High Commissioner: António Guterres, Portugal (since June 2005) (elected by the UN General Assembly on the nomination of the Secretary-General)

Purpose

UNHCR's work is humanitarian and non-political. Its principal functions are to provide international protection to refugees and other persons of concern, including stateless people, and to seek durable solutions for them. Protection includes preventing 'refoulement' (the involuntary return of a refugee or a person of concern to a country where he or she may have a well-founded fear of persecution) and ensuring that host countries follow international norms in the treatment of refugees. In seeking durable solutions to refugees' problems, UNHCR helps those who wish to go home to do so once circumstances permit, assisting them to reintegrate into their home communities. Where this is not feasible, UNHCR seeks other solutions, whether in the countries where refugees have already found asylum or in third countries. Emergency and other material assistance is provided in collaboration with government, other inter-government and non-government partners, in the form of food, shelter, medical aid, education and other social services.

While its mandate specifically covers refugees, UNHCR has also frequently been asked by the UN Secretary-General to protect and assist internally displaced persons (IDPs) in conflict-generated emergencies. A comprehensive inter-agency agreement in 2005 reinforced and made more explicit the role of the UN and other humanitarian agencies involved in helping IDPs. Under this mechanism UNHCR has assumed leadership for protection, emergency shelter and camp management in conflict-related situations of internal displacement.

Evolution

By GA res. 319 (IV) (1949) the General Assembly decided to appoint a UN High Commissioner for Refugees (UNHCR) to protect the interests of refugees after the International Refugee Organization terminated its activities. The Statute of the Office of the UN High Commissioner for Refugees, detailing its functions and responsibilities, was embodied in GA res. 428 (V) (1950), and the Office came into being on 1 January 1951.

In 2003, following periodic extensions, the General Assembly removed the time limitation on the organisation's mandate and extended it "until the refugee problem is solved" (GA res. 58/153 (2004)). The General Assembly also decided that the High Commissioner should make an annual oral report to ECOSOC on the coordination aspects of the Office's work, and that it should continue the existing practice of presenting an annual written report to the General Assembly, as established in para. 11 of its Statute. This would be on the understanding that every 10 years, beginning with the 68th session, the report would include a strategic review of the global situation of refugees and the role of the Office, prepared in consultation with the Secretary-General and the Executive Committee of the High Commissioner's Programme.

Executive Committee of the High Commissioner's Programme

The Executive Committee (ExCom) determines the general policies under which UNHCR plans, develops and administers refugee projects and programmes. It advises the High Commissioner, on request, on the discharge of his or her duties under the Statute of the Office. It approves the use of UNHCR annual programme funds and reviews all UNHCR programmes and projects.

ExCom holds an annual plenary session in Geneva every October. The 58th plenary session is scheduled to be held from 1 to 5 October 2007. Meetings of ExCom's Standing Committee are held at various dates throughout the year.

Membership

Excom membership is on the widest possible geographical basis from those states (members of the UN and others) with a demonstrated interest in, and devotion to, solving refugee problems. New members requesting admission may be admitted by ECOSOC election if a request to enlarge the Executive Committee's membership has been approved by the General Assembly. The 72 members are:

Algeria	Greece	Pakistan
Argentina	Guinea	Philippines
Australia	Holy See	Poland
Austria	Hungary	Portugal
Bangladesh	India	ROK
Belgium	Iran	Romania
Brazil	Ireland	Russian Federation
Canada	Israel	Serbia
Chile	Italy	Somalia
China	Japan	South Africa
Colombia	Jordan	Spain
Costa Rica*	Kenya	Sudan
Côte d'Ivoire	Lebanon	Sweden
Cyprus	Lesotho	Switzerland
DR Congo	Madagascar	Thailand
Denmark	Mexico	Tunisia
Ecuador	Morocco	Turkey
Egypt	Mozambique	UK
Estonia*	Namibia	UR of Tanzania
Ethiopia	Netherlands	USA
Finland	New Zealand	Uganda
France	Nicaragua	Venezuela
Germany	Nigeria	Yemen
Ghana	Norway	Zambia

Note

*   In accordance with GA res. A/61/136 (2006), the Council elected Costa Rica and Estonia to the Executive Committee on 25 April 2007.

UN Relief and Works Agency for Palestine Refugees in the Near East (UNRWA)

UNRWA Headquarters (Gaza)
PO Box 140157
Amman 11814
Jordan
Telephone: (+972 8) 677 7333
Fax: (+972 8) 677 7555
Email: unrwa-pio@unrwa.org
Internet: www.unrwa.org
Commissioner-General: Karen Koning AbuZayd (since 2005) (appointed by the UN Secretary-General)

Purpose

UNRWA was established by GA res. 302 (IV) on 8 December 1949, following the 1948 Arab-Israeli conflict, to carry out direct relief and works programmes for Palestine refugees. The Agency began operations on 1 May 1950. In the absence of a solution to the Palestine refugee problem, the General Assembly has repeatedly renewed UNRWA's mandate, most recently extending it until 30 June 2008.

UNRWA provides essential services for all eligible registered Palestine refugees in its fields of operation: Jordan, Lebanon, the Syrian AR and the Occupied Palestinian Territory. The

Agency defines Palestine refugees as people whose normal residence was in Palestine for a minimum of two years before the 1948 conflict and who, because of the Arab–Israeli hostilities, lost their homes and means of livelihood. Their descendants are registered as refugees through the male line. To be eligible for assistance, a refugee must live in one of the five areas where UNRWA operates and be in need. In 2006 more than 4.4 million refugees were registered with UNRWA.

Evolution

UNRWA has been conducting emergency operations in the West Bank and Gaza since the outbreak of strife in the Occupied Palestinian Territory in September 2000.

Today UNRWA's principal areas of activity are education, health, relief, social services and micro-credit programmes. UNRWA is by far the largest UN operation in the Middle East. It has more than 28,000 staff, most of them local refugees.

Structure
- Office of the Commissioner-General (headquarters)
- Field Offices
- Liaison Offices
- Advisory Commission.

The Commissioner-General is the head of all UNRWA operations and is accountable to the General Assembly. The Office of the Commissioner-General supports both the Commissioner-General and the Deputy Commissioner-General, and acts as the coordinating office to ensure that all of UNRWA's substantive actions and activities conform with the Agency's governing objectives and rules. The Office is also the focal point for coordination between UNRWA and host authorities, donor governments, other UN organs and organisations, and inter-government bodies.

UNRWA's headquarters is split between the Gaza Strip and Jordan. There are five UNRWA field offices, located in the West Bank, the Gaza Strip, Jordan, Lebanon and Syria. A Director heads each office and is accountable to the Commissioner-General. The responsibilities and functions of each field office include directing the implementation of UNRWA programmes and services, advising and making recommendations to the Commissioner-General on matters affecting UNRWA operations in the field, and providing advice and assistance to the Commissioner-General on relations with government authorities, and government and non-government organisations. UNRWA also maintains liaison offices in New York, Geneva and Cairo.

Membership

The Advisory Commission was established under the same General Assembly resolution as UNRWA itself. It advises and assists the UNTWA Commissioner-General in the execution of the Agency's programme.

There are now 21 Advisory Commission members. This follows the General Assembly's decision on 9 December 2005 to include those countries whose contributions to the Agency have exceeded an annual average of $5 million over the past three years (*). The Commission members are:

Australia*	Italy*	Spain*
Belgium	Japan	Sweden

Canada*	Jordan	Switzerland*
Denmark*	Lebanon	Syrian AR
Egypt	Netherlands*	Turkey
France	Norway*	UK
Germany*	Saudi Arabia*	USA

The European Community, the League of Arab States and the Palestine Liberation Organization attend Advisory Commission meetings as observers.

UN Human Settlements Programme (UN–HABITAT)

PO Box 30030
Nairobi 00100
Kenya
Telephone: (+254 20) 62 1234
Fax: (+254 20) 62 3477/4266/4267
Email: infohabitat@unhabitat.org
Internet: www.unhabitat.org
Executive Director: Anna Kajumulo Tibaijuka, Tanzania (2002–10) (appointed by the UN Secretary-General)

Purpose

GA res. 32/162 (1977) established the UN Commission on Human Settlements and its secretariat, the UN Centre for Human Settlements. The Centre has its headquarters in Nairobi, Kenya. It is charged with coordinating human settlement activities within the UN system and for facilitating the global exchange of information on shelter and sustainable human settlement development. It also assists countries with policy and technical advice in solving their human settlement problems.

UN-HABITAT has four main objectives, to:
• Promote the development of socially and environmentally sustainable human settlements and the achievement of adequate shelter for all
• Support governments and other partners of the Programme to improve the shelter conditions of the world's poor, particularly within the cities and towns of developing countries
• Support governments and other partners to adopt operationally effective, socially integrated, inclusive, transparent and accountable local governance and management systems as frameworks for ensuring sustainable human settlements development
• Promote international cooperation in shelter and sustainable human settlements development in the attainment of MDG Goal 7, Target 11, on slum upgrading and improvement.

The agency helps governments create policies and strategies aimed at strengthening management capacity at both national and local levels. It focuses on promoting shelter for all, improving urban governance, reducing urban poverty, improving the living environment, and managing disaster mitigation and post-conflict rehabilitation.

Evolution

The Second UN Conference on Human Settlements (Habitat II) was held in Istanbul, Turkey, in 1996. The Conference formulated the Habitat Agenda and the Istanbul Declaration, through which governments committed themselves to the goals of adequate shelter for all and sustainable human settlements development in an urbanising world.

The 25th Special Session of the General Assembly for an Overall Review and Appraisal of the Implementation of the Habitat Agenda, known as Istanbul+5, was held in New York in 2001. The special session adopted the Declaration on Cities and Other Human Settlements in the New Millennium.

GA res. 56/206 (2001) upgraded the Commission on Human Settlements and its secretariat into the UN Human Settlements Programme (UN-HABITAT). The Commission became the Governing Council of UN-HABITAT, which was moved from ECOSOC to be a subsidiary organ of the General Assembly.

UN-HABITAT continues its predecessor's role as the focal point for the implementation of the Habitat Agenda. It will be guided in its work by the Declaration on Cities and Other Human Settlements in the New Millennium. GA res. 56/206 (2001) reaffirmed that the Governing Council's objectives, functions and responsibilities would remain as mandated by GA res. 32/162 (1977) and para. 222 of the Habitat Agenda.

Structure

Every two years UN-HABITAT's work and relationships with its partners are examined in detail by a Governing Council comprising 58 Member States. This is a ministerial-level forum at which the organisation's policy guidelines and budget are established for the next two-year period. The Council approves UN-HABITAT's work programme (the medium-term plan and the two-year work programme) and the budget. It also provides overall policy guidance, direction and supervision to UN-HABITAT.

The Governing Council reports to the General Assembly through ECOSOC, which coordinates the work of the General Assembly's subsidiary bodies. The governments have representatives in Nairobi with whom senior UN-HABITAT officials meet regularly throughout the year in the Committee of Permanent Representatives (CPR).

Resources

The programme's resources come from the UN regular budget, voluntary contributions from governments and the private sector. Total contributions received in 2006 were approximately $135 million.

Meetings

The Governing Council meets once every two years. The 21st session was held in Nairobi from 16 to 20 April 2007.

Membership

The Governing Council's 58 members are each elected by ECOSOC for a four-year term. The membership is made up of 16 members from African states, 13 from Asian states, six from Eastern European states, 10 from Latin American and Caribbean states, and 13 from Western European and Other states.

The following officers were elected to the Governing Council Bureau during the 21st Governing Council:

President	Vice-Presidents	Rapporteur
Kumari Selja, India	Daniel Chuburu, Argentina	Andrey Pronin, Russian Federation
	Ross Hynes, Canada	
	Michael Werikhe, Uganda	

	Previous membership	Current membership

African states

	Previous membership	Current membership
Algeria	1983–85 1996–2003	
Benin	1978–80 1996–2003	
Botswana	1985–95	
Burkina Faso	2003–06	
Burundi	1978–83 85–91 2003–06	2007–10
Cameroon	1979–81 1987–2002	
Central African Republic	1978–80 84–86	
Congo		2004–07
DR Congo	1986–88 1999–2006	
Egypt	1977–82 88–94 2001–04	
Ethiopia	1997–2004	
Equatorial Guinea		2007–10
Gabon	1984–90 1995–2002	
Gambia	1995–2002	
Ghana	1984–86 92–95	2005–08
Guinea	1981–86 2001–04	
Kenya	1979–2003	2004–07
Lesotho	1980–82 85–87 89–96	
Liberia	1982–84 1997–2000	
Libyan AJ	1983–85 93–96	2005–08
Madagascar	1987–90 93–96 2001–04	
Malawi	1979–81 1986–2000 2003–06	
Mali	1999–2002	
Mauritania		2007–10
Morocco	1982–84 86–88 2000–03	
Namibia	1997–2000	
Niger		2007–10
Nigeria	1977–88 91–98	2004–07
Rwanda	1978–80 84–86	2005–08
Senegal	1979–81 1999–2006	2007–10
Sierra Leone	1977–85 87–94 2003–06	
Somalia	1981–83 89–96	
South Africa		2004–07
Sudan	1978–80 82–84 92–99	
Swaziland	1981–83 86–92	2004–07
Togo	1979–81 87–90	
Tunisia	1977–79 85–87 89–92 96–99	
UR of Tanzania	1978–86 88–95 2001–04	2005–08
Uganda	1977–85 87–98 2000–03	2005–08
Zambia	1981–83 1997–2000	
Zimbabwe	1982–84 91–98	2007–10

Asian states

	Previous membership	Current membership
Bangladesh	1979–94 1997–2004	2005–08
China	1989–2004	2005–08
Cyprus	1982–91	
India	1979–2003	2004–07
Indonesia	1980–2000 03–06	2007–10
Iran	1978–80 1988–2006	2007–10
Iraq	1977–81 84–86 89–92 2001–04	
Japan	1978–2006	2007–10

	Previous membership	Current membership
Jordan	1979–2003	2004–07
Kazakhstan	1995–98	
Lebanon	1983–85	
Malaysia	1977–88 92–95 2000–03	
Nepal	1988	
Pakistan	1978–2006	2007–10
Papua New Guinea	1977–85 93–96	
Philippines	1978–90 1992–2003	2004–07
ROK	1997–2000	
Saudi Arabia		2004–07
Sri Lanka	1979–2003	2004–07
Syrian AR	1977–79 81–83 89–92	
UAE	1993–99 2001–04	2005–08
Viet Nam	1979–81 1999–2000	

Note: one Asian seat is currently vacant.

Eastern European states[1, 2]

	Previous membership	Current membership
Azerbaijan	1993–96	
Belarus	1982–84 88–95 1997–2000	2004–07
Bulgaria	1977–79 81–90 92–99	2004–07
Croatia	2000–03	
Czech Republic	1996–2003	2005–08
Hungary	1980–96	
Lithuania	1999–2002	
Poland	1979–81 86–88 90–91 1997–2000 03–06	2007–10
Republic of Moldova	2001–04	
Romania	1982–84 91–98	
Russian Federation	1978–2006	2007–10
Slovakia		2005–08
The Former Yugoslav Republic of Macedonia	2001–04	
Ukraine	1985–87	

Latin American and Caribbean states

	Previous membership	Current membership
Antigua and Barbuda	1991–94	2005–08
Argentina	1978–83 87–90 1999–2006	2007–10
Bahamas	1993–96	
Barbados	1981–83 1992–2003	
Bolivia	1982–84 86–92 1999–2002	
Brazil	1987–2006	
Chile	1979–87 1991–2006	2007–10
Colombia	1977–85 1987–2003	
Costa Rica	1995–98 2004–07	2007–10
Cuba	1977–85	
Dominican Republic	1986–88 95–98	
Ecuador	1978–80 87–90 1997–2000 03–06	
El Salvador	1982–84	
Grenada		2007–10
Guatemala	1979–81 89–92	
Haiti	1984–86 92–95 2001–04	2005–08
Honduras	1984–86	
Jamaica	1978–83 85–91 1993–2004	

	Previous membership	Current membership
Mexico	1978–83 1985–2003	2004–07
Nicaragua	1984–86	
Panama	1986–88	
Paraguay	1989–92	2004–07
Peru	1977–85 88–91	
Trinidad and Tobago	2001–04	2004–07
Venezuela	1979–81 84–86 1993–2000	2007–10

Western European and Other states

	Previous membership	Current membership
Australia	1979–81	
Austria	1977–79 92–95 2001–04	
Belgium	1980–82 1997–2004	2005–08
Canada	1977–96	2005–08
Denmark	1981–83 86–91 96–99	
Finland	1977–79 1981–2002	2007–10
France	1977–2004	2005–08
Germany	1979–2003	2004–07
Greece	1979–2003	2004–07
Israel		2004–07
Italy	1979–84 1986–2004	2007–10
Netherlands	1977–2000 2003–06	2007–10
New Zealand	1982–84	
Norway	1980–2003	2004–07
Portugal	1978–80	
Spain	1981–86 1996–2003	2004–07
Sweden	1978–80 1983–2004	2005–08
Turkey	1984–2006	
UK	1978–80 1987–2006	
USA	1978–2006	2007–10

Notes

There is currently one vacant seat on the Governing Council.

[1] The former Socialist Federal Republic of Yugoslavia served on the Governing Council from 1978 to 1980 and from 1989 to 1992. It was not automatically succeeded by any of the new states created following its dissolution.

[2] Czechoslovakia served on the Governing Council from 1979 to 1981.

World Food Programme (WFP)

Via Cesare Giulio Viola 68/70
Parco de Medici
00148 Rome
Italy
Telephone: (+39 06) 65131
Fax: (+39 06) 6513 2840
Email: wfpinfo@wfp.org
Internet: www.wfp.org
Executive Director: Josette Sheeran, USA (appointed in 2006 jointly by the UN Secretary-General and FAO Director-General)

Purpose

The WFP was established in 1961 by the General Assembly and the UN Food and Agriculture Organization (FAO) Conference as the UN system's food aid organisation.

The WFP is the largest international food aid organisation in the world. It provides food aid primarily to low-income, food-deficit countries to assist in the implementation of economic and social development projects, and to meet the relief needs of victims of natural and other disasters. The Programme also administers the International Emergency Food Reserve (IEFR), established by the Assembly with a minimum target of 500,000 tonnes of cereals. In 2005 its operational expenditure was $3.1 billion. All contributions to the Programme are on a voluntary basis.

Evolution

By GA res. 50/227 (1995) the FAO and the WFP absorbed the functions of the World Food Council, which was discontinued.

Structure

The supervision of the Programme is vested in the Executive Board, which meets four times a year in Rome. The Executive Board became effective on 1 January 1996. It replaced the Committee on Food Aid Policies and Programmes (CFA), which was established in 1975 by General Assembly resolutions and the FAO Conference on the recommendation of the 1974 World Food Conference. The CFA had itself replaced the Inter-government Committee (IGC) of the World Food Programme. The membership of the WFP Executive Board has been reduced from 42 to 36. The Board:

- Provides a forum for inter-government consultations on national and international food aid programmes and policies
- Reviews general trends in food aid requirements and availability
- Formulates proposals for effective coordination of multilateral, bilateral and non-government food aid programmes, including emergency food aid
- Examines and approves projects and programmes submitted to it by the Executive Director
- Examines and approves the administrative and project budget of the Programme.

The Board reports to ECOSOC and the FAO Council on its yearly activities.

Membership

The members of the Executive Board for 2007 are:

Elected by the FAO Council

Elected by ECOSOC

Term of office expiring
31 Dec 2007

Canada	Australia
Congo	China
Germany	Cuba
Haiti	Ethiopia
Kuwait	Norway
Niger	Tunisia

Term of office expiring
31 Dec 2008

Austria	Indonesia
Colombia	Japan
Slovenia	Mexico
Sudan	Ukraine
Switzerland	UK
UR of Tanzania	Zimbabwe

Term of office expiring
31 Dec 2009

Netherlands	Cape Verde
Pakistan	India
Peru	Iran
Philippines	New Zealand
USA	Russian Federation
Zambia	Sweden

OTHER UN ENTITIES

Office of the United Nations High Commissioner for Human Rights (OHCHR)

Palais des Nations
1211 Geneva 10
Switzerland
Telephone: (+41 22) 917 9000
Fax: (+41 22) 917 9012
Email: InfoDesk@ohchr.org
Internet: www.ohchr.org
High Commissioner: Louise Arbour (July 2004–June 2008) (appointed by the UN Secretary-General)

Purpose

GA res. 48/141 (1993) established the post of High Commissioner for Human Rights to promote and protect the effective enjoyment by all people of all civil, cultural, economic, political and social rights, including the right to development. It further held that the High Commissioner should function as the UN official with principal responsibility for global human rights efforts. The High Commissioner acts under the direction and authority of the Secretary-General. GA res. 48/141 (1993) lists the activities that comprise the High Commissioner's mandate.

OHCHR represents the world's commitment to universal ideals of human rights and has been given a unique mandate by the international community to promote and protect all human rights.

GA res. 60/251 (2006) decided the new Human Rights Council would assume the role and responsibilities of the former Commission on Human Rights relating to the work of the OHCHR, as decided by the General Assembly in its res. 48/141 (1993).

The High Commissioner is appointed by the Secretary-General and approved by the General Assembly, with regard to geographical rotation. Appointments are for a fixed term of four years, with the possibility of one renewal for another fixed term of four years.

Joint United Nations Programme on HIV/AIDS (UNAIDS)

20 Avenue Appia
1211 Geneva 27
Switzerland
Telephone: (+41 22) 791 3666
Fax: (+41 22) 791 4187
Email: unaids@unaids.org
Internet: www.unaids.org
Executive Director: Dr Peter Piot, Belgium (since 1995) (appointed by the UN Secretary-General on the recommendation of the Committee of Co-sponsoring Organisations)

Purpose

UNAIDS leads, strengthens and supports an expanded response aimed at preventing the transmission of HIV. It works to provide care and support, reduce the vulnerability of individuals and communities to AIDS, and alleviate the impact of the epidemic.

The UNAIDS Secretariat supports a more effective global response to AIDS through:
- Leadership and advocacy for effective action on the epidemic
- Strategic information to guide the efforts of partners
- Tracking, monitoring and evaluating the epidemic and responses to it
- Civil society engagement and partnership development
- Mobilisation of resources.

Evolution

The need for a programme to take collective action against AIDS was outlined by a resolution of the World Health Assembly in 1993 and further endorsed by ECOSOC res. 1994/24.

The Joint UN Programme on HIV/AIDS (UNAIDS) began operations on 1 January 1996. Early that year a Memorandum of Understanding was signed by the six original co-sponsors of UNAIDS: the UN Children's Fund (UNICEF), the UN Development Programme (UNDP), the UN Population Fund (UNFPA), the UN Educational, Scientific and Cultural Organization (UNESCO), the World Health Organization (WHO) and the World Bank.

These agencies were joined in 1999 by the UN International Drug Control Programme (UNDCP) – now an integral part of the UN Office on Drugs and Crime (UNODC), in 2001 by the International Labour Organization (ILO), in 2003 by the World Food Programme (WFP) and in 2004 by the UN High Commissioner for Refugees (UNHCR).

Structure

UNAIDS has a secretariat headquartered in Geneva and offices in more than 60 countries.

The organisation is guided by a Programme Coordination Board (PCB), which serves as its governing body. This comprises 22 Member States elected by ECOSOC with a regional distribution (five African states, five Asian, two Eastern European, three Latin American and Caribbean, and seven Western European and Other), as well as the six co-sponsors and five NGOs, including associations of people living with HIV/AIDS.

The current PCB members are:

African states

DR Congo	Libyan AJ	Zambia
Kenya	Senegal	

Asian states

India	Myanmar	Thailand
Japan	Nepal	

Eastern European states

Russian Federation	Slovakia

Latin American and Caribbean states

Brazil	El Salvador	Grenada

Western European and Other states

Australia	Norway	Vacant
Belgium	Sweden	
Germany	USA	

NGOs for:

Africa: Rwanda Women's Network, Rwanda	Latin America/Caribbean: Rede Latinoamericana de Reducao de Danos (RELARD), Brazil	North America: Interagency Coalition on AIDS and Development, Canada
Asia/Pacific: Asia Pacific Network of People Living with HIV/AIDS (APN+), China		
Europe: You Act, Portugal		

Committee of Cosponsoring Organizations (CCO)

The CCO comprises representatives from the 10 UNAIDS co-sponsors and the UNAIDS Secretariat. It meets twice a year to consider matters concerning UNAIDS and to provide co-sponsor input into UNAIDS' policies and strategies. The UNAIDS Executive Director is Secretary of the CCO. From 1 July each co-sponsor rotates annually as Chair of the CCO (currently WFP, UNHCR as of 1 July 2007, to be followed by WHO). The PCB membership (six seats) also rotates among co-sponsors.

UN Office on Drugs and Crime (UNODC)

Vienna International Centre
PO Box 500
A–1400 Vienna
Austria
Telephone: (+43 1) 26 0600
Fax: (+43 1) 26 060 5866
Email: unodc@unodc.org
Internet: www.unodc.org
Under-Secretary-General and Executive Director: Antonio Maria Costa, Italy (since May 2002)
(appointed by the UN Secretary-General)

218

Purpose

UNODC's mandate is to support Member States in the prevention of illicit drugs, crime and terrorism. The three pillars of the Office's work programme are:

- Research and analytical work to increase knowledge and understanding of drugs and crime issues
- Assistance for states in ratifying and implementing relevant international treaties, developing domestic legislation on drugs, crime and terrorism, and providing secretariat and other services to the treaty-based and governing bodies
- Field-based technical cooperation projects to enhance the capacity of Member States to counteract illicit drugs, crime and terrorism.

UNODC is the secretariat of the Conference of the States Parties to the UN Convention against Transnational Organized Crime and its three supplementary Protocols on: Trafficking in Persons, especially Women and Children; Smuggling of Migrants; and Illicit Manufacturing of and Trafficking in Firearms.

UNODC is promoting the ratification and implementation of the UN Convention against Corruption. It acts as the secretariat of the Conference of the States Parties to the Convention, which held its inaugural session in December 2006. UNODC's Global Programme against Corruption assists countries to assess the problem and make public sector actions more transparent. It focuses on judiciaries and criminal justice systems, and helps establish national anti-corruption agencies and other watchdog bodies.

The UNODC Terrorism Prevention Branch provides, through its Global Programme against Terrorism, technical and legal assistance to Member States seeking to ratify and implement international legal instruments relating to the prevention and suppression of terrorism.

Evolution

The UN International Drug Control Programme (UNDCP), the predecessor of UNODC, was established under GA res. 45/179 (1990) as the body responsible for coordinated international action in the field of drug abuse control.

The authority for the Programme's fund was conferred on the Executive Director by GA res. 46/185C (1991).

The Crime Prevention and Criminal Justice Programme was established under GA res. 46/152 (1991). From 1992 it was implemented, under ECOSOC res. 1992/1, by the Commission on Crime Prevention and Criminal Justice (CCPCJ). On 15 March 2004 the Secretary-General (ST/SGB/2004/6) established the UN Office on Drugs and Crime (UNODC) to implement the two programmes in an integrated manner.

Prior to 1 October 2002, the Office was known as the Office for Drug Control and Crime Prevention.

Structure

UNODC has 21 country and regional field offices around the world. They represent the operational arm of the organisation. Field staff work directly with institutions, civil society organisations and local communities to develop and implement drug control and crime prevention programmes that are tailored to the needs of assisted countries. UNODC also maintains liaison offices in New York and Brussels.

UNODC country offices

Kabul, Afghanistan	Vientiane, Lao PDR	Lima, Peru
La Paz, Bolivia	Yangon, Myanmar	Ha Noi, Viet Nam
Bogota, Colombia	Abuja, Nigeria	
Tehran, Iran	Islamabad, Pakistan	

UNODC regional offices

Brazil and South Cone: Brasilia, Brazil	East Asia and the Pacific Office: Bangkok, Thailand	South Africa Office: Pretoria, South Africa
Caribbean Office: Bridgetown, Barbados	Mexico and Central America Office: Mexico City, Mexico	South Asia Office: New Delhi, India
Central Asia Office: Tashkent, Uzbekistan	North Africa and the Middle East Office: Cairo, Egypt	West and Central Africa Office: Dakar, Senegal
East Africa Office: Nairobi, Kenya	Russia and Belarus Office: Moscow, Russian Federation	

Liaison offices

Brussels, Belgium	New York, USA

UN Office for Project Services (UNOPS)

UNOPS
Midtermolen 3
PO Box 2695
DK–2100 Copenhagen
Denmark
Telephone: (+45) 3546 7500
Fax: (+45) 3546 7501
Email: hq@unops.org
Internet: www.unops.org
Executive Director: Gilberto Flores, Canada (since 2005) (appointed by the UN Secretary-General)

Purpose

UNOPS was established by GA res. 48/501 (1994) to provide management and operational services for projects and programmes undertaken by UN system organisations and Member States. It is self-financing.

The services of UNOPS include:
- Overall project management
- Loan administration and supervision on behalf of international financial institutions and global funds
- Operational management and administrative services for the implementation of projects or components of projects funded by or through other UN organisations or by national institutions
- Management services for multilateral, bilateral and beneficiary-financed projects
- Procurement services.

Structure

The UNDP/UNFPA Executive Board provides overall policy guidance and supervision for UNOPS. The Management Coordination Committee (MCC) provides operational guidance and management direction. The MCC is composed of the Administrator of UNDP (Chair), the Under-Secretary-General for Management and the Under-Secretary-General for

Economic and Social Affairs. It was expanded in 2002 following a decision by the Secretary-General to include the UN Controller and representatives of the International Fund for Agricultural Development, the UN Office of Legal Affairs and the UN Department of Peacekeeping Operations.

The Office is headed by an Executive Director who reports to the Secretary-General and the UNDP/UNFPA Executive Board through the MCC. The Executive Director represents UNOPS at meetings of the Executive Board. The Executive Board of the UNDP/UNFPA is the governing body for UNOPS. See page 194 for more information on the UNDP/UNFPA Executive Board.

Resources

UNOPS is funded by fees earned for services rendered, with no assessed or voluntary budget funding. The management fees are determined on a case-by-case basis and take into account level of effort, complexity and risk of the services delivered.

United Nations University (UNU)

53–70, Jingumae 5-chome
Shibuya-ku
Tokyo 150–8925
Japan
Telephone: (+81 3) 3499 2811
Fax: (+81 3) 3499 2828
Email: mbox@hq.unu.edu
Internet: http://www.unu.edu
Rector: Professor Hans J A van Ginkel, Netherlands (1997–2007) (appointed by the UN Secretary-General with the concurrence of the Director-General of UNESCO)

Purpose

UNU was established by GA res. 2951 (XXVII) (1972) as an autonomous organ of the General Assembly. The resolution provided that the University:
*   Be a system of academic institutions, rather than an inter-government organisation
*   Comprise a programming and coordinating central organ along with a decentralised system of affiliated institutions
*   Be integrated into the world university community and devoted to research into the problems of human survival, development and welfare, and to postgraduate training of young scholars and research workers (particularly those from developing countries)
*   Have a special mandate to alleviate the intellectual isolation of academics in developing countries by organising worldwide networks of collaborating scholars and research institutions
*   Be funded by voluntary contributions from governments, foundations, universities and individuals.

Under the UNU Charter, the University has five key roles. It functions as:
*   An international community of scholars
*   A bridge between the UN and the international academic community
*   A think-tank for the UN system
*   A contributor to capacity-building, particularly in developing countries
*   A platform for dialogue and new and creative ideas.

Structure

The University's academic activities are coordinated and carried out by the UNU Centre and 13 UNU Research and Training Centres and Programmes (RTC/Ps), as well as through a global network of several associated institutions and hundreds of cooperating institutions and scholars.

Membership

The UNU Council has 28 members. Twenty-four appointed members serve in their individual capacities for six-year terms. The UNU Rector is also a Council member, and there are three ex officio members: the UN Secretary-General, the Director-General of UNESCO and the Executive Director of the UN Institute for Training and Research (UNITAR). The appointed members of the UNU Council, with terms expiring at the end of the year indicated, are:

Rafaa Ben Achour, Tunisia (2007)

Sheikha Abdulla Al-Misnad, Qatar (2010)

Lidia R Arthur Brito, Mozambique (2010)

Jayantha Dhanapala, Sri Lanka (2010)

Gloria Cristina Florez, Peru (2010)

Eduardo Carrega Marçal Grilo, Portugal (2010)

Ahmad Jalali, Iran (2007)

Ji Fusheng, China (2010)

Peter H Katjavivi, Namibia (2007)

Marju Lauristin, Estonia (2010)

Andrei Marga, Romania (2010)

Dorothy L Njeuma, Cameroon (2007)

Otto S R Ongkosongo, Indonesia (2010)

Jocelyne Perard, France (2007)

José Raymundo Martins Romeo, Brazil (2007)

Akilagpa Sawyerr, Ghana (2010)

Dagmar Schipanski, Germany (2007)

Vappu Taipale, Finland (2007)

Terusuke Terada, Japan (2010)

Juan Vela Valdes, Cuba (2007)

Lyudmila A Verbitskaya, Russian Federation (2007)

Hebe Maria Cristina Vessuri, Venezuela (2010)

David Ward, USA (2010)

Alison Wolf, UK (2010)

RESEARCH AND TRAINING INSTITUTES

UN Institute for Disarmament Research (UNIDIR)

Palais des Nations
1211 Geneva 10
Switzerland
Telephone: (+41 22) 917 3186
Fax: (+41 22) 917 0176
Email: unidir@unog.ch
Internet: www.unidir.org
Director: Dr Patricia Lewis, UK (since 1997) (appointed by the UN Secretary-General in consultation with the Advisory Board on Disarmament Matters)

Purpose

UNIDIR is an autonomous body of the UN, established by the General Assembly to carry out independent research on disarmament and related international security issues.

The Institute was established in 1980 and its Statute was approved by the General Assembly in res. 39/148H (1984). The Statute stipulates that UNIDIR should aim to:

- Provide the international community with more diversified and complete data on problems relating to international security, the armaments race and disarmament in all fields, particularly nuclear, to facilitate progress through negotiations towards greater security for all states, and the economic and social development of all peoples
- Promote informed participation by all states in disarmament efforts

- Assist with negotiations on disarmament and continued efforts to ensure greater international security at a progressively lower level of armaments, particularly nuclear, by means of objective, factual studies and analyses
- Carry out more in-depth, forward-looking and long-term research on disarmament, to provide a general insight into the problems involved and stimulate initiatives for new negotiations.

UNIDIR's research programme addresses global security issues such as weapons of mass destruction, missile proliferation and defences, and treaty implementation. Human security issues are prominent in the Institute's work, particularly through its work on small arms, peacebuilding and disarmament as humanitarian action. UNIDIR also focuses on aspects of regional security and disarmament.

The Institute publishes books and the quarterly journal *Disarmament Forum* (also available online), holds research seminars and conferences, and cooperates with research institutes, universities and non-government organisations around the world. Its internship programme enables young researchers to work within the Institute and develop their capabilities.

UNIDIR is one of the three founding partners of the Geneva Forum, a process for information exchange and informal discussion among the diplomatic and research communities in Geneva.

The Institute is funded by voluntary contributions from UN Member States and foundations, and receives a small contribution from the UN budget.

The Director of UNIDIR reports annually to the General Assembly on the activities of the Institute. The UN Secretary-General's Advisory Board on Disarmament Matters functions as UNIDIR's Board of Trustees.

UN Institute for Training and Research (UNITAR)

Palais des Nations
1211 Geneva 10
Switzerland
Telephone: (+41 22) 917 8455
Fax: (+41 22) 917 8047
Internet: www.unitar.org
Executive Director: Carlos Lopes, Guinea-Bissau (since 2007) (appointed by the UN Secretary-General)

Purpose

In GA res. 1934 (XVIII) (1963), on the recommendation of ECOSOC, the General Assembly asked the Secretary-General to establish UNITAR and to explore possible sources of finance for it, both government and private.

The UNITAR Statute, promulgated by the Secretary-General in 1965 (annexed to the Executive Director's report in Document E/42000 of 5 May 1966), describes the Institute's purpose as being to assist the UN in achieving its major objectives, in particular the maintenance of international peace and security, and the promotion of economic and social development.

The Institute provides training, particularly to people from developing countries, for assignments with the UN or specialised agencies, and for assignments in their national services that are connected with the work of the UN. It also conducts research related to training.

UNITAR organises more than 200 training workshops a year, as well as distance and e-learning courses, benefiting close to 30,000 participants. It designs and carries out training in:

- International affairs management
- Climate change
- Chemicals and waste management
- Debt and financial management
- Environmental law
- Peacemaking and preventive diplomacy
- Decentralised cooperation
- UNOSAT satellite imagery (a UN programme created to provide enhanced access to satellite imagery and Geographic Information System services, used mainly in humanitarian relief, disaster prevention and post crisis reconstruction).

The training and capacity-building programmes are intended for diplomats and personnel from Member States, as well as staff from local governments.

Evolution

The Institute began operating in 1966. By GA res. 47/227 (1993) the General Assembly adopted a number of restructuring measures, including shifting the Institute's headquarters from New York to Geneva, and, from 1 January 1994, that all expenditures should be covered from voluntary contributions, donations and special purpose grants. The resolution also provided for the designation of a liaison officer to organise and coordinate training programmes in New York. In 2002, an office in Hiroshima was opened for Asia and the Pacific.

GA res. 47/227 (1993) reaffirms that the Institute should focus on providing training programmes and research activities related to training.

Membership

The Board of Trustees is responsible for the basic policies of the Institute, and for reviewing and adopting the annual budget proposals submitted by the Executive Director. It consists of up to 30 members appointed in their personal capacity by the UN Secretary-General. At present the Board is made up of 20 trustees. They come from:

Brazil	Ghana	Russian Federation
Burkina Faso	Japan	South Africa
China	Kuwait	Switzerland
Arab Republic of Egypt	Mexico	Thailand
Estonia	Morocco	USA (2)
France (3)	Nigeria	

Ex officio members are the UN Secretary-General, the President of the UN General Assembly, the President of ECOSOC and the Executive Director of UNITAR.

UN International Research and Training Institute for the Advancement of Women (INSTRAW)

PO Box 21747
Santo Domingo
Dominican Republic
Telephone: (+1809) 685 2111
Fax: (+1809) 685 2117
Email: instraw@un-instraw.org
Internet: www.un-instraw.org
Director: Carmen Moreno, Mexico (since 2003) (appointed by the UN Secretary-General after consultation with the Executive Board)

Purpose

INSTRAW was established by ECOSOC res. 1998 (LX) (1976) following a recommendation made by the World Conference on the International Women's Year in Mexico in 1975. ECOSOC's decision was endorsed in GA res. 31/135 (1976).

The Institute is an autonomous body of the UN, funded by voluntary contributions. It is the only UN Institute working at an international level to promote and undertake research and training programmes contributing to the advancement of women and gender equality worldwide. It works in partnership with governments, the UN system, civil society and academia.

The Institute's headquarters has been in the Dominican Republic since 1983.

Structure

The Institute Statute, adopted by its Board of Trustees at its fourth session, was endorsed in GA res. 39/249 (1985).

In 2003 ECOSOC res. 2003/57 amended article III of the Institute's Statute to replace its Board of Trustees with an Executive Board. The Board comprises 10 members, with two elected by the Council from each regional group, serving in their national capacities for three-year terms. The Director of the Institute, the Under-Secretary-General of the Department of Economic and Social Affairs, a representative of each of the Regional Commissions of the Economic and Social Council and a representative of the host country serve as ex officio members of the Board.

The Board, which meets at least once a year at UN Headquarters in New York, formulates the principles, policies and guidelines for the Institute's activities, considers its work programme and budget proposals, and reports to ECOSOC and, where appropriate, to the General Assembly.

Membership

Current Board members and their terms are:

African states

Egypt	2006–09
Zimbabwe	2006–09

Asian states

Syria (Vice-President)	2006–09
Philippines (Vice-President/Rapporteur)	2003–09

Eastern European states

Belarus	2007–09
Slovakia	2007–09

Latin American and Caribbean states

Grenada	2006–09
Honduras (President)	2006–09

Western European and Other states (plus Japan)

Israel	2006–09
Spain	2003–09

UN Interregional Crime and Justice Research Institute (UNICRI)

Viale Maestri del Lavoro 10
10127 Turin
Italy
Telephone: (+39 011) 653 7111
Fax: (+39 011) 631 3368
Email: information@unicri.it
Internet: www.unicri.it
Officer in Charge: Doris Buddenberg, Germany (since February 2007)

Purpose

UNICRI was established as the UN Social Defence Research Institute (UNSDRI) in 1968. Its task was to undertake and promote action-oriented research aimed at preventing crime and treating offenders.

The Institute's area of competence was expanded to include technical cooperation and training on the basis of a recommendation of the Committee on Crime Prevention and Criminal Justice, and through the adoption of a new Statute established by ECOSOC res. 1989/56.

UNICRI aims to formulate and implement improved policies in crime prevention and criminal justice. It does this through research, training, field activities and collecting, exchanging and disseminating information.

The Institute's specific goals are to:
*   Advance understanding of crime-related problems
*   Foster just and efficient criminal justice systems
*   Support respect for international instruments and other standards
*   Facilitate international law enforcement cooperation and judicial assistance.

UNICRI's principal areas of focus are:
*   Organised crime, in particular trafficking in persons
*   Security governance/counter-terrorism
*   Criminal justice reform, with a special focus on juvenile justice
*   Corruption
*   Exchange and dissemination of documentation and information.

UNICRI conducts training courses for judges, prosecutors and law enforcement officials.

The Institute and the University of Turin Faculty of Law jointly offer a Master of Laws (LLM) in international organisations, international criminal law and crime prevention.

Structure

UNICRI is governed by a Board of Trustees with 11 members. Seven are selected by the Commission on Crime Prevention and Criminal Justice on the principle of equitable geographical distribution. They are nominated by the Secretary-General and endorsed by ECOSOC. Representatives of the host country, the Secretary-General, the Administrator of UNDP and the Director of the Institute serve as ex officio members of the Board.

Current Board members, other than ex officio members, and the date of membership expiry are:

Ann-Marie Begler, Sweden (2009)

Pedro David, Argentina (2008)

Iskandar Ghattas, Egypt (2007)

Željko Horvatic, Croatia (2007)

Michèle Ramis-Plum, France (2011)

Takayuki Shiibashi, Japan (2008)

Elizabeth Verville, USA (2009)

UN Research Institute for Social Development (UNRISD)

Palais des Nations
1211 Geneva 10
Switzerland
Telephone: (+41 22) 917 3020
Fax: (+41 22) 917 0650
Email: info@unrisd.org
Internet: www.unrisd.org
Director: Thandika Mkandawire, Sweden (since 1998) (appointed by the UN Secretary-General)

Purpose

UNRISD is an autonomous body of the UN established in 1963 by a decision of the Secretary-General (ST/SGB/126). It was created to:

- Conduct research into problems and policies of social development during different phases of economic growth
- Carry out studies that are urgent and important to the work of the UN Secretariat in the field of social policy, social development planning and balanced economic and social development, and to regional and national institutes in the fields of economic and social development.

UNRISD works through an extensive global network of researchers and institutes to promote original enquiry, strengthen research capacity in developing countries and carry out multi-disciplinary research on development challenges in six broad areas:

- Social policy and development
- Democracy, governance and well-being
- Markets, business and regulation
- Civil society and social movements
- Identities, conflict and cohesion
- Gender and development.

Through its research, events and publications, UNRISD provides government agencies, inter-government organisations, non-government organisations and scholars with a better understanding of how development policies and processes affect different social groups. It works to stimulate dialogue and contributes to policy debates within and outside the UN system.

Structure

As an autonomous body of the UN, UNRISD is not associated with any particular specialised agency. It is funded entirely by voluntary contributions. Its work is coordinated with specialised agencies, and is supervised by a Board. This is composed of a Chair, appointed by the Secretary-General, eight ex officio members and 10 members (one post currently vacant) nominated by the Commission for Social Development and confirmed by ECOSOC.

Membership

Board membership is for four years, with the possibility of extension for a further two years. Current members are:

Lourdes Arizpe, Mexico (Chair)	Rosalind Eyben, UK	Pasuk Phongpaichit, Thailand
Christian Comeliau, Belgium/France	Asma Jahangir, Pakistan	Anna Sundén, Sweden
Yakin Ertürk, Turkey	Elizabeth Jelin, Argentina	Zenebeworke Tadesse, Ethiopia
Peter Evans, USA	Marina Pavlova-Silvanskaya, Russian Federation	

Ex officio members

A representative of the Secretary-General

Director, Latin American and Caribbean Institute for Economic and Social Planning

Director, African Institute for Economic Development and Planning

Director, Asian and Pacific Development Centre

Executive Secretary, ESCWA

Representatives of two of the following agencies appointed in rotation: FAO, ILO, UNESCO, WHO

Director of the Institute

TREATY AND RELATED BODIES

HUMAN RIGHTS AND TREATY BODIES

Committee Against Torture (CAT)

Office of the High Commissioner for Human Rights
United Nations Office at Geneva
1211 Geneva 10
Switzerland
Telephone: (+41 22) 917 9000
Fax: (+41 22) 917 9022
Email: InfoDesk@ohchr.org
Internet: www.ohchr.org/english/bodies/cat
Chair: Andreas Maurommatis, Cyprus (until 31 December 2007)

Purpose

CAT is the body of independent experts that monitors implementation of the Convention Against Torture and Other Cruel, Inhuman or Degrading Treatment or Punishment by its States Parties. The Convention was adopted by GA res. 39/46 (1984) and entered into force on 26 June 1987. As at 6 December 2006 the Convention had been ratified or acceded to by 144 states.

The Committee may make general comments on the regular reports of States Parties and inform the other States Parties and the General Assembly in this regard.

Under article 20, if the Committee receives reliable information indicating that torture is being systematically practised in the territory of a State Party, it may decide to make an enquiry – including, with that state's agreement, a visit to the state concerned. Under article 21 a State Party may declare that it recognises the Committee's competence to receive and consider communications from a State Party claiming that another State Party is not fulfilling its obligations under the Convention.

Under article 22 a State Party may declare that it recognises the Committee's competence to receive and consider communications from, or on behalf of, individuals subject to its jurisdiction who claim to be victims of a violation of the provisions of the Convention by a State Party. The provisions of articles 21 and 22 entered into force in 1987 for those states that had made the requisite declarations.

Evolution

At its 57th session (2002) the General Assembly adopted an Optional Protocol to the Convention Against Torture that provides for regular visits by independent international and national bodies to places of detention in order to prevent torture. The Optional Protocol entered into force on 22 June 2006. As at 19 April 2007 it had 57 signatories and 34 States Parties.

Meetings

The Committee normally meets twice a year, in Geneva. It held its 38th session from 30 April to 18 May 2007. The 39th session is scheduled to be held from 5 to 23 November 2007.

Membership

Article 17 provides for the establishment of CAT consisting of 10 experts of high moral standing and recognised competence in the field of human rights, serving in their personal capacity. The experts are elected by States Parties to the Convention. Consideration is given to equitable geographical distribution and the legal experience of candidates.

Members of the Committee, who serve for four years, are:

Term expiring 31 Dec 2007	Term expiring 31 Dec 2009
Guibril Camara, Senegal	Essadia Belmir, Morocco
Luis Gallegos Chiriboga, Ecuador	Alexander Kovalev, Russian Federation
Felice Gaer, USA	Fernando Marino Menendez, Spain
Claudio Grossman, Chile	Nora Sveaass, Norway
Andreas Mavrommatis, Cyprus, Chair	Wang Xuexian, China

Committee on the Elimination of Discrimination against Women (CEDAW)

Division for the Advancement of Women
Department of Economic and Social Affairs
United Nations Headquarters
New York, NY 10017
United States of America
Telephone: (+1 212) 963 3153
Fax: (+1 212) 963 3463
Email: daw@un.org
Internet: www.un.org/womenwatch/daw/cedaw
Chair: Dubravka Simonvic, Croatia

Purpose

The Convention on the Elimination of All Forms of Discrimination against Women was adopted by GA res. 34/180 (1979) and entered into force on 3 September 1981. It is often described as an international bill of rights for women. The Convention defines discrimination against women and outlines a comprehensive range of measures to end it.

On 31 May 2007 there were 185 States Parties to the Convention. In 2006 Brunei Darussalam, Cook Islands, Marshall Islands and Oman acceded to the Convention, and Montenegro succeeded to it. Countries are legally bound to put the Convention's provisions into practice if they have ratified, acceded or succeeded to it. They are also committed to submit national reports, at least every four years, on measures they have taken to comply with their treaty obligations.

The Committee on the Elimination of Discrimination against Women (CEDAW) reports annually to the General Assembly through ECOSOC and is charged with considering progress made in implementing the Convention, including through reports submitted by States Parties. In 2006–07 CEDAW was meeting three times a year to consider the large number of outstanding State Party reports. It held its 38th session from 14 May to 1 June 2007.

An Optional Protocol to the Convention was adopted by GA res. A/54/4 (1999). The protocol contains two procedures:

- A communication procedure allows individual women, or groups of women, to submit claims of violations of rights protected under the Convention to CEDAW
- An inquiry procedure enables CEDAW to initiate inquiries into grave or systematic violations of the rights of women.

On 21 May 2007 there were 86 States Parties to the Optional Protocol.

Structure

Article 17 provides that CEDAW consist of 23 experts of high moral standing and competence in the fields covered by the Convention. Experts are elected to the Committee by States Parties to the Convention from among their nationals, and serve in their personal capacity. Consideration is given to equitable geographical distribution and the representation of different cultures, as well as of the principal legal systems.

Membership

Members of the Committee, who serve for four years, are:

Term ending 31 Dec 2008	Term ending 31 Dec 2010*
Magalys Arocha Dominguez, Cuba	Ferdous Ara Begum, Bangladesh
Mary Shanthi Dairiam, Malaysia (Rapporteur)	Meriem Belmihoub-Zerdani, Algeria
Françoise Gaspard, France (Vice-Chair)	Saisuree Chutikul, Thailand
Tiziana Maiolo, Italy	Dorcas Ama Frema Coker-Appiah, Ghana
Silvia Pimentel, Brazil	Cornelius Flinterman, Netherlands
Hanna Beate Schöpp-Schilling, Germany	Naela Gabr Mohamed Gabre Ali, Egypt (Vice-Chair)
Heisoo Shin, ROK	Ruth Halperin-Kaddari, Israel
Glenda Simms, Jamaica	Violeta Neubauer, Slovenia
Anamah Tan, Singapore	Pramila Patten, Mauritius
Maria Regina Tavares da Silva, Portugal	Fumiko Saiga, Japan
Zou Xiaoqiao, China	Dubravka Simonovic, Croatia (Chair)

Note

* These members took up their positions on 1 January 2007.
  Hazel Gumede Shelton, South Africa, resigned from the Committee effective May 2007. At 31 May 2007 a new expert remained to be determined in accordance with article 17.7 of the Convention.

Committee on Economic, Social and Cultural Rights (CESCR)

Office of the High Commissioner for Human Rights
United Nations Office at Geneva
1211 Geneva 10
Switzerland
Telephone: (+41 22) 917 9000
Fax: (+41 22) 917 9022
Email: InfoDesk@ohchr.org
Internet: www.ohchr.org/english/bodies/cescr

Purpose

CESCR is the body of independent experts that monitors implementation of the International Covenant on Economic, Social and Cultural Rights by its States Parties. The Covenant was adopted by GA res. 2200 A (1966) and entered into force on 3 January 1976. As at 19 April 2007 there were 156 States Parties to the Covenant.

Evolution

ECOSOC res. 1985/17 renamed the Working Group the Committee on Economic, Social and Cultural Rights (CESCR). It comprises 18 experts of recognised competence in human rights, serving in their personal capacities.

All States Parties are obliged to submit regular reports to the Committee on how the Covenant is being implemented. States must report initially within two years of accepting the Covenant, and every five years after that. The Committee examines each report and addresses its concerns and recommendations to the State Party in the form of 'concluding observations'.

While other core international human rights instruments have treaty bodies to examine States Parties' reports, the Covenant obliges States Parties to report to ECOSOC on its implementation. ECOSOC res. 1988 (LX) (1976) laid down the procedures for this. ECOSOC decision 1978/10 established the Sessional Working Group on the Implementation of the International Covenant on Economic, Social and Cultural Rights to assist in the consideration of reports submitted by States Parties.

The Committee's reports to ECOSOC include observations on each State Party's report, with a view to helping the Council fulfil its responsibilities under articles 21 and 22 of the Covenant.

Meetings

CESCR normally meets twice a year in Geneva. Its 38th session was held from 30 April to 18 May 2007 and its 39th session is scheduled for November 2007.

Membership

Consideration is given to equitable geographical distribution of membership and to the representation of different social and legal systems. Fifteen seats are distributed equally among the regional groups, while the other three are allocated in accordance with the increase in the total number of States Parties per regional group. Members of the Committee are elected by ECOSOC by secret ballot from a list of people nominated by States Parties to the Covenant.

Members of the Committee, who serve for four years, are:

Term ending 31 Dec 2008	Term ending 31 Dec 2010
Mohamed Ezzeldin Abdel-Moneim, Egypt	Clement Atangana, Cameroon
Rocío Barahona Riera, Costa Rica (Vice-Chair)	Maria Virginia Bras Gómes, Portugal
Ariranga Govindasamy Pillay, Mauritius	Virginia Bonoan-Dandan, Philippines (Chair)
Sergei Martynov, Belarus	Chandrashekhar Dasgupta, India
Andrzej Rzeplinski, Poland	Azzouz Kerdoun, Algeria (Vice-Chair)
Walid Sa'di, Jordan	Yuri Kolosov, Russian Federation (Rapporteur)
Philippe Texier, France	Jaime Marchan Romero, Ecuador
Barbara Elaine Wilson, Switzerland	Eibe Riedel, Germany
Daode Zhan, China	Alvaro Tirado Mejia, Colombia

Committee on the Elimination of Racial Discrimination (CERD)

Office of the High Commissioner for Human Rights
United Nations Office at Geneva
1211 Geneva 10
Switzerland
Telephone: (+41 22) 917 9309
Fax: (+41 22) 917 9022
Email: nprouvez@ohchr.org
Internet: www.ohchr.org/english/bodies/cerd
Chair: Regis de Gouttes, France

Purpose

CERD is the body of independent experts that monitors implementation of the International Convention on the Elimination of All Forms of Racial Discrimination by its States Parties. The Convention was adopted by GA res. 2106A (1965) and entered into force on 4 January 1969. As at 18 July 2007 there were 173 States Parties to the Convention.

Under article 14 a State Party may declare that it recognises the competence of the Committee to consider communications from individuals or groups of individuals within its jurisdiction who claim to be victims of a violation by that State Party of any of the rights set forth in the Convention. As at 24 April 2007, 51 States Parties had made a declaration under article 14.

The Committee reports annually to the General Assembly and may make suggestions and recommendations based on its examination of the reports and information provided by States Parties.

Evolution

GA res. 47/111 (1992) made an amendment to the Convention's fund provisions so that it would enter into force when it had been accepted by two-thirds of the States Parties.

Meetings

The Committee normally meets twice a year. The 70th session took place in Geneva from 19 February to 9 March 2007. The 71st session was scheduled to take place in Geneva from 30 July to 18 August 2007.

Membership

Article 8 established CERD, consisting of 18 experts of high moral standing and acknowledged impartiality elected by States Parties from amongst their nationals. Members serve in their personal capacity. Consideration is given to equitable geographical distribution and the representation of different cultures, as well as of the principal legal systems.

Members of the Committee, who serve for four years, are:

Term ending 19 Jan 2008	Term ending 19 Jan 2010
Alexei Avtonomov, Russian Federation	Mahmoud Aboul-Nasr, Egypt
Jose Francisco Cali Tzay, Guatemala	Nourredine Amir, Algeria
Fatimata Binta Victoire Dah, Burkina Faso (Vice-Chair)	Regis de Gouttes, France (Chair)
	Kokou Mawuena Ika Kana Ewomsan, Togo
Patricia Nozipho January-Bardill, South Africa	Anwar Kemal, Pakistan
Raghavan Pillai, India (Vice-Chair)	Morten Kjaerum, Denmark
Pierre-Richard Prosper, USA	Jose A Lindgren Alves, Brazil
Chengyuan Tang, China	Linos Alexander Sicilianos, Greece
Luis Valencia Rodriguez, Ecuador	Patrick Thornberry, UK (Rapporteur)
Mario J Yutzis, Argentina (Vice-Chair)	

Committee on the Protection of the Rights of All Migrant Workers and Members of Their Families (CMW)

Office of the UN High Commissioner for Human Rights
1211 Geneva 10
Switzerland
Telephone: (+41 22) 917 9241
Fax: (+41 22) 917 9022
Email: cedelenbos@ohchr.org
Internet: www.ohchr.org/english/bodies/cmw
Chair: Prasad Kariyawasam, Sri Lanka

Purpose

CMW is the body of independent experts that monitors implementation of the International Convention on the Protection of the Rights of All Migrant Workers and Members of Their Families. The Convention was adopted by GA res. 45/158 on 18 December 1990 and entered into force on 1 July 2003. As at 7 June 2007 there were 37 States Parties to the Convention.

Under article 73 the Committee is charged with examining the reports submitted by each State Party on the measures it has adopted to give effect to the rights recognised in the Convention. Reports indicate factors and difficulties, if any, affecting implementation of the Convention and include information on migration flows involving the State Party concerned. The first report is to be submitted within one year after the entry into force of the Convention for the State Party concerned and subsequently every five years.

Under article 77 a State Party may declare that it recognises the competence of the Committee to receive and consider communications from or on behalf of individuals subject to its jurisdiction who claim that their rights under the Convention have been violated by that State Party. As at 31 March 2006 no State Party had made this declaration.

Structure

The Committee normally meets once a year in Geneva for three weeks, although it may decide to have two shorter sessions each year instead. It held its first session in 2004. Its sixth session took place in April 2007.

Membership

Article 72 provides for the establishment of CMW, consisting of 10 experts of high moral standing, impartiality and recognised competence in the field covered by the Convention. CMW membership will increase to 14 when there are 41 States Parties to the Convention. Members are elected by secret ballot by States Parties from among their nationals and serve in their personal capacity. Consideration is given to equitable geographical distribution, as well as to the principal legal systems. Members are elected for four-year terms, but the terms of five of the members elected in the first election expire at the end of two years.

Members of the Committee are:

Term ending 31 Dec 2007	Term ending 31 Dec 2009
Francisco Alba, Mexico	Ana María Dieguez Arévalo, Guatemala
Francisco Carríon-Mena, Ecuador	José Serrano Brillantes, Philippines
Ana Elizabeth Cubias Medina, El Salvador	Prasad Kariyawasam, Sri Lanka (Chair)
Ahmed Hassan El-Borai, Egypt	Mehmet Sevim, Turkey
Abdelhamid El Jamri, Morocco	Asad Taghizadet, Azerbaijan

OTHER BODIES

Committee on the Rights of the Child (CRC)

Office of the UN High Commissioner for Human Rights
1211 Geneva 10
Switzerland
Telephone: (+41 22) 917 9000
Fax: (+41 22) 917 9022
Email: InfoDesk@ohchr.org
Internet: www.ohchr.org/english/bodies/crc
Chair: Yanghee Lee, ROK

Purpose

CRC is the body of independent experts that monitors implementation of the Convention on the Rights of the Child. The Convention was adopted by GA res. 44/25 on 20 November 1989 and entered into force on 2 September 1990. It also monitors implementation of two optional protocols to the Convention on the involvement of children in armed conflict and on the sale of children, child prostitution and child pornography.

The Committee is charged with examining progress made by States Parties towards achieving the obligations undertaken in the Convention. States Parties are required to submit reports on the measures they have adopted that give effect to the rights recognised in the Convention and on the progress made on the enjoyment of those rights. The first report is to be submitted within two years of the entry into force of the Convention for the State Party concerned. Subsequent reports are to be submitted every five years.

Evolution

The Optional Protocol to the Convention on the involvement of children in armed conflict and the Optional Protocol to the Convention on the sale of children, child prostitution and child pornography were adopted by GA res. 54/263 (2000) and opened for signature and ratification or accession in New York on 5 June 2000. They entered into force on 12 February and 18 January 2002 respectively. As at 24 April 2007 there were 193 parties to the Convention, 121 parties to the Optional Protocol on the Sale of Children, and 117 parties to the Optional Protocol on Children in Armed Conflict.

Meetings

The Committee normally meets three times a year in Geneva. It held its 44th session from 15 January to 2 February 2007. Its 45th session took place from 21 May to 8 June 2007.

Membership

Article 43 provides for the establishment of a Committee on the Rights of the Child (CRC), consisting of 10 experts of high moral standing and recognised competence in the field covered by the Convention. The members of the Committee are elected by States Parties from among their nationals and serve in their personal capacity. Consideration is given to equitable geographical distribution, as well as to representation of the principal legal systems. An amendment to article 43.2 to increase the membership of the Committee from 10 to 18 experts was adopted by the Conference of the States Parties on 12 December 1995. GA res. 50/55 (1995) approved this amendment, which entered into force on 19 November 2002.

Members of the Committee, who serve for four years, are:

Term ending Feb 2009	Term ending Feb 2011
Ghalia Mohd. Bin Hamad Al-Thani, Qatar	Agnes Akosua Aidoo, Ghana
Joyce Aluoch, Kenya	Luigi Citarella, Italy
Yanghee Lee, ROK (Chair)	Kamel Filali, Algeria
David Brent Parfitt, Canada	Maria Herczog, Hungary
Awich Pollar, Uganda	Moushira Khattab, Egypt
Kamal Siddiqui, Bangladesh	Hatem Kotrane, Tunisia
Lucy Smith, Norway	Lothar Friedrich Krappmann, Germany
Nevena Vuckovic-Sahovic, Serbia	Rosa María Ortiz, Paraguay
Jean Zermatten, Switzerland	Dainius Puras, Lithuania

Human Rights Committee (HRC)

Office of the UN High Commissioner for Human Rights
1211 Geneva 10
Switzerland
Telephone: (+41 22) 917 9332
Fax: (+41 22) 917 9022
Email: InfoDesk@ohchr.org
Internet: www.ohchr.org/english/bodies/hrc
Chair: Rafael Rivas Posada, Columbia

Purpose

HRC is the body of independent experts that monitors implementation of the International Covenant on Civil and Political Rights by its States Parties. The Convention was adopted by GA res. 2200 A (1966) and came into force on 23 March 1976. As at 19 April 2007, 160 states had ratified or acceded to the Covenant.

The Committee is mandated to consider reports from States Parties on measures adopted and progress made in achieving the observance of the rights enshrined in the Covenant. In addition, under the (First) Optional Protocol to the Covenant, which also came into force on 23 March 1976, 109 states have recognised the competence of the Committee to consider communications from individuals regarding alleged violations of their rights under the Covenant. The Second Optional Protocol, aimed at the abolition of the death penalty, entered into force on 11 July 1991 and at 23 March 2007 had 60 States Parties.

Meetings

The Committee normally meets three times a year. Usually there are two sessions in Geneva and one in New York. Its 89th session was held in New York from 12 to 30 March 2007. Its 90th session was scheduled to be held in Geneva from 9 to 27 July 2007.

Membership

The first meeting of States Parties, in accordance with the provisions of articles 28 to 32 of the Covenant, elected an 18-member Committee. This comprises nationals of States Parties to the Covenant who are of high moral character and recognised competence in human rights. Given the legal nature of the Committee's work, most of its members are lawyers, judges or professors of law. Committee members are elected by States Parties and serve in their personal capacity.

Members of the Committee, who serve for four years, are:

Term ending 2008	Term ending 2010
Maurice Glele Ahanhanzo, Benin (Vice-Chair)	Abdelfattah Amor, Tunisia (Rapporteur)
Rajsoomer Lallah, Mauritius	Prafullachandra Natwarlal Bhagwati, India
Edwin Johnson Lopez, Ecuador	Christine Chanet, France (Chair)
Ahmed Tawfik Khalil, Egypt (Vice-Chair)	Yuji Iwasawa, Japan
Michael O'Flaherty, Ireland	Walter Kälin, Switzerland
Elisabeth Palm, Sweden (Vice-Chair)	Zonke Zanele Majodina, South Africa
Rafael Rivas Posada, Colombia (Chair)	Iulia Antoanelle Motoc, Romania
Nigel Rodley, UK	Nigel Rodley, UK
Ivan Shearer, Australia (Vice-Chair)	José Luis Sanchez-Cerro, Peru
	Ruth Wedgwood, USA

LAW OF THE SEA TREATY BODIES

Commission on the Limits of the Continental Shelf

Division for Ocean Affairs and the Law of the Sea
Office of Legal Affairs
United Nations
2 United Nations Plaza, DC2–0438
New York, NY 10017
United States of America
Telephone: (+1 212) 963 3194
Fax: (+1 212) 963 5847
Email: doalos@un.org
Internet: www.un.org/depts/los/clcs_new/clcs_home.htm

Purpose

The Commission on the Limits of the Continental Shelf was established in accordance with Part VI and Annex II of the UN Convention on the Law of the Sea (UNCLOS) of 10 December 1982.

The Commission's functions are to:
- Consider data and other material submitted by coastal states concerning the outer limits of the continental shelf in areas where those limits extend beyond 200 nautical miles
- Make recommendations to coastal states on matters related to the establishment of the outer limits of their continental shelf, in accordance with article 76 and the Statement of Understanding adopted on 29 August 1980 by the Third United Nations Conference on the Law of the Sea
- Provide scientific and technical advice if requested by the coastal state during its preparation of data.

Meetings

The Commission's eighteenth session was held from 21 August to 15 September 2006, during which time sub-commissions established to consider submissions by Brazil, Australia and Ireland continued to meet. The Commission also began considering a submission made by New Zealand and a joint submission by France, Ireland, Spain and the UK, through sub-commissions established for this purpose.

The nineteenth session was held from 5 March to 13 April 2007. At this session the Commission began considering the submission made by Norway, through a sub-commission established for this purpose. The Commission also adopted the recommendations concerning the submissions made by Brazil and Ireland respectively. The twentieth session of the Commission was scheduled to be held from 27 August to 14 September 2007.

Membership

The Commission comprises 21 members who are experts in the field of geology, geophysics or hydrography. They are elected by States Parties to UNCLOS but serve in their personal capacities. There must be no fewer than three members from each geographical group. Members are elected for terms of five years and may be re-elected.

The current members of the Commission, elected by the seventeenth meeting of States Parties on 14 June 2007, are:

Alexandre Tagore Medeiros de Albuquerque, Brazil

Osvaldo Pedro Astiz, Argentina

Lawrence Folajimi Awosika, Nigeria

Harald Brekke, Norway

Galo Carrera Hurtado, Mexico

Francis L Charles, Trinidad and Tobago

Peter F Croker, Ireland

Indurlall Fagoonee, Mauritius

Mihai Silviu German, Romania

Abu Bakar Jaafar, Malaysia

George Jaoshvili, Georgia

Emmanuel Kalngui, Cameroon

Yuri Borisovitch Kazmin, Russian Federation

Wenzheng Lu, China

Isaac Owusu Oduro, Ghana

Yong-Ahn Park, ROK

Fernando Manuel Maia Pimentel, Portugal

Sivaramakrishnan Rajan, India

Michael Anselme Marc Rosette, Seychelles

Philip Alexander Symonds, Australia

Kensaku Tamaki, Japan

The election of the new officers, including the Commission Chair, will take place at the twentieth session of the Commission.

International Seabed Authority (ISA)

14–20 Port Royal Street
Kingston
Jamaica
Telephone: (+1876) 922 9105
Fax: (+1876) 922 0195
Email: postmaster@isa.org.jm
Internet: www.isa.org.jm
Secretary-General: Satya N Nandan, Fiji (1996–2008) (elected by the Assembly of the International Seabed Authority)

Purpose

The ISA is an autonomous international organisation that organises and controls activities in 'the Area' – the seabed and ocean floor beyond the limits of national jurisdiction. It was established under Part XI of the UN Convention on the Law of the Sea (UNCLOS) of 10 December 1982 and the Agreement relating to the Implementation of Part XI adopted by GA res. 48/263 (1994).

Structure

The principal organs of the Authority are the Assembly, the Council and the Secretariat. The Authority has 153 members, including all States Parties to the Convention.

The Council comprises 36 Member States, selected in accordance with five categories, ensuring representation of:
- Countries with the greatest global consumption

- Those that have made significant investment in seabed activities
- Those that produce and export minerals sourced from the seabed
- Those with special interests
- Others, with due regard to equitable geographical distribution.

Meetings

The thirteenth session of the International Seabed Authority was held from 9 to 20 July 2007 in Kingston, Jamaica.

Members

Elections for the Council were held on 16 August 2006 to replace half of the members of each group. The terms of office of the new Council members, who were elected for a term of four years, began on 1 January 2007.

The composition of the Council[1] for 2007 is as follows. Members whose terms expire in 2008 are noted in parentheses.

Group A (4)[2]

China (2008)	Japan (2008)	Russian Federation
Italy[1]		

Group B (4)

France	India (2008)	UK (2008)
Germany		

Group C (4)

Canada[3]	Portugal (2008)	South Africa (2008)
Indonesia		

Group D (6)

Brazil (2008)	Fiji	Malaysia (2008)
Egypt	Jamaica	Sudan

Group E (18)

Argentina (2008)	Honduras[4]	Poland (2008)
Cameroon	Kenya (2008)	Qatar
Côte d'Ivoire	Mexico	ROK
Czech Republic (2008)	Namibia (2008)	Senegal (2008)
Gabon (2008)	Netherlands (2008)	Spain (2008)
Guyana (2008)	Nigeria	Viet Nam

Notes

[1] The agreed allocation of seats on the Council is 10 seats to the African Group, nine seats to the Asian Group, eight seats to the Western European and Others Group, seven seats to the Latin American and Caribbean Group and three seats to the Eastern European Group. Since the total number of seats allocated according to that formula is 37, it is understood that for the period 2005–08 each regional group other than the Eastern European Group will relinquish a seat in rotation as follows:

a. In 2005 Trinidad and Tobago will relinquish its seat in Group E on behalf of the Group of Latin American and Caribbean states, which will occupy six seats in that year

b.   In 2006 Canada will relinquish its seat on behalf of the Group of Western European and Other states, which will occupy seven seats in that year

c.   In 2007 Senegal will relinquish its seat on behalf of the African Group, which will occupy nine seats in that year

d.   In 2008, the Asian Group will occupy eight seats. The Asian Group will nominate the member that will relinquish a seat in 2008.

2   The arrangements for Groups A and B are without prejudice to future elections for the two groups and any interim arrangements for the substitutions in those groups.

3   Canada will relinquish its seat in Group C to Australia from 1 January 2009 for two years.

4   Honduras will relinquish its seat in Group E to Chile from 1 January 2009 for two years.

The 15 members of the Finance Committee, elected by the Assembly in 2006 for a five-year term commencing on 1 January 2007 are:

Neeru Chadha, India

Hasjim Djalal, Indonesia

Trecia Elliot, Jamaica

Domenico Da Empoli, Italy

Juliet Semambo Kalema, Uganda

Pavel Kavina, Czech Republic

Jean-Pierre Lévy, France

Jian Liu, China

Olav Myklebust, Norway

Denis Fontes De Souza Pinto, Brazil

Oleg Alekseevich Safronov, Russian Federation

Alexander Stedtfeld, Germany

Kyaw Moe Tun, Myanmar

Christopher Adrian Whomersley, UK

Shinichi Yamanaka, Japan

The 25 members of the Legal and Technical Commission, elected by the Council on 14 August 2006 for a five-year term commencing on 1 January 2007 are:

Frida María Armas Pfirter, Argentina

Jean-Marie Auzende, France

David Stewart Martin Billett, UK

Laleta Davis-Mattis, Jamaica

Walter De Sá Leitão, Brazil

Baïdy Diène, Senegal

Miguel Dos Santos Alberto Chissano, Mozambique

Elva G Escobar, Mexico

Sergey Ivanovich Fyodorov, Russian Federation

Kennedy Hamutenya, Namibia

Said S Hussein, Kenya

Yoshiaki Igarashi, Japan

Asif Inam, Pakistan

Emmanuel Kalngui, Cameroon

Woong-Seo Kim, ROK

Eusebio Lopera Caballero, Spain

Andrzej Przybycin, Poland

Mahmoud Samy, Egypt

Elena Sciso, Italy

Sudhakar Maruthadu, India

Isikeli Uluinairai Mataitoga, Fiji

Sandor Mulsow Flores, Chile

Adam Mulawarman Tugio, Indonesia

Michael Wiedicke-Hombach, Germany

Hongtao Zhang, China

International Tribunal for the Law of the Sea

Am Internationalen Seegerichtshof 1
22609 Hamburg
Germany
Telephone: (+49 40) 35 607 0
Fax: (+49 40) 35 607 245/275
Email: itlos@itlos.org
Internet: www.itlos.org or www.tidm.org
Registrar: Philippe Gautier, Belgium (2006–11) (elected by the Tribunal)

Purpose

The International Tribunal for the Law of the Sea is an international court dealing with the peaceful settlement of disputes relating to use of the seas and oceans and their resources. It was constituted in 1996 and functions in accordance with the relevant provisions of Part XV and Part XI, section 5, of the UN Convention on the Law of the Sea (UNCLOS) and its Statute, contained in Annex VI to the Convention.

The Tribunal deals with cases submitted to it in accordance with the Convention and all matters specifically provided for in any other international agreement that confers jurisdiction on the Tribunal. Cases may be submitted by or against States Parties to the Convention, and (in relation to cases concerning 'the Area' – the seabed and ocean floor beyond the limits of national jurisdiction – or submitted pursuant to other agreements) by other states, international organisations and entities other than states, including natural or juridical persons.

The Tribunal's budget, as well as contributions by States Parties and the International Seabed Authority, is decided by the Meeting of States Parties to UNCLOS.

Structure

The Tribunal has compulsory jurisdiction to deal with requests for the prompt release of vessels and crew submitted by or on behalf of the vessel's flag state. It may prescribe provisional measures (interim injunction) to preserve the rights of the parties to a dispute or to prevent serious harm to the marine environment in the relevant circumstances.

The Seabed Disputes Chamber of the Tribunal (composed of 11 elected members of the Tribunal) has certain compulsory jurisdiction with respect to disputes arising out of the exploitation and exploration of the Area. The Chamber gives advisory opinions, at the request of the International Seabed Authority Assembly or Council, on legal questions arising within the scope of their activities.

Membership

The Tribunal comprises 21 independent members (judges), elected from among those enjoying the highest reputation for fairness and integrity, and with recognised competence in the law of the sea. The Statute of the Tribunal requires equitable geographical distribution, and the judges must represent the principal legal systems of the world. There must be no fewer than three judges from each geographical group established by the UN General Assembly and no two judges may be of the same nationality.

The members are elected for nine years and may be re-elected. Every three years the terms of office of one-third of the 21 members expire. Elections to replace seven of the Tribunal's members were held during the fifteenth Meeting of State Parties, from 16 to 24 June 2005.

Members of the Tribunal, whose terms end on 30 September of the year shown, are listed below in order of precedence.

Rüdiger Wolfrum, Germany, President	2008	Tafsir Malick Ndiaye, Senegal	2011
Joseph Akl, Lebanon, Vice-President	2008	Jose Luis Jesus, Cape Verde	2008
Hugo Caminos, Argentina	2011	Xu Guangjian, China	2011
Vicente Marotta Rangel, Brazil	2008	Jean-Pierre Cot, France	2011
Alexander Yankov, Bulgaria	2011	Anthony Amos Lucky, Trinidad and Tobago	2011[1]
Anatoly Lazarevich Kolodkin, Russian Federation	2008	Stanislaw Pawlak, Poland	2014
Choon-Ho Park, ROK	2014	Shunji Yanai, Japan	2014
Paul Bamela Engo, Cameroon	2008	Helmut Türk, Austria	2014
L Dolliver M Nelson, Grenada	2014	James Kateka, UR of Tanzania	2014
P Chandrasekhara Rao, India	2008	Albert Hoffman, South Africa	2014
Tullio Treves, Italy	2011		

Note

[1] Judge Lucky was elected on 2 September 2003 by a special Meeting of States Parties to fill the vacancy created by the passing away of Judge Lennox Fitzroy Ballah (Trinidad and Tobago).

ENVIRONMENTAL BODIES

Intergovernmental Panel on Climate Change (IPCC)

C/– World Meteorological Organization
7 bis Avenue de la Paix
Case Postale 2300
1211 Geneva 2
Switzerland
Telephone: (+41 22) 730 8208
Fax: (+41 22) 730 8025
Email: ipcc-sec@wmo.int
Website: www.ipcc.ch
Secretary: Dr Renate Christ, Austria (since 2004) (appointed by the Secretary-General of WMO, in consultation with the Executive Director of UNEP)

Purpose

The IPCC was established in 1988 by the UN Environment Programme (UNEP) and the World Meteorological Organization (WMO) to:

*   Assess available information on the science, impacts and economics of climate change, and on the response options available to address it
*   Assess, and develop as needed, methodologies such as the IPCC Guidelines for National Greenhouse Gas Inventories
*   Provide, on request, scientific, technical and socio-economic advice to the Conference of the Parties to the UN Framework Convention on Climate Change (UNFCCC) and its bodies.

Since its inception the IPCC has produced four multi-volume assessment reports. The first, in 1990, confirmed the scientific basis for concern about climate change. The second, in 1995, concluded that the balance of evidence suggested a discernible human influence on global climate. The third, in 2001, concluded that there was new evidence that most of the warming observed over the past 50 years was attributable to human activities. The IPCC is finalising its fourth assessment report during 2007. The three working group contributions (on The Physical Science Basis; Impacts, Adaptation and Vulnerability; and Mitigation of Climate Change) were finalised in the first half of the year. The Synthesis Report is due in November 2007. All components of the IPCC's fourth assessment report are available on the IPCC website.

The IPCC also publishes special reports/methodology reports, often in response to a request from parties to the UNFCCC. In 2005 and 2006 the IPCC completed reports on safeguarding the ozone layer and the global climate system, on carbon dioxide capture and storage, and guidelines for national greenhouse gas inventories.

Structure

All Member States of the UN and WMO are members of the IPCC. The Panel has three working groups:

*   Working Group I (WG1) assesses the physical scientific aspects of the climate system and climate change
*   Working Group II (WG2) assesses the vulnerability of natural and socio-economic systems to climate change and its observed and projected effects on them, along with adaptation options

- Working Group III (WG3) assesses options for mitigating climate change through limiting or preventing greenhouse gas emissions and enhancing activities that remove them from the atmosphere.

The Task Force on National Greenhouse Gas Inventories (TFI) develops methodology and software for the calculation and reporting of national greenhouse gas (GHG) emissions and removals.

The Panel makes decisions at its plenary sessions and is assisted by a bureau comprising 30 members. The IPCC Bureau is currently chaired by Rajendra Pachauri, India. Bureau members are normally elected for the duration of the preparation of an IPCC assessment report (five to six years). A new Bureau is to be elected in 2008.

Secretariat for the Vienna Convention for the Protection of the Ozone Layer and the Montreal Protocol on Substances that Deplete the Ozone Layer (the Ozone Secretariat)

PO Box 30552
United Nations Avenue
Gigiri, Nairobi 00100
Kenya
Telephone: (+254 20) 762 3850/51
Fax: (+254 20) 762 4691/92/93
Email: ozoneinfo@unep.org
Internet: www.unep.org/ozone
Executive Secretary: Marco González, Costa Rica (since 2002) (appointed by the Executive Director of UNEP)

Purpose

The Ozone Secretariat services the Vienna Convention for the Protection of the Ozone Layer and its Montreal Protocol on Substances that Deplete the Ozone Layer. The Ozone Secretariat was established and its duties defined by article 7 of the Vienna Convention and articles 12 and 14 of the Montreal Protocol.

The Vienna Convention was adopted in 1985 following negotiations facilitated by the UN Environment Programme (UNEP), in cooperation with the World Meteorological Organization (WMO). The Vienna Convention, which had been ratified by 191 countries as at March 2007, lays down a general commitment to protect the ozone layer and focuses on scientific cooperation. It is governed by a Conference of the Parties, which meets every three years. The last meeting was held in Dakar, Senegal, in December 2005. The next meeting will be held in 2008.

The Montreal Protocol sets targets for phasing out production and consumption of ozone-depleting substances, and includes other measures for the protection of the ozone layer. These include controls on trade in ozone-depleting substances and a multilateral fund for meeting the incremental costs faced by developing countries in implementing the control measures. As at March 2007, 191 parties had ratified the Protocol.

The Montreal Protocol is subject to the 1990 London Amendment, which at March 2007 had been ratified by 185 parties. The 1992 Copenhagen Amendment has been ratified by 177 parties, the 1997 Montreal Amendment by 154 parties and the 1999 Beijing Amendment by 126 parties.

The seventeenth annual meeting of the parties to the Montreal Protocol was held in Dakar, Senegal, in December 2005. The eighteenth meeting of the parties was held in New Delhi, India, in November 2006.

The Multilateral Fund for the Implementation of the Montreal Protocol was established under article 10 of the Protocol. The Fund made an initial interim allocation of $200 million to developing countries to cover the period 1991 to 1993. This was to enable them to meet present and future Protocol requirements by covering the agreed incremental costs they incurred from the phasing-out of production and consumption of ozone-depleting substances, and the adoption of non-ozone-depleting alternatives.

Since 1991 the parties to the Montreal Protocol have decided to replenish the Fund six times, to a total of $2.475 billion. In 2005 the parties decided to replenish the Fund by an additional $400.4 million for the three-year period 2006 to 2008. Funds are contributed by developed countries on an assessed basis.

Secretariat of the Basel Convention on the Control of Transboundary Movements of Hazardous Wastes and their Disposal (SBC)

International Environment House
13–15 Chemin des Anémones
1219 Châtelaine, Geneva
Switzerland
Telephone: (+41 22) 917 8218
Fax: (+41 22) 797 3454
Email: sbc@unep.ch
Internet: www.basel.int
Executive Secretary: Katharina Kummer Peiry, Switzerland

Purpose

The Basel Convention on the Control of Transboundary Movements of Hazardous Wastes and their Disposal was adopted at Basel in March 1989 and entered into force in May 1992. There were 170 parties (169 States Parties and the European Community) to the Convention at the end of May 2007.

The main goal of the Convention is to protect human health and the environment from the adverse effects that may result from handling, transporting and disposing of hazardous and other wastes. To achieve this, the Convention pursues four objectives:
- Reducing transboundary movements of hazardous wastes to a minimum consistent with their environmentally sound management
- Treating and disposing of such wastes as close as possible to their source of generation
- Promoting the environmentally sound management (ESM) of hazardous wastes
- Minimising the generation of hazardous wastes.

Evolution

A decision containing the Amendment to the Convention on the Control of Transboundary Movements of Hazardous Wastes and their Disposal (Ban Amendment) was adopted during the third meeting of the Conference of the Parties (COP) in Geneva on 22 September 1995. The objective of this Amendment is to prohibit exports of hazardous wastes from ratifying countries. The Amendment has not yet entered into force. This will take place upon ratification by at least three-quarters of the parties that accepted it. Sixty-two states and the European Community had ratified by May 2007.

The Basel Protocol on Liability and Compensation for Damage Resulting from Transboundary Movements of Hazardous Wastes and their Disposal (Basel Protocol) was adopted at the fifth meeting of the Conference of the Parties (COP5) in Basel on 10 December 1999. The objective of the Protocol is to provide for a liability and compensation regime for damage resulting from the transboundary movement of hazardous wastes and other wastes. Thirteen countries have signed and eight have ratified the Protocol. The Protocol has not yet entered into force. Entry into force is dependent on ratification by 20 parties.

In addition COP5 adopted the Basel Ministerial Declaration on Environmentally Sound Management (ESM), which guides the activities of the Convention and outlines the main areas of focus during the next decade. The Declaration covers prevention, minimisation, recycling, recovery and disposal of hazardous and other wastes, active promotion and use of cleaner technologies, and further reduction of transboundary movements of hazardous and other wastes.

COP6 adopted a strategic plan for the implementation of the Basel Declaration to 2010.

A Ministerial Statement on Partnership for Meeting the Global Waste Challenge was adopted at COP7 in 2004. The Ministerial Statement acknowledged the importance of focusing on four policy directions:
- Minimisation of hazardous waste
- A life-cycle approach
- A regional approach and integrated waste management.

COP7 also saw the adoption of General Technical Guidelines for the environmentally sound management of wastes containing persistent organic pollutants (POPs), and the technical guidelines for the environmentally sound management of wastes containing polychlorinated biphenyls (PCBs), polychlorinated terphenyls (PCTs) or polybrominated biphenyls (PBBs).

The eighth meeting of the COP was held from 27 November to 1 December 2006 in Nairobi, Kenya. It adopted a decision, and issued a Presidential statement, on the dumping of hazardous waste in Abidjan, Côte d'Ivoire; the Nairobi Declaration on the Environmentally Sound Management of Electrical and Electronic Waste (e-waste); the cooperation between the Basel Convention and the International Maritime Organization related to the scope of MARPOL 73/78; and the enhancing of cooperation and coordination among the Basel, Rotterdam and Stockholm Conventions.

Structure

The Convention provides for a COP, the supreme decision-making body, and a secretariat. The COP's subsidiary bodies are the Expanded Bureau, the Open-ended Working Group and the Compliance Committee.

Under article 14 of the Basel Convention, 14 Regional Centres for Training and Technology Transfer (BCRCs) have been established in Latin America and the Caribbean, Asia and the Pacific, Africa, and Central and Eastern Europe.

Secretariat of the Convention on Biological Diversity (CBD)

World Trade Centre
413 Saint Jacques Street, Suite 800
Montreal, Quebec
Canada H2Y 1N9
Telephone: (+1 514) 288 2220
Fax: (+1 514) 288 6588
Email: secretariat@cbd.int
Internet: www.cbd.int
Executive Secretary: Dr Ahmed Djoghlaf, Algeria

Purpose

The Convention on Biological Diversity (CBD) was negotiated under the auspices of the UN Environment Programme (UNEP) and opened for signature at the Earth Summit (UN Conference on Environment and Development) held in Rio de Janeiro in June 1992. It entered into force on 29 December 1993. As at June 2007, 189 states and the European Community were parties to the Convention.

The Convention has three objectives:
- Conservation of biological diversity
- The sustainable use of its components
- The fair and equitable sharing of the benefits arising from the use of genetic resources.

The Cartagena Protocol on Biosafety was adopted at the first extraordinary meeting of the Conference of the Parties (COP) held in 2000. It was opened for signature in May 2000 and entered into force on 11 September 2003. The Protocol aims at ensuring adequate protection in the safe transfer, handling and use of living modified organisms resulting from modern biotechnology that may adversely effect the conservation and sustainable use of biological diversity, taking into account risks to human health and specifically focusing on transboundary movements. As at June 2007, 143 states and the European Community were parties to the Protocol.

The COP has held eight ordinary meetings. It has adopted work programmes on thematic areas (forest biodiversity, inland waters, marine and coastal areas, dry and sub-humid lands, agricultural biodiversity, mountains and island ecosystems), as well as on cross-cutting issues such as technology transfer and cooperation, traditional biodiversity-related knowledge, access to genetic resources, and public awareness and education.

The ninth COP meeting will be held in Bonn, Germany in May 2008. It will be preceded by the fourth meeting of the parties to the Cartagena Protocol on Biosafety. The UN General Assembly has declared 22 May each year as the International Day for Biological Diversity and 2010 as the International Year on Biodiversity.

Evolution

In 2002 the COP committed itself to achieving the 2010 Biodiversity Target of a significant reduction in the current rate of biodiversity loss at global, regional and national levels, as a contribution to poverty alleviation and for the benefit of all life on Earth.

The eighth meeting of the COP, held in March 2006 in Curitiba, Brazil, launched a new phase of enhanced implementation of the Convention's three objectives. The parties adopted the work programme for island biodiversity. They agreed to finalise the negotiations for an international regime on access to genetic resources and the fair and equitable sharing of the benefits no later than 2010.

Measures adopted at the third meeting of the parties to the Cartagena Protocol, also held in Curitiba in March 2006, included requirements for documentation accompanying living modified organisms intended for direct use as food or feed, or for processing; recommended measures for enhancing risk assessment and risk management; and a revised action plan for effective implementation of the Protocol.

Structure

The Secretariat services the COP and its subsidiary bodies, performs functions assigned to it by any protocol, and coordinates with other international bodies and processes. A Clearing-House Mechanism was established under article 18.3 of the Convention to promote and facilitate technical and scientific cooperation. Article 21 establishes a mechanism for providing financial resources to developing countries for the purposes of the Convention. The Global Environment Facility (GEF) acts as the financial mechanism of the Convention.

Meetings

The COP is the supreme body of the Convention and meets once every two years. The Subsidiary Body on Scientific, Technical and Technological Advice (SBSTTA) meets every year and provides advice to the COP. The twelfth meeting of the SBSTTA was held in Paris in July 2007.

The parties have also established a working group on article 8j related to indigenous and local communities that, as at June 2007, had held four meetings. The parties also established an Ad hoc Open-ended Working Group on Access and Benefit Sharing that, as at June 2007, had held four meetings. The parties also established an Open-ended Working Group on Review of the Implementation of the Convention. Its second meeting was held in July 2007.

Secretariat of the UN Convention to Combat Desertification in Countries Experiencing Serious Drought and/or Desertification, especially in Africa (UNCCD)

UNCCD Secretariat
PO Box 260129
D–53153 Bonn
Germany
Telephone: (+49 228) 815 2800
Fax: (+49 228) 815 2898/99
Email: secretariat@unccd.int
Internet: www.unccd.int
Executive Secretary: Appointment pending

Purpose

UNCD, established by GA res. 47/188 (1992), was adopted in June 1994 and entered into force in December 1996. It seeks to combat desertification and mitigate the effects of drought in affected countries, particularly in Africa. It establishes a framework for national, sub-regional and regional programmes to counter land degradation in arid, semi-arid and dry sub-humid areas. It coordinates effective action at all levels, supported by international cooperation and partnership arrangements including financial and technological transfer, research and training programmes.

The Convention pursues long-term, integrated strategies that focus on improving land productivity and rehabilitation, conservation, and sustainable management of land and water resources, with a view to achieving sustainable development in affected areas.

As recognised by the World Summit on Sustainable Development, the Convention plays a key role in efforts to reach the Millennium Development Goals (MDGs), particularly with regard to the eradication of extreme poverty and hunger.

Structure
- Permanent Secretariat
- Conference of the Parties (COP)
- Global Environment Facility (GEF).

The Permanent Secretariat was established in 1999 and, in conformity with decision five of the first COP, was relocated to headquarters in Bonn. The Secretariat services the COP and subsidiary bodies such as the Committee on Science and Technology (CST), and facilitates the implementation of national, sub-regional and regional programmes.

The COP is the supreme governing body of the UNCCD and the Permanent Secretariat is accountable to it. It has met every two years since 2001. The seventh session of the COP was held in Nairobi, Kenya, from 17 to 28 October 2005. The eighth session was scheduled to take place in Madrid, Spain, from 3 to 14 September 2007.

The following bodies established by the UNCCD are accountable to the COP:
- The Global Mechanism, housed at the International Fund for Agricultural Development (IFAD) in Rome, promotes actions leading to the mobilisation and channelling of substantial financial resources, including its own resources
- The Committee on Science and Technology provides the COP with information and advice on scientific and technological matters relating to combating desertification and mitigating the effects of drought
- The Committee for the Review of the Implementation of the Convention (CRIC), established by COP5, reviews and analyses national reports submitted to the COP that describe the status of the Convention's implementation by parties and observers. This is done to improve the coherence, impact and effectiveness of policies and programmes aimed at restoring the agro-ecological balance in the dry lands. CRIC-5 was held from 12 to 21 March 2007 in Buenos Aires, Argentina.

Since 2003 the Global Environment Facility (GEF) has served as a financial mechanism to the Convention. To strengthen the implementation of the Convention, an Operational Programme on Sustainable Land Management is being implemented by the GEF and its implementing agencies. An envelope of $282 million has been made available by the GEF during the current cycle to address desertification and deforestation.

Membership
As of March 2007 there were 191 parties to the Convention.

Secretariat of the Convention on International Trade in Endangered Species of Wild Fauna and Flora (CITES)

International Environment House
Chemin des Anémones
1219 Châtelaine
Geneva
Switzerland
Tel: (+41 22) 917 8139/8140
Fax: (+41 22) 797 3417
Email: info@cites.org
Internet: www.cites.org
Secretary-General: Willem Wijnstekers, Netherlands (since 1999) (appointed by the Executive Director of UNEP)

Purpose

The Secretariat services the Convention on International Trade in Endangered Species of Wild Fauna and Flora (CITES). The Convention's objective is to ensure that no species of wild fauna or flora becomes, or remains, subject to unsustainable exploitation because of international trade. In this way it provides an international, as well as national, regulatory framework. The Convention was adopted in March 1973 and entered into force in July 1975. It had been ratified by 172 countries as of June 2007. About 5000 animal species and 28,000 plant species are protected by CITES.

Structure

The Convention is governed by the Conference of the Parties (COP) and serviced by a standing committee and a secretariat. The Animals and Plants Committees comprise experts who can fill gaps in biological and other specialised knowledge regarding species of animals and plants that are, or might become, subject to CITES trade controls. Their role is to provide technical support to decision-making about these species.

Meetings

The thirteenth meeting of the COP was held in Bangkok, Thailand, from 2 to 14 October 2004. The fourteenth meeting was held in The Hague, Netherlands, from 3 to 15 June 2007.

Secretariat of the UN Framework Convention on Climate Change (UNFCCC)

Haus Carstanjen
Martin Luther King Strasse 8
PO Box 260124
D–53153 Bonn
Germany
Telephone: (+49 228) 815 1000
Fax: (+49 228) 815 1999
Email: secretariat@unfccc.int
Internet: www.unfccc.int
Executive Secretary: Yvo de Boer, Netherlands (since 2006) (appointed by the UN Secretary-General)

Purpose

The Convention opened for signature at the Earth Summit (UN Conference on Environment and Development) in Rio de Janeiro in June 1992. It entered into force in March 1994. As of April 2007, 190 parties had ratified the Convention.

The ultimate objectives of the Convention are to:

- Stabilise greenhouse gas concentrations in the atmosphere at a level that will prevent dangerous human interference with the climate system, and within a time-frame sufficient to allow ecosystems to adapt naturally to climate change
- Ensure that food production is not threatened
- Enable economic development to proceed in a sustainable manner.

Evolution

The first Conference of the Parties (COP1), held in Berlin in April 1995, agreed that the Convention commitments were inadequate for meeting its objectives. In a decision known as the Berlin Mandate they agreed to establish a process to negotiate strengthened commitments for developed countries. The result of these negotiations, the Kyoto Protocol, was adopted by consensus at COP3 in Kyoto in December 1997. The Protocol includes legally binding emission targets for developed country (Annex I) parties for the six major greenhouse gases, to be reached in the period 2008 to 2012.

The eleventh COP was held in conjunction with the first meeting of the parties to the Kyoto Protocol in Montreal in December 2005. Decisions were adopted that outlined the path to future international action on climate change. Under the Kyoto Protocol a new working group was established to discuss future commitments for developed countries for the period after 2012. The parties to the Kyoto Protocol also formally adopted the 'rulebook' of the 1997 Kyoto Protocol, the Marrakesh Accords, which set the framework for implementing the Protocol.

The twelfth COP was held in conjunction with the second meeting of the parties to the Kyoto Protocol in Nairobi in November 2006. The meeting agreed on activities for the next five years under the Nairobi Work Programme on Impacts, Vulnerability and Adaptation. These activities will help enhance decision-making on adaptation action and improved assessment of vulnerability and adaptation to climate change.

The Nairobi Framework, an initiative involving six UN agencies, was also announced at the meeting by then-UN Secretary-General Kofi Annan. It provides additional support for developing countries to successfully develop projects for the clean development mechanism of the Kyoto Protocol.

The Protocol entered into force on 16 February 2005, 90 days after it had been ratified by 55 parties to the Convention, some of them major developed country emitters of carbon dioxide. The Protocol was open for signature from 16 March 1998 to 15 March 1999. As at April 2007, 171 parties had ratified or acceded to the Kyoto Protocol.

Structure

A Conference of the Parties is the supreme body under the Convention. There are also subsidiary bodies for implementation, and for scientific and technological advice, and a secretariat. At the first COP1 session, held in Berlin in April 1995, it was decided that the Convention Secretariat would be based in Bonn and institutionally linked to the UN but not fully integrated in any department or programme.

UNEP/CMS Secretariat of the Convention on the Conservation of Migratory Species of Wild Animals (CMS or Bonn Convention)

UNEP/CMS Secretariat
United Nations Premises
Hermann-Ehlers-Strasse 10
53113 Bonn
Germany
Telephone: (+49 228) 815 2401/2
Fax: (+49 228) 815 2449
Email: secretariat@cms.int
Internet: www.cms.int
Executive Secretary: Robert Hepworth, UK (since 2004) (appointed by the UN Secretary-General)

Purpose

The CMS or Bonn Convention originated in Recommendation 32 of the 1972 United Nations Conference on the Human Environment and was adopted the same year. The Convention was concluded in 1979 and entered into force on 1 November 1983. As of 1 April 2007 there were 102 States Parties to the Convention.

The objective of the Convention is to conserve migratory species and their habitat by:
- Providing strict protection measures for migratory species listed as endangered in its Appendix I
- Concluding multilateral agreements for the conservation and management of migratory species listed in Appendix II (such as water birds, terrestrial and marine mammals, reptiles and bats) that have an unfavourable conservation status or would benefit significantly from international cooperation
- Undertaking joint research and monitoring activities.

Structure

The Convention is governed by the Conference of the Parties (COP), which meets every three years. A standing committee provides policy and administrative guidance between regular meetings of the COP. A scientific council gives advice on scientific matters.

Meetings

The eighth COP was held in Nairobi, Kenya, in November 2005. The next COP will take place in Italy in 2008. The Standing Committee meets at least annually and the Scientific Council meets annually.

Secretariat of the Convention on Wetlands (Ramsar Convention)

Rue Mauverney 28
1196 Gland
Switzerland
Telephone: (+41 22) 999 0170
Fax: (+41 22) 999 0169
Email: ramsar@ramsar.org
Internet: www.ramsar.org/
Secretary-General: Anada Tiéga, Niger (from 2007) (appointed by the Ramsar Convention Standing Committee)

Purpose

The Convention on Wetlands of International Importance Especially as Waterfowl Habitat, commonly referred to as the Convention on Wetlands or the Ramsar Convention, was adopted in Ramsar, Iran, in February 1971 and entered into force on 21 December 1975.

The Ramsar Convention provides a framework for national action and international cooperation for the conservation and sustainable use of wetlands and their resources. To accede to the Convention, potential contracting parties must designate at least one wetland for inclusion in the Ramsar List of Wetlands of International Importance. Contracting parties are also expected to manage all wetlands within their territories in accordance with the principles of sustainable use, and to engage in international cooperation to further the Convention's objectives.

The Conference of the Parties (COP) to the Ramsar Convention meets every three years. Kampala, Uganda, was the venue for COP9 in November 2005 and COP10 is scheduled to take place in Changwong, ROK, in late 2008.

Evolution

The Convention text has been modified twice, first by the Paris Protocol of 3 December 1982, which outlined an amendment procedure for the Convention, and in 1987 at an extraordinary Conference of the Contracting Parties in Regina, Canada, when institutional and financial arrangements were adopted. The Regina Amendments entered into force in May 1994.

Structure

A Standing Committee of 18 runs for a period of a three-year term. The current term runs from 2006 to 2008. It consists of 16 elected contracting parties as regional representatives, as well as the host countries of the previous and forthcoming COPs. The Committee meets annually to supervise the implementation of the Convention and the work of the Secretariat.

A subsidiary body called the Scientific and Technical Review Panel (STRP) comprises six independent experts from each of the Convention's regions and six experts in thematic areas of work, as well as representatives of the Convention's five international organisation partners. The STRP advises the Standing Committee and the COP on technical issues. It met most recently in Gland, Switzerland, from 26 to 30 March 2007.

As at 3 April 2007, the Convention had 154 contracting parties, which had designated 1651 wetlands to the Ramsar List. These covered almost 150 million hectares.

Global Environment Facility (GEF)

1818 H Street NW
Washington DC 20433
United States of America
Telephone: (+1 202) 473 0508
Fax: (+1 202) 522 3240
Email: gef@thegef.org
Internet: www.thegef.org
Chief Executive Officer: Monique Barbut, France (July 2006–09) (appointed by the GEF Council on the recommendation of the Implementing Agencies)

Purpose

The GEF provides grants and concessional funding to eligible countries for projects and programmes that protect the global environment and promote sustainable development.

The Facility, originally set up as a pilot programme in 1991, was restructured and replenished by more than $2 billion in 1994, $2.75 billion in 1998 and $3 billion in 2002. It funds the agreed incremental costs of activities that benefit the global environment in six focal areas:

- Biological diversity
- Climate change
- International waters
- The ozone layer
- Persistent organic pollutants
- Land degradation.

The GEF is the designated financial mechanism for the Framework Convention on Climate Change, the Convention on Biological Diversity, the Stockholm Convention on Persistent Organic Pollutants and the Convention to Combat Desertification.

GEF funds come from participant countries. Co-financing for particular projects comes from bilaterals, governments hosting projects, non-government organisations and the private sector.

GEF projects and programmes are managed through three implementing agencies: the UN Development Programme (UNDP), the UN Environment Programme (UNEP) and the World Bank. Seven other specialised UN agencies and regional development banks also administer GEF projects:
- Food and Agriculture Organization (FAO)
- Industrial Development Organization (UNIDO)
- International Fund for Agricultural Development (IFAD)
- African Development Bank (ADB)
- Asian Development Bank (ADB)
- European Bank for Reconstruction and Development (EBRD)
- Inter-American Development Bank (IDB).

The GEF Secretariat, which is independent of the three implementing agencies, reports to and serves the Council and Assembly of the GEF.

Structure
- Council
- Assembly
- Scientific and Technical Advisory Panel (STAP).

The Council, the main governing body, comprises 32 members, of which 16 represent developing countries, 14 developed countries and two economies in transition.

The Assembly, which meets every four years, consists of representatives of all participating countries. The first GEF Assembly met in New Delhi in April 1998, the second in October 2002 in Beijing and the third in South Africa in August 2006.

The STAP provides expert advice to the GEF.

The GEF has 178 participating countries. Countries may be eligible for GEF funds if:
- They are eligible for financial assistance through the Climate Change Convention, the Convention on Biological Diversity or the Stockholm Convention on Persistent Organic Pollutants
- They are eligible to borrow from the World Bank (IBRD and/or IDA) or receive technical assistance grants from UNDP through a country programme.

A country must be a party to the Climate Change Convention, the Convention on Biological Diversity, the Stockholm Convention on Persistent Organic Pollutants or the Convention to Combat Desertification to receive funds from the GEF in the relevant focal area.

Membership

Member countries and date of entry into the GEF:

Afghanistan	7 Apr 1994	Denmark	9 Jun 1994
Albania	6 May 1994	Djibouti	24 May 1994
Algeria	13 May 1994	Dominica	8 Jun 1994
Antigua and Barbuda	29 Mar 1994	Dominican Republic	21 Apr 1994
Argentina	12 May 1994	Ecuador	23 Jun 1994
Armenia	16 Jun 1994	Egypt	8 Jun 1994
Australia	27 Jun 1994	El Salvador	20 May 1994
Austria	21 Jun 1994	Equatorial Guinea	20 Jun 2003
Azerbaijan	24 Jul 1995	Eritrea	27 Dec 1995
Bahamas	19 Apr 1994	Estonia	12 May 1994
Bangladesh	22 Jun 1994	Ethiopia	27 Oct 1994
Barbados	13 May 1994	Fiji	10 May 1994
Belarus	30 Mar 1994	Finland	9 Jun 1994
Belgium	30 Jan 1995	France	20 Jun 1994
Belize	29 Apr 1994	Gabon	20 Mar 1998
Benin	29 Jun 1994	Gambia	16 Aug 1994
Bhutan	12 Dec 1995	Georgia	8 Jul 1994
Bolivia	17 Jun 1994	Germany	23 Jun 1994
Bosnia and Herzegovina	29 Oct 2001	Ghana	16 Jan 1997
Botswana	12 Jul 1994	Greece	11 May 1994
Brazil	13 Jun 1994	Grenada	20 Apr 1994
Bulgaria	22 Mar 1994	Guatemala	20 May 1994
Burkina Faso	24 Aug 1994	Guinea	17 Oct 1994
Burundi	30 Mar 1998	Guinea-Bissau	2 May 1995
Cambodia	31 Jan 1995	Guyana	12 May 1994
Cameroon	31 Oct 1994	Haiti	10 May 1994
Canada	6 Jul 1994	Honduras	6 Sep 1994
Cape Verde	18 Jul 1994	Hungary	22 Jun 1994
Central African Republic	23 Mar 1995	India	12 May 1994
Chad	27 Jul 1994	Indonesia	29 Jun 1994
Chile	1 Jul 1994	Iran	25 May 1994
China	16 May 1994	Ireland	14 Jun 1994
Colombia	28 Jun 1994	Israel	19 Mar 1995
Comoros	5 Sep 1995	Italy	28 Jun 1994
Congo	22 Sep 1995	Jamaica	29 Jun 1994
Cook Islands	6 May 1994	Japan	27 Jun 1994
Costa Rica	19 May 1994	Jordan	10 May 1994
Côte d'Ivoire	24 Jun 1994	Kazakhstan	30 Mar 1998
Croatia	4 Mar 1994	Kenya	25 May 1994
Cuba	4 Apr 1994	Kiribati	10 May 1994
Czech Republic	30 Jun 1994	Kyrgyzstan	9 Jan 1997
DPRK	6 May 1994	Lao PDR	2 Aug 1994
DR Congo	6 Feb 1997	Latvia	27 Jun 1994

Lebanon	21 Jul 1994
Lesotho	29 Jun 1994
Liberia	5 Dec 2000
Libyan AJ	13 Dec 1994
Lithuania	13 May 1994
Luxembourg	28 Apr 1995
Madagascar	14 Jul 1994
Malawi	23 Feb 1996
Malaysia	4 May 1994
Maldives	25 Aug 1994
Mali	4 Jul 1994
Malta	27 Jul 1994
Marshall Islands	15 Apr 1994
Mauritania	8 May 1994
Mauritius	4 Jul 1994
Mexico	17 May 1994
Micronesia	26 Apr 1994
Mongolia	14 Apr 1994
Montenegro	25 Aug 2006
Morocco	29 Jun 1994
Mozambique	27 Dec 1995
Myanmar	13 May 1994
Namibia	30 Apr 2001
Nauru	5 May 1994
Nepal	10 Aug 1994
Netherlands	20 Jun 1994
New Zealand	18 May 1994
Nicaragua	19 May 1994
Niger	23 Aug 1994
Nigeria	12 Jul 1994
Niue	4 May 1994
Norway	1 Jul 1994
Pakistan	8 Apr 1994
Palau	12 Oct 1998
Panama	7 Apr 1994
Papua New Guinea	6 May 1994
Paraguay	15 Feb 1995
Peru	14 Jun 1994
Philippines	16 Jun 1994
Poland	18 Apr 1994
Portugal	17 Jun 1994
ROK	3 May 1994
Republic of Moldova	27 Oct 1995
Romania	29 Jul 1994
Russian Federation	23 Jun 1994
Rwanda	11 Jun 2002
Saint Kitts and Nevis	25 Jul 1994
Saint Lucia	31 Mar 1994
Saint Vincent and the Grenadines	4 May 1994
Samoa	28 Mar 1994
Sao Tome and Principe	7 Jun 2002
Senegal	7 Apr 1994
Serbia[1]	16 Sep 2001
Seychelles	20 Sep 2001
Sierra Leone	6 Sep 1994
Slovakia	1 Nov 1994
Slovenia	12 Jul 1994
Solomon Islands	16 Apr 1994
Somalia	11 April 2007
South Africa	6 Jul 1994
Spain	9 Jun 1994
Sri Lanka	26 May 1994
Sudan	14 Jun 1994
Suriname	12 May 1994
Swaziland	16 May 1994
Sweden	28 Jun 1994
Switzerland	1 Jul 1994
Syrian AR	15 Apr 1996
Tajikistan	1 Oct 1999
Thailand	30 Jun 1994
The Former Yugoslav Republic of Macedonia	7 Jul 1994
Timor-Leste	6 Oct 2003
Togo	21 Jul 1994
Tonga	4 May 1994
Trinidad and Tobago	19 May 1994
Tunisia	13 May 1994
Turkey	6 Jul 1994
Turkmenistan	29 May 1997
Tuvalu	3 May 1994
Uganda	28 Jun 1994
Ukraine	15 Jun 1994
UK	13 Jun 1994
UR of Tanzania	26 Mar 1996
USA	24 Jun 1994
Uruguay	22 Apr 1994
Uzbekistan	5 Apr 1995
Vanuatu	19 May 1994
Venezuela	1 Jul 1994

Viet Nam	12 May 1994	Zambia	13 Jun 1994
Yemen	30 Mar 1994	Zimbabwe	7 Jul 1994

Note

[1] On 3 June 2006 the Republic of Serbia notified the UN that the membership of the State Union of Serbia and Montenegro in the UN, including all organs and organisations of the UN system, was continued by the Republic of Serbia on the basis of article 60 of the Constitutional Charter of Serbia and Montenegro, activated by the Declaration of Independence adopted by the National Assembly of Montenegro on 3 June 2006.

SPECIALISED AGENCIES AND OTHER RELATED BODIES

SPECIALISED AGENCIES

International Labour Organization (ILO)

4 Route des Morillons
1211 Geneva 22
Switzerland
Telephone: (+41 22) 799 6111
Fax: (+41 22) 798 8685
Email: ilo@ilo.org
Internet: www.ilo.org
Director-General: Juan Somavia, Chile (1999–2009) (appointed by the Governing Body)

Purpose

The ILO was established in 1919, its Constitution forming a part of the Treaty of Versailles. In 1946 it became a specialised agency of the UN. It is unique among inter-government agencies in that its composition is tripartite, made up of representatives of governments, employers and workers.

The Organization's primary aim is to advance social justice through policies and programmes designed to improve the working conditions of both women and men. Its action is structured around the Decent Work Agenda, which integrates four strategic objectives:
- The promotion of standards and fundamental principles and rights at work
- The creation of employment
- The enhancement of social protection
- The strengthening of social dialogue.

Structure

- International Labour Conference
- Governing Body
- International Labour Office.

The International Labour Conference meets each year to debate world social and labour problems, and draw up and adopt international labour conventions and recommendations. Each member state is entitled to be represented by four delegates: two representatives of the government and one representative each of employers and workers. The Conference's work is divided between sittings of the plenary, and standing and technical committees. The 96th session met in Geneva from 30 May to 15 June 2007.

The governing body is the ILO executive board. It formulates the Organization's policies and programmes, guides the activities of the various conferences and committees, and adopts the draft programme and budget for submission to the Conference. It meets twice a year (in March and November) for a full session. A one-day session is held in June, in conjunction with the International Labour Conference.

The Governing Body is elected by the Conference every three years. It comprises 56 regular members (28 government, 14 employer and 14 worker representatives) and 66 deputy members (28 government, 19 employer and 19 worker representatives). All are elected by their respective electoral colleges, meeting during the Conference. Governments holding non-elective seats do not participate in the vote in their group.

Ten of the regular government seats are held permanently by the main industrialised states (Brazil, China, France, Germany, India, Italy, Japan, Russian Federation, UK and USA). The remaining 18 are appointed by the government electoral college, taking into account geographical distribution. The distribution of the 18 seats of government regular members for 2005 to 2008 (the result of consultations among the regions) is: six from Africa, five from the Americas (plus two non-elective seats), four from Asia–Pacific (plus three non-elective seats) and three from Europe (plus five non-elective seats). The electoral college also elects 28 deputy members.

The employers' and workers' electoral colleges consist, respectively, of the employers' and workers' delegates to the Conference. They elect their regular and deputy members in their individual capacities.

The International Labour Office is the ILO's permanent secretariat and the focal point of the activities it carries out under the scrutiny of the Governing Body and leadership of the Director-General. The office employs more than 1900 people in Geneva and in 40 field offices around the world.

Membership

The following list of ILO members includes their previous and current terms of office on the Governing Body:

	Previous terms	Current terms
Afghanistan		
Albania		
Algeria	1969–72 81–87 1996–2002	
Angola	1978–87	
Antigua and Barbuda	1987–90	
Argentina[2]	1969–99 2002–05	2005–08
Armenia		
Australia[1]	1972–96	2005–08
Austria	1975–78 84–87 96–99	
Azerbaijan		
Bahamas	2002–05	
Bahrain	1981–84	
Bangladesh	1978–84 87–93 1996–2005	
Barbados[2]	1981–84 2002–05	2005–08
Belarus[1]	1987–93 2002–05	2005–08
Belgium	1969–72 81–84 90–93 2002–05	
Belize		
Benin	1972–75 84–90 1999–2002	
Bolivia	1972–75 84–87 90–93	
Bosnia and Herzegovina		
Botswana	1984–90	
Brazil[3]		
Brunei Darussalam		
Bulgaria	1969–75 81–84 90–93 1999–2005	
Burkina Faso	1969–72 84–87 1999–2002	
Burundi[2]	1975–78 84–90 2002–05	2005–08
Cambodia[2]		2005–08

	Previous terms	Current terms
Cameroon[1]	1975–81 87–93 2002–05	2005–08
Canada[1]	1969–81 1984–2005	2005–08
Cape Verde		
Central African Republic	1969–72 96–99	
Chad	1999–2002	
Chile[1]	1969–72 1993–2002	2005–08
China[3]		
Colombia	1969–84 87–90 1996–2002	
Comoros		
Congo	1969–72 90–99	
Costa Rica	1990–93 96–99	
Côte d'Ivoire[2]	1978–81 96–99	2005–08
Croatia	1996–2002	
Cuba[1]	1975–78 81–90 1993–2002	2005–08
Cyprus	1984–87 1999–2002	
Czech Republic[2]	1993–96	2005–08
DR Congo	1975–78	
Denmark	1969–72 82–84 90–93 1999–2002	
Djibouti	1984–87	
Dominica		
Dominican Republic	1999–2002 02–05	
Ecuador	1969–75 81–84 87–90 2002–05	
Egypt	1978–84 93–99	
El Salvador[1]	1999–2005	2005–08
Equatorial Guinea		
Eritrea		
Estonia		
Ethiopia[2]	1981–87 1996–2005	2005–08
Fiji		
Finland[2]	1972–75 84–87 96–99	2005–08
France[3]		
Gabon	1972–75 78–81 93–96 1999–2005	
Gambia		
Georgia		
Germany[3]		
Ghana	1972–75 81–87 93–96 1999–2005	
Greece[2]	1975–78 87–90	2005–08
Grenada		
Guatemala	1999–2002	
Guinea	1975–78 87–90 96–99	
Guinea-Bissau		
Guyana	1978–81	
Haiti		
Honduras[2]	1975–81 90–93	2005–08
Hungary[2]	1975–78 81–87 93–99	2005–08
Iceland		
India[3]		
Indonesia	1969–78 81–87 1990–2005	
Iran[2]	1969–81 84–90 1993–2005	2005–08
Iraq	1984–87	
Ireland[2]	1972–75 90–93	2005–08
Israel		
Italy[3]		

	Previous terms	Current terms
Jamaica	1972–75 84–87	
Japan[3]		
Jordan[2]	1972–75 96–99 2002–05	2005–08
Kazakhstan		
Kenya[1]	1969–72 78–84 90–96 2002–05	2005–08
Kiribati		
Kuwait[2]	1975–78 87–90	2005–08
Kyrgyzstan		
Lao PDR		
Latvia		
Lebanon	1978–81	
Lesotho	1988–93	
Liberia	1975–78	
Libyan AJ	1984–90 1999–2005	
Lithuania	1999–2005	
Luxembourg	2002–05	
Madagascar	1972–75 81–84 90–93	
Malawi[1]	1990–93 2002–05	2005–08
Malaysia	1987–90 1996–2002	
Mali	1981–84 93–96 2002–05	
Malta	1978–81 90–93	
Mauritania	1972–75	
Mauritius	1975–78 93–99	
Mexico[2]	1972–87 1990–2005	2005–08
Mongolia	1981–87 96–99	
Montenegro		
Morocco[1]	1972–75 87–93 2002–05	2005–08
Mozambique[2]	1978–84	2005–08
Myanmar	1981–84	
Namibia	1996–2002	
Nepal		
Netherlands[2]	1981–84 93–96 1999–2002	2005–08
New Zealand	1990–96 1999–2005	
Nicaragua	1978–81 84–90 93–96	
Niger	1978–81 90–96 2002–05	
Nigeria[1]	1969–72 78–84 90–93 1996–2005	2005–08
Norway	1975–78 84–87 93–96 2002–05	
Oman	2002–05	
Pakistan[2]	1969–72 75–81 84–87 1990–2005	2005–08
Panama	1972–78 81–84 93–99	
Papua New Guinea		
Paraguay		
Peru[1]	1978–81 90–93 1996–2002	2005–08
Philippines[1]	1978–84 1990–2005	2005–08
Poland[2]	1972–78 93–99	2005–08
Portugal	1981–84 93–96 1999–2002	
Qatar	1993–96	
ROK[2]	1996–2005	2005–08
Republic of Moldova		
Romania[1]	1969–72 75–81 90–96 2002–05	2005–08
Russian Federation[3]		
Rwanda	1972–75	
Saint Kitts and Nevis		

	Previous terms	Current terms
Saint Lucia		
Saint Vincent and the Grenadines		
Samoa		
San Marino		
Sao Tome and Principe	1984–87	
Saudi Arabia[1]	1996–2005	2005–08
Senegal[2]	1981–84 96–99	2005–08
Serbia[4]		
Seychelles		
Sierra Leone	1975–81	
Singapore[2]	2002–05	2005–08
Slovakia	1996–2002	
Slovenia	2002–05	
Solomon Islands		
Somalia	1969–72 75–78 87–90	
South Africa[1]	1996–2005	2005–08
Spain[1]	1972–75 78–81 84–87 93–99 2002–05	2005–08
Sri Lanka[1]	1972–78 87–90	2005–08
Sudan	1969–72 75–78 93–96 1999–2005	
Suriname	1996–99	
Swaziland	1993–99	
Sweden	1978–81 87–90 96–99	
Switzerland	1978–81 87–90 1999–2002	
Syrian AR	1969–72 96–99	
Tajikistan		
Thailand	1975–81 84–90 1996–2002	
The Former Yugoslav Republic of Macedonia	1975–81 84–90	
Timor-Leste		
Togo	1975–78 90–93	
Trinidad and Tobago[2]	1975–78 1999–2002	2005–08
Tunisia[2]	1975–81 90–96	2005–08
Turkey	1975–78 87–90 96–99 2002–05	
Turkmenistan		
Uganda[2]	1969–75 87–90 96–99	2005–08
Ukraine	1972–75 81–87 1996–2002	
UAE	1990–93 1999–2002	
UK[3]		
UR of Tanzania	1975–78 87–90 1999–2002	
USA[3]		
Uruguay	1969–72 78–84 87–96 2002–05	
Uzbekistan		
Vanuatu		
Venezuela[2]	1969–72 75–96 1999–2005	2005–08
Viet Nam[2]	1969–72 2002–05	2005–08
Yemen	1999–2002	
Zambia	1972–75 78–81	
Zimbabwe	1981–87 93–96	

Notes

Czechoslovakia served on the Governing Body 1969–1972, 1978–1981 and 1984–1992.

The former Socialist Federal Republic of Yugoslavia served on the ILO Governing Body from 1975–1981 and 1984–1990. It was not automatically succeeded by any of the new states created following its dissolution.

1   Currently elected regular member.
2   Currently elected deputy member.
3   Members holding non-elective seats as 'states of chief industrial importance'.
4   On 3 June 2006 the Republic of Serbia notified the UN that the membership of the State Union of Serbia and Montenegro in the UN, including all organs and organisations of the UN system, was continued by the Republic of Serbia on the basis of article 60 of the Constitutional Charter of Serbia and Montenegro, activated by the Declaration of Independence adopted by the National Assembly of Montenegro on 3 June 2006.

Workers' Group members

N Adyanthaya, India

S Burrow, Australia

B Byers, Canada

R Diallo, Guinea

U Edström, Sweden

U Engelen-Kefer, Germany

J Gómez Esguerra, Colombia

S Nakajima, Japan

A Oshiomhole, Nigeria

A Sidi Saïd, Algeria

E Sidorov, Russian Federation

S Steyne, UK

R Trotman, Barbados

J Zellhoefer, USA

Deputy members

K Ahmed, Pakistan

M Al-Ma'ayta, Jordan

H Anderson Nevárez, Mexico

L Basnet, Nepal

M Blondel, France

C Brighi, Italy

B Canak, Serbia

T Etty, Netherlands

A Garcia, Angola

N Goulart, Brazil

B Hossu, Romania

A Husain, Bahrain

G Martinez, Argentina

L Ongaba, Uganda

A Palanga, Togo

C Pandeni, Namibia

E Patel, South Africa

R Silaban, Indonesia

H Yacob, Singapore

Employers' Group members

P Anderson, Australia

A Dahlan, Saudi Arabia

D Funes de Rioja, Argentina

R Goldberg, USA

R Hornung-Draus, Germany

A Jeetun, Mauritius

E Julien, France

D Lima Godoy, Brazil

A M'Kaissi, Tunisia

A Moore, UK

B Nacoulma, Burkina Faso

T Suzuki, Japan

A Tabani, Pakistan

G Trogen, Sweden

Deputy members

I Anand, India

F Awassi Atsimadja, Gabon

M Barde, Switzerland

L Chen, China

B de Arbeloa, Venezuela

J de Regil, Mexico

O Eremeev, Russian Federation

A Finlay, Canada

S Goh Hock Li, Singapore

W Hilton-Clarke, Trinidad and Tobago

L Horvatic, Croatia

J Lacasa Aso, Spain

K Mattar, UAE

E Megateli, Algeria

O Oshinowo, Nigeria

C Renique, Netherlands

G Ricci Muadi, Guatemala

L Traore, Mali

V Van Vuuren, South Africa

Food and Agriculture Organization (FAO)

Viale Delle Terme di Caracalla
00153 Rome
Italy
Telephone: (+39 06) 57051
Fax: (+39 06) 57053 152
Email: fao-hq@fao.org
Internet: www.fao.org
Director-General: Jacques Diouf, Senegal (1994–2011) (elected by the FAO membership)

Purpose

The preamble of the Food and Agriculture Organization (FAO) Constitution defines the aim of the members as being to:
- Raise levels of nutrition and standards of living
- Secure improvements in food production and distribution
- Better the conditions of rural people
- Contribute toward an expanding world economy and ensure freedom from hunger.

Evolution

The FAO was established in 1945, when 44 governments accepted the Constitution as drafted by an interim commission. The functions and assets of the former International Institute of Agriculture in Rome were transferred to the new body. By GA res. 50/227 (1996) the FAO and the World Food Programme absorbed the functions of the World Food Council, which was discontinued.

Structure

- Conference
- Council
- Committees of the Council
- Other inter-government bodies
- Secretariat.

The Conference, which consists of all FAO members, meets in regular session every two years to determine the Organization's policies, approve the budget, and make recommendations to members and international organisations. The 34th Conference session is scheduled to be held in Rome from 17 to 24 November 2007.

The Council is the executive organ of the Conference and exercises powers delegated to it by the Conference. It meets at least four times between the two-yearly Conference sessions. There are 49 Member States, elected by the Conference for three-year terms. One-third of the members retire each year.

An independent Council chair is appointed by the Conference for a renewable two-year term. The present Chair is Mohammad Saeid Noori Naeini, Iran, who was appointed by the Conference in 2005. The 132nd session was held in Rome from 18 to 22 June 2007.

The FAO Council has three elected committees concerned with particular aspects of management. Members are:

Programme Committee, Nov 2005 to Nov 2007

A R Ayazi, Afghanistan	V Heard, UK (Chair)	R Parasuram, India
J Barfield, Australia	J Melanson, Canada	R S Recide, Philippines
Z Budham, Jamaica	Y Olaniran, Nigeria	A A Zaied, Libyan AJ
M A Caamaño, Dominican Republic		

Finance Committee, Nov 2005 to Nov 2007

A A Khawaja, Pakistan, Chair	L Brudvig, USA	V Takaendesa Mutiro, Zimbabwe
A I Al Abdulla, Qatar	E W Hein, Germany	S Yokoi, Japan
A M Baiardi Quesnel, Paraguay	R Seminario Portocarrero, Peru	A Zodda, Italy
A Bakayoko, Côte d'Ivoire	S Skafte, Denmark	

Committee on Constitutional and Legal Matters, Nov 2005 to Nov 2007

Belgium	Guatemala	USA
Czech Republic	Philippines	
Gabon	Syrian AR	

The Council also has five major committees covering the Organization's activities. Each is non-elective and open to all Member States:
• Committee on Commodity Problems
• Committee on Fisheries
• Committee on Forestry
• Committee on Agriculture
• Committee on World Food Security.

The FAO has a wide range of other inter-government and expert bodies, of both a global and regional nature, dealing with aspects of agriculture, fisheries and food. Some of these also include the private sector.

Membership

For the purpose of Council elections, the membership of the FAO is divided into seven regional groups, each with a fixed number of seats. Terms of office on the 49-member Council are also shown.

	Previous terms	Current terms
Africa (48 members, 12 seats)		
Algeria[1]	1978–80 87–89 95–98	2005–07
Angola	1981–83 89–94 2003–06	
Benin	1973–75 83–85	
Botswana	1979–81	
Burkina Faso	1969–72 81–84 93–96 1999–2004	
Burundi	1975–77 85–92	
Cameroon[1,6]	1961–63 79–82 85–92 1995–2003	2005–07
Cape Verde[1]	1981–84 91–96	2005–07
Central African Republic	1967–70	
Chad	1965–67 77–80	
Comoros		

	Previous terms	Current terms
Congo	1973–76 81–86 89–98 2003–06	
Côte d'Ivoire[2]	1979–82 91–93 2003–05	2005–08
DR Congo	1971–73 77–80 87–89 93–95	
Equatorial Guinea		
Eritrea[1]	1997–2000	2005–07
Ethiopia[3]	1965–70 73–75 81–84 89–91 1999–2002	2007–09
Gabon[3]	1973–77 1987–2004	2007–09
Gambia	1975–77 83–89	
Ghana	1959–62 77–81 89–92 95–98 2001–04	
Guinea	1973–76 87–90	
Guinea-Bissau	1977–79	
Kenya	1965–68 71–74 81–83 87–93 2001–03	
Lesotho	1973–75 81–84 87–90 1999–2002	
Liberia	1953–56 77–80 85–90	
Madagascar[2]	1961–64 79–81 87–95 1999–2001	2005–08
Malawi	1975–78 83–85	
Mali[1]	1967–69	2005–07
Mauritania	1997–2002	
Mauritius	1975–78 95–98 2003–05	
Morocco	1959–65 71–74 81–83 89–92 1999–2001	
Mozambique		
Namibia	1997–2000	
Niger	1975–78 85–88	
Nigeria[2]	1963–65 69–71 81–83 87–90 93–95 1999–2001 03–05	2005–08
Rwanda	1977–79 83–85 92–94	
Sao Tome and Principe	1983–86	
Senegal	1963–66 79–81 85–87 1997–2002	
Seychelles		
Sierra Leone	1983–86	
South Africa[3]	1947–59 97–99	2007–09
Swaziland	1993–96 2003–05	
Togo	1971–73	
Tunisia	1965–68 75–77 83–86 93–95 2001–04	
Uganda	1967–68 83–86 93–99 2003–06	
UR of Tanzania	1969–72 77–80 85–87 91–97 2001–04	
Zambia[2]	1969–71 79–82 85–88 91–93	2005–08
Zimbabwe	1985–87 95–97 2001–03	

Asia (23 members, 9 seats)

	Previous terms	Current terms
Bangladesh[3]	1977–88 1991–2000 2003–06	2007–09
Bhutan		
Cambodia		
China[3]	1947–48 1973–2006	2007–09
DPRK		
India[2]	1947–2005	2005–08
Indonesia[2]	1955–64 1967–2000 03–05	2005–08
Japan[3]	1953–61 1965–2006	2007–09
Kazakhstan		
Lao PDR		
Malaysia[3]	1965–67 79–91 93–97 1999–2002	2007–09
Maldives		
Mongolia		
Myanmar	1949–52	

	Previous terms	Current terms
Nepal	1967–70	
Pakistan[2]	1949–55 57–93 1997–2005	2005–08
Philippines	1947–49 53–58 61–64 67–79 81–93 2001–06	
ROK[3]	1965–67 1989–2006	2007–09
Sri Lanka	1961–64 71–81 93–96 2001–03	
Thailand[3]	1973–2006	2007–09
Timor-Leste		
Uzbekistan		
Viet Nam		

Europe (47 members, 10 seats)

	Previous terms	Current terms
Albania		
Armenia	2003–06	
Austria	1961–64 83–86 1999–2001	
Azerbaijan		
Belarus		
Belgium	1949–52 55–58 61–64 69–71 77–80 93–95	
Bosnia and Herzegovina		
Bulgaria	1973–80 83–86 2001–04	
Croatia		
Cyprus	1983–85 91–94 2001–03	
Czech Republic	2001–03	
Denmark	1947–51 61–63 73–75 85–87 97–99	
Estonia	1995–97	
European Community[4] (Member organisation)		
Finland	1951–54 63–66 75–78 87–90 2003–05	
France[2]	1947–2005	2005–08
Georgia		
Germany[3]	1959–61 1965–2006	2007–09
Greece	1965–67 77–79 89–91 1997–2000	
Hungary	1971–74 77–80 87–89 91–94 1999–2001	
Iceland	1999–2002	
Ireland	1961–64 81–83 1995–2002	
Israel	1967–68	
Italy[2]	1947–65 1971–2005	2005–08
Latvia		
Lithuania		
Luxembourg		
Malta[1]	1977–80	2005–07
Monaco		
Netherlands[1]	1947–49 53–55 59–61 75–77 89–92	2005–07
Norway	1957–60 69–72 81–84 93–96	
Poland	1965–67 69–71 81–83 89–92 1997–2000	
Portugal	1979–82 89–92 95–98 2001–04	
Republic of Moldova		2007–09
Romania	1967–73 81–83 95–98 2003–06	
Russian Federation – attended the first meeting as a full FAO member in 2006		
San Marino		
Serbia[5]		
Slovakia	1993–95	
Slovenia[1]		2005–07
Spain	1953–58 75–77 83–85 87–89 93–95 1999–2001	
Sweden[2]	1953–57 67–69 79–81 91–93	2005–08

	Previous terms	Current terms
Switzerland	1953–57 71–74 87–89 2001–04	
The Former Yugoslav Republic of Macedonia		
Turkey	1955–58 67–70 85–88 95–97	
Ukraine[3]		2007–09
UK[2]	1947–55 1957–2005	2005–08

Latin America and Caribbean (33 members, 9 seats)

	Previous terms	Current terms
Antigua and Barbuda		
Argentina	1953–58 61–67 1971–2000	
Bahamas		
Barbados	1981–83 1995–2004	
Belize		
Bolivia[1]	2001–04	2005–07
Brazil[1]	1947–53 1957–2004	2005–07
Chile[3]	1947–56 59–64 67–75 1995–2006	2007–09
Colombia	1953–61 65–95	
Costa Rica	1955–57 63–71 91–93	
Cuba[1]	1947–49 51–54 57–63 1977–2004	2005–07
Dominica		
Dominican Republic		
Ecuador	1975–78 81–87	
El Salvador[2]	1979–81	2005–08
Grenada		
Guatemala	1999–2005	
Guyana		
Haiti		
Honduras	1993–99	
Jamaica	1977–80	
Mexico[1]	1947–51 57–62 1973–2004	2005–07
Nicaragua	1985–91	
Panama[3]	1963–65 73–85 2003–06	2007–09
Paraguay	1999–2001	
Peru	1965–76 87–90 2001–06	
Saint Kitts and Nevis		
Saint Lucia		
Saint Vincent and the Grenadines		
Suriname		
Trinidad and Tobago[1]	1975–77 83–95	2005–07
Uruguay[3]	1953–56 67–70 95–97	2007–09
Venezuela	1949–52 63–66 71–75 1977–2000	

Near East (21 members, 6 seats)

	Previous terms	Current terms
Afghanistan	1965–71 77–83 85–87	
Bahrain		
Djibouti		
Egypt[2]	1947–63 1967–2005	2005–08
Iran[3]	1957–65 71–74 87–90 1995–2006	2007–09
Iraq	1953–56 69–71 77–91	
Jordan	1963–66 75–77	
Kuwait	1973–75 79–81 1995–2001	
Kyrgyzstan		

	Previous terms	Current terms
Lebanon[2]	1953–56 59–65 75–79 81–98	2005–08
Libyan AJ	1975–78 87–95 2001–04	
Oman[1]		2005–07
Qatar	1999–2004	
Saudi Arabia[2]	1969–72 1979–2005	2005–08
Somalia	1967–69	
Sudan	1965–68 73–78 81–84 91–93	
Syrian AR	1957–58 71–74 79–82 1993–2005	
Tajikistan		
Turkmenistan		
UAE[1]		2005–07
Yemen	1983–86	

North America (2 members, 2 seats)

	Previous terms	Current terms
Canada[1]	1947–2004	2005–07
USA[1]	1947–2004	2005–07

South-West Pacific (16 members, 1 seat)

	Previous terms	Current terms
Australia[2]	1947–57 61–63 67–69 73–75 79–81 1985–2005	2005–08
Cook Islands		
Fiji		
Kiribati		
Marshall Islands		
Micronesia		
Nauru		
New Zealand	1957–60 63–66 69–72 75–78 81–84	
Niue		
Palau		
Papua New Guinea		
Samoa		
Solomon Islands		
Tonga		
Tuvalu		
Vanuatu		

Notes

[1] Term of office until the conclusion of the 34th session of the Conference, November 2007.

[2] Term of office until 31 December 2008.

[3] Term of office until the conclusion of the 35th Session of the Conference, November 2009.

[4] The EC has the right to participate in matters within its competence in any meeting of the Organization, other than those bodies with restricted membership, in which any of its Member States are entitled to participate. It exercises membership rights in those meetings on an alternative basis with those of its Member States that are members of the Council, or other bodies concerned in the areas of their respective competencies. The EC is not eligible for election or designation to any such body in its own right, nor is it entitled to participate in voting for elective places or to hold office itself. The EC is not entitled to participate in the Programme Committee, Finance Committee or Committee on Constitutional and Legal Matters.

[5] On 3 June 2006 the Republic of Serbia notified the UN that the membership of the State Union of Serbia and Montenegro in the UN, including all organs and organisations of the UN system, was continued by the Republic of Serbia on the basis of article 60 of the Constitutional Charter of Serbia and Montenegro, activated by the Declaration of Independence adopted by the National Assembly of Montenegro on 3 June 2006.

[6] Replaced the Democratic Republic of the Congo until November 2007.

FAO/WHO Codex Alimentarius Commission

Viale delle Terme di Caracalla
00153 Rome
Italy
Telephone: (+39 06) 57051
Fax: (+39 06) 5705 4593
Email: Codex@fao.org
Internet: www.codexalimentarius.net

Purpose

The Commission was established by the FAO and WHO governing bodies in 1961/1963 to implement the Joint FAO/WHO Food Standards Programme. The Programme's mandate is to protect the health of consumers and ensure fair practices in the food trade by initiating and guiding the preparation, publication and revision of international food standards and by promoting the coordination of all food standards work undertaken by international organisations.

To date, the Commission has adopted some 200 standards (for single commodities, groups of commodities or horizontal subjects such as labelling or hygiene), and around 100 codes of practice and guidelines, as well as thousands of maximum residue limits for pesticides and veterinary drugs in foods. Together these texts form the Codex Alimentarius, which is freely available on the internet (www.codexalimentarius.net) but also published on CD and in extracts in booklet format.

The Codex Alimentarius promotes the harmonisation of import requirements for foods and, in so doing, protects the health of consumers and ensures fair practices in international food trade. Codex standards, guidelines and codes of practice contribute to the standards used in implementing the World Trade Organization (WTO) Agreement on the Application of Sanitary and Phytosanitary Measures and have relevance as international standards in the Agreement on Technical Barriers to Trade.

Structure

The Commission is assisted by a Rome-based secretariat and an executive committee. The technical work is done by some 20 Codex specialist committees and task forces, which prepare draft standards and related texts for adoption by the Commission. The Committees rely heavily rely on independent scientific advice provided by FAO and WHO expert groups – the Joint FAO/WHO Expert Committee on Food Additives (JECFA), Joint FAO/WHO Expert Meetings on Microbiological Risk Assessment (JEMRA), Joint FAO/WHO Meetings on Pesticide Residues (JMPR) and ad hoc consultations. Six regional coordinating committees collect information on regional implementation of Codex standards and other regional issues, and also prepare standards that are of regional relevance.

Membership

Membership of the Commission is open to members and associate members of the FAO and WHO. Current membership covers 99 percent of the world's population and consists of 174 countries and the European Community.

United Nations Educational, Scientific and Cultural Organization (UNESCO)

7 Place de Fontenoy
75352 Paris 07–Sp
France
Telephone: (+33 1) 4568 1000
Fax: (+33 1) 4567 1690
Email: bpi@unesco.org
Internet: www.unesco.org
Director-General: Koïchiro Matsuura, Japan (1999–2009) (elected by the General Conference on the recommendation of the Executive Board)

Purpose

UNESCO was established in 1945 to promote the aims set out in article 1, para. 3 of the Charter of the UN. Its purpose, as stated in article 1 of its Constitution, is to contribute to peace and security by promoting collaboration among nations through education, science and culture.

Structure

- General Conference
- Executive Board
- Secretariat.

The General Conference, the Organization's supreme body, meets every two years. Its 33rd session was held in Paris from 3 to 21 October 2005. The 34th session is scheduled to be held in Paris in October 2007.

The Executive Board is elected by the General Conference and consists of 58 Member States. Each Member State appoints a representative with competence in fields related to UNESCO and qualified to fulfil the administrative and executive duties of the Board. Alternates may also be appointed. Members are elected for a four-year term.

The Board meets in regular sessions at least four times in any two-year period. As a general rule there are at least two regular sessions per year, normally in April and October. There is a system of electoral grouping by which each region is allocated a specific number of Board seats. At present these are allocated: Group I, nine seats; Group II, seven seats; Group III, 10 seats; Group IV, 12 seats; Group V(a), 14 seats; Group V(b), six seats. The current Board Chair is Xinsheng Zhang, China.

Membership

As at 1 March 2007, UNESCO had 192 Member States and six Associate Members. The following list shows the members of UNESCO and their terms of office on the Executive Board:

	Previous terms	Current terms
Group I		
Andorra		
Austria	1972–76 95–99	
Belgium	1946–51 56–64 74–78 80–89 95–99	
Canada	1946–51 68–74 83–87 89–93 1997–2001	2003–07
Cyprus	1987–91	

OTHER BODIES

	Previous terms	Current terms
Denmark	1952–58 78–83 91–95	
Finland	1966–74 87–91 1997–2001	
France	1948–2003	2003–07
Germany	1954–68 1970–2005	
Greece	1946–51 56–64 83–87 1999–2003	
Iceland	1983–87 2001–05	
Ireland		
Israel	1962–70	
Italy	1948–58 62–70 72–89 93–97 1999–2003	2003–07
Luxembourg		2005–09
Malta	1995–99	
Monaco		
Netherlands	1946–47 51–56 66–74 91–95 1999–2003	
Norway	1946–52 74–78 89–93	2005–09
Portugal	1976–80 91–95	2005–09
San Marino		
Spain	1954–60 70–76 80–85 87–91 93–97 1999–2003	
Sweden	1958–66 85–89 95–99	
Switzerland	1950–54 64–72 76–80 87–91 93–97	2003–07
Turkey	1946–52 58–66 78–83 91–95 2001–05	
UK	1946–85 1997–2005	2005–09
USA		2003–07

Group II[1]

	Previous terms	Current terms
Albania		
Armenia		
Azerbaijan		2005–09
Belarus	1989–93 1999–2005	
Bosnia and Herzegovina		
Bulgaria	1972–76 85–89 93–97	
Croatia		
Czech Republic	1995–99	2003–07
Estonia		
Georgia	1999–2003	
Hungary	1964–72 78–83 95–99	2003–07
Latvia		
Lithuania	1997–2001	2005–09
Montenegro[2]		
Poland	1946–50 56–64 76–80 87–91 93–97 1999–2003	
Republic of Moldova		
Romania	1962–68 76–80 91–95 1999–2003	
Russian Federation	1954–2003	2003–07
Serbia[3]		2005–09
Slovakia	1995–99 2001–05	
Slovenia		2003–07
Tajikistan		
The Former Yugoslav Republic of Macedonia		
Ukraine	1980–85 95–99 2001–05	
Uzbekistan		

Group III

	Previous terms	Current terms
Antigua and Barbuda	1985–89	
Argentina	1962–70 72–76 78–83 85–93 95–99	
Bahamas	2001–05	2005–09
Barbados	1976–80 1997–2001	
Belize		
Bolivia	1995–99	
Brazil	1946–52 54–62 64–72 74–78 80–89 91–95 2001–05	2005–09
Chile	1962–70 72–76 93–97 1999–2003	
Colombia	1948–54 70–76 80–89 91–95 1997–2001	2005–09
Costa Rica	1966–74 80–85 89–97	
Cuba	1974–78 80–85 87–91 95–99 2001–05	
Dominica	2001–05	
Dominican Republic	1999–2003	
Ecuador	1947–48 54–62 76–80	2003–07
El Salvador	1956–64 93–97	
Grenada		
Guatemala	1978–83 89–93	2003–07
Guyana	1983–87 93–97	
Haiti	1980–85 1997–2001	
Honduras	1997–2001	
Jamaica	1970–76 80–85 91–95 2001–05	
Mexico	1946–54 58–66 68–74 76–80 83–87 89–97 1999–2003	2005–09
Nicaragua	1989–93	
Panama	1962–68 76–80	
Paraguay		
Peru	1952–54 64–72 76–80 85–89 1999–2003	
Saint Kitts and Nevis		2005–09
Saint Lucia	1997–2001	
Saint Vincent and the Grenadines		2005–09
Suriname	1987–91 2001–05	
Trinidad and Tobago	1985–89 93–97	
Uruguay	1952–58 72–76 89–93 1997–2001	2003–07
Venezuela	1946–52 56–64 76–80 83–91	2003–07

Group IV

	Previous terms	Current terms
Afghanistan	1968–74	2003–07
Australia	1946–50 56–60 74–78 85–89 91–95 1999–2005	
Bangladesh	1983–87 1995–2003	2003–07
Bhutan		
Brunei Darussalam		
Cambodia		2003–07
China	1946–50 1972–2005	2005–09
Cook Islands		
DPRK		
Fiji		2005–09
India	1946–2005	2005–09
Indonesia	1954–62 76–80 85–89 95–99	2003–07
Iran	1952–58 64–68 74–78 1999–2003	
Japan	1952–95 1997–2005	2005–09
Kazakhstan	1997–2001	
Kiribati		

	Previous terms	Current terms
Kyrgyzstan		
Lao PDR		
Malaysia	1978–83 87–91 93–97 1999–2003	
Maldives		
Marshall Islands		
Micronesia		
Mongolia	1983–87	
Myanmar		
Nauru		
Nepal	1974–78 95–99	2005–09
New Zealand	1960–64 78–83 95–99	
Niue		
Pakistan	1951–66 68–74 1978–2003	2003–07
Palau		
Papua New Guinea	1989–93	
Philippines	1950–54 58–62 74–78 83–87 91–95 1999–2003	
ROK	1987–2003	
Samoa	1997–2001	
Solomon Islands		
Sri Lanka	1968–74 87–91	2003–07
Thailand	1952–56 80–85 89–93 95–99	2005–09
Timor-Leste		
Tonga	1993–97	
Turkmenistan		
Tuvalu		
Vanuatu	2001–05	
Viet Nam	1978–83 2001–05	
Group V		
Algeria	1968–74 80–89 91–95 2001–05	2005–09
Angola	1993–97	
Bahrain	1991–95	2003–07
Benin	1972–76 85–89 93–97 1999–2003	2005–09
Botswana	1991–95	
Burkina Faso	1974–78 89–93 2001–05	
Burundi	1978–83 89–93	
Cameroon	1962–68 80–89 95–99	2003–07
Cape Verde	1989–93	2003–07
Central African Republic	1983–87	
Chad	1962–70 76–80 89–93 1999–2003	
Comoros		
Congo	1968–74 85–89	2003–07
Côte d'Ivoire	1964–72 76–80 85–89 91–95 1997–2001	
DR Congo	1970–76 80–85	2005–09
Djibouti		
Egypt	1946–51 54–80 1985–2005	2005–09
Equatorial Guinea	1987–91	
Eritrea		
Ethiopia	1968–74 85–89 93–97 1999–2003	2005–09
Gabon	1974–78 83–87 1997–2001	
Gambia	1989–93	
Ghana	1970–76 80–85 91–95 1997–2001	2003–07
Guinea	1980–85 89–93 1997–2001	

	Previous terms	Current terms
Guinea-Bissau	1980–85	
Iraq	1978–83 89–93	
Jordan	1976–80 85–89 93–97 2001–05	
Kenya	1972–76 87–91 95–99 2001–05	
Kuwait	1983–87 1999–2003	
Lebanon	1950–58 66–74 83–87 1997–2001	2005–09
Lesotho	1978–83 95–99	
Liberia	1953–56 76–80	
Libyan AJ	1976–80 1997–2001	
Madagascar	1960–64 83–87 91–95 1999–2003	
Malawi	1987–91 1999–2003	
Mali	1962–70 85–89 93–97	2003–07
Mauritania	1974–78 87–91	
Mauritius	1976–80 95–99	2003–07
Morocco	1958–66 78–83 93–97 1999–2003	2003–07
Mozambique	1987–91 2001–05	
Namibia	1993–97	2003–07
Niger	1983–87 93–97	
Nigeria	1962–70 76–85 87–91 93–97 1999–2003	2005–09
Oman	1991–95 1999–2003	
Qatar	1987–91	
Rwanda	1976–80 2001–05	
Sao Tome and Principe		
Saudi Arabia	1972–76 95–99	
Senegal	1966–74 78–83 85–89 95–99 2001–05	
Seychelles	1991–95	
Sierra Leone	1976–80	
Somalia	1987–91	
South Africa	1997–2001	2005–09
Sudan	1962–66 78–87	
Swaziland	1983–87 2001–05	
Syrian AR	1951–54 74–78 83–87	
Togo	1972–76 87–91 1997–2001	2005–09
Tunisia	1974–78 80–85 91–95 1999–2003	
Uganda	1974–78 87–91 1997–2001	2005–09
UAE	1980–85 95–99	
UR of Tanzania	1964–72 80–85 89–93 95–99 2001–05	
Yemen	1989–93 95–99	2003–07
Zambia	1966–74 91–95	
Zimbabwe	1983–87 95–99	

Associate members

Aruba	Cayman Islands	Netherlands Antilles
British Virgin Islands	Macau, China	Tokelau

Observer status

Holy See	Palestine	Singapore

Sub-organs

The following are some of the inter-government bodies that are sub-organs of the UNESCO General Conference:

- Inter-governmental Council of the International Hydrological Programme

- International Coordinating Council of the Programme on Man and the Biosphere
- International Geoscience Programme
- Inter-governmental Oceanographic Commission
- Inter-governmental Council for the Information for All Programme
- Inter-governmental Council of the International Programme for the Development of Communication
- Inter-governmental Committee for Physical Education and Sport
- Inter-governmental Committee for Promoting the Return of Cultural Property to its Countries of Origin or its Restitution in the Case of Illicit Appropriation
- Inter-governmental Council of the Management of Social Transformations Programme
- Inter-governmental Bioethics Committee.

Notes

[1] The former Socialist Federal Republic of Yugoslavia occupied a seat on the Executive Board as a member of Group II from 1951–53, 1972–76, 1983–87, 1989–91 and 1991–92.

[2] Montenegro became a member state of UNESCO on 1 March 2007. Its place among the electoral groups will be confirmed by the General Conference at its 34th session in October 2007.

[3] On 3 June 2006 the Republic of Serbia notified the UN that the membership of the State Union of Serbia and Montenegro in the UN, including all organs and organisations of the UN system, was continued by the Republic of Serbia on the basis of article 60 of the Constitutional Charter of Serbia and Montenegro, activated by the Declaration of Independence adopted by the National Assembly of Montenegro on 3 June 2006.

World Heritage Committee (WHC)

http://whc.unesco.org/ab_comm.htm

Purpose

The WHC is a part of UNESCO. It is responsible for inscribing sites on the World Heritage List, monitoring their state of conservation, inscribing properties on the List of World Heritage in Danger and determining the use of the World Heritage Fund. As of 1 March 2007, 830 sites – 644 cultural, 162 natural and 24 mixed sites – in 138 countries were inscribed on the World Heritage List.

The 1972 Convention concerning the Protection of the World Cultural and Natural Heritage had 183 States Parties as at October 2006.

Structure

The UNESCO World Heritage Centre in Paris is the Secretariat to the World Heritage Committee. It was established in 1992 to develop an integrated, multi-disciplinary approach to the conservation of both cultural and natural heritage of outstanding universal value.

The General Assembly of States Parties meets during the ordinary session of the UNESCO General Conference to elect the 21 members to the WHC.

Membership

According to the World Heritage Convention, a committee member's term of office is for six years. In practice most States Parties choose voluntarily to serve for only four years to give other States Parties an opportunity to be on the Committee. All members elected at the fifteenth General Assembly (2005) have voluntarily decided to reduce their period of term from six to four years.

Current WHC members are as follows. The year indicates the expiry of their term in office:

Benin	2007	Mauritius	2009
Canada	2009	Morocco	2009
Chile	2007	Netherlands	2007
Cuba	2009	New Zealand	2007
India	2007	Norway	2007
Israel	2009	Peru	2009
Japan	2007	Spain	2009
Kenya	2009	ROK	2009
Kuwait	2007	Tunisia	2009
Lithuania	2007	USA	2009
Madagascar	2009		

The WHC meets annually. Its 2007 meeting was held in Christchurch, New Zealand, from 23 June to 2 July.

World Health Organization (WHO)

20 Avenue Appia
1211 Geneva 27
Switzerland
Telephone: (+41 22) 791 2111
Fax: (+41 22) 791 3111
Email: info@who.int
Internet: www.who.int
Director-General: Margaret Chan, China (since January 2007) (appointed by the World Health Assembly for a five-year term on 9 November 2006)

Purpose

Representatives of 61 states adopted the Constitution of the WHO in 1946. The Organization formally came into existence on 7 April 1948 and became a specialised agency on 10 July 1948.

Article 1 of the Constitution defines WHO's objective as "the attainment by all peoples of the highest possible level of health". The detailed functions are set out in article 2 of the Constitution.

Structure
- World Health Assembly
- Executive Board
- Secretariat.

The World Health Assembly takes place annually, usually in Geneva. The 60th session was held in Geneva from 14 to 23 May 2007.

The Executive Board is composed of 34 individuals technically qualified in the health field, each one designated by a Member State elected to do so by the World Health Assembly. Member States are elected for three-year terms. The Board meets at least twice a year in Geneva. The Chair for 2007 and 2008 is B Sadasivan, Singapore.

Membership

At 1 March 2007 there were 193 Member States. The following is a list of WHO members, showing terms on the Executive Board:

	Previous terms	Current terms
Africa (46 members)		
Algeria	1969–72 95–98	
Angola	1977–80 96–99	
Benin	1966–69 96–99	
Botswana	1977–80 96–99	
Burkina Faso	1969–72 96–99	
Burundi	1978–81 1997–2000	
Cameroon	1964–67 92–95	
Cape Verde	1978–81 1998–2001	
Central African Republic	1969–72 1998–2001	
Chad	1978–81 1999–2002	
Comoros	1978–81 1999–2002	
Congo	1979–82 1999–2002	
Côte d'Ivoire	1967–70 84–87 1999–2002	
DR Congo	1972–75 93–96	
Equatorial Guinea	1984–87 2000–03	
Eritrea	1983–86 2001–04	
Ethiopia	1969–73 2001–04	
Gabon	1980–83 2002–05	
Gambia	1980–83 2002–05	
Ghana	1960–63 83–86 2002–05	
Guinea	1965–68 84–87 2002–05	
Guinea-Bissau	1981–84 2003–06	
Kenya	1970–73 84–87 2004–07	
Lesotho	1971–74 85–88 2004–07	
Liberia	1951–54 57–60 86–89	2005–08
Madagascar	1961–64 86–89	2005–08
Malawi	1973–76 87–90	2007–10
Mali	1963–66 87–90	2006–09
Mauritania	1975–78 87–90	
Mauritius	1974–77 87–90	
Mozambique	1981–84 88–91	
Namibia		2005–08
Niger	1972–75 89–92	
Nigeria	1961–62 66–69 89–92	
Rwanda	1975–78 90–93	2005–08
Sao Tome and Principe	1981–84 90–93	2007–10
Senegal	1961–64 90–93	
Seychelles	1981–84 90–93	
Sierra Leone	1963–66 91–94	
South Africa	1948–51 54–57	
Swaziland	1975–78 92–95	
Togo	1975–77 93–96	
Uganda	1968–71 93–96	
UR of Tanzania	1975–78 93–96	
Zambia	1976–79 94–97	
Zimbabwe	1982–85 95–98	

OTHER BODIES

The Americas (35 members)

	Previous terms	Current terms
Antigua and Barbuda		
Argentina	1955–58 60–62 66–69 74–77 83–86 88–91 95–98	
Bahamas	1989–92	2007–10
Barbados	1995–98	
Belize		
Bolivia	1977–80 91–94 2004–07	
Brazil	1948–51 52–55 58–61 63–66 80–83 87–90 95–98 2000–07	
Canada	1952–59 62–65 68–71 75–78 80–83 85–88 92–95 1997–2000 03–06	
Chile	1950–53 54–57 61–62 68–72 82–85 89–92 1998–2001	
Colombia	1962–65 72–75 79–82 89–92 2001–04	
Costa Rica	1953–56 93–96	
Cuba	1951–54 77–80 85–88 94–97 2001–04	
Dominica		
Dominican Republic		
Ecuador	1955–58 71–74 85–87 2003–06	
El Salvador	1950–53	2006–09
Grenada	2001–04	
Guatemala	1958–61 74–77 80–83 1999–2002	
Guyana	1975–76 86–89	
Haiti	1962–65	
Honduras	1976–79 96–99	
Jamaica	1968–71 79–82 92–95 2004–07	
Mexico	1948–50 56–59 65–68 78–81 86–89 92–95	2005–08
Nicaragua	1970–73 88–91	
Panama	1967–70 83–86	
Paraguay	1964–67	2007–10
Peru	1959–62 65–68 76–79 1997–2000	2007–10
Saint Kitts and Nevis		
Saint Lucia		
Saint Vincent and the Grenadines		
Suriname		
Trinidad and Tobago	1971–74 82–85 1998–2001	
USA	1949–52 54–56 58–60 62–64 66–68 70–72 74–76 78–80 82–85 87–89 91–93 95–97 1999–2001 03–05	2006–09
Uruguay	1971–74 91–94	
Venezuela	1949–52 59–62 74–77 83–86 2000–03	

Eastern Mediterranean (21 members)

	Previous terms	Current terms
Afghanistan	1972–75 91–94	2006–09
Bahrain	1978–81 95–98 2004–07	
Djibouti	1983–86	2006–09
Egypt	1949–51 57–60 67–70 84–87 95–98 2001–04	
Iran	1948–49 52–55 58–61 63–66 73–76 79–82 88–91 2000–03	
Iraq	1953–56 61–64 82–85 87–93	2005–08
Jordan	1960–63 74–77 87–90 2000–03	
Kuwait	1964–67 80–83 94–97 2002–05	
Lebanon	1951–54 68–71 86–89 1999–2002	

	Previous terms	Current terms
Libyan AJ	1964–67 77–80 88–91 2004–07	
Morocco	1965–68 82–85 93–96	
Oman	1979–82 1997–2000	
Pakistan	1950–53 55–58 61–63 67–70 76–79 82–85 94–97 2003–06	
Qatar	1976–79 92–95 1998–2001	
Saudi Arabia	1954–57 70–73 86–89 2001–04	
Somalia	1966–69 75–78	
Sudan	1959–62 75–77 89–92 2003–06	
Syrian AR	1956–58 71–74 83–86 92–95	
Tunisia	1958–59 62–65 77–80 91–94	2007–10
UAE	1981–84 96–99	2007–10
Yemen	1965–68 73–76 80–83 85–88 90–92 1998–2001	

Europe (53 members)[1,2]

	Previous terms	Current terms
Albania		
Andorra		
Armenia		
Austria	1953–56 70–73 88–91	
Azerbaijan		2005–08
Belarus	1948–50	
Belgium	1951–54 68–71 83–86 1999–2002	
Bosnia and Herzegovina		
Bulgaria	1969–72 81–84 91–94	
Croatia	1995–98	
Cyprus	1969–72 85–88 1997–2000	
Czech Republic	2003–06	
Denmark	1952–55 71–74 91–94	2006–09
Estonia		
Finland	1955–58 75–78 94–97	
France	1948–2001 03–06	
Georgia		
Germany	1957–60 67–70 73–80 85–88 1997–2000	
Greece	1951–54 76–79 91–94	
Hungary	1972–75 84–87	
Iceland	1961–63 83–86 2003–06	
Ireland	1959–62 95–98	
Israel	1961–64 93–96	
Italy	1950–53 56–59 61–64 71–74 2000–03	
Kazakhstan	2001–04	
Kyrgyzstan		
Latvia		2006–09
Lithuania	2000–03	
Luxembourg	1959–62 2004–07	
Malta	1985–88	
Monaco		
Montenegro[3]		
Netherlands	1948–51 63–66 79–82 1997–2000	
Norway	1948–49 63–66 79–82 1997–2000	
Poland	1948–51 61–64 73–76 85–88 1996–2000	
Portugal	1955–58 77–80 92–95	2005–08
Republic of Moldova		2007–10
Romania	1967–70 80–83 2004–07	

	Previous terms	Current terms
Russian Federation	1948–50 1958–2005	
San Marino		
Serbia[4]	1948–51 64–67 75–78 89–92	
Slovakia		
Slovenia		2006–09
Spain	1961–64 81–84 89–92 2002–05	
Sweden	1949–52 67–70 87–90 2000–03	
Switzerland	1953–56 73–76 1999–2002	
Tajikistan		
The Former Yugoslav Republic of Macedonia		
Turkey	1949–52 64–67 79–82 93–96	2006–09
Turkmenistan		
Ukraine		
UK	1948–99 2001–04	2007–10
Uzbekistan		

South-East Asia (11 members)

	Previous terms	Current terms
Bangladesh	1975–78 87–90 1998–2001	
Bhutan	1995–98	2005–08
DPRK	1990–93 2000–03	
India	1948–51 56–59 65–68 77–80 88–91 1999–2002	
Indonesia	1953–56 63–66 72–75 84–88 96–99	2007–10
Maldives	1981–84 91–94 2002–05	
Myanmar	1954–57 66–69 78–81 90–93 2001–04	
Nepal	1959–62 69–72 83–86 93–96 2003–06	
Sri Lanka	1948–49 51–54 62–65 74–77 86–89 1997–2000	2006–09
Thailand	1950–53 60–63 71–74 84–87 94–97 2004–07	
Timor-Leste		

Western Pacific (27 members)

	Previous terms	Current terms
Australia	1948–49 57–60 67–70 75–78 85–88 95–98 2004–07	
Brunei Darussalam		
Cambodia		
China	1948–50 73–76 78–85 1990–2005	2006–09
Cook Islands	1997–2000	
Fiji	1976–79	
Japan	1954–57 61–64 69–72 75–76 81–84 87–90 1992–2003	2005–08
Kiribati		
Lao PDR	1970–73 1998–2001	
Malaysia	1964–67 82–85	
Marshall Islands		
Micronesia		
Mongolia	1968–71 80–83 92–95	
Nauru		
New Zealand	1952–55 63–66 72–75 79–82	2007–10
Niue		
Palau		
Papua New Guinea	1989–92	
Philippines	1949–52 55–58 66–69 76–79 91–94 2001–04	
ROK	1960–63 84–87 95–98 2001–04	2007–10
Samoa	1979–82	

Previous terms	Current terms
Singapore	2006–09
Solomon Islands	
Tonga 1985–86 88–91 2004–07	
Tuvalu	
Vanuatu 1999–2002	
Viet Nam 1958–61 93–96 2003–06	

Associate members

Puerto Rico
Tokelau

Notes

[1] The former Socialist Federal Republic of Yugoslavia served on the Executive Board from 1948–1951, 1964–1967, 1975–1978 and 1989–1992.

[2] Czechoslovakia served on the Executive Board from 1965–1968, 1976–1979 and 1988–1991.

[3] On 29 August 2006 Montenegro became a member of the UN, including all organs and organisations of the UN system.

[4] On 3 June 2006 the Republic of Serbia notified the UN that the membership of the State Union of Serbia and Montenegro in the UN, including all organs and organisations of the UN system, was continued by the Republic of Serbia on the basis of article 60 of the Constitutional Charter of Serbia and Montenegro, activated by the Declaration of Independence adopted by the National Assembly of Montenegro on 3 June 2006.

International Civil Aviation Organization (ICAO)

999 University Street
Montreal, Quebec
Canada H3C 5H7
Telephone: (+1 514) 954 8219
Fax: (+1 514) 954 6077
Email: icaohq@icao.int
Internet: www.icao.int
Secretary-General: Taïeb Chérif, Algeria (reappointed by the Council for a term of three years, beginning 1 August 2006)

Purpose

The Convention on International Civil Aviation, which provided for the establishment of ICAO, was signed in Chicago in 1944. The Organization came into existence on 4 April 1947 after 26 states had ratified the Convention.

Under article 44 of the Convention, ICAO is charged with developing the principles and techniques of international air navigation, and fostering the planning and development of international air transport to ensure the safe and orderly growth of international civil aviation throughout the world.

Structure

- Assembly
- Council
- Committees of the Council
- Air Navigation Commission
- Secretariat.

The Assembly is the Organization's sovereign body. It meets not less than once in three years to review its work and establish guidelines for future activities. The 36th session is scheduled to be held in Montreal from 18 to 28 September 2007.

The Council is the executive body of ICAO. It comprises 36 contracting states elected by the ordinary session of the Assembly for a three-year term. The current President of the Council is Roberto Kobeh González, Mexico. In electing the members of the Council, the Assembly gives adequate representation to states of chief importance to air transport, states not otherwise included that make the largest contribution to the provision of facilities for international civil air navigation, and states whose designation will ensure that all major geographical areas of the world are represented.

ICAO's committees are: the Air Transport Committee, Legal Committee, Committee on Joint Support of Air Navigation Services, Finance Committee, Committee on Unlawful Interference, Technical Cooperation Committee and the Committee on Aviation Environmental Protection. All committee members, except those of the Legal Committee, are appointed by the Council. Membership of the Legal Committee is open to all Member States.

The Air Navigation Commission is the principal body concerned with the development of Standards and Recommended Practices (SARPs). It comprises 19 people qualified and experienced in the science and practice of aeronautics. Its members are nominated by Contracting States and are appointed by the Council.

Membership

As at 31 March 2007 ICAO had 190 members. The following is a list of ICAO members' terms on the Council:

	Previous terms	Current terms
Afghanistan		
Albania		
Algeria	1980–86 1998–2004	
Andorra		
Angola	1995–98	
Antigua and Barbuda		
Argentina	1947–2004	2004–07
Armenia		
Australia	1947–2004	2004–07
Austria		2004–07
Azerbaijan		
Bahamas		
Bahrain		
Bangladesh		
Barbados		
Belarus		
Belgium	1983–86 92–95	
Belize		
Benin		
Bhutan		
Bolivia	1995–98	
Bosnia and Herzegovina		
Botswana	1998–2001	
Brazil	1947–2004	2004–07

	Previous terms	Current terms
Brunei Darussalam		
Bulgaria		
Burkina Faso		
Burundi		
Cambodia		
Cameroon	1980–83 1992–2004	2004–07
Canada	1947–2004	2004–07
Cape Verde		
Central African Republic		
Chad		
Chile	1947–50 89–92 2002–04	2004–07
China	1974–2004	2004–07
Colombia	1962–86 1992–2001	2004–07
Comoros		
Congo	1962–74	
Cook Islands		
Costa Rica	1974–77 2001–04	
Côte d'Ivoire		
Croatia		
Cuba	1986–89 1998–2004	
Cyprus		
Czech Republic	1993–95 2001–04	
DPRK		
DR Congo		
Denmark	1980–83 95–98	
Djibouti		
Dominican Republic		
Ecuador	1992–95	
Egypt	1947–2004	2004–07
El Salvador	1980–83 95–98	
Equatorial Guinea		
Eritrea		
Estonia		
Ethiopia	2001–04	2004–07
Fiji		
Finland	1977–80 89–92	2004–07
France	1948–2004	2004–07
Gabon		
Gambia		
Georgia		
Germany	1959–2004	2004–07
Ghana	1986–92	2004–07
Greece		
Grenada		
Guatemala		
Guinea		
Guinea-Bissau		
Guyana		
Haiti		
Honduras	1977–80 89–92	2004–07
Hungary		2004–07
Iceland	1992–2001	
India	1947–2004	2004–07

	Previous terms	Current terms
Indonesia	1968–2001	
Iran		
Iraq	1980–92	
Ireland	1947–59 2001–04	
Israel		
Italy	1950–2004	2004–07
Jamaica	1977–86	
Japan	1956–2004	2004–07
Jordan		
Kazakhstan		
Kenya	1983–89 1992–2001	
Kiribati		
Kuwait		
Kyrgyzstan		
Lao PDR		
Latvia		
Lebanon	1953–86 1992–2004	2004–07
Lesotho		
Liberia		
Libyan AJ		
Lithuania		
Luxembourg		
Madagascar	1974–86	
Malawi		
Malaysia		
Maldives		
Mali		
Malta		
Marshall Islands		
Mauritania		
Mauritius	2001–04	
Mexico	1962–2004	2004–07
Micronesia		
Monaco		
Mongolia		
Montenegro[1]		
Morocco	1974–80 92–98	
Mozambique		2004–07
Myanmar		
Namibia		
Nauru		
Nepal		
Netherlands	1980–83 89–92 1998–2001	
New Zealand		
Nicaragua	1971–74 92–95	
Niger		
Nigeria	1962–2004	2004–07
Norway	1983–86 1998–2001	
Oman		
Pakistan	1973–2004	2004–07
Palau		
Panama	1986–2001	
Papua New Guinea		
Paraguay	2001–04	

	Previous terms	Current terms
Peru	1986–89	2004–07
Philippines	1959–68	
Poland		
Portugal	1947–62	
Qatar		
ROK	2001–04	2004–07
Republic of Moldova		
Romania	1995–98	
Russian Federation	1972–2004	2004–07
Rwanda		
Saint Kitts and Nevis		
Saint Lucia		2004–07
Saint Vincent and the Grenadines		
Samoa		
San Marino		
Sao Tome and Principe		
Saudi Arabia	1986–2004	2004–07
Senegal	1968–2004	
Serbia[2]		
Seychelles		
Sierra Leone		
Singapore	2002–04	2004–07
Slovakia	1998–2001	
Slovenia		
Solomon Islands		
Somalia		
South Africa	1950–65 2002–04	2004–07
Spain	1951–2004	2004–07
Sri Lanka		
Sudan		
Suriname		
Swaziland		
Sweden	1986–89 2001–04	
Switzerland	1986–89 95–98	
Syrian AR		
Tajikistan		
Thailand		
The Former Yugoslav Republic of Macedonia		
Timor-Leste		
Togo		
Tonga		
Trinidad and Tobago	1972–77 89–98	
Tunisia	1986–92	2004–07
Turkey	1947–50	
Turkmenistan		
Uganda	1980–83	
Ukraine		
UAE		
UK	1947–2004	2004–07
UR of Tanzania	1977–80 83–95	
USA	1947–2004	2004–07

Previous terms		Current terms
Uruguay	1998–2001	
Uzbekistan		
Vanuatu		
Venezuela	1980–92 95–98 2001–04	
Viet Nam		
Yemen		
Zambia		
Zimbabwe		

Notes

[1] Montenegro became a Member State on 14 March 2007.

[2] On 3 June 2006 the Republic of Serbia notified the UN that the membership of the State Union of Serbia and Montenegro in the UN, including all organs and organisations of the UN system, was continued by the Republic of Serbia on the basis of article 60 of the Constitutional Charter of Serbia and Montenegro, activated by the Declaration of Independence adopted by the National Assembly of Montenegro on 3 June 2006.

Universal Postal Union (UPU)

International Bureau
Case postale 13
3000 Berne 15
Switzerland
Telephone: (+41 31) 350 3111
Fax: (+41 31) 350 3110
Email: info@upu.int
Internet: www.upu.int
Director-General: Edouard Dayan, France (since 2005) (elected by the 2004 Bucharest UPU Congress)

Purpose

The UPU was established by the Berne Treaty of 1874 and became a specialised agency of the United Nations in 1948. Article 1 of the Vienna Constitution 1964 states that the aim of the Union is to secure the organisation and improvement of the postal services, promote the development of international collaboration and undertake, as far as possible, technical assistance in postal matters requested by member countries. To this end, the countries that have adopted the Constitution comprise a single postal territory.

Structure

• Universal Postal Congress
• Council of Administration
• Postal Operations Council (POC)
• Consultative Committee (CC)
• International Bureau.

The Universal Postal Congress is the four-yearly conference at which the general legislation, except the Constitution, is revised, and members of the Council of Administration and the Postal Operations Council are elected. An extraordinary Congress may be held at the request of two-thirds of the members. The provisions in force were those approved by the 23rd Universal Postal Congress in Bucharest in 2004 and came into effect on 1 January 2006. The 24th Congress is to be held in Nairobi, Kenya, in 2008.

The Council of Administration, formerly the Executive Council, carries on the work of the Union between Congresses. Forty members are elected by the Congress on the basis of equitable geographical distribution and may not hold office for more than two consecutive terms. The 41st member is the representative of the Congress host country, which automatically becomes the Chair. Romania was the host country of the 2004 Bucharest Congress.

The POC is responsible for operational, commercial, technical and economic postal matters. Its 40 members are elected by the Congress on a geographical basis. The POC members elect the Chair during the Congress. The chair for 2004 to 2008 is the USA.

The CC was created by the 2004 Bucharest Congress. It gives postal stakeholders other than public postal operators and regulators a voice in the organisation's deliberations. It consists of non-government organisations, delivery service providers, workers' organisations, suppliers of goods and services to the postal sector, and other organisations that have an interest in international postal services. The Chair is currently the President of the United States Direct Marketing Association.

The International Bureau is the permanent secretariat of the Union and the UPU's headquarters. Located in Berne, Switzerland, it provides logistical and technical support for the UPU's bodies. It also serves as an office of liaison, information and consultation, and promotes technical cooperation among Union members.

Membership

As at 1 April 2007 the UPU had 191 member countries:

Member countries	Membership of UPU bodies	Member countries	Membership of UPU bodies
Zone 1 – Western Hemisphere			
Antigua and Barbuda		Guyana	
Argentina		Haiti	
Bahamas		Honduras	
Barbados	Postal Operations Council Consultative Committee	Jamaica	
Belize		Mexico	
Bolivia		Netherlands	
Brazil	Council of Administration Postal Operations Council	Antilles and Aruba	
Canada	Postal Operations Council	Nicaragua	
Colombia	Council of Administration	Panama	Council of Administration
Chile	Council of Administration	Paraguay	
Costa Rica	Council of Administration	Peru	
Cuba	Council of Administration Postal Operations Council	Saint Kitts and Nevis	
Dominica		Saint Lucia	
Dominican Republic		Saint Vincent and the Grenadines	
Ecuador	Council of Administration	Suriname	
El Salvador		Trinidad and Tobago	Council of Administration
Grenada		USA	Chair of Postal Operations Council
Guatemala		Uruguay	
		Venezuela	

OTHER BODIES

Member countries	Membership of UPU bodies

Zone 2 – Eastern Europe and Northern Asia

Armenia	Council of Administration
Azerbaijan	Council of Administration
Belarus	
Bosnia and Herzegovina	
Bulgaria	
Czech Republic	
Estonia	
Georgia	
Hungary	Council of Administration Postal Operations Council
Kazakhstan	Council of Administration
Kyrgyzstan	
Latvia	
Lithuania	

Zone 3 – Western Europe

Albania	Council of Administration
Austria	
Belgium	Council of Administration Postal Operations Council
Croatia	
Cyprus	
Denmark	
Finland	
France	Postal Operations Council
Germany	Council of Administration Postal Operations Council
Greece	Postal Operations Council
Iceland	
Ireland	
Italy	Council of Administration Postal Operations Council
Liechtenstein	
Luxembourg	

Zone 4 – Southern Asia, Oceania

Afghanistan	
Australia	Council of Administration Postal Operations Council
Bahrain	
Bangladesh	
Bhutan	

Member countries	Membership of UPU bodies

Montenegro	
Poland	Council of Administration
Republic of Moldova	
Romania	Chair of Council of Administration Postal Operations Council
Russian Federation	Postal Operations Council
Serbia[1]	
Slovakia	
Tajikistan	
The Former Yugoslav Republic of Macedonia	
Turkmenistan	
Ukraine	Postal Operations Council
Uzbekistan	

Malta	
Monaco	
Netherlands	Postal Operations Council
Norway	
Portugal	Council of Administration Postal Operations Council
San Marino	
Slovenia	
Spain	Council of Administration Postal Operations Council Consultative Committee
Sweden	Postal Operations Council
Switzerland	Postal Operations Council
Turkey	
UK	Council of Administration Postal Operations Council Consultative Committee
Vatican	

Brunei Darussalam	
Cambodia	
China[2]	Council of Administration Postal Operations Council
DPRK	
Fiji	

Member countries	Membership of UPU bodies
India	Postal Operations Council
Indonesia	Council of Administration
	Postal Operations Council
Iran	Council of Administration
Iraq	
Israel	
Japan	Council of Administration
	Postal Operations Council
	Consultative Committee
Jordan	
Kiribati	
Kuwait	
Lao PDR	
Lebanon	
Malaysia	Council of Administration
	Postal Operations Council
Maldives	
Mongolia	
Myanmar	
Nauru	
Nepal	
New Zealand	Postal Operations Council
Oman	

Member countries	Membership of UPU bodies
Pakistan	Council of Administration
	Postal Operations Council
Papua New Guinea	
Philippines	
Qatar	
ROK	Council of Administration
	Postal Operations Council
	Consultative Committee
Samoa	
Saudi Arabia	
Singapore	Postal Operations Council
Solomon Islands	
Sri Lanka	
Syrian AR	
Thailand	Postal Operations Council
Timor-Leste	
Tonga	
Tuvalu	
UAE	Council of Administration
Vanuatu	
Viet Nam	Council of Administration
Yemen	

Zone 5 – Africa

Member countries	Membership of UPU bodies
Algeria	
Angola	Council of Administration
Benin	Council of Administration
	Consultative Committee
Botswana	
Burkina Faso	Postal Operations Council
Burundi	
Cameroon	Council of Administration
Cape Verde	
Central African Republic	
Chad	
Comoros	
Congo	
Côte d'Ivoire	Postal Operations Council
DR Congo	
Djibouti	
Egypt	Postal Operations Council
Equatorial Guinea	
Eritrea	

Member countries	Membership of UPU bodies
Ethiopia	
Gabon	
Gambia	
Ghana	Postal Operations Council
Guinea	
Guinea-Bissau	
Kenya	Postal Operations Council
Lesotho	
Liberia	
Libyan AJ	
Madagascar	
Malawi	
Mali	
Mauritania	
Mauritius	
Morocco	Council of Administration
	Postal Operations Council
Mozambique	
Namibia	

Member countries	Membership of UPU bodies	Member countries	Membership of UPU bodies
Niger		South Africa	
Nigeria	Council of Administration	Sudan	Council of Administration
Rwanda		Swaziland	
Saudi Arabia	Postal Operations Council	Tunisia	Council of Administration Postal Operations Council
Sao Tome and Principe			
Senegal	Council of Administration	Uganda	Council of Administration
Seychelles		UR of Tanzania	
Sierra Leone		Zambia	
Somalia		Zimbabwe	Council of Administration

Notes

[1] On 3 June 2006 the Republic of Serbia notified the UN that the membership of the State Union of Serbia and Montenegro in the UN, including all organs and organisations of the UN system, was continued by the Republic of Serbia on the basis of article 60 of the Constitutional Charter of Serbia and Montenegro, activated by the Declaration of Independence adopted by the National Assembly of Montenegro on 3 June 2006.

[2] Host country and Chair.

International Telecommunication Union (ITU)

Place des Nations
1211 Geneva 20
Switzerland
Telephone: (+41 22) 730 5111
Fax: (+41 22) 733 7256
Email: itumail@itu.int
Internet: www.itu.int
Secretary-General: Hamadoun Touré, Mali (since 2007) (elected for a four-year term by Member States, commencing on 1 January 2007)

Purpose

The ITU was founded in 1865 in Paris as the International Telegraph Union. The 1932 Madrid Plenipotentiary Conference decided the current name, which came into force on 1 January 1934.

The ITU is an inter-government organisation that brings together governments and industry to coordinate the establishment and operation of global telecommunication networks and services. It consists of Member States and Sector Members representing public and private companies and organisations with an interest in telecommunications.

The purposes of the Union are to:
- Extend international cooperation among Member States for the improvement and rational use of telecommunications of all kinds
- Promote and enhance participation of entities and organisations in the activities of the Union and foster cooperation and partnership between them and Member States
- Promote and offer technical assistance to developing countries in telecommunications
- Promote the development of technical facilities and their most efficient operation
- Promote the extension of the benefits of information and communication technologies to all the world's inhabitants
- Promote the use of telecommunication services with the aim of facilitating peaceful relations

- Harmonise the actions of Member States and promote cooperation and partnership between Member States and Sector Members
- Promote internationally a broader approach to telecommunications issues by cooperating with other inter-government organisations and those non-government organisations concerned with telecommunications.

The ITU pursues its objectives by means of:

- The promotion of international cooperation in the delivery of technical assistance to developing countries
- Policy papers and reports designed to provide a focus on topics of current interest to regulators, policy-makers and the broader ITU membership
- The global coordination of radio frequency spectrum usage and orbital satellite positions, and the adoption of international regulations and treaties governing all uses of the frequency spectrum within which countries frame their national legislation
- The adoption of technical standards that foster global inter-connectivity and inter-operability with as low rates as possible, consistent with efficient service
- Policy advice and technical assistance to developing countries
- Measures for ensuring the safety of life
- Promotion of preferential and favourable lines of credit for the development of social projects aimed at extending telecommunication services to the most isolated areas.

The ITU's current areas of focus are:

- Facilitating implementation of the outcomes of the World Summit on the Information Society
- Building telecommunication/ICT infrastructure to connect under-served and remote communities
- Promoting cybersecurity and confidence in online transactions
- Strengthening emergency telecommunications.

Structure

The Union comprises:

- Plenipotentiary Conference
- Council
- World conferences on international telecommunications (see Sectors below)
- General Secretariat.

The Constitution provides that a Plenipotentiary Conference, the supreme organ of the Union, be convened every four years. The next is scheduled to take place in Mexico in 2010. Plenipotentiary Conferences are composed of delegations from the Union's Member States. They adopt the underlying policies of the organisation and determine its structure and activities. Plenipotentiary conferences determine the direction of the Union and its activities, and make decisions relating to the structure of the organisation through a treaty called the Constitution and Convention of the International Telecommunication Union.

The Council acts on behalf of the Plenipotentiary Conference. It comprises up to 25 percent of the total number of Member States, elected by the Plenipotentiary Conference with due regard to the equitable distribution of Council seats among the five world regions (Americas, eight seats; Western Europe, eight seats; Eastern Europe, five seats; Africa, 13 seats; Asia and Australasia, 12 seats). The current Council comprises 46 Member States, and meets annually. The 2007 session was scheduled to be held from 4 to 14 September.

The role of the Council is to consider, in the interval between Plenipotentiary Conferences, broad telecommunication policy issues and ensure that the Union's activities, policies and strategies respond fully to the rapidly changing telecommunication environment. In addition, the Council reports on policy and strategic planning, and is responsible for ensuring the smooth day-to-day running of the Union, coordinating work programmes, approving budgets and controlling finances.

The ITU has three main Sectors, encompassing its main conferences:
- The Radiocommunication Sector comprises the world and regional radio communication conferences, radio communication assemblies, study groups, the Radio Regulations Board, the Radiocommunication Advisory Group and the Radiocommunication Bureau
- The Telecommunication Standardization Sector comprises the world telecommunication standardisation assemblies, study groups, the Telecommunication Standardization Advisory Group and the Telecommunication Standardization Bureau
- The Telecommunication Development Sector comprises the world and regional telecommunication development conferences, study groups, the Telecommunication Development Advisory Group and the Telecommunication Development Bureau.

The General Secretariat of the ITU is headed by the organisation's Secretary-General, Hamadoun Touré, Mali, who is assisted by a Deputy Secretary-General and three elected Directors.

Membership

ITU membership consists of 191 Member States and over 600 Sector Members. Sector Members are public and private companies and organisations with an interest in telecommunications that are entitled to participate, with specific rights and obligations, in the work of one or more Sectors of the ITU.

Currently more than 130 Associates are also taking part in some work of the ITU under special arrangements with the Sectors. It is up to each Sector to admit Associates as partners in their activities.

The following list of Member States sets out terms of office on the Council:

	Previous terms	Current terms
The Americas		
Antigua and Barbuda		
Argentina	1947–2006	2006–10
Bahamas	1994–98	
Barbados		
Belize		
Bolivia		
Brazil	1947–2006	2006–10
Canada	1947–2006	2006–10
Chile	1994–98	
Colombia	1982–94	
Costa Rica		
Cuba	1989–2006	2006–10
Dominica		
Dominican Republic		
Ecuador		
El Salvador		
Grenada		

	Previous terms	Current terms
Guatemala		
Guyana		
Haiti		
Honduras		
Jamaica	1989–94	
Mexico	1952–2006	2006–10
Nicaragua		
Panama		
Paraguay		
Peru	1982–89	
Saint Lucia	1998–2002	
Saint Vincent and the Grenadines		
Saint Kitts and Nevis		
Suriname	2006–10	
Trinidad and Tobago	1973–82	2006–10
USA	1947–2006	2006–10
Uruguay		
Venezuela	1965–2006	2006–10

Western Europe

	Previous terms	Current terms
Andorra		
Austria		
Belgium		
Bosnia and Herzegovina		
Croatia		
Cyprus		
Denmark	1994–2002	
Estonia		
Finland		
France	1947–2006	2006–10
Germany	1959–2006	2006–10
Greece	1989–94	
Holy See		
Hungary	1973–82	
Iceland		
Ireland	1965–73	
Italy	1947–2006	2006–10
Latvia		
Liechtenstein		
Lithuania		
Luxembourg		
Malta		
Monaco		
Netherlands		
Norway	2002–06	
Portugal	1947–52 1994–2006	2006–10
San Marino		
Slovenia		
Spain	1973–2006	2006–10
Sweden	1973–94	2006–10
Switzerland	1947–2006	2006–10
Turkey	2002–06	2006–10
UK	1947–89 1994–2002	

Eastern Europe and Northern Asia[1, 2]

	Previous terms	Current terms
Albania		
Armenia		
Azerbaijan		
Belarus		
Bulgaria	1989–2006	2006–10
Czech Republic	1993–2006	2006–10
Georgia		
Kazakhstan		
Kyrgyzstan		
Poland	1965–82 1994–2006	
Republic of Moldova		
Romania	1973–89 1994–2006	2006–10
Russian Federation	1947–2006	2006–10
Serbia[3]		
Slovakia		
Tajikistan		
The Former Yugoslav Republic of Macedonia		
Turkmenistan		
Ukraine	1994–98	2006–10
Uzbekistan	1947–59	

Africa

	Previous terms	Current terms
Algeria	1965–2006	2006–10
Angola		
Benin	1982–98	
Botswana		
Burkina Faso	1989–2006	2006–10
Burundi		
Cameroon	1973–2006	2006–10
Cape Verde	1989–98	
Central African Republic		
Chad		
Comoros		
Congo		
Côte d'Ivoire	1998–2002	
DR Congo	1973–82	
Djibouti		
Egypt	1973–2006	2006–10
Equatorial Guinea		
Eritrea		
Ethiopia	1959–89	
Gabon	1998–2002	
Gambia		
Ghana	2002–06	2006–10
Guinea		
Guinea-Bissau		
Kenya	1982–2006	2006–10
Lesotho		
Liberia		
Libyan AJ		

	Previous terms	Current terms
Madagascar	1965–73	
Malawi		
Mali	1989–2006	2006–10
Mauritania		
Mauritius		
Morocco	1959–2006	2006–10
Mozambique		
Namibia		
Niger		
Nigeria	1965–98 2002–06	2006–10
Rwanda		
Sao Tome and Principe		
Senegal	1973–2006	2006–10
Seychelles		
Sierra Leone		
Somalia		
South Africa	1994–2006	2006–10
Sudan		
Swaziland		
Togo		
Tunisia	1959–2006	2006–10
Uganda	1965–73 2002–06	
UR of Tanzania	1973–2002	2006–10
Zambia	1982–89	
Zimbabwe		

Asia and Australasia

	Previous terms	Current terms
Afghanistan		
Australia	1959–2006	2006–10
Bahrain		
Bangladesh		
Bhutan		
Brunei Darussalam		
Cambodia		
China	1947–2006	2006–10
DPRK		
Fiji		
India	1952–2006	2006–10
Indonesia	1982–98 2002–06	2006–10
Iran	1973–82	2002–06
Iraq		
Israel		
Japan	1959–2006	2006–10
Jordan		
Kiribati		
Kuwait	1982–2002	
Lao PDR		
Lebanon	1965–89	
Malaysia	1973–82 1989–2006	2006–10
Maldives		
Marshall Islands		
Micronesia		
Mongolia		

Previous terms	Current terms

Myanmar
Nauru
Nepal
New Zealand
Oman
Pakistan........................1982–2006.........................2006–10
Papua New Guinea
Philippines.....................1982–2002.........................2006–10
Qatar
ROK.............................1989–2006.........................2006–10
Samoa
Saudi Arabia...................1965–2006.........................2006–10
Singapore
Solomon Islands
Sri Lanka
Syria
Thailand........................1973–2006.........................2006–10
Tonga
Tuvalu
UAE...2006–10
Vanuatu
Viet Nam.......................1994–2006
Yemen

OTHER BODIES

Notes

1   Czechoslovakia served on the Council from 1989–1992.

2   The former Socialist Federal Republic of Yugoslavia served on the Council from 1989–92.

3   On 3 June 2006 the Republic of Serbia notified the UN that the membership of the State Union of Serbia and Montenegro in the UN, including all organs and organisations of the UN system, was continued by the Republic of Serbia on the basis of article 60 of the Constitutional Charter of Serbia and Montenegro, activated by the Declaration of Independence adopted by the National Assembly of Montenegro on 3 June 2006.

World Meteorological Organization (WMO)

7 bis Avenue de la Paix
Case Postale 2300
1211 Geneva 2
Switzerland
Telephone: (+41 22) 730 8111
Fax: (+41 22) 730 8181
Email: wmo@wmo.int
Internet: www.wmo.ch
Secretary-General: M Jarraud, France (2008–11) (re-appointed by the fifteenth WMO Congress)

Purpose

The WMO is the successor to the International Meteorological Organization, which was established in 1873. It formally came into existence in 1950 and became a specialised agency of the UN in 1951.

Article 2 of the WMO Convention, which was signed in Washington in 1947 and came into force on 23 March 1950, defined the Organization's purposes as being to:
*   Facilitate worldwide cooperation in the establishment of networks of stations for making meteorological observations, as well as hydrological and other geophysical observations

related to meteorology, and to promote the establishment and maintenance of centres charged with the provision of meteorological and related services

- Promote the establishment and maintenance of systems for rapid exchange of meteorological and related information
- Promote standardisation of meteorological and related observations and ensure the uniform publication of observations and statistics
- Further the application of meteorology to aviation, shipping, water problems, agriculture and other human activities
- Promote activities in operational hydrology and further close cooperation between meteorological and hydrological services
- Encourage research and training in meteorology and, as appropriate, in related fields and to assist in coordinating the international aspects of such research and training.

Structure

- World Meteorological Congress
- Executive Council
- Six regional associations (Africa, Asia, South America, North America, Central America and the Caribbean, South-West Pacific and Europe)
- Eight technical commissions (atmospheric sciences, aeronautical meteorology, agricultural meteorology, basic systems, hydrology, instruments and methods of observation, oceanography and marine meteorology, and climatology)
- Secretariat.

The World Meteorological Congress, the supreme body of the Organization, meets once every four years. The fifteenth Congress was held from 7 to 25 May 2007. The sixteenth Congress is to be held from 16 May to 3 June 2011.

The 37 members of the Executive Council are the President and three Vice-Presidents of the Organization, the six Presidents of the regional associations who are ex officio members, and 27 Directors of members' national meteorological or hydrometeorological services. Elections to the Council are held at the World Meteorological Congress, except that the Presidents of regional associations are elected by their respective associations. Apart from the Presidents of regional associations, the members of the Council serve from the end of one Congress to the end of the next. When a vacancy occurs among the 27 elected members between sessions of the Congress, an acting member is designated by the Executive Council. Current membership is:

President	First Vice-President	Second Vice-President
A I Bedritsky, Russian Federation	A M Noorian, Iran	T W Sutherland, British Caribbean Territories

Third Vice-President

A D Moura, Brazil

Presidents of regional associations

Region I, Africa: M L Bah, Guinea
Region II, Asia: A M H Isa, Bahrain
Region III, South America: C R J Viñas García, Venezuela
Region IV, North America, Central America and the Caribbean: C Fuller, Belize
Region V, South-West Pacific: A Ngari, Cook Islands (Acting)
Region VI, Europe: D K Keuerleber-Burk, Switzerland

Membership

Membership of the WMO comprises 182 Member States and six territories. The following is a list of the current members and their terms of office on the Executive Council:

	Previous terms	Current terms
Afghanistan		
Albania		
Algeria	1987–91	
Angola	1979–80	
Antigua and Barbuda		
Argentina	1975–2000 03–07	2007–11
Armenia		
Australia	1958–2007	2007–11
Austria	1994–98	
Azerbaijan		
Bahamas		
Bahrain	2000–04	2005–08
Bangladesh		
Barbados		
Belarus		
Belgium	1963–71	
Belize	2002–03	2005–08
Benin	1997–2001	
Bhutan		
Bolivia		
Bosnia and Herzegovina		
Botswana	1995–2003	
Brazil	1974–99 2001–07	2007–11
British Caribbean Territories	1983–2007	2007–11
Brunei Darussalam		
Bulgaria		
Burkina Faso	2005	
Burundi	1993–97	
Cambodia		
Cameroon	1979–81 86–95 2001–03	
Canada	1975–2007	2007–11
Cape Verde		
Central African Republic		
Chad		
Chile	1980–82 89 2007	
China	1973–2007	2007–11
Colombia	1971–83 91–92 95–99	
Comoros		
Congo	1981–87 1999–2001	
Cook Islands	2005–06	2006–10
Costa Rica	1986–91 2003–07	
Côte d'Ivoire	1986–87 90–95	
Croatia		
Cuba	1983–84	
Cyprus		
Czech Republic	1995–99 2004–07	
DPRK		
DR Congo		
Denmark	1999–2003	

	Previous terms	Current terms
Djibouti		
Dominica		
Dominican Republic		
Ecuador	1963–71 2000–03	
Egypt	1955–85 87–91 95–99 2003–06	2007–11
El Salvador		
Eritrea		
Estonia		
Ethiopia	1982–90 2003–05	
Fiji	1995–2003	
Finland	1983–90	2007–11
France	1951–2006	2007–11
French Polynesia		
Gabon		
Gambia	1994–95	
Georgia		
Germany	1963–2007	2007–11
Ghana	1979–81 87–91 2003–06	
Greece	1989–94	
Guatemala	1973–77	
Guinea	2002–07	2007–11
Guinea-Bissau		
Guyana		
Haiti		
Honduras	1991–93	
Hong Kong, China		
Hungary	1979–81 2000–01	
Iceland		
India	1979–99 2002–07	2007–11
Indonesia	1993–99 2001–02	2007–11
Iran	1969–79 1991–2007	2007–11
Iraq	1979–82	
Ireland		
Israel	1995–2002	
Italy	1983–95 1998–2000 03–07	2007–11
Jamaica		
Japan	1967–2007	2007–11
Jordan	1987–91 2003–06	
Kazakhstan		
Kenya	1971–2007	2007–11
Kiribati		
Kuwait		
Kyrgyzstan		
Lao PDR		
Latvia		
Lebanon		
Lesotho	1994–95 2003–07	
Liberia		
Libyan AJ		
Lithuania	2002–05	
Luxembourg	1955–71	
Macau, China		
Madagascar		

	Previous terms	Current terms
Malawi	1981–82 91–95	
Malaysia	1979–86 95–96 1998–2001 03–05 06–07	2007–11
Maldives		
Mali	1990–2001 06–07	
Malta		
Mauritania		2007–11
Mauritius	1975–79	2007–11
Mexico	1979–85 1995–2002	2007–11
Micronesia		
Monaco		
Mongolia	1975 1994–2000	
Montenegro		
Morocco	1983–87 1999–2003	
Mozambique	2006–07	
Myanmar	1982–84	
Namibia		2007–11
Nepal	1983–87	
Netherlands	1991–95	
Netherlands Antilles and Aruba	1993–95 1997–2005	
New Caledonia	1962–71	
New Zealand	1986–88 2003–07	
Nicaragua		
Niger	1985–91	
Nigeria	1973–83 91–93 1995–2002	
Niue		
Norway	1979–83 90–94	
Oman		
Pakistan	1971–91 2003–07	
Panama	1987–91	
Papua New Guinea		
Paraguay	1959–63 91–99 2003–05	
Peru	1983–87	2007–11
Philippines	1974–95 97–99	
Poland	1971–75 1991–2003	2007–11
Portugal	1984–87 2001–02	
Qatar	1986–95	
Republic of Moldova		
ROK	2000	2007–11
Romania		
Russian Federation	1951–2003 04–07	2007–11
Rwanda	1991–92 98–99 2006–07	2007–11
Saint Lucia		
Samoa		
Sao Tome and Principe		
Saudi Arabia	1983–2002	2007–11
Senegal	1975–85 95–97 2001–04	
Serbia[1]		
Seychelles		
Sierra Leone		
Singapore	1967–74 89–92 02–06	
Slovakia		
Slovenia		

	Previous terms	Current terms
Solomon Islands		
Somalia		
South Africa	1995–2005	2007–11
Spain	1983–96 1999–2000 03–07	2007–11
Sri Lanka		
Sudan	1959–63 91–95	
Suriname		
Swaziland		
Sweden	1955–79	
Switzerland	1971–75 2003–05	2005–08
Syrian AR	1979–84 2001–03	
Tajikistan		
Thailand		
The Former Yugoslav Republic of Macedonia		
Togo	1983–90	
Tonga		
Trinidad and Tobago	1994–97	
Tunisia	1975–79 91–95	
Turkey		
Turkmenistan		
Uganda	1971–79	
Ukraine		
UAE		
UK	1979–2007	2007–11
UR of Tanzania	1975–79 1995–2007	
USA	1951–2007	2007–11
Uruguay	1982–91 1999–2000 03–05	
Uzbekistan		
Vanuatu		
Venezuela	1971–79 86–88 94–95 1999–2003	2006–10
Viet Nam		
Yemen		
Zambia	1983–87	
Zimbabwe	1987–91	

Notes

The former Socialist Federal Republic of Yugoslavia served on the Executive Council from 1963 to 1991.

[1] On 3 June 2006 the Republic of Serbia notified the UN that the membership of the State Union of Serbia and Montenegro in the UN, including all organs and organisations of the UN system, was continued by the Republic of Serbia on the basis of article 60 of the Constitutional Charter of Serbia and Montenegro, activated by the Declaration of Independence adopted by the National Assembly of Montenegro on 6 June 2006.

International Maritime Organization (IMO)

Temporary address due to refurbishment: Aug 2006–Feb 2008
55 Victoria St
London SW1H 0EU
United Kingdom
Telephone: (+44 0) 20 7735 7611
Fax: (+44 0) 20 7587 3210
Email: info@imo.org
Internet: www.imo.org

Permanent address:
4 Albert Embankment
London SE1 7SR
United Kingdom

Secretary-General: Efthimios Mitropoulos, Greece (since 2004, mandate renewed November 2006)
(elected by the IMO Council)

Purpose

The IMO is the UN specialised agency responsible for the safety of life at sea and protection of the marine environment through prevention of pollution of the sea caused by ships and other craft. It facilitates cooperation among governments to achieve the highest practicable standards of maritime safety and security, and efficiency in navigation. It deals with legal matters connected with international shipping, including liability and compensation regimes, as well as with facilitation of international maritime traffic. It is also responsible for providing technical assistance in maritime matters to developing countries.

The IMO is responsible for convening international conferences on shipping matters and for drafting international conventions or agreements on this subject. The current emphasis is on ensuring relevant conventions and treaties are properly implemented by the countries that have accepted them.

The Convention on the International Maritime Organization (IMO) concluded at Geneva in 1948 and came into force in 1958. The first IMO Assembly was convened in London in 1959. Prior to 22 May 1982 (the date of entry into force of the 1975 amendments to the IMO Convention), the Organization's name was the Inter-governmental Maritime Consultative Organization (IMCO).

Structure

*   Assembly
*   Council
*   Committees
*   Secretariat.

The Assembly, consisting of all Member States, usually meets every two years. The 24th session was held from 21 November to 2 December 2005. The 25th session is scheduled to take place from 19 to 30 November 2007.

The 40-member Council is the Executive Organ of the IMO. It is responsible, under the Assembly, for supervising the work of the Organization. Between Assembly sessions, the Council performs all the functions of the Assembly except making recommendations to governments on maritime safety and pollution prevention. This function is reserved for the Assembly by article 15(j) of the Convention.

The IMO Council is also responsible for appointing the Secretary-General, subject to the approval of the Assembly. Council members are elected by the Assembly for two-year terms beginning after each regular session of the Assembly. Member States are elected from three categories:

*   Category A: 10 states with the largest interest in providing international shipping services

- Category B: 10 other states with the largest interest in international seaborne trade
- Category C: 20 states not elected under either category (A) or (B) that have special interests in maritime transport or navigation, and whose election will ensure the representation of all major areas of the world.

All IMO committees are open to all member governments on an equal basis. They are:

Maritime Safety Committee

This Committee, established under the IMO Convention, is the highest technical body of the IMO. Much of its work is carried out through subsidiary bodies. Subjects dealt with include maritime security, flag state implementation, navigation safety, radio communications, life-saving appliances and arrangements, search and rescue, ship design and equipment, fire protection, standards of training and watch keeping, containers and cargoes, and the carriage of dangerous goods.

Marine Environment Protection Committee

This Committee was set up in 1973 to coordinate and administer IMO activities for the prevention and control of marine pollution from ships. All members of the IMO are entitled to take part, as are representatives of non-IMO states that are parties to treaties linked to Committee work. It was institutionalised in 1982.

The Maritime Safety Committee and the Marine Environment Protection Committee are assisted by nine sub-committees, which are open to all member states.

Legal Committee

Set up in 1967, this Committee considers any legal matters within the IMO's scope and submits to the Council its drafts of international conventions and other international treaty instruments. It was institutionalised in 1982. Subjects dealt with include liability and compensation regimes for damage caused at sea by hazardous and noxious substances, wreck removal and seafarer claims.

Technical Cooperation Committee

This Committee was set up in 1969 to establish directives and guidelines for the IMO's programme of assistance to developing countries in maritime transport (particularly shipping and ports), monitor the programme's progressive development and review the results. It was institutionalised in 1984.

Facilitation Committee

This Committee, established in 1972, is responsible for facilitating international maritime traffic through reducing the formalities and simplifying the documentation required of ships when entering or leaving ports or other terminals. It has not yet been institutionalised.

Consultative Meeting of Contracting Parties to the London Convention

The IMO also acts as a secretariat in respect of the Convention on the Prevention of Marine Pollution by Dumping of Wastes and Other Matter, adopted in London in 1972, which regulates the disposal into the sea of waste materials generated on land. Consultative meetings are normally held once a year. A Protocol amending the Convention was adopted in 1996 and entered into force on 24 March 2006. Thirty of the 81 states that have ratified the Convention have now acceded to the Protocol, which is expected ultimately to replace the Convention.

Membership

The IMO has 167 members and three associate members. The Council has 40 members. The following list of all members shows their membership terms on the Council:

	Previous terms	Current terms
African states		
Algeria[3]	1971–79 83–99 2004–05	2006–07
Angola		
Benin		
Cameroon		
Cape Verde		
Comoros		
Congo		
Côte d'Ivoire		
DR Congo		
Djibouti		
Egypt[3]	1978–2005	2006–07
Equatorial Guinea		
Eritrea		
Ethiopia		
Gabon	1984–87	
Gambia		
Ghana	1986–87 96–97 2002–05	
Guinea		
Guinea-Bissau		
Kenya[3]	1978–79 2002–03	2006–07
Liberia	1978–91 98–99	
Libyan AJ		
Madagascar	1964–71	
Malawi		
Mauritania		
Mauritius		
Morocco	1980–81 84–87 89–97 2000–01	
Mozambique		
Namibia		
Nigeria	1974–85 88–95 2002–05	
Sao Tome and Principe		
Senegal		
Seychelles		
Sierra Leone		
Somalia		
South Africa[3]	1998–2005	2006–07
Sudan		
Togo		
Tunisia	1998–99	
UR of Tanzania		
Zimbabwe		
Asian states		
Bahrain		

OTHER BODIES

	Previous terms	Current terms
Bangladesh[2]	1981–87 2002–05	2006–07
Brunei Darussalam		
Cambodia		
China[1]	1975–81 83–87 1989–2005	2006–07
Cyprus[3]	1991–2005	2006–07
DPRK		
Fiji		
India[2]	1959–83 1985–2005	2006–07
Indonesia[3]	1974–79 1985–2005	2006–07
Iran	1991–97	
Iraq		
Japan[1]	1959–2005	2006–07
Jordan		
Kazakhstan		
Kuwait	1978–91 93–95	
Lebanon	1981–91 2002–03	
Malaysia[3]		2006–07
Maldives		
Marshall Islands		
Mongolia		
Myanmar		
Nepal		
Oman		
Pakistan	1978–81 87–93	
Papua New Guinea		
Philippines[3]	1989–93 1998–2005	2006–07
Qatar		
ROK[1]	1991–2005	2006–07
Samoa		
Saudi Arabia[3]	1982–97 2004–05	2006–07
Singapore[3]	1993–2005	2006–07
Solomon Islands		
Sri Lanka		
Syrian AR		
Thailand[3]		2006–07
Timor-Leste		
Tonga		
Turkmenistan		
Tuvalu		
UAE		
Vanuatu		
Viet Nam		
Yemen		

Eastern European states

Albania		
Azerbaijan		
Bosnia and Herzegovina		
Bulgaria	1984–85	
Croatia		
Czech Republic		
Estonia		
Georgia		

OTHER BODIES

Hungary
Latvia
Lithuania
Montenegro
Poland 1980–83 85–91 93–99 2002–05
Republic of Moldova
Romania 1978–79
Russian Federation[1] 1959–2005 2006–07
Serbia
Slovakia
Slovenia
The Former Yugoslav Republic
   of Macedonia
Ukraine

Latin American and Caribbean states

Antigua and Barbuda
Argentina[2] 1975–79 1983–2005 2006–07
Bahamas[3] 1991–95 2000–05 2006–07
Barbados 1989–91
Belize
Bolivia
Brazil[2] 1967–2005 2006–07
Chile[3] 1984–85 2002–05 2006–07
Colombia
Costa Rica
Cuba 1979–81 83–85
Dominica
Dominican Republic
Ecuador
El Salvador
Grenada
Guatemala
Guyana
Haiti
Honduras 2002–03
Jamaica 1980–83
Mexico[3] 1978–79 82–83 86–87 1989–2005 2006–07
Nicaragua
Panama[1] 1980–83 85–89 91–93 1995–2005 2006–07
Paraguay
Peru 1978–81 87–89
Saint Kitts and Nevis
Saint Lucia
Saint Vincent and the Grenadines
Suriname
Trinidad and Tobago 1983–89
Uruguay
Venezuela 2002–05

Western European and Other states

Australia[3] 1985–2005 2006–07

	Previous terms	Current terms
Austria		
Belgium[3]	1959–75	2006–07
Canada[2]	1959–2005	2006–07
Denmark[3]	2002–05	2006–07
Finland	1998–2001	
France[2]	1959–2005	2006–07
Germany[2]	1959–2005	2006–07
Greece[1]	1979–2005	2006–07
Iceland		
Ireland		
Israel		
Italy[1]	1982–83 1986–2005	2006–07
Luxembourg		
Malta[3]	1978–79 2000–05	2006–07
Monaco		
Netherlands[2]	1984–87 1991–2005	2006–07
New Zealand		
Norway[1]	1959–2005	2006–07
Portugal[3]	2004–05	2006–07
San Marino		
Spain[2]	1974–75 1980–2005	2006–07
Sweden[2]	1988–2005	2006–07
Switzerland		
Turkey[3]	2000–05	2006–07
UK[1]	1959–2005	2006–07

Members outside of UNGA regional groupings

Kiribati		
USA[1]	1959–2005	2006–07

Associate IMO members

Faroe Islands, Denmark
Hong Kong, China
Macau, China

Notes

[1] Category A: 10 states with the largest interest in providing international shipping services.

[2] Category B: 10 other states with the largest interest in providing international seaborne trade.

[3] Category C: 20 states not elected under category A or B that have special interests in maritime transport or navigation, and whose election would ensure the representation of all geographic areas of the world.

World Intellectual Property Organization (WIPO)

34 Chemin des Colombettes
PO Box 18
CH 1211 Geneva 20
Switzerland
Telephone: (+41 22) 338 9111
Fax: (+41 22) 733 5428
Email: wipo.mail@wipo.int
Internet: www.wipo.int
Director-General: Dr Kamil Idris, Sudan (2003–09) (re-elected by the WIPO General Assembly)

Purpose

WIPO was established by a Convention signed in Stockholm in 1967 that entered into force in 1970. GA res. 3346 (XXIX) (1974), adopted unanimously by the General Assembly, established WIPO as the fourteenth specialised agency of the UN.

The Organization was established to promote through international cooperation the creation, dissemination, use and protection of works of the human spirit for the economic, cultural and social progress of all mankind. It was also intended to ensure administrative cooperation among the Unions established to afford protection in the field of intellectual property.

The principal Unions established are those of Paris and Berne. The Paris Union, officially the International Union for the Protection of Industrial Property, is composed of States Parties to a convention concluded at Paris in 1883 and last revised in 1979. The Berne Union, officially the International Union for the Protection of Literary and Artistic Works, is composed of States Parties to a convention concluded at Berne in 1886 and last revised in 1979.

Structure

- General Assembly
- Conference
- Coordination Committee
- Secretariat.

States Members of WIPO and of either the Paris Union or the Berne Union meet in an ordinary session of the General Assembly once every two years and in extraordinary session every other year. The General Assembly has 175 members. The 33rd session was held from 25 to 29 September 2006 and the 34th session is due to be held from 24 September to 3 October 2007.

WIPO States Members, whether or not they are members of any of the Unions, are entitled to participate in the Conference, which meets at the same time as the General Assembly. The Conference has 184 members.

The Paris and Berne Unions elect executive committees from among their members. The joint membership of these two committees constitutes the Coordination Committee of WIPO. The 82 members meet in ordinary session once a year.

The WIPO Secretariat had 891 regular staff as at 1 March 2007.

International Fund for Agricultural Development (IFAD)

Via del Serafico 107
00142 Rome
Telephone: (+39 06) 54591
Fax: (+39 06) 5043463
Email: ifad@ifad.org
Internet: www.ifad.org
President: Lennart Båge, Sweden (2001–09) (elected by the Governing Council)

Purpose

IFAD is an international financial institution and a UN specialised agency dedicated to eradicating poverty in rural areas of developing countries. It was established in 1977 as one of the major outcomes of the 1974 World Food Conference.

Through low-interest loans and grants, IFAD develops and finances programmes and projects that fit within national systems and respond to the needs, priorities and constraints identified by governments and poor rural people themselves.

IFAD-supported programmes and projects ensure that poor rural people have better access, and the skills and organisation needed, to take advantage of:
- Natural resources, especially secure access to land and water, and improved natural resource management and conservation practices
- Improved agricultural technologies and effective production services
- A broad range of financial services
- Transparent and competitive markets for agricultural inputs and produce
- Opportunities for rural off-farm employment and enterprise development
- Local and national policy and programming processes.

The Millennium Development Goals (MDGs) guide IFAD's work, in particular the first goal that aims to halve the proportion of people suffering from hunger and extreme poverty by 2015.

The vast majority of IFAD's resources are provided to low-income countries on highly concessional terms. Loans are typically repayable over 40 years, with a 10-year grace period, at zero percent interest and a 0.75 percent service charge. Since starting operations, IFAD has invested US$9.5 billion in 731 programmes and projects that have helped over 300 million people achieve better lives for themselves and their families. Co-financing has been provided by governments, project participants, multilateral and bilateral donors, and other partners.

Structure

The Governing Council is IFAD's highest decision-making authority. Each Member State is represented in the Council by a Governor and/or an Alternate Governor. The Council meets in Rome in February each year. IFAD res. 86/XVIII adopted a new voting system for the Council. Member States now have two types of votes – membership votes and votes based on the size of their cumulative paid contributions.

The Executive Board is responsible for overseeing IFAD's general operations and approving its programme of work. It meets three times a year, in April, September and December. The Board consists of 18 elected Members and 18 Alternate Members, all of whom have a three-year term of office. Membership is determined by the Governing Council. At present it comprises eight Members and eight Alternate Members from List A, four Members and four Alternate Members from List B, and six Members and six Alternate Members from

List C. The total number of votes in the Executive Board is now calculated by membership and contributions.

The President is the head of staff and conducts the business of the organisation under the control and direction of the Governing Council and the Executive Board. The President chairs the Executive Board and is IFAD's legal representative.

Membership

IFAD membership is open to any state that is a member of the UN or its specialised agencies, or the International Atomic Energy Agency (IAEA). Countries may join the agency after approval by IFAD's Governing Council and accession to the Agreement Establishing IFAD.

Following a change to IFAD's governance structure approved by the twentieth session of the Governing Council in 1997 (IFAD res. 86/XVIII), countries in former Category I (OECD) were reclassified as List A, former Category II (OPEC) as List B, and former Category III (Developing Countries) as List C. This list has three sub-listings: C1 for countries in Africa; C2 for Europe, Asia and the Pacific; and C3 for Latin America and the Caribbean.

IFAD has a total membership of 165 countries: 23 in List A, 12 in List B and 130 in List C. Executive Board Member States for 2007, with the Alternate Members in brackets, are:

List A	List B	List C
Canada (Finland)	Kuwait (UAE)	Brazil (Guatemala)
France (Belgium)	Nigeria (Qatar)	China (Pakistan)
Germany (Switzerland)	Saudi Arabia (Indonesia)	Egypt (Mali)
Italy (Greece)	Venezuela (Algeria)	India (Yemen)
Japan (Denmark)		Mexico (Argentina)
UK (Netherlands)		South Africa (Cameroon)
USA (Spain)		

UN Industrial Development Organization (UNIDO)

Vienna International Centre
PO Box 300
A–1400 Vienna
Austria
Telephone: (+43 1) 260260
Fax: (+43 1) 2692669
Email: unido@unido.org
Internet: www.unido.org
Director-General: Kandeh K Yumkella, Sierra Leone (2005–09) (elected by the General Conference on the recommendation of the Industrial Development Board)

Purpose

UNIDO was established by GA res. 2152 (XXI) (1966) to act as the central coordinating body for industrial activities within the UN system and to promote industrial development and cooperation at global, regional, national and sectoral levels. UNIDO became the sixteenth specialised agency of the UN in 1985.

UNIDO aims to relieve poverty by fostering productivity growth. A business plan adopted at the 1997 UNIDO General Conference groups the Organization's activities into two areas:
• Strengthening industrial capacities
• Promoting cleaner and sustainable industrial development.

The Business Plan provides for UNIDO's activities to be focused:

- Geographically on Least Developed Countries, particularly in Africa
- Sectorally on small- and medium-sized agro-based industries.

These activities have two main aspects: technical cooperation and 'global forum', and three thematic priorities: poverty reduction through productive activities, trade capacity building, and environment and energy.

Technical cooperation is directed at building policy and institutional capacities in developing countries. Global forum activities generate and disseminate knowledge relating to industrial matters and provide a platform for the public and private sector and civil society to enhance cooperation, establish dialogue and develop partnerships.

Structure

- General Conference
- Industrial Development Board
- Programme and Budget Committee.

The General Conference is open to all Member States and meets every two years to approve the budgets and work programme. The eleventh session was held in Vienna from 28 November to 2 December 2005. The next session is scheduled to be held from 3 to 7 December 2007.

The Industrial Development Board comprises 53 Member States elected by the General Conference. Thirty-three are from developing countries, 15 from market economy countries and five from Eastern European countries. The Board meets once in General Conference years and twice in other years to review the implementation of the work programme and the budget, which is prepared by the Programme and Budget Committee.

The Programme and Budget Committee is a subsidiary organ of the Industrial Development Board. It comprises 27 Member States elected by the General Conference. Fifteen are from developing countries, nine from market economy countries and three from Eastern European countries. It normally meets once a year.

Resources

UNIDO's operations are budgeted on a biennial basis. Operating expenses are funded by assessed contributions and technical cooperation by voluntary contributions. The estimated volume of UNIDO operations for 2006 to 2007 is some $490.7 million, drawn from the regular budget ($208.1 million), the operational budget ($27.6 million) and voluntary contributions ($255 million). In 2006 voluntary contributions totalled some $104 million, the bulk of which ($51.4 million) came from Member States, the Montreal Protocol ($36.7 million) and the Global Environment Facility ($15.2 million). In 2006 UNIDO implemented projects to the value of $113 million.

Membership

As of 22 November 2006, UNIDO had 172 members:

Afghanistan[2]	Austria[2,3]	Belarus
Albania	Azerbaijan	Belgium[1]
Algeria[2,3]	Bahamas	Belize
Angola	Bahrain	Benin
Argentina	Bangladesh	Bhutan
Armenia	Barbados	Bolivia[2]

Bosnia and Herzegovina
Botswana
Brazil[1]
Bulgaria
Burkina Faso[2, 3]
Burundi
Cambodia
Cameroon
Cape Verde
Central African Republic
Chad
Chile[1]
China[1, 3]
Colombia[1]
Comoros
Congo
Costa Rica
Côte d'Ivoire[2, 3]
Croatia
Cuba[2, 3]
Cyprus
Czech Republic[2]
DPRK[3]
Denmark
Djibouti
Dominica
Dominican Republic
DR Congo
Ecuador
Egypt[2]
El Salvador
Equatorial Guinea
Eritrea
Ethiopia[2, 3]
Fiji
Finland
France[1, 3]
Gabon
Gambia
Georgia
Germany[1, 3]
Ghana[1]
Greece[2, 3]
Grenada
Guatemala[2, 3]
Guinea
Guinea-Bissau
Guyana
Haiti
Honduras
Hungary[3]
India[2]

Indonesia[1]
Iran[2, 3]
Iraq
Ireland[2]
Israel
Italy[1, 3]
Jamaica
Japan[1, 3]
Jordan
Kazakhstan
Kenya[2]
Kuwait
Kyrgyzstan
Lao PDR
Lebanon
Lesotho
Liberia
Libyan AJ
Lithuania
Luxembourg[2]
Madagascar
Malawi
Malaysia
Maldives
Mali
Malta
Mauritania
Mauritius
Mexico[1, 3]
Monaco
Mongolia
Montenegro[5]
Morocco[1]
Mozambique
Myanmar
Namibia
Nepal
Netherlands[1]
New Zealand
Nicaragua
Niger
Nigeria[2]
Norway[1]
Oman
Pakistan[1, 3]
Panama
Papua New Guinea
Paraguay[2, 3]
Peru
Philippines
Poland[1, 3]
Portugal

Qatar
Republic of Moldova
ROK[1, 3]
Romania
Russian Federation[2, 3]
Rwanda
Saint Kitts and Nevis
Saint Lucia
Saint Vincent and the
  Grenadines
Sao Tome and Principe
Saudi Arabia[2]
Senegal[1]
Serbia[4]
Seychelles
Sierra Leone
Slovakia[1]
Slovenia
Somalia
South Africa[1, 3]
Spain[2]
Sri Lanka[2]
Sudan
Suriname
Swaziland
Sweden
Switzerland[2, 3]
Syrian AR[1]
Tajikistan
Thailand[2]
The Former Yugoslav Republic
  of Macedonia
Timor-Leste
Togo
Tonga
Trinidad and Tobago
Tunisia[1, 3]
Turkey[2, 3]
Turkmenistan
UAE
Uganda
Ukraine[1]
UK[1, 3]
UR of Tanzania
Uruguay[2]
Uzbekistan
Vanuatu
Venezuela
Viet Nam
Yemen
Zambia
Zimbabwe[1]

Notes

[1] Denotes member of the Industrial Development Board (as of 2 December 2005): one of 26 states whose term of office expires at the end of the twelfth regular session of the General Conference, in 2007 (see decision GC.10/Dec.8 of 5 December 2003).

² Denotes member of the Industrial Development Board (as of 2 December 2005): one of 27 states whose term of office expires at the close of the thirteenth regular session of the General Conference, in 2009 (see decision GC.11/Dec.7 of 2 December 2005).

³ Denotes member of the Programme and Budget Committee (as of 2 December 2005). The current members of the Committee hold office until the close of the twelfth regular session of the General Conference, in 2007 (see decision GC.11/Dec.8 of 2 December 2005).

⁴ On 3 June 2006 the Republic of Serbia notified the UN that the membership of the State Union of Serbia and Montenegro in the UN, including all organs and organisations of the UN system, was continued by the Republic of Serbia on the basis of article 60 of the Constitutional Charter of Serbia and Montenegro, activated by the Declaration of Independence adopted by the National Assembly of Montenegro on 3 June 2006.

⁵ On 22 November 2006 Montenegro became a member of UNIDO.

World Tourism Organization (UNWTO/OMT)

Capitán Haya, 42
28020 Madrid
Spain
Telephone: (+34 91) 567 8100
Fax: (+34 91) 571 3733
Email: omt@unwto.org
Internet: www.unwto.org
Secretary-General: Francesco Frangialli, France (2006–09) (elected by the General Assembly)

Purpose

UNWTO is the only inter-government organisation whose activities cover all aspects of tourism on a worldwide basis.

It was established in 1974 on entry into force of Statutes adopted on 27 September 1970 in Mexico City. Following a resolution adopted by its first General Assembly in May 1975, UNWTO established its headquarters in Madrid in January 1976, at the invitation of the Spanish Government.

In GA res. 32/156 (1977) the General Assembly adopted an agreement on the relationship between the UN and UNWTO. The Organization became a specialised agency of the UN in December 2003, pursuant to GA res. 58/232.

The Organization helps its members participate in tourism, the world's largest industry. By promoting and developing tourism, it aims to stimulate economic growth and job creation, provide incentives for protecting the environment and heritage of destinations, and promote peace and understanding. Particular attention is paid to the interests of developing countries. UNWTO's General Programme of Work comprises:

- Cooperation for development
- Human resource development
- Sustainable development of tourism
- Quality of tourism development
- Statistics and economic measurement of tourism
- Market intelligence and promotion
- New information technologies
- Communications and documentation
- Activities of the affiliate members.

UNWTO acts as an executing agency for the UNDP and has cooperation agreements with a UN programme (UNEP), UN regional commissions (ECA and ESCAP) and other UN specialised agencies (FAO, ICAO, IMO, UNESCO, WMO, WHO).

UNWTO's two acronyms relate to its English and Spanish names.

Structure
- General Assembly
- Executive Council
- Committees of the Council
- Affiliate Members (UNWTO Business Council)
- Secretariat.

The General Assembly, the supreme body of the Organization, meets every two years to approve UNWTO's budget and work programme. The next session is scheduled to be held in Cartagena de Indias, Colombia, in November 2007. The General Assembly has established six Regional Commissions covering Africa, the Americas, Europe, the Middle East, East Asia and the Pacific, and South Asia. These subsidiary organs normally meet once a year.

The Executive Council is UNWTO's governing body. It meets at least twice a year and has one member elected on the basis of equitable geographical distribution for every five full members of UNWTO. There are currently 30 countries elected to the Board. Other Council participants, without voting rights, are an associate member selected by UNWTO Associate Members and a representative of the affiliate members (Business Council). Spain, the Organization's host country, also sits on the Council as a permanent voting member.

The Council's work is carried out by its subsidiary committees: the Programme Committee, the Committee on Budget and Finance (CBF), the Sustainable Development of Tourism Committee, the Committee on Statistics and Macroeconomic Analysis of Tourism, the Quality Support Committee, the Committee on Market Intelligence and Promotion, the Education Council and the World Committee on Tourism Ethics.

Affiliate members constituted into the UNWTO Business Council participate in UNWTO's activities, make recommendations to its bodies and carry out, by means of studies and seminars, their own activities within the framework of the UNWTO General Programme of Work.

The Secretariat is led by the Secretary-General. The Secretariat is responsible for implementing UNWTO's work programme.

Membership
UNWTO has three categories of members:
- Full members: 150 Member States
- Associate members: seven territories or groups of territories not responsible for their external relations but whose membership is approved by the state assuming responsibility for their external relations
- Affiliate members: some 350 inter-government and non-government entities with specialised interests in tourism, and commercial and non-commercial bodies and associations with activities related to the aims of UNWTO or falling within its competence.

Permanent Observer status, with the right to speak but without the right to vote, was given to the Holy See at the General Assembly in 1979. Palestine has Special Observer status, granted in 1999.

Full members

Afghanistan	Gabon	Pakistan
Albania	Gambia	Panama
Algeria	Georgia	Papua New Guinea
Andorra	Germany	Paraguay
Angola	Ghana	Peru
Argentina	Greece	Philippines
Armenia	Guatemala	Poland
Australia	Guinea	Portugal
Austria	Guinea-Bissau	Qatar
Azerbaijan	Haiti	ROK
Bahamas	Honduras	Republic of Moldova
Bahrain	Hungary	Romania
Bangladesh	India	Russian Federation
Belarus	Indonesia	Rwanda
Benin	Iran	San Marino
Bhutan	Iraq	Sao Tome and Principe
Bolivia	Israel	Saudi Arabia
Bosnia and Herzegovina	Italy	Senegal
Botswana	Jamaica	Serbia
Brazil	Japan	Seychelles
Bulgaria	Jordan	Sierra Leone
Burkina Faso	Kazakhstan	Slovakia
Burundi	Kenya	Slovenia
Cambodia	Kuwait	South Africa
Cameroon	Kyrgyzstan	Spain
Canada	Lao PDR	Sri Lanka
Cape Verde	Latvia	Sudan
Central African Republic	Lebanon	Swaziland
Chad	Lesotho	Switzerland
Chile	Libyan AJ	Syrian AR
China	Lithuania	Thailand
Colombia	Madagascar	The Former Yugoslav Republic
Congo	Malawi	of Macedonia
Costa Rica	Malaysia	Timor-Leste
Côte d'Ivoire	Maldives	Togo
Croatia	Mali	Tunisia
Cuba	Malta	Turkey
Cyprus	Mauritania	Turkmenistan
Czech Republic	Mauritius	Uganda
DPRK	Mexico	Ukraine
DR Congo	Monaco	UK
Djibouti	Mongolia	UR of Tanzania
Dominican Republic	Morocco	Uruguay
Ecuador	Mozambique	Uzbekistan
Egypt	Namibia	Venezuela
El Salvador	Nepal	Viet Nam
Equatorial Guinea	Netherlands	Yemen
Eritrea	Nicaragua	Zambia
Ethiopia	Niger	Zimbabwe
Fiji	Nigeria	
France	Oman	

Associate members

Aruba	Hong Kong, China	Netherlands Antilles
Flemish Community of Belgium	Macau, China	Puerto Rico
	Madeira	

Permanent Observer
Holy See
Special Observer
Palestine

International Centre for the Study of the Preservation and Restoration of Cultural Property (ICCROM)

Via di San Michele, 13
I–00153 Rome
Italy
Telephone: (+39 06) 58 5531
Fax: (+39 06) 58 553349
Email: iccrom@iccrom.org
Internet: www.iccrom.org
Director-General: Dr Mournir Bouchenaki, Algeria (since 1 May 2006) (appointed by the ICCROM General Assembly in November 2005, term expiring on 31 December 2011)

Purpose

ICCROM is an inter-government organisation founded by the ninth UNESCO General Conference in New Delhi in 1956 and established in Rome in 1959. Its mandate is to promote the conservation of all types of cultural heritage, both movable and immovable, through its five main areas of activity: training, research, information, cooperation and advocacy.

Structure

- General Assembly
- Council
- Secretariat.

ICCROM is governed by a General Assembly made up of delegates from its Member States. The General Assembly determines the general policies of ICCROM. This includes approving its biennial programme of activities and budget, electing the Council members and appointing the Director-General. Other functions include approving reports on Council and ICCROM Secretariat activities, determining Member State contributions, adopting ICCROM's financial regulations and approving changes to the Statutes. The General Assembly meets in ordinary session every two years and in extraordinary session if the Council, or at least one-third of its Member States, so request.

The ICCROM Council comprises 25 members elected by the General Assembly. The ICCROM Council also has ex officio members with voting power: the Italian Government, Istituto Centrale per Il Restauro and UNESCO. Ex officio members with no voting power are the International Council on Monuments and Sites (ICOMOS), and the International Council of Museums (ICOM).

The Secretariat of ICCROM is based in Rome, Italy, and is headed by the Director-General.

Membership

There are 119 Member States:

Albania	Angola	Australia
Algeria	Argentina	Austria
Andorra	Armenia	Azerbaijan

OTHER BODIES

316

Bahrain
Barbados
Belgium
Benin
Bolivia
Bosnia and Herzegovina
Botswana
Brazil
Brunei Darussalam
Bulgaria
Burkina Faso
Cambodia
Cameroon
Canada
Chad
Chile
China
Colombia
Congo
Côte d'Ivoire
Croatia
Cuba
Cyprus
Czech Republic
Denmark
Dominican Republic
Ecuador
Egypt
Estonia
Ethiopia
Finland
France
Gabon
Gambia
Georgia
Germany
Ghana

Greece
Guatemala
Guyana
Haiti
Honduras
Hungary
India
Iran
Ireland
Israel
Italy
Japan
Jordan
Kenya
Kuwait
Lao PDR
Lebanon
Libyan AJ
Lithuania
Luxembourg
Madagascar
Malaysia
Mali
Malta
Mauritius
Mexico
Mongolia
Morocco
Mozambique
Myanmar
Namibia
Nepal
Netherlands
New Zealand
Nicaragua
Nigeria
Norway

Oman
Pakistan
Paraguay
Peru
Philippines
Poland
Portugal
ROK
Romania
Rwanda
Saudi Arabia
Senegal
Serbia[1]
Seychelles
Slovakia
Slovenia
South Africa
Spain
Sri Lanka
Sudan
Sweden
Switzerland
Syrian AR
Thailand
The Former Yugoslav Republic
    of Macedonia
Togo
Tunisia
Turkey
UK
UR of Tanzania
USA
Uruguay
Venezuela
Viet Nam
Zambia
Zimbabwe

Note

[1] On 3 June 2006 the Republic of Serbia notified the UN that the membership of the State Union of Serbia and Montenegro in the UN, including all organs and organisations of the UN system, was continued by the Republic of Serbia on the basis of article 60 of the Constitutional Charter of Serbia and Montenegro, activated by the Declaration of Independence adopted by the National Assembly of Montenegro on 3 June 2006.

WORLD BANK GROUP

Headquarters:
1818 H Street NW
Washington DC 20433
United States of America
Telephone: (+1 202) 473 1000
Fax: (+1 202) 477 6391
Email: pic@worldbank.org
Internet: www.worldbank.org

The World Bank Group comprises the:
- International Bank for Reconstruction and Development (IBRD)
- International Development Association (IDA)
- International Finance Corporation (IFC)
- Multilateral Investment Guarantee Agency (MIGA)
- International Centre for the Settlement of Investment Disputes (ICSID).

The term 'World Bank' refers specifically to the first two of these institutions, the IBRD and IDA.

International Bank for Reconstruction and Development (IBRD)

1818 H Street NW
Washington DC 20433
United States of America
Telephone: (+1 202) 473 1000
Fax: (+1 202) 477 6391
Internet: www.worldbank.org
President: Robert Zoellick, USA (since 1 July 2007) (appointed by the Executive Directors)

Purpose

The IBRD was established to promote the international flow of capital for productive purposes and assist in financing the rebuilding of nations devastated by World War II.

The articles of the IBRD were drawn up at the Bretton Woods Conference in 1944 and the Bank began operation in 1946–47. Its main objective now is to lend for productive projects or to finance reform programmes that will lead to economic growth in its less developed Member States. The Bank is also attempting to increase the proportion of its lending that directly assists the poorest people in developing countries.

Capital

The Bank's authorised capital stock was 1,581,724 shares as of 31 March 2007. Subscribed share capital amounted to $189.8 billion at that date, of which $11.5 billion was paid-in and $178.3 billion was on call.

The Bank obtains the bulk of its funds from borrowing on international capital markets, in effect using the callable capital as its security. As at 31 March 2007 it had outstanding borrowings (after net swaps) totalling $84.2 billion.

Structure

The Board of Governors of the World Bank Group comprises one Governor and one alternate appointed by each member country. The 2006 Annual Meeting of the Board, in conjunction with the Board of Governors of the IMF, is scheduled to be held in Washington DC on 20 and 21 October 2007.

The Joint Ministerial Committee of the Boards of Governors of the Bank and the Fund on the Transfer of Real Resources to Developing Countries (Development Committee) meets in April and September each year. Each member country (or executive group of member countries) represented on the two Boards appoints a member of the Development Committee.

Because the World Bank Governors only meet annually, they delegate specific duties to 24 Executive Directors who work at the Bank in Washington. Five of the Executive Directors are appointed by the members with the largest number of shares. The other 19 are elected every two years at the time of the Annual Meeting by the governors of the remaining members.

Membership

Membership of the IBRD is restricted to members of the International Monetary Fund (IMF) that have ratified the articles of the Bank and accept the terms laid down by it.

IBRD membership as at 31 March 2007 totalled 185. A list is available on the World Bank website.

International Development Association (IDA)

1818 H Street NW
Washington DC 20433
United States of America
Telephone: (+1 202) 473 1000
Fax: (+1 202) 477 6391
Internet: www.worldbank.org/ida
President: Robert Zoellick, USA (since 1 July 2007) (appointed by the Executive Directors)

Purpose

The purpose of the IDA, which began operations in 1960, is to promote economic development by providing finance to the world's less developed areas on much more concessionary terms than conventional loans. It is designed specifically to finance projects or reform programmes in countries that are not able to service loans from the IBRD.

Capital

The initial subscriptions of all members are proportioned to their subscriptions to the capital stock of the IBRD, but under the article of agreement members of the IDA are divided into two groups. Part One involves the more economically advanced countries and Part Two involves the less developed nations. A Part One country pays its entire subscription in convertible currency, all of which may be used for IDA lending. A Part Two country pays only one-tenth of its subscriptions in convertible currency. The remaining portion is paid in the member's own currency and may not be used without the member's consent.

IDA lending resources have been supplemented since 1960 by a series of replenishments in which Part One and an increasing number of Part Two member countries contribute funds to IDA. Beginning with the IDA13 Replenishment, it was agreed that between 18 and 21 percent of the total funds subscribed would be given as grants rather than credits. Total IDA sources of development resources (including original subscriptions and subsequent contributions to all replenishments) totalled $135 billion at 31 March 2007.

Structure

The Association is affiliated to the IBRD. Each member country is represented by the same Governor and Executive Director as represent it for the Bank, and IDA shares the same President, management and staff as the Bank.

Membership

Membership is open to IBRD member countries. As at 31 March 2007 there were 166 members. A list is available on the World Bank website.

International Finance Corporation (IFC)

2121 Pennsylvania Ave NW
Washington DC 20433
United States of America
Telephone: (+1 202) 473 3800
Fax: (+1 202) 973 4384
Internet: www.ifc.org
Chair: Robert Zoellick, USA (since 1 July 2007)

Purpose

The IFC is empowered to invest in productive private or part-government enterprises in association with private investors, and without government guarantee of repayment in cases where sufficient private capital is not available on reasonable terms. It also serves as a clearing-house to bring together investment opportunities, private capital (both foreign and domestic) and experienced management. Its primary purpose is to promote the growth of the private sector and to assist productive private enterprises in developing member countries, where such enterprises can advance economic development.

Evolution

The IFC was established in 1956 and became a specialised agency of the UN in 1957. Although affiliated to the International Bank for Reconstruction and Development (IBRD), it is a separate legal entity and its capital is entirely separate from that of the Bank. It borrows its funds for re-lending from both the IBRD and private capital markets.

Capital

An increase in the IFC's authorised capital from $650 million to $1.3 billion was approved in 1985, which permitted it to expand its operations into more developing member countries, particularly lower-income countries, and into new sectors such as agro-business, energy and minerals. Since then, further increases totalling $150 million to the IFC's capital have been approved. As at 31 March 2007 the IFC's cumulative commitments totalled $60.5 billion from its own account and $26.3 billion in syndications, making a total of $86.80 billion in 140 countries.

Structure

The IFC is affiliated to the IBRD. Each member country is represented by the same Governor and Executive Director as represents it for the Bank. The IFC also shares the same President, but has its own management and staff.

Membership

As at 31 March 2007 IFC membership totalled 179 countries. A list is available on the IFC website.

Multilateral Investment Guarantee Agency (MIGA)

1818 H Street NW
Washington DC 20433
United States of America
Telephone: (+1 202) 473 1000
Fax: (+1 202) 522 0316
Email: migainquiry@worldbank.org
Internet: www.miga.org
Chair: Robert Zoellick, USA (since 1 July 2007)

Purpose

The objective of MIGA is to encourage the flow of productive investments among member countries, in particular to developing countries. MIGA guarantees or insures eligible investments against losses resulting from non-commercial risk such as unexpected restrictions on currency transfer, expropriation, contract repudiation by governments and armed conflict. It charges premiums for these services. MIGA also carries out research and promotional activities related to foreign direct investment.

The international Convention establishing this body took effect on 12 April 1988.

Capital

As at 31 March 2006 MIGA's subscribed capital was $1.88 billion and net income before provisioning was $46.6 million. MIGA assumed a total of $4.74 billion gross exposure in respect of its guarantee programme. The maximum level of guarantees outstanding may not exceed $10.15 billion.

Membership

As at 31 March 2007, 173 countries had signed and ratified the Convention.

International Centre for the Settlement of Investment Disputes (ICSID)

1818 H Street NW
Washington DC 20433
United States of America
Telephone: (+1 202) 458 1534
Fax: (+1 202) 522 2615
Internet: www.worldbank.org/icsid
Chair: Robert Zoellick, USA (since 1 July 2007)

Membership of ICSID is dependent on the ratification of the Convention on the Settlement of Investment Disputes between States and Nationals of Other States, which was opened for signature in Washington DC on 18 March 1965. The Convention, serviced by the Centre, provides a voluntary mechanism for settling disputes between governments and foreign investors. As at 31 March 2007, 143 nations had ratified the Convention and 155 had signed it.

INTERNATIONAL MONETARY FUND (IMF)

700 19th Street NW
Washington DC 20431
United States of America
Telephone: (+1 202) 623 7300
Fax: (+1 202) 623 6278
Email: publicaffairs@imf.org
Internet: www.imf.org
Managing Director: Rodrigo de Rato, Spain (since June 2004)

Purpose

The IMF is an organisation of 185 countries that works to foster global monetary cooperation, secure financial stability, facilitate international trade, promote high employment and sustainable economic growth, and reduce poverty. As at 31 March 2006 the IMF had $28 billion in loans outstanding to 74 countries. Of this, $6 billion was on concessional terms to 56 countries.

The IMF Articles of Agreement were drawn up at the Bretton Woods Conference in 1944. Membership is open to all countries. Ratification of the Articles and acceptance of conditions laid down by the Fund are conditions of membership.

The purposes of the Fund are to:
- Promote international monetary cooperation through consultation and collaboration
- Facilitate the expansion and balanced growth of international trade, and thereby contribute to the promotion and maintenance of high levels of employment and real income
- Promote exchange stability and orderly exchange arrangements
- Assist in the establishment of a multilateral system of payments and the elimination of foreign exchange restrictions
- Assist members through the temporary provision of financial resources to correct maladjustments in their balance of payments.

Quotas and drawing facilities

Each member has an assessed quota that is subscribed and determines voting power. Access to use of the Fund's resources is also determined in relation to quota, taking account of the member's balance of payments need and the strength of the policies it agrees to implement to restore balance of payments viability. The total of members' quotas as at the end of March 2006 was approximately $308 billion.

Members may draw from the general resources of the Fund, which are derived from quota subscriptions, under credit tranches (of 25 percent of quota each) or special facilities such as the Compensatory Financing Facility (CFF) for temporary export shortfalls. For purchases under the CFF, repurchases are subject to the same expectations and obligations as under a stand-by arrangement (see below).

Drawings (or 'purchases') in the upper credit tranches – in other words, beyond the first credit tranche – are subject to the terms of a stand-by arrangement agreed with the member. This arrangement specifies the precise economic policy conditions that the member must meet to qualify for each purchase, and the scheduling of purchases. Stand-by arrangements usually cover a 12- to 18-month period, but may be as long as three years. Members are expected to meet their repurchase expectations, but the Fund may extend them on request by the member if the Executive Board agrees that the member's external position was not sufficiently strong for it to repay early without undue hardship or risk.

There is also an Extended Fund Facility, under which members with structural maladjustments and experiencing balance of payments difficulties can enter into extended arrangements with the Fund for periods of up to 36 months. These can be in amounts larger than is possible under the credit tranches.

A Supplemental Reserve Facility was established on 17 December 1997. It provides temporary financial assistance to members experiencing exceptional balance of payments difficulties owing to a short-term financing need resulting from a sudden and disruptive loss of market confidence reflected in the pressure on the capital account and the members' reserves.

In September 1999, a new Poverty Reduction and Growth Facility (PRGF) replaced and strengthened the former Enhanced Structural Adjustment Facility (ESAF). The ESAF had provided concessional loans to qualifying low-income countries, aimed at strengthening balance of payments and fostering growth. The PRGF has broadened this initiative to explicitly include lasting poverty reduction as well as to encourage sustainable growth. The PRGF provides a vehicle for integrating mutually reinforcing macroeconomic, structural and social policies, and is geared much more towards the objective of using social indicators to measure progress.

These changes were agreed in tandem with commitments to enhance the Heavily Indebted Poor Countries (HIPC) initiative.

Special Drawing Rights

The Fund has created and allocated Special Drawing Rights (SDRs) to supplement member countries' reserves and thereby improve the liquidity of the international monetary system. Members may use SDRs to acquire currency from other members for use in alleviating balance of payments difficulties, and in a variety of other transactions. Members in strong balance of payments positions may be designated to accept SDRs from other members with a weak balance of payments in exchange for currency.

Allocations of SDRs are made over two basic periods that generally run to five years. The US dollar value of the SDR is posted daily on the IMF's website.

Evolution

The Articles have been amended three times, in 1969, 1978 and 1992. The first amendment provided for the creation and allocation of SDRs. The second amendment implemented a review of the Fund's responsibilities and operations that was conducted from 1972 to 1976 following the collapse of the fixed exchange rate system. The third amendment empowers the Fund to suspend the voting and certain related rights of a member who fails to fulfil any of the obligations under the Articles, other than obligations with respect to SDRs.

In addition to these amendments, the Board of Governors of the IMF approved in September 1997 another amendment for a special one-time allocation of SDRs so as to equalise members' ratio of cumulative allocations to their ninth review quotas. This Fourth Amendment of the Articles of the IMF will enter into force when the amendment is accepted by three-fifths of the members of the IMF, having 85 percent of the total voting power. As at the end of March 2007, 131 members, having some 77 percent of total voting power, had accepted the amendment.

Structure

The Board comprises one Governor appointed by each member country – typically a minister of finance or governor of a central bank. Substantive or policy matters are transmitted in the form of a report and draft resolution to the Governors for their vote, when one is required. An annual meeting of the Board in conjunction with that of the World Bank Group is held in late September/early October. The International Monetary and Financial Committee (IMFC) of the Board meets in April and September. Its terms of reference are the supervision of the international monetary system, including the operation of the adjustment process and global liquidity. The Development Committee (the Joint Ministerial Committee of the Boards of Governors of the Bank and the Fund on the Transfer of Real Resources to Developing Countries) generally meets at the same time as the IMFC. It advises and reports to the Boards of Governors of the World Bank and the Fund on all aspects of the real transfer of resources to developing countries. Each member country or group of member countries represented on the Executive Board (see below) appoints a member of the Committee.

This Board is responsible for the daily business of the Fund, including requests for financial assistance, economic consultations with member countries, and the development of Fund policies. It consists of the Managing Director as Chair and 24 Executive Directors. Of these, eight are appointed by members having the largest quotas – USA, Germany, Japan, UK, France, Russia, China and Saudi Arabia – while the remainder are elected to represent the interests of constituencies made up of several countries. Elections are held every two years.

Membership

As at 31 March 2007 IMF membership totalled 185. Members are listed on the IMF website.

Executive Directors/Alternates

Abdallah S Alazzaz/Ahmed A Al Nassar, Saudi Arabia

Klaus D Stein/ Stephan von Stenglin, Germany

Pierre Duquesne/ Bertrand Dumont, France

Vacant/Meg Lundsager, USA

Shigeo Kashiwagi/ Michio Kitahara, Japan

Willy Kiekens, Belgium/ Johann Prader, Austria

Age F P Bakker, Netherlands/ Yuriy G Yakusha, Ukraine

Paulo Nogueira Batista Jr, Brazil/Maria Ines Agudelo, Colombia

Jonathan Freid, Canada/ Peter Charleton, Ireland

Abbas Mirakhor, Iran/ Mohammed Daïri, Morocco

Adarsh Kishore, India/ Amal Uthum Herat, Sri Lanka

Aleksei V Mozhin/Andrei Lushin, Russian Federation

Richard Murray, Australia/ Wilhelmina C Manalac, Philippines

Peter Gakunu, Kenya/ Samura Kamara, Sierra Leone

Laurean W Rutayisire, Rwanda/ Kossi Assimaidou, Togo

Arrigo Sadun, Italy/ Miranda Xafa, Greece

Perry Warjiyo, Indonesia/ Chantavarn Sucharitakul, Thailand

Tom Scholar/Jens Larsen, UK

Roberto Guarnieri, Venezuela/ Ramon Guzman, Spain

A Shakour Shaalan, Egypt/ Samir El-Khouri, Lebanon

Javier Silva-Ruete, Peru/ Héctor R Torres, Argentina

Ge Huayong/He Jianxiong, China

Thomas Moser, Switzerland/ Andrzej Raczko, Poland

International Atomic Energy Agency (IAEA)

Vienna International Centre
PO Box 100
A–1400 Vienna
Austria
Telephone: (+43 1) 26 000
Fax: (+43 1) 26 007
Email: official.mail@iaea.org
Internet: www.iaea.org
Director General: Mohamed ElBaradei, Egypt (1997–2009) (appointed by the Board of Governors with the approval of the General Conference)

Purpose

The IAEA's purpose is to seek to accelerate and enlarge the contribution of atomic energy to peace, health and prosperity throughout the world. It is charged with ensuring the assistance it provides is not used to further any military purpose. The Agency groups its activities under the three pillars of science and technology, safety and security, and safeguards and verification. Specifically, it seeks to act as a catalyst for the development and transfer of peaceful nuclear technologies, build and maintain a global nuclear safety regime, and assist in global efforts to prevent the proliferation of nuclear weapons.

The Statute of the International Atomic Energy Agency (IAEA) entered into force in 1957. It is not a specialised agency, but an independent inter-government organisation under the aegis of the UN.

The Agency is authorised to:
- Encourage and assist research on atomic energy for peaceful purposes worldwide
- Act as an intermediary in the supply of materials, services, equipment and facilities
- Foster the exchange of scientific and technical information
- Encourage the exchange and training of scientists and experts
- Establish and administer safeguards against the misuse of aid provided by IAEA
- Establish safety standards.

Evolution

The IAEA is charged with drawing up and implementing the Nuclear Non-Proliferation Treaty (NPT) safeguards provisions, as well as those of the Treaty of Tlatelolco (the Latin American Nuclear Weapon Free Zone), the Treaty of Pelindaba (the African Nuclear Weapon Free Zone), the Treaty of Bangkok (the ASEAN Nuclear Weapon Free Zone) and the Treaty of Rarotonga (the South Pacific Nuclear Free Zone). These safeguard activities are a relatively new concept in international law and form one of the most important aspects of the IAEA's role and functions. The aim of safeguards is to assist states in demonstrating their compliance with international obligations in the interest of preventing the further proliferation of nuclear weapons. There are now some 1122 nuclear installations and other locations under IAEA safeguards. This represents about 95 percent of the world's nuclear facilities and materials outside the five NPT nuclear weapon states.

The IAEA's role in nuclear safety has increased as nuclear power programmes have grown and public attention has focused on the issue. Although the IAEA is not a regulatory body, its recommendations have been used by many countries as a basis for national standards and rules. The Agency also has important functions under international conventions related to emergency response and preparedness in the event of a nuclear accident. These conventions include the Convention on Early Notification of a Nuclear Accident, which entered into force on 27 October 1986 and had 99 parties as at 14 November 2006; and the Convention on Assistance in the Case of a Nuclear Accident or Radiological Emergency, which entered into force on 26 February 1987 and had 97 parties as at 14 November 2006.

In 1994, an IAEA Diplomatic Conference adopted the Convention on Nuclear Safety. It entered into force on 24 October 1996. As at 11 May 2006 it had 59 parties.

Other conventions adopted under the auspices of the IAEA are (dates indicate last change of status):

- The Convention on Physical Protection of Nuclear Material, which entered into force on 8 February 1987 (122 parties as at 15 December 2006) – an Amendment to this Convention was adopted on 8 July 2005 but has not yet entered into force (seven contracting states as at 6 February 2007)
- The Joint Convention on the Safety of Spent Fuel Management and on the Safety of Radioactive Waste Management, which entered into force on 18 June 2001 (44 parties as at 18 December 2006)
- The Vienna Convention on Civil Liability for Nuclear Damage, which entered into force on 12 November 1977 (33 parties as at 15 May 2005)
- The Joint Protocol relating to the Application of the Vienna Convention and the Paris Convention, which entered into force on 27 April 1992 (25 parties as at 26 March 2007)
- The Protocol to Amend the Vienna Convention on Civil Liability for Nuclear Damage, which entered into force on 4 October 2003 (five parties as at 4 July 2003)
- The Optional Protocol concerning the Compulsory Settlement of Disputes to the Vienna Convention on Civil Liability for Nuclear Damage, which entered into force on 3 May 1999 (two parties as at 13 April 1999)
- The Convention on Supplementary Compensation for Nuclear Damage, which was adopted on 12 September 1997 but has not yet entered into force (three parties as at 14 November 2000).

Structure

- General Conference
- Board of Governors
- Director General
- Secretariat
- Laboratories, safeguards offices (Tokyo, Toronto), UN liaison offices.

The IAEA meets annually. The 50th regular session of the General Conference took place in Vienna from 18 to 22 September 2006.

The Board has 35 members. Thirteen members are designated each year by the Board to serve for one year and 22 (11 each year) are elected by the General Conference to serve for two years. The term of all members runs from the end of a regular session of the General Conference until the end of the next or second subsequent regular session. Article VI of the IAEA Statute requires the Board to designate the 10 members most advanced in the technology of atomic energy, including the production of source materials. It also requires the Board to designate the member most advanced in the technology of atomic energy, including the production of source materials, in each of the following areas: North America,

Latin America, Western Europe, Eastern Europe, Africa, the Middle East and South Asia, South East Asia and the Pacific, and the Far East.

The members elected by the General Conference are representatives from the following areas: five from Latin America, four from Western Europe, three from Eastern Europe, four from Africa, two from the Middle East and South Asia, one from South East Asia and the Pacific, and one from the Far East. In addition, one member is elected from the Middle East and South Asia, or South East Asia and the Pacific, or the Far East; and one other member from Africa, or the Middle East and South Asia, or South East Asia and the Pacific.

In 1999, the General Conference approved an amendment to the Statute concerning the size and distribution of seats on the Board of Governors, by which Board membership would be expanded from 35 to 43 seats. This amendment will enter into force when two-thirds of all IAEA Member States have accepted it and other conditions are met.

The Board of Governors Chair for 2006–07 is Ernest Petri, Slovenia. Vice-Chairs for 2006–07 are Thomas Stelzer, Austria, and Milenko E Skoknic, Chile.

The following table lists IAEA Member States and terms on the IAEA Board:

	Previous terms	Current terms
Afghanistan	1963–65	
Albania		
Algeria	1967–69 73–74 81–83 85–96 1999–2001 04–06	
Angola		
Argentina	1957–2006	2006–07
Armenia		
Australia	1957–2006	2006–07
Austria	1965–67 77–79 83–85 90–92 1999–2001	2006–08
Azerbaijan		
Bangladesh	1975–77 81–83	
Belarus	1999–2001	2005–07
Belgium	1958–73 76–78 83–85 89–92 95–99 2003–06	
Belize		
Benin		
Bolivia	1999–2001	2006–08
Bosnia and Herzegovina		
Botswana		
Brazil	1957–2006	2006–07
Bulgaria	1959–61 67–69 73–75 77–79 82–84 86–88 91–93 95–97 2001–03	
Burkina Faso	2001–03	
Cameroon	1990–92	
Canada	1957–2006	2006–07
Central African Republic		
Chad		
Chile	1964–66 70-77 79–81 1983–2003	2006–08
China	1984–2006	2006–07
Colombia	1961–63 65–67 71–73 75–77 81–83 87–89 93–98 2001–03	2005–07
Costa Rica	1973–75	
Côte d'Ivoire	1984–86 88–90	
Croatia		2006–08
Cuba	1983–85 1987–2004	2005–07

	Previous terms	Current terms
Cyprus		
Czech Republic	1996–98 2002–04	
DR Congo	1963–65 71–76 82–84 91–93	
Denmark	1958–59 62–63 66–67 70–71 73–77 82–84 88–90 95–97 2002–04	
Dominican Republic		
Ecuador	1977–79 84–86 91–93 2004–06	
Egypt	1957–60 64–66 71–73 1976–2004	2005–07
El Salvador	1960–62	
Eritrea		
Estonia		
Ethiopia	1993–95	2006–08
Finland	1960–61 64–65 68–69 72–73 78–80 85–87 92–95 1999–2002	2006–08
France	1957–2006	2006–07
Gabon	1973–75	
Georgia		
Germany[1]	1960–62 66–68 1972–2006	2006–07
Ghana[2]	1962–63 65–67 73–74 77–79 88–90 1994–2002 04–06	
Greece	1961–63 71–73 78–80 84–86 91–93 1998–2000	2005–07
Guatemala	1957–58 78–80 85–87	
Haiti		
Holy See		
Honduras		
Hungary	1961–63 69–71 73–75 78–80 83–85 87–89 92–94 97–99 2003–05	
Iceland		
India	1957–2006	2006–07
Indonesia	1957–60 62–64 66–68 72–95 1999–2001	2005–07
Iran	1962–64 68–70 74–79 90–92 2001–03	
Iraq	1960–62 74–76 80–91	
Ireland	1973–74 79–81 86–88 93–95 2000–02	
Israel		
Italy	1957–58 62–64 68–70 73–86 89–91 93–94 97–99 2003–05	
Jamaica		
Japan	1957–2006	2006–07
Jordan	1984–86 1998–2000	
Kazakhstan		
Kenya	1979–81 82–84	
Kuwait	1977–79 87–89 95–97 2001–03	
Kyrgyzstan		
Latvia		
Lebanon	1966–68 73–74 80–82 93–95	
Liberia		
Libyan AJ	1975–77 82–84 87–89 92–94 2000–02	2005–07
Liechtenstein		
Lithuania		
Luxembourg		
Madagascar	1967–69 86–88	
Malawi		
Malaysia	1976–78 80–82 84–86 88–90 92–94 96–98 2002–04	
Mali		

327

OTHER BODIES

	Previous terms	Current terms
Malta		
Marshall Islands		
Mauritania		
Mauritius		
Mexico	1959–64 1966–2005	
Monaco		
Mongolia	1985–87	
Montenegro		
Morocco	1963–65 69–71 78–80 84–86 90–92 94–99 2001–03	2006–08
Mozambique		
Myanmar		
Namibia	1996–98	
Netherlands	1958–60 64–66 70–72 75–77 81–83 88–90 95–98 2002–05	
New Zealand	1996–98 2002–04	
Nicaragua	1995–97	
Niger	1976–81	
Nigeria	1969–71 76–78 80–97 1999–2001 2003–05	2006–08
Norway	1959–60 63–64 67–68 71–72 77–79 84–86 91–93 1998–2000	2005–07
Pakistan	1957–59 61–63 65–67 69–71 1973–2005	2006–08
Palau		
Panama	1976–78 81–83 2002–04	
Paraguay	1992–94	
Peru	1957–60 67–69 73–75 77–82 84–86 88–90 97–99 2000–05	
Philippines	1959–61 67–69 73–77 79–81 83–85 89–91 93–95 2001–03	
Poland	1958–73 75–77 80–82 85–87 89–91 93–95 99–2001 03–05	
Portugal	1957–72 76–78 82–84 90–92 96–98 2004–06	
Qatar		
ROK	1957–59 65–67 73–75 77–79 81–83 85–89 91–93 1995–2001 03–05	2005–07
Republic of Moldova		
Romania	1957–59 63–65 71–73 77–79 81–83 91–93 95–97 2001–03	
Russian Federation	1957–2006	2006–07
Saudi Arabia	1972–74 78–80 1986–2000 02–04	
Senegal	1975–78 87–89	
Seychelles		
Sierra Leone		
Singapore	1968–70 1998–2000 04–06	
Slovakia	1994–96 1998–2000 04–06	
Slovenia	1997–99	2005–07
South Africa	1957–77 1995–2006	2006–07
Spain	1959–61 69–71 74–76 81–83 86–89 92–96 2000–04	
Sri Lanka	1959–61 67–69 71–73 2004–06	
Sudan	1973–75 80–82 85–87 1998–2000 02–04	
Sweden	1957–58 61–62 65–66 69–70 73–75 80–82 85–94 1997–2000 04–06	2006–07
Switzerland	1963–65 73–75 79–81 86–89 93–97 2000–03	
Syrian AR	1970–72 83–85 92–94 1999–2001	2005–07
Tajikistan		

	Previous terms	Current terms
Thailand	1960–62 64–66 70–72 74–76 78–80 82–84 86–88 90–92 94–96 2000–02	2006–08
The Former Yugoslav Republic of Macedonia		
Togo[3]		
Tunisia	1962–632 65–67 77–79 83–85 89–91 93–98 2003–05	
Turkey	1957–59 67–69 74–76 80–82 87–89 94–96 2001–03	
Uganda		
Ukraine	1990–92 93–95 2000–02	
UAE	1996–98	
UK	1957–2006	2006–07
UR of Tanzania	1978–80	
USA	1957–2006	2006–07
Uruguay	1963–65 69–71 74–76 80–82 90–92 94–96 1998–2000	
Uzbekistan		
Venezuela	1958–60 68–70 74–76 78–80 82–84 86–91 2004–06	
Viet Nam	1961–63 69–71 91–93 97–99 2003–05	
Yemen	2004–06	
Zambia	1974–76 81–83	
Zimbabwe		

Notes

The former Socialist Federal Republic of Yugoslavia served on the Board from 1965–67, 1975–77, 1979–81, 1983–85 and 1987–89.

Czechoslovakia served on the Board from 1957–74, 1976–78, 1981–83, 1985–87 and 1989–91.

The Democratic People's Republic of Korea (DPRK), which joined the IAEA in 1974, withdrew its membership of the Agency on 13 June 1994. Cambodia, which joined the IAEA in 1958, withdrew its membership of the Agency on 26 March 2003.

[1] Prior to 3 October 1990, the German Democratic Republic had been a member of the Board from 1974–76, 1979–81, 1984–86 and 1988–90.

[2] One year as an observer.

[3] Membership has been approved by the IAEA General Conference and will take effect once the state deposits the necessary legal instruments with the IAEA.

International Criminal Court (ICC)

PO Box 19 519
2500 CM The Hague
The Netherlands
Telephone: (+31 70) 515 8515
Fax: (+31 70) 515 8555
Email: pio@icc-cpi.int
Internet: www.icc-cpi.int
Registrar: Bruno Cathala, France (since 2003)

Purpose

The ICC is a permanent international court with the power to exercise its jurisdiction over individuals who, since 1 July 2002, have committed the most serious crimes of concern to the international community as a whole. The provisions of the Rome Statute govern the jurisdiction and functioning of the Court. States decide to accept the jurisdiction of the Court by becoming party to the Rome Statute, to which there were 104 States Parties as of 31 May 2007. The Court may exercise jurisdiction only if either the state in which the suspected crime occurred or the state of nationality of the person suspected of having committed the crime is a party to the Rome Statute. The Court may exercise jurisdiction over a crime only when national legal systems are unable or unwilling to do so.

Evolution

The ICC was established as a new international organisation by the Rome Statute of the ICC, which was adopted on 17 July 1998 by the United Nations Diplomatic Conference of Plenipotentiaries on the Establishment of an International Criminal Court (1998). The Conference was convened pursuant to GA res. 51/207 (1996) and GA res. 52/160 (1997).

The ICC is not a body of the UN, but an independent organisation. Its relationship with the UN is governed by a separate relationship agreement.

Structure

The ICC is composed of the Presidency, the Chambers, the Office of the Prosecutor and the Registry. Its seat is in The Hague, although the Court may sit elsewhere whenever it considers it desirable to do so.

The 18 judges of the ICC are elected by the Assembly of States Parties and are chosen from two lists:
- Those with established competence in criminal law and procedure, and the necessary relevant experience – whether as judge, prosecutor, advocate or in other similar capacity in criminal proceedings
- Those with established competence in relevant areas of international law, such as international humanitarian law and the law of human rights, and extensive experience in a professional legal capacity that is relevant to the judicial work of the court.

In the selection of judges, States Parties must take into account the need for the representation of the principal legal systems of the world, equitable geographical distribution and a fair representation of female and male judges.

Judges are elected for terms of nine years and may not be re-elected. Every three years the terms of office of one-third of the 18 judges expire. There are currently two judicial vacancies, which will be filled by election at the Assembly of States Parties in late 2007.

The present members of the Court, whose terms end in March of the year shown, are, in order of precedence:

Philippe Kirsch, Canada, President	2009	Sang-Hyun Song, ROK	2015
Akua Kuenyehia, Ghana, First Vice-President	2015	Hans-Peter Kaul, Germany	2015
Rene Blattmann, Bolivia, Second Vice-President	2009	Mauro Politi, Italy	2009
		Erkki Kourula, Finland	2015
Claude Jorda, France	2009	Fatoumata Dembele Diarra, Mali	2012
Georghios M Pikis, Cyprus	2009	Anita Usacka, Latvia	2015
Elizabeth Odio Benito, Costa Rica	2012	Adrian Fulford, UK	2012
Navanethem Pillay, South Africa	2009	Sylvia Steiner, Brazil	2012
		Ekaterina Trendafilova, Bulgaria	2015

The Office of the Prosecutor is an independent organ of the Court headed by the Prosecutor, who can be assisted by one or more Deputy Prosecutors. The Prosecutor is elected by the Assembly of States Parties and the Deputy Prosecutors are elected in the same way from a list of candidates provided by the Prosecutor. The Prosecutor and Deputy Prosecutors must be of different nationalities. Unless a shorter term is decided upon at the time of their election, the Prosecutor and Deputy Prosecutors hold office for a term of nine years and are not eligible for re-election.

Luis Moreno Ocampo, Argentina, was elected Prosecutor by the Second Resumed First Session of the Assembly of States Parties in April 2003, for a term of nine years. Serge Brammertz, Belgium, was elected Deputy Prosecutor and Head of Investigations by the Assembly of States Parties in November 2003, for a term of six years. Fatou Bensouada, Gambia, was elected Deputy Prosecutor and Head of Prosecutions in September 2004, for a term of nine years.

The Registry is headed by the Registrar, who is the principal administrator of the Court. The Registrar is elected by the judges of the Court, taking into account any recommendation by the Assembly of States Parties. If the need arises and the Registrar so recommends, the judges may also elect a Deputy Registrar. Bruno Cathala, France, was elected Registrar of the Court by the judges in a plenary meeting in June 2003 and holds office for five years.

Organisation for the Prohibition of Chemical Weapons (OPCW)

Johan de Wittlaan 32
2517 JR The Hague
The Netherlands
Telephone: (+31 70) 416 3300
Fax: (+31 70) 306 3535
Email: media@opcw.org
Internet: www.opcw.org
Director-General: Rogelio Pfirter, Argentina (2006–10) (appointed by the Conference on the recommendation of the Executive Council)

Purpose

The OPCW was created under the Convention on the Prohibition of the Development, Production, Stockpiling and Use of Chemical Weapons (CWC), negotiated in the Conference on Disarmament and entered into force on 29 April 1997. Its role is to ensure implementation of the Convention's provisions, including those for international compliance, and to provide a forum for consultation and cooperation. It is not a specialised UN agency but an independent inter-government organisation. An Agreement Concerning the Relationship between the UN and the OPCW was signed on 17 October 2000. It was approved by the Conference of States Parties in May 2001 and the UN General Assembly in GA res. 55/283 (2001).

The CWC is a global disarmament agreement that bans the development, production, stockpiling and use of chemical weapons, and provides for the destruction of existing chemical weapons stockpiles and related facilities within a specific time-frame. States Parties undertake never to:
- Develop, produce, otherwise acquire, stockpile or retain chemical weapons, or transfer, directly or indirectly, chemical weapons to anyone
- Use chemical weapons
- Engage in military preparations to use chemical weapons
- Assist, encourage or induce, in any way, anyone to engage in any activity prohibited to a State Party under the Convention.

States Parties also undertake:

- To destroy chemical weapons they own or possess, or which are located in any place under their jurisdiction or control, in accordance with the provisions of the Convention
- To destroy all chemical weapons they abandoned on the territory of another State Party
- To destroy any chemical weapons production facilities they own or possess, or that are located in any place under their jurisdiction or control
- Not to use riot control agents as a method of warfare.

The Convention also regulates the production, processing, consumption and, to some degree, the international transfer of toxic chemicals that can be converted into, or used to produce, chemical weapons. To this end, the OPCW monitors the chemical industry by means of compulsory annual national declarations by States Parties, controls on the transfer of some chemicals listed in the Convention, and a system of routine visits and challenge inspections by OPCW Technical Secretariat inspectors.

Structure

- Conference
- Executive Council.

The Conference of States Parties meets annually in The Hague. The twelfth session is scheduled to be held from 5 to 9 November 2007, and the thirteenth session in December 2008. The second Review Conference will take place from 7 to 18 April 2008.

The Executive Council (EC) considers any issues or matters within its competence affecting the Convention and its implementation, including concerns regarding compliance. It brings non-compliance cases to the attention of the Conference as appropriate. The EC consists of 41 members sitting on a rotational basis, with regard to equitable geographical distribution and the importance of the chemical industry, as well as to political and security interests. Its membership comprises nine African states, nine Asian states, five Eastern European states, seven Latin American and Caribbean states, 10 Western European and Other states, plus one further seat rotating between Asia, and Latin America and the Caribbean. Nominations for election are made from within each region respectively.

The EC Chair is Romeo Arguelles, Philippines, for one year from May 2007. Vice-Chairs are Algeria, Chile, Ireland and the Russian Federation.

Membership

As at 31 May 2007, 182 countries were members of the OPCW. A further eight countries had signed, but not yet ratified, the Convention. These countries will become members upon ratification. Members' terms of appointment to the Executive Council are from May to May of the years shown:

	Previous terms	Current terms
Afghanistan		
Albania		
Algeria	1997–2006	2006–08
Andorra		
Antigua and Barbuda		
Argentina	1997–2007	2007–09
Armenia		
Australia	1997–2000	2006–08

	Previous terms	Current terms
Austria	2000–02	
Azerbaijan		
Bahrain		
Bangladesh	1997–2004	
Barbados		
Belarus	1997–98 2002–04	2006–08
Belgium	1998–2000 02–04	2006–08
Belize		
Benin	2002–04	
Bhutan		
Bolivia		
Bosnia and Herzegovina		2006–08
Botswana	2001–03	
Brazil	1997–2007	2007–09
Brunei Darussalam		
Bulgaria	1997–98 2001–03	2007–09
Burkina Faso		
Burundi		
Cambodia		
Cameroon	1997–2005	2007–09
Canada	2000–04	
Cape Verde		
Central African Republic		
Chad		
Chile	1997–2004	2006–08
China	1997–2007	2007–09
Colombia	2002–07	
Comoros		
Cook Islands		
Costa Rica		
Côte d'Ivoire	1997–2001	
Croatia	2001–03	
Cuba	1998–2002 04–06	2006–08
Cyprus		
Czech Republic	1998–2000 03–05	2007–09
DR of Congo		
Denmark	2002–04	
Djibouti		
Dominica		
Ecuador	1997–2000	
El Salvador		
Equatorial Guinea		
Eritrea		
Estonia		
Ethiopia	1997–2001	
Fiji		
Finland	1998–2000	2006–08
France	1997–2007	2007–09
Gabon	2005–07	
Gambia		
Georgia		
Germany	1997–2007	2007–09
Ghana	2005–07	2007–09

	Previous terms	Current terms
Greece	2004–06	2006–08
Grenada		
Guatemala		
Guinea		
Guyana		
Haiti		
Holy See		
Honduras		
Hungary	1997–99 2002–04	
Iceland		
India	1997–2007	2007–09
Indonesia	2000–02	
Iran	1998–2006	2006–08
Ireland		2006–08
Italy	1997–2007	2007–09
Jamaica		
Japan	1997–2007	2007–09
Jordan		
Kazakhstan		
Kenya	1997–2000 04–06	2006–08
Kiribati		
Kuwait	2003–05	
Kyrgyzstan		
Lao PDR		
Latvia		
Lesotho	2005–07	2007–09
Liberia		
Libyan AJ		
Liechtenstein		
Lithuania		
Luxembourg		
Madagascar		
Malawi		
Malaysia	2004–06	2007–09
Maldives		
Mali		
Malta	1997–98	
Marshall Islands		
Mauritania		
Mauritius		
Mexico	1997–2007	2007–09
Micronesia		
Monaco		
Mongolia		
Montenegro		
Morocco	1999–2006	2006–08
Mozambique		
Namibia	2000–02	
Nauru		
Nepal		
Netherlands	1997–98 2000–02 04–06	
New Zealand	2004–06	
Nicaragua		

335

OTHER BODIES

	Previous terms	Current terms
Niger		
Nigeria	2001–05	
Niue		
Norway	1997–98 2004–06	
Oman	1997–98	
Pakistan	1998–2006	2006–08
Palau		
Panama	2000–06	
Papua New Guinea		
Paraguay		
Peru	1997–2006	2006–08
Philippines	1997–2000	2006–08
Poland	1997–2002 05–07	
Portugal	2002–04	
Qatar		
ROK	1997–2007	2007–09
Republic of Moldova		
Romania	1997–2001 05–07	
Russian Federation	1998–2006	2006–08
Rwanda		
Saint Kitts and Nevis		
Saint Lucia		
Saint Vincent and the Grenadines		
Samoa		
San Marino		
Sao Tome and Principe		
Saudi Arabia	1997–2007	2007–09
Senegal		
Serbia	2004–06	
Seychelles		
Sierra Leone		
Singapore		
Slovakia	1998–2000 03–05	
Slovenia	2000–02	
Solomon Islands		
South Africa	1997–2006	2006–08
Spain	1997–2002 04–06	
Sri Lanka	1997–2006	
Sudan	2001–07	2007–09
Suriname	1997–98	
Swaziland		
Sweden	2000–02	
Switzerland	1998–2000	2006–08
Tajikistan		
Thailand		2006–08
The Former Yugoslav Republic of Macedonia		
Timor-Leste		
Togo		
Tonga		
Trinidad and Tobago		
Tunisia	1997–2007	2007–09
Turkey	2002–04	

	Previous terms	Current terms
Turkmenistan		
Tuvalu		
Uganda		
Ukraine	1999–2001 04–06	
UAE		
UK	1997–2007	2007–09
UR of Tanzania		
USA	1997–2007	2007–09
Uruguay	1997–98 2001–06	
Uzbekistan		
Vanuatu		
Venezuela	1998–2000	
Viet Nam		
Yemen		
Zambia	2003–05	
Zimbabwe	1997–2001	

Preparatory Commission for the Comprehensive Nuclear-Test-Ban Treaty Organization (CTBTO Preparatory Commission)

Vienna International Centre
PO Box 1200
A–1400 Vienna
Austria
Telephone: (+43 1) 26030 6200
Fax: (+43 1) 26030 5823
Email: info@ctbto.org
Internet: www.ctbto.org
Executive Secretary: Tibor Tóth, Hungary (since August 2005) (elected and appointed by Preparatory Commission)
Chair: Ana Teresa Dengo, Costa Rica

Purpose

The CTBTO Preparatory Commission was established by the States Signatories to the Treaty on 19 November 1996. It is mandated to carry out the necessary preparations for the entry into force and effective implementation of the Comprehensive Nuclear-Test-Ban Treaty (CTBT). This includes the establishment of a global verification regime to monitor compliance with the Treaty.

Evolution

The CTBT was adopted by the UN General Assembly on 10 September 1996 and opened for signature on 24 September 1996. Article I prohibits all nuclear weapons test explosions or any other nuclear explosions. Each State Party further undertakes to refrain from causing, encouraging or in any way participating in the carrying out of any such test or explosion.

The Treaty will enter into force 180 days after it has been signed and ratified by the 44 States listed in Annex 2 to the Treaty. These countries possessed nuclear reactors or research reactors and participated in negotiations for the Treaty in 1996. Under article XIV, if the Treaty has not entered into force three years after its opening for signature, a conference on Facilitating the Entry into Force of the CTBT will be convened. The last conference was held in September 2005 in New York. The next conference is scheduled to be held in Vienna on 17 and 18 September 2007.

Structure

The Preparatory Commission for the CTBTO consists of two main organs:
- A plenary body composed of all States Signatories, also known as the Preparatory Commission
- The Provisional Technical Secretariat (PTS).

The plenary body has three subsidiary organs:
- Working Group A on budgetary and administrative matters
- Working Group B on verification issues
- An Advisory Group consisting of financial experts from States Signatories.

The Preparatory Commission's main task is the verification regime. This is made up of a 337-facility International Monitoring System (IMS) consisting of seismic, infrasound, hydroacoustic and radionuclide stations, as well as radionuclide laboratories. The IMS stations send data to the International Data Centre (IDC) in Vienna, where they are processed and forwarded to states for review. As of 30 April 2007 more than 200 of the facilities had been certified and were sending data continuously to the IDC. The verification regime also includes on-site inspections in the event of a nuclear explosion, a consultation and clarification process, and confidence-building measures.

Membership

A state becomes a member of the Preparatory Commission for the CTBTO upon signing of the CTBT. Member States oversee the work of the Preparatory Commission and fund its activities. As at 30 April 2007 there were 177 States Signatories. Of these, 138 had deposited their instruments of ratification. Thirty-four of the 44 Annex II States had ratified the Treaty including the three nuclear weapon states France, Russian Federation and the UK.

International Narcotics Control Board (INCB)

PO Box 500
A–1400 Vienna
Austria
Telephone: (+43 1) 260600
Fax: (+43 1) 26060 5867/5868
Email: secretariat@incb.org
Internet: www.incb.org
Secretary: Koli Kouame, Côte d'Ivoire (since 2004) (appointed by the UN Secretary-General in consultation with the Board)

Purpose

The task of the INCB is to monitor international and domestic movement of narcotic drugs and psychotropic substances used for medical and scientific needs, and promote compliance by governments with the various drug control treaties. It is also the Board's responsibility to supervise international trade in precursors and essential chemicals, prevent their diversion to illicit channels and serve as a link between national competent authorities in these matters, in accordance with article 12 of the UN Convention Against Illicit Traffic in Narcotic Drugs and Psychotropic Substances 1988.

Evolution

Establishment of the Board was provided for in the Single Convention on Narcotic Drugs of 1961, which entered into force on 13 December 1964. Under ECOSOC res. 1106 (XL)

(1966) the Board took over the functions of the Permanent Central Narcotics Board and the Drug Supervisory Body.

Structure

Pursuant to article 9 of the 1961 Convention, ECOSOC, with regard to the principle of equitable geographical representation, considers the importance of including people on the Board with knowledge of the drug situation in the producing, manufacturing and consuming countries. Board members were originally elected for a three-year period. This was increased to five years by the 1972 Protocol amending the 1961 Convention, which also strengthened the INCB's powers and enlarged its membership from 11 to 13.

Board members serve in their personal capacity and do not represent their governments. They are elected by ECOSOC as follows: three members with medical, pharmacological or pharmaceutical experience from a list of at least five nominated by the World Health Organization; and 10 members from a list of people nominated by UN members and by parties to the Single Convention on Narcotic Drugs that are not UN members.

The Board meets three times a year in Vienna. The meetings are held in closed session, but the Board publishes an annual report on its work. This is supplemented by two detailed technical reports containing data on the lawful movement of narcotic drugs and psychotropic substances required for medical and scientific purposes, as well as an annual publication on the implementation of article 12 of the 1988 Convention. The 88th session was held from 29 January to 2 February 2007 and the 89th session from 7 to 18 May 2007. The 90th session is scheduled to be held from 30 October to 16 November 2007.

Board members, whose mandates expire on 1 March of the year shown, are:

Joseph Bediako Asare, Ghana	2010	Melvyn Levitsky, USA	2012
Sevil Atasoy, Turkey	2010	Maria-Elena Medina Mora, Mexico	2012
Tatiana Borisovna Dmitrieva, Russian Federation	2010	Sri Suryawati,* Indonesia	2012
		Camilo Uribe Granja, Colombia	2010
P O Emafo,* Nigeria	2010	Brian Watters, Australia	2010
Hamid Ghodse,* Iran	2012	Raymond Yans, Belgium	2012
Carola Lander, Germany	2012	Xin Yu, China	2012

Note

*   Elected by ECOSOC from among nominees submitted by WHO.

International Trade Centre (ITC)

Palais des Nations
1211 Geneva 10
Switzerland
Telephone: (+41 22) 730 0111
Fax: (+41 22) 733 4439
Email: itcreg@intracen.org
Internet: www.intracen.org
Executive Director: Patricia Francis, Jamaica (2006–09) (appointed by the UN Secretary-General)

Purpose

The ITC is the joint technical cooperation agency of the World Trade Organization (WTO) and the UN Conference on Trade and Development (UNCTAD) for business aspects of trade development. The ITC's mission is to enable small business export success in developing countries by providing, with partners, trade development solutions to the private sector, trade support institutions and policy-makers.

The ITC's strategic objectives are to:
- Strengthen the international competitiveness of enterprises
- Develop the capacity of trade service providers to support businesses
- Support policy-makers in integrating the business sector into the global economy.

ITC technical programmes include:
- Strategic and operational market research
- Business advisory services
- Trade information management
- Export training capacity development
- Sector-specific product and market development
- Trade in services
- International purchasing and supply chain management.

The ITC's regular programme is financed in equal parts by the WTO and the UN. The ITC also implements projects, at the demand of beneficiary countries, with voluntary contributions from donor governments and civil society institutions.

Evolution

The ITC was created in 1964 through a decision of General Agreement on Tariff and Trade (GATT) Contracting Parties. In 1968 UNCTAD joined GATT as co-sponsor of the ITC. Its legal status was formally confirmed by the General Assembly in 1974 as a joint subsidiary organ of GATT and the UN, the latter acting through UNCTAD.

Structure

The ITC's annual inter-government gathering in Geneva is called the Joint Advisory Group (JAG) meeting. The ITC JAG is open to all members of the WTO and UNCTAD, as well as UN specialised agencies and bodies, other inter-government organisations with observer status, and NGOs with an interest in trade promotion. This meeting, held in Geneva, reviews ITC's technical cooperation programme over the preceding year and makes recommendations for its future work programme. The 40th session of the JAG was held from 25 to 27 April 2007.

Membership

Because of its legal status, the ITC does not have a membership of its own. However, its de facto members are the Member States of the WTO and of UNCTAD.

OTHER BODIES

International Union for the Protection of New Varieties of Plants (UPOV)

34 Chemin des Colombettes
1211 Geneva 20
Switzerland
Telephone: (+41 22) 338 9111
Fax: (+41 22) 733 0336
Email: upov.mail@upov.int
Internet: www.upov.int
Secretary-General: Dr Kamil Idris, Sudan (1997–2009) (the Council of UPOV appoints the Director-General of WIPO as Secretary-General of UPOV by virtue of an agreement between the two organisations)

Purpose

The purpose of UPOV is to ensure that members of the Union:
- Recognise and secure to breeders of new varieties of plants an intellectual property right (plant breeder's right)
- Encourage cooperation between members in their administration of such rights on the basis of a set of uniform and clearly defined principles.

Evolution

UPOV was established by a Convention adopted in Paris in 1961 and entered into force in 1968. The Convention was revised in 1972, 1978 and 1991. The 1991 Act entered into force on 24 April 1998. UPOV is an independent inter-government organisation.

Structure

- Council
- Committees
- Secretariat.

The Council of UPOV is responsible for safeguarding the interests and encouraging the development of the Union. It is also responsible for adopting the Union's work programme and budget. The Council meets annually and consists of the representatives of all members. Each state member has one vote in the council.

Three committees assist the Council with its work – the Consultative Committee (which prepares the sessions of the Council), the Administrative and Legal Committee, and the Technical Committee. Several working groups have been established under the Technical Committee.

The Secretariat is called the Office of the Union and is directed by UPOV's Secretary-General.

Membership

The 63 members as of 24 November 2006 were:

Albania	Brazil	Denmark
Argentina	Bulgaria	Ecuador
Australia	Canada	Estonia
Austria	Chile	European Community
Azerbaijan	China	Finland
Belarus	Colombia	France
Belgium	Croatia	Germany
Bolivia	Czech Republic	Hungary

Iceland
Ireland
Israel
Italy
Japan
Jordan
Kenya
Kyrgyzstan
Latvia
Lithuania
Mexico
Morocco
Netherlands

New Zealand
Nicaragua
Norway
Panama
Paraguay
Poland
Portugal
ROK
Republic of Moldova
Romania
Russian Federation
Singapore
Slovakia

Slovenia
South Africa
Spain
Sweden
Switzerland
Trinidad and Tobago
Tunisia
Ukraine
UK
USA
Uruguay
Uzbekistan
Viet Nam

REGIONAL DEVELOPMENT BANKS

REGIONAL DEVELOPMENT BANKS

African Development Bank (ADB)

Temporary Address:
ADB Temporary Relocation Agency (Tunis)
African Development Bank Angle des trois rues
Avenue du Ghana, Rue Pierre de Coubertin, Rue Hedi Nouira
BP 323 1002
Tunis Belvedère
Tunisia
Telephone: (+216) 71 333 511 / 7110 3450
Fax: (+216) 71 351 933

Headquarters:
Rue Joseph Anoma
01 BP 1387 Abidjan 01
Côte d'Ivoire
Telephone: (+225) 2020 4444
Fax: (+225) 2020 4959

Email: afdb@afdb.org
Internet: www.afdb.org
President: Donald Kaberuka, Rwanda (since 2005) (elected by the Board of Governors on the recommendation of the Board of Directors)

Purpose

The ADB is a regional multilateral development bank that promotes the economic development and social progress of its regional member countries (RMCs) in Africa. The ADB is dedicated to combating poverty and improving living conditions across the continent.

The agreement establishing the ADB was drawn up under the auspices of the Economic Commission for Africa and entered into force in 1964. The Bank began operations in 1966. Its principal functions are to:

- Make loans and equity investments for the economic and social advancement of the RMCs
- Provide technical assistance for the preparation and execution of development projects and programmes
- Promote investment of public and private capital for development purposes
- Respond to requests for assistance in coordinating development policies and plans of RMCs.

The Bank is also required to give special attention to national and multinational projects and programmes that promote regional integration.

The ADB is also working to play a leading role in the New Partnership for Africa's Development (NEPAD) initiative, which aims to reduce the gaps that exist between Africa and the developed world and to reach the Millennium Development Goals (MDGs). The Bank is coordinating activities in the area of infrastructure, banking and finance, and corporate governance.

Structure

The shareholders are the 53 countries in Africa, as well as 24 countries in the Americas, Europe and Asia.

The Board of Governors is the Bank's supreme organ and comprises mostly the ministers of finance and economy of Member State governments. It issues general directives concerning the Bank's operational policies.

The Board of Directors comprises 18 members holding the title of executive director. They are elected by the Board of Governors for a period of three years, renewable once. Regional members have 12 directors while states outside the region have six.

The President is elected by the Bank's Board of Governors on the recommendation of the Board of Directors for a five-year term, renewable once. The President acts as the Bank's Chief Executive and conducts the current business of the Bank, as well as being its legal representative.

Membership

Any African country that has the status of an independent state may become a member of the Bank. The agreement defines 'Africa' or 'African' as comprising the continent of Africa and African islands. The 53 regional members are:

Algeria	Ethiopia	Niger
Angola	Gabon	Nigeria
Benin	Gambia	Rwanda
Botswana	Ghana	Sao Tome and Principe
Burkina Faso	Guinea	Senegal
Burundi	Guinea-Bissau	Seychelles
Cameroon	Kenya	Sierra Leone
Cape Verde	Lesotho	Somalia
Central African Republic	Liberia	South Africa
Chad	Libyan AJ	Sudan
Comoros	Madagascar	Swaziland
Congo	Malawi	Togo
Côte d'Ivoire	Mali	Tunisia
DR Congo	Mauritania	Uganda
Djibouti	Mauritius	UR of Tanzania
Egypt	Morocco	Zambia
Equatorial Guinea	Mozambique	Zimbabwe
Eritrea	Namibia	

There are 24 non-regional members:

Argentina	France	Portugal
Austria	Germany	ROK
Belgium	India	Saudi Arabia
Brazil	Italy	Spain
Canada	Japan	Sweden
China	Kuwait	Switzerland
Denmark	Netherlands	UK
Finland	Norway	USA

Inter-American Development Bank (IDB)

1300 New York Avenue NW
Washington DC 20577
United States of America
Telephone: (+1 202) 623 1000
Fax: (+1 202) 623 3096
Email: pic@iadb.org
Internet: www.iadb.org
President (Executive Head): Luis Alberto Moreno, Colombia (since 2005)

Purpose

The IDB, the oldest and largest regional multilateral development institution, was established in December 1959 to help accelerate economic and social development in Latin America and the Caribbean.

The Bank's Charter states that its principal functions are to:
- Use its own capital, funds raised in financial markets and other resources, for financing the development of borrowing member countries
- Supplement private investment when private capital is not available on reasonable terms and conditions
- Provide technical assistance for the preparation, financing and implementation of development plans and projects.

The Bank's operations cover the entire spectrum of economic and social development. Current key areas of concentration include poverty reduction and social equity, modernisation of the state, integration and competitiveness, and promoting private sector growth.

The Bank's financial resources consist of ordinary capital resources comprising subscribed capital, reserves and funds raised through borrowings, and 44 Trust Funds in Administration. These Trust Funds are established by contributions made by member countries.

Member countries' subscriptions to the Bank's capital fund consist of paid-in and callable capital. A paid-in subscription is in the form of a cash payment and represents a minor portion of a member's subscription (4.3 percent). The major part of a member's subscription is in the form of callable capital or guarantees of the Bank's borrowings in the world's financial markets. The Bank also has a Fund for Special Operations for lending on concessional terms for projects in countries classified as economically less developed.

The Bank has borrowed funds for its ordinary operations from the capital markets of Europe, Japan, Latin America, the Caribbean and the USA. The Bank's debt is AAA rated by the three major rating services in the USA and is accorded equivalent status in the other major capital markets. In 46 years of operation the IDB has approved loans worth $145 billion. Bank financing has contributed to development projects with a total cost of over $335 billion. Lending totalled $6.3 billion in 2006.

Structure

The IDB is an Official Observer to the United Nations. It has country offices in each of its regional member countries, as well as in Paris and Tokyo. Headquarters are in Washington DC.

The Board of Governors, on which each member country is represented, is the Bank's highest authority. The 47 Governors are usually ministers of finance, presidents of central banks or officers of comparable rank. The Board of Governors has delegated many of its operational powers to the 14 members of the Board of Executive Directors, which is responsible for the conduct of the Bank's operations.

An Office of Institutional Integrity spearheads the fight against fraud and corruption. This Office investigates all allegations of fraud and corruption in connection with any Bank activities or operations, manages investigations, imposes appropriate sanctions and coordinates their implementation, and determines when matters need to be referred to national authorities for civil or criminal prosecution.

Membership

Forty-seven countries are members of the Bank:

Argentina	El Salvador	Panama
Austria	Finland	Paraguay
Bahamas	France	Peru
Barbados	Germany	Portugal
Belgium	Guatemala	ROK
Belize	Guyana	Slovenia
Bolivia	Haiti	Spain
Brazil	Honduras	Suriname
Canada	Israel	Sweden
Chile	Italy	Switzerland
Colombia	Jamaica	Trinidad and Tobago
Costa Rica	Japan	UK
Croatia	Mexico	USA
Denmark	Netherlands	Uruguay
Dominican Republic	Nicaragua	Venezuela
Ecuador	Norway	

Associated organisations

The Inter-American Development Bank Group includes four organisations that complement the work of the Private Sector Department to help meet the needs of the region's growing private sector:
- Inter-American Investment Corporation (IIC)
- Multilateral Investment Fund (MIF)
- Institute for the Integration of Latin America and the Caribbean (INTAL)
- Inter-American Institute for Social Development (INDES).

Inter-American Investment Corporation (IIC)

1350 New York Avenue NW
Washington DC 20577
United States of America
Telephone: (+1 202) 623 3900
Fax: (+1 202) 623 3815
Internet: www.iadb.org
General Manager: Jacques Rogozinski, Mexico (since 1999)

The IIC is a multilateral financial institution that is an autonomous affiliate of the Inter-American Development Bank Group (IDB). It began operations in 1989 to promote the economic development of its Latin American and Caribbean member countries by financing private enterprise, preferably small and medium in scale. It provides financing in the form of equity investments, loans and guarantees and provides advisory services to private enterprise in the region. The IIC has 43 member countries.

The IIC works directly with the private sector and neither seeks nor requires government guarantees for its loans, equity investments or lines of credit. IIC investments leverage significant capital flows to Latin America. In 2006 the IIC approved $338 million in direct loan and equity for transactions totalling $511 million in project costs. Since its establishment the IIC's cumulative lending has reached $2.3 billion.

Multilateral Investment Fund (MIF)

1300 New York Avenue NW
Washington DC 20577
United States of America
Telephone: (+1 202) 942 8211
Fax: (+1 202) 942 8100
Internet: www.iadb.org
Manager: Donald F Terry, USA (since 1992)

The MIF is a special fund administered by the Inter-American Development Bank (IDB), which promotes private sector development and private investment in Latin America and the Caribbean. The MIF began operations in 1993 with funds committed by 20 countries amounting to $1.145 billion. MIF operations are concentrated in three areas:
*   Fostering efficient institutions and regulatory frameworks
*   Raising the productivity of human resources
*   Improving smaller enterprises' access to sources of finance and technical assistance.

Today there are 37 donor countries. Since its inception a total of 889 operations have been approved, representing a total commitment of $1.1 billion. MIF projects have put over $2.2 billion to work, making the Fund the largest provider of technical assistance in the region.

Institute for the Integration of Latin America and the Caribbean (INTAL)

Esmeralda 130
Casilla de Correo 39
Buenos Aires
Argentina
Telephone: (+54 11) 4320 1850
Fax: (+54 11) 4320 1865
Internet: www.iadb.org/intal
Director: Ricardo Carciofi (since 2005)

INTAL has been in operation since 1964. It provides services of specialised technical cooperation, conferences, policy research and publications in the field of integration and trade, both to IDB member countries and to regional organisations.

Inter-American Institute for Social Development (INDES)

1350 New York Avenue NW
Washington DC 20577
United States of America
Telephone: (+1 202) 623 2420
Fax: (+1 202) 623 2633
Internet: www.iadb.org/indes
Director: Nohra Rey de Marulanda, Colombia (since 1994)

INDES, part of the Inter-American Development Bank (IDB), was created in 1994 as a training institute and forum dedicated to developing knowledgeable social policy-makers and social managers who are committed to sustainable social reform. INDES trains public sector decision-makers and managers as well as staff of non-government organisations and other civil society organisations, both at IDB Headquarters in Washington and in specially customised programmes in Latin America and the Caribbean.

Asian Development Bank (ADB)

PO Box 789
0980 Manila
Philippines
Telephone: (+63 2) 632 4444
Fax: (+63 2) 636 2444
Email: information@adb.org
Internet: www.adb.org
President and Chairman of the Board of Directors: Haruhiko Kuroda, Japan (since 2005) (elected by the Board of Directors)

Purpose

The ADB's mission is to help its developing member countries (DMCs) reduce poverty and improve their living conditions and quality of life. Established in 1966 through a multilateral agreement ratified by 31 countries, the Bank has a strategic agenda that focuses on sustainable economic growth, inclusive social development, and good governance. It has cross-cutting themes relating to private sector development, supporting regional cooperation for development, gender and development, and environmental sustainability.

The ADB's main instruments in providing help to its DMCs are policy dialogues, loans, technical assistance, grants, guarantees and equity investments.

The Bank offers a range of lending avenues and terms. All loans involve conditions aimed at improving development performance. About 73 percent of ADB's cumulative lending comes from its ordinary capital resources. These comprise paid-in capital, reserves, funds raised through borrowings, and accumulated retained income. The ADB also provides loans from its Special Funds resources, including the Technical Assistance Special Fund, Japan Special Fund and ADB Institute Special Fund.

The Asian Development Fund (ADF) is a special window for loans on concessional terms to members with low per capita gross national product and weak debt repayment capacity. The ADF is financed by periodic voluntary contributions from donors.

Other funds managed by the ADB are the Japan Scholarship Program, Japan Fund for Poverty Reduction, Japan Fund for Information and Communication Technology, and other untied grant funds provided in lump sums by bilateral donors to pursue objectives determined by the donor country and agreed to by the ADB. In recent years, thematic trust funds focusing on governance, poverty reduction, water, energy and environment have been established to support technical assistance operations and selected components of loan projects.

The ADB is also involved in channel financing of grants provided by bilateral donors to support technical assistance and soft components of loans. Most technical assistance grants are used for preparing projects and supporting advisory activities in areas such as law and policy reform, fiscal strengthening, good governance, capacity-building and natural resource management.

At the end of 2006 the ADB's authorised capital stock was $53.169 billion and its subscribed capital stock was $3.739 billion. For purposes of the Bank's financial statements, capital stock is valued in terms of Special Drawing Rights at the rate in current US dollars, as computed by the International Monetary Fund.

Total lending in 2006 reached $6.8 billion. In 2006 the ADB approved 71 loans, of which 26 ordinary capital resources loans amounted to $5.5 billion and 45 ADF loans totalled $1.3 billion.

The ADB has an AAA rating and typically raises about $4 billion to $5 billion a year from bond issues. It actively mobilises financial resources through its co-financing operations, tapping official, commercial and export credit sources.

Structure

The ADB has its headquarters in the Philippines and has other offices in Afghanistan, Azerbaijan, Bangladesh, Cambodia, China, India, Indonesia, Kazakhstan, Kyrgyzstan, Lao PDR, Mongolia, Nepal, Pakistan, Papua New Guinea, Sri Lanka, Tajikistan, Thailand, Uzbekistan and Viet Nam. The Bank also maintains three sub-regional offices in the Pacific, a country office in the Philippines, a special office in Timor-Leste and a field office in Kazakhstan. It has representative offices for Europe (based in Frankfurt), Japan (Tokyo) and North America (Washington DC).

The Bank's highest policy-making body is its Board of Governors, which meets annually and comprises one representative from each member. The Governors elect the 12 members of the Board of Directors, with each Director appointing an alternate. The President is elected by the Board of Governors for a five-year term and is Chair of the Board of Directors. The President, assisted by three Vice-Presidents, manages the business of the ADB.

The total voting power of each ADB member consists of the sum of its basic and proportional votes. Each member receives a number of basic votes. In addition, each member is allocated a number of proportional votes equal to the number of shares of ADB capital stock held by that member.

In June 2006 the ADB established a panel of eminent persons to advise it on key trends and development challenges in the fast changing Asia–Pacific region, and on the Bank's long-term role. The six-person group is to be chaired by Supachai Panitchpakdi, the Secretary-General of the UN Conference on Trade and Development.

The Bank's Board of Directors and constituencies are:

Executive Director	Alternate Executive Director	Members represented
Phil Bowen	Richard Moore	Australia; Azerbaijan; Cambodia; Georgia; Hong Kong, China; Kiribati; Federated States of Micronesia; Nauru; Palau; Solomon Islands; Tuvalu
Howard Brown	Pasi Hellman	Canada; Denmark; Finland; Ireland; Netherlands; Norway; Sweden
Sebastian Paust	Ugur Salih Uçar	Austria; Germany; Luxembourg; Turkey; UK
Ceppie Kurniadi Sumadilaga	Richard Stanley	Cook Islands; Fiji; Indonesia; Kyrgyzstan; New Zealand; Samoa; Tonga
Chol-Hwi Lee	Tsuen-Hua Shih	ROK; Papua New Guinea; Sri Lanka; Taipei, China; Uzbekistan; Vanuatu; Viet Nam

Executive Director	Alternate Executive Director	Members represented
Marita Magpili-Jimenez	Sibtain Fazal Halim	Kazakhstan; Maldives; Marshall Islands; Mongolia; Pakistan; Philippines; Timor-Leste
Patrick Pillon	João Simões de Almeida	Belgium; France; Italy; Portugal; Spain; Switzerland
Masaki Omura	Atsushi Mizuno	Japan
Ashok Saikia	Nima Wangdi	Afghanistan; Bangladesh; Bhutan; India; Lao PDR; Tajikistan; Turkmenistan
Curtis S Chin	Paul Curry	USA
Md. Saad Hashim	Aw Siew Juan	Brunei Darussalam; Malaysia; Myanmar; Nepal; Singapore; Thailand
Wencai Zhang	Fangyu Liu	China

Membership

Membership is open to members and associate members of the UN Economic and Social Commission for Asia and the Pacific (UNESCAP), and other regional countries and non-regional developed countries that are members of the UN or any of its specialised agencies. The ADB has 66 members, of which 47 are in Asia and the Pacific and 19 are from other parts of the world. The 47 regional members, with year of joining, are:

Afghanistan	1966	Myanmar	1973
Armenia	2005	Nauru	1991
Australia	1966	Nepal	1966
Azerbaijan	1999	New Zealand	1966
Bangladesh	1973	Pakistan	1966
Bhutan	1982	Palau	2003
Brunei Darussalam	2006	Papua New Guinea	1971
Cambodia	1966	Philippines	1966
China	1986	ROK	1966
Cook Islands	1976	Samoa	1966
Fiji	1970	Singapore	1966
Hong Kong, China	1969	Solomon Islands	1973
India	1966	Sri Lanka	1966
Indonesia	1966	Taipei, China	1966
Japan	1966	Tajikistan	1998
Kazakhstan	1994	Thailand	1966
Kiribati	1974	Timor-Leste	2002
Kyrgyzstan	1994	Tonga	1972
Lao PDR	1966	Turkmenistan	2000
Malaysia	1966	Tuvalu	1993
Maldives	1978	Uzbekistan	1995
Marshall Islands	1990	Vanuatu	1981
Micronesia	1990	Viet Nam	1966
Mongolia	1991		

The 19 non-regional members, with year of joining, are:

Austria	1966	Netherlands	1966
Belgium	1966	Norway	1966
Canada	1966	Portugal	2002
Denmark	1966	Spain	1986
Finland	1966	Sweden	1966
France	1970	Switzerland	1967
Germany	1966	Turkey	1991
Ireland	2006	UK	1966
Italy	1966	USA	1966
Luxembourg	2003		

Caribbean Development Bank (CDB)

PO Box 408
Wildey
St Michael
Barbados BB11000
Telephone: (+1 246) 431 1600
Fax: (+1 246) 426 7269
Email: info@caribank.org
Internet: www.caribank.org
President and Chair of Board of Directors: Dr Compton Bourne, Guyana (2001–11) (appointed by the Board of Governors)

Purpose

The Caribbean Development Bank (CDB) was established in 1970. It aims to contribute to the economic growth and development of member countries in the Caribbean and promote economic cooperation and integration among them. The needs of the less developed member countries are a particular concern.

Special operations are financed from the Bank's Special Development Fund and other special funds. The Special Development Fund is used to make or guarantee loans of high developmental priority that call for longer maturities, longer deferred commencement of repayment of principal and lower interest rates than those determined for ordinary operations. The Fund amounted to $634 million at 31 December 2006.

The Bank can also accept contributions or loans for other special funds that it may administer on terms agreed with its donors, as long as the purposes are consistent with its objectives and functions. Other special funds resources in active operation include the Basic Needs Trust Fund, which finances small social and economic infrastructure projects geared to the alleviation of poverty in the less developed borrowing member countries.

At 31 December 2006 the Bank's authorised capital was $714.9 million. The subscribed capital, including additional subscriptions, was $705 million, of which $155.7 million was paid-up and $549.3 million callable. Subscribed capital is held or available for subscription in the proportion of not less than 60 percent by regional members and not more than 40 percent by non-regional members.

Non-member contributors to the resources of the Bank have included Netherlands, New Zealand, Nigeria, Sweden and USA.

Evolution

The resolution adopted by the Board of Governors of the Inter-American Development Bank (IDB) in 1974 provided for an amendment to the IDB Charter to enable the Bank to lend through the CDB to all the latter's borrowing member countries, whether or not those countries were members of the IDB. The resolution entered into force in 1977.

Structure

The Board of Governors comprises one governor and one alternate governor for each member country. For this purpose, the member territories of Anguilla, British Virgin Islands, Cayman Islands, Montserrat, and Turks and Caicos Islands are regarded as one member. Voting power is approximately proportional to shares subscribed, with a slight weighting in favour of the smaller member territories.

The Board of Directors comprises 17 directors, 12 representing the regional members and five representing non-regional members. Directors hold office for a term of two years and are eligible for reappointment. The Board meets five times a year. The current members are:

Director	Alternate directory	Country or group of countries
Locksley Smith	Vacant	Jamaica
Anthony Bartholomew	Maurice Suite	Trinidad and Tobago
Ruth Millar	George Rodgers	Bahamas
Alberto de Brigard	Adolfo Meisel	Colombia
Vanessa Rubio Márquez	Vacant	Mexico
Vacant	Carlos Pérez	Venezuela
Havelock Brewster	Neermal Rekha	Guyana
Bentley Gibbs	June Simpson-Clarke	Barbados
Carla Barnett	I Hartley Coalbrooke	Belize and Anguilla Islands, Montserrat, and the Turks and Caicos Islands
Whitfield Harris Jr	Janet Harris	Antigua and Barbuda and Saint Kitts and Nevis
Isaac Anthony	Rosamund Edwards	Dominica and Saint Lucia
Crispin Frederick	Maurice Edwards	Grenada and Saint Vincent and the Grenadines
Non-regional		
Kathryn Dunlop	Nalini Ablack	Canada
Sandra Pepera	Lindsey Block	UK
Adolfo Di Carluccio	Pablo Facchinei	Italy
Uwe Wolff	Julia Lehmann	Germany
Jin Qi	Wang Lin	China

Membership

CDB membership is open to states and territories of the region and to non-regional states that are members of the UN or its specialised agencies, or the International Atomic Energy Agency (IAEA). The members are:

Borrowing member countries

Anguilla	Barbados	Cayman Islands
Antigua and Barbuda	Belize	Dominica
Bahamas	British Virgin Islands	Grenada

Guyana
Haiti
Jamaica
Montserrat

Saint Kitts and Nevis
Saint Lucia
Saint Vincent and the
    Grenadines

Trinidad and Tobago
Turks and Caicos Islands

Other

Colombia

Mexico

Venezuela

Non-regional

Canada
China

Germany
Italy

UK

BUDGET AND SCALES OF ASSESSMENT

BUDGET AND SCALES OF ASSESSMENT

UN BUDGET

The budget for 2006–07 continues to implement the budget process set in train by GA res. 41/213 (1986). The budget outline for 2006–07 was approved by GA res. 59/278. By its res. 61/253A (2006) the General Assembly revised approved appropriations totalling $4,173,895,900. The total was allocated amongst principal expenditure sections as follows:

Appropriation section	(thousands of US dollars)
Part I: Overall Policy-Making, Direction and Coordination	
1 Overall Policy-Making, Direction and Coordination	77,003.7
2 General Assembly Affairs and Conference Services	602,512.5
Total, Part I	**679,516.2**
Part II: Political Affairs	
3 Political Affairs	686,871.0
4 Disarmament	20,471.5
5 Peacekeeping Operations	96,670.6
6 Peaceful Uses of Outer Space	6175.7
Total, Part II	**810,188.8**
Part III: International Justice and Law	
7 International Court of Justice	36,785.0
8 Legal Affairs	42,153.0
Total, Part III	**78,938.0**
Part IV: International Cooperation for Development	
9 Economic and Social Affairs	157,474.1
10 Least Developed Countries, Landlocked Developing Countries and Small Island Developing States	5052.7
11 UN Support for the New Partnership for Africa's Development	10,803.1
12 Trade and Development	117,152.9
13 International Trade Centre, UNCTAD/WTO	26,901.5
14 Environment	12,286.6
15 Human Settlements	18,289.4
16 International Drug Control, Crime Prevention and Criminal Justice	32,838.4
Total, Part IV	**380,798.7**

Part V: Regional Cooperation for Development

Part VI: Human Rights and Humanitarian Affairs

Part VII: Public Information

Part VIII: Common Support Services

Part IX: Internal Oversight

Part X: Jointly Financed Administrative Activities and Special Expenses

Part XI: Capital Expenditures

Part XII: Safety and Security

Part XIII: Development Account

34	Development Account	16,480.9
	Total, Part XIII	**16,480.9**

Part XIV: Staff Assessment

35	Staff Assessment	436,347.5
	Total, Part XIV	**436,347.5**

GA res. 61/253 B (2006) approved an estimate of income, other than assessments on Member States, totalling $486,369.9 for 2006–07. This total was apportioned amongst the various income sections as follows:

Appropriation section	(thousands of US dollars)
1 Income from Staff Assessment	440,787.5
2 General Income	41,641.4
3 Services to the Public	3941.0
Total, Income Sections	**486,369.9**

SCALES OF ASSESSMENT

UN Regular Budget

Contributions from Member States to the UN regular budget are determined by reference to a scale of assessments approved by the General Assembly on the basis of advice from the Committee on Contributions. GA res. 55/5B (2000) substantially revised the scale of assessments, lowering the ceiling on the maximum contribution by any Member State to the regular budget to 22 percent. It reaffirmed the floor for the minimum contribution at 0.001 percent and the maximum contribution from Least Developed Countries at 0.01 percent. It also reaffirmed the low per capita income adjustment with a threshold per capita income limit of the average per capita gross national product of all Member States and a gradient of 80 percent.

GA res. 61/237(2006) set out the scale of assessments for 2007, 2008 and 2009. The following table lists the scale of assessments for contributions to the regular budget for the period 2007 to 2009:

Member States	Percentage contribution	Member States	Percentage contribution
Afghanistan	0.001	Bahamas	0.016
Albania	0.006	Bahrain	0.033
Algeria	0.085	Bangladesh	0.010
Andorra	0.008	Barbados	0.009
Angola	0.003	Belarus	0.020
Antigua and Barbuda	0.002	Belgium	1.102
Argentina	0.325	Belize	0.001
Armenia	0.002	Benin	0.001
Australia	1.787	Bhutan	0.001
Austria	0.887	Bolivia	0.006
Azerbaijan	0.005	Bosnia and Herzegovina	0.006

Member States	Percentage contribution	Member States	Percentage contribution
Botswana	0.014	Ghana	0.004
Brazil	0.876	Greece	0.596
Brunei Darussalam	0.026	Grenada	0.001
Bulgaria	0.020	Guatemala	0.032
Burkina Faso	0.002	Guinea	0.001
Burundi	0.001	Guinea-Bissau	0.001
Cambodia	0.001	Guyana	0.001
Cameroon	0.009	Haiti	0.002
Canada	2.977	Honduras	0.005
Cape Verde	0.001	Hungary	0.244
Central African Republic	0.001	Iceland	0.037
Chad	0.001	India	0.450
Chile	0.161	Indonesia	0.161
China	2.667	Iran	0.180
Colombia	0.105	Iraq	0.015
Comoros	0.001	Ireland	0.445
Congo	0.001	Israel	0.419
Costa Rica	0.032	Italy	5.079
Côte d'Ivoire	0.009	Jamaica	0.010
Croatia	0.050	Japan	16.624
Cuba	0.054	Jordan	0.012
Cyprus	0.044	Kazakhstan	0.029
Czech Republic	0.281	Kenya	0.010
DPRK	0.007	Kiribati	0.001
DR Congo	0.003	Kuwait	0.182
Denmark	0.739	Kyrgyzstan	0.001
Djibouti	0.001	Lao PDR	0.001
Dominica	0.001	Latvia	0.018
Dominican Republic	0.024	Lebanon	0.034
Ecuador	0.021	Lesotho	0.001
Egypt	0.088	Liberia	0.001
El Salvador	0.020	Libyan AJ	0.062
Equatorial Guinea	0.002	Liechtenstein	0.010
Eritrea	0.001	Lithuania	0.031
Estonia	0.016	Luxembourg	0.085
Ethiopia	0.003	Madagascar	0.002
Fiji	0.003	Malawi	0.001
Finland	0.564	Malaysia	0.190
France	6.301	Maldives	0.001
Gabon	0.008	Mali	0.001
Gambia	0.001	Malta	0.017
Georgia	0.003	Marshall Islands	0.001
Germany	8.577	Mauritania	0.001

Member States	Percentage contribution	Member States	Percentage contribution
Mauritius	0.011	Seychelles	0.002
Mexico	2.257	Sierra Leone	0.001
Micronesia	0.001	Singapore	0.347
Monaco	0.003	Slovakia	0.063
Mongolia	0.001	Slovenia	0.096
Montenegro[1]	0.001	Solomon Islands	0.001
Morocco	0.042	Somalia	0.001
Mozambique	0.001	South Africa	0.290
Myanmar	0.005	Spain	2.968
Namibia	0.006	Sri Lanka	0.016
Nauru	0.001	Sudan	0.010
Nepal	0.003	Suriname	0.001
Netherlands	1.873	Swaziland	0.002
New Zealand	0.256	Sweden	1.071
Nicaragua	0.002	Switzerland	1.216
Niger	0.001	Syrian AR	0.016
Nigeria	0.048	Tajikistan	0.001
Norway	0.782	Thailand	0.186
Oman	0.073	The Former Yugoslav Republic of Macedonia	0.005
Pakistan	0.059	Timor-Leste	0.001
Palau	0.001	Togo	0.001
Panama	0.023	Tonga	0.001
Papua New Guinea	0.002	Trinidad and Tobago	0.027
Paraguay	0.005	Tunisia	0.031
Peru	0.078	Turkey	0.381
Philippines	0.078	Turkmenistan	0.006
Poland	0.501	Tuvalu	0.001
Portugal	0.527	Uganda	0.003
Qatar	0.085	Ukraine	0.045
ROK	2.173	UAE	0.302
Republic of Moldova	0.001	UK	6.642
Romania	0.070	UR of Tanzania	0.006
Russian Federation	1.200	USA	22.000
Rwanda	0.001	Uruguay	0.027
Saint Kitts and Nevis	0.001	Uzbekistan	0.008
Saint Lucia	0.001	Vanuatu	0.001
Saint Vincent and the Grenadines	0.001	Venezuela	0.200
Samoa	0.001	Viet Nam	0.024
San Marino	0.003	Yemen	0.007
Sao Tome and Principe	0.001	Zambia	0.001
Saudi Arabia	0.748	Zimbabwe	0.008
Senegal	0.004		
Serbia[1]	0.021	**Grand Total**	**100.00**

In accordance with GA res. 58/1B (2003) the Holy See, which is not a member of the UN but which participates in some of its activities, is called upon to contribute towards the expenses of the organisation on the basis of 50 percent of the notional assessment rate of 0.001 percent that would have been charged if it were a member.

Note

[1]   On 3 June 2006 the Republic of Serbia notified the UN that the membership of the State Union of Serbia and Montenegro in the UN, including all organs and organisations of the UN system, was continued by the Republic of Serbia on the basis of article 60 of the Constitutional Charter of Serbia and Montenegro, activated by the Declaration of Independence adopted by the National Assembly of Montenegro on 3 June 2006.

AD HOC SCALE OF ASSESSMENTS FOR UN PEACEKEEPING BUDGETS

By GA res. 55/235 (2000) the General Assembly reformed its methodologies for apportioning the expenses of peacekeeping operations, replacing the ad hoc arrangements in place since GA res. 3101 XXVIII (1973). The Assembly took into account that the financing of peacekeeping operations was the collective responsibility of Member States, and a different procedure was required from that used under the regular budget. The economically more developed countries were in a position to make relatively larger contributions and the economically less developed countries had a relatively limited capacity to contribute towards such operations. It also reaffirmed the special responsibilities of the Security Council's permanent Member States, as indicated in GA res. 1874 (S–IV) (1963), in connection with their contributions to the financing of peace and security operations.

To reflect these principles, the Assembly decided on the parameters of a new set of 10 levels for Member States for the purposes of apportioning the costs of peacekeeping, to be implemented on a phased basis from 1 July 2001. The resulting distribution of Member States among the 10 levels was set out in an annex to the resolution. The apportionments range from a premium payable by permanent Member States of the Security Council (Level A), to a 90 percent discount for Least Developed Countries (Level J). GA res. 61/243 (2006) established the updated composition of levels of contribution for peacekeeping operations for the period 2007 to 2009. The membership of the 10 groups is as follows:

Assignment of contribution levels for 2007–09

Level A

Permanent Members of the Security Council

China	Russian Federation	USA
France	UK	

Level B

Andorra	Cyprus	Iceland
Australia	Denmark	Ireland
Austria	Estonia	Israel
Bahamas	Finland	Italy
Bahrain	Germany	Japan
Belgium	Greece	Liechtenstein
Canada	Hungary	Luxembourg

Malta
Monaco
Netherlands
New Zealand

Norway
Portugal
San Marino
Slovenia

Spain
Sweden
Switzerland

Transition to Level B
ROK

Level C

Brunei Darussalam
Kuwait

Qatar
Singapore

UAE

Level D
(None)

Level E
Barbados

Level F

Antigua and Barbuda
Oman

Saudi Arabia

Seychelles

Level G

Czech Republic

Saint Kitts and Nevis

Transition to Level G
Trinidad and Tobago

Level H[*1]

Bulgaria
Latvia
Lithuania

Poland
Romania
Slovakia

Uruguay

Level H[1]

Mexico

Palau

Level I

Albania
Algeria
Argentina
Armenia
Azerbaijan
Belarus
Belize
Bolivia
Bosnia and Herzegovina
Botswana
Brazil
Cameroon
Chile
Colombia
Congo

Costa Rica
Côte d'Ivoire
Croatia
Cuba
DPRK
Dominica
Dominican Republic
Ecuador
Egypt
El Salvador
Fiji
Gabon
Georgia
Ghana
Grenada

Guatemala
Guyana
Honduras
India
Indonesia
Iran
Iraq
Jamaica
Jordan
Kazakhstan
Kenya
Kyrgyzstan
Lebanon
Libyan AJ
Malaysia

Marshall Islands
Mauritius
Micronesia
Mongolia
Montenegro
Morocco
Namibia
Nauru
Nicaragua
Nigeria
Pakistan
Panama
Papua New Guinea
Paraguay

Peru
Philippines
Republic of Moldova
Saint Lucia
Saint Vincent and
   the Grenadines
Serbia
South Africa
Sri Lanka
Suriname
Swaziland
Syrian AR
Tajikistan
Thailand

The Former Yugoslav Republic
   of Macedonia
Tonga
Tunisia
Turkey
Turkmenistan
Ukraine
Uruguay
Uzbekistan
Venezuela
Viet Nam
Zimbabwe

Level J

The Least Developed Countries

Afghanistan
Angola
Bangladesh
Benin
Bhutan
Burkina Faso
Burundi
Cambodia
Cape Verde
Central African Republic
Chad
Comoros
DR Congo
Djibouti
Equatorial Guinea
Eritrea
Ethiopia

Gambia
Guinea
Guinea-Bissau
Haiti
Kiribati
Lao PDR
Lesotho
Liberia
Madagascar
Malawi
Maldives
Mali
Mauritania
Mozambique
Myanmar
Nepal
Niger

Rwanda
Samoa
Sao Tome and Principe
Senegal
Sierra Leone
Solomon Islands
Somalia
Sudan
Timor-Leste
Togo
Tuvalu
Uganda
UR of Tanzania
Vanuatu
Yemen
Zambia

Notes

1   Category H* comprises countries that have voluntarily moved to category H.

LIST OF ACRONYMS AND INDEX

GUIDE TO THE INDICES

The United Nations Handbook 2007/08 contains two indices: one locating the names, bodies and programmes of the UN by acronym, the other by name and keyword order. Recently terminated or renamed bodies and programmes mentioned in the text under other headings are included to help the reader determine their current status.

LIST OF ACRONYMS

W

INDEX

A

B

D

E

F

G

H

I

J

K

L

M

R

S

T

U

V

W